SERIES PREFACE

The United Nations' designation of 1979 as the International Year of the Child marked the first global effort undertaken to heighten awareness of the special needs of children. Activities initiated during this special year were designed to promote purposive and collaborative actions for the benefit of children throughout the world. Michigan State University's celebration of the International Year of the Child was held from September 1979 through June 1980. A variety of activities focused attention on the multiplicity of factors affecting the welfare of today's children as well as the children of the future. Many people involved with the university were concerned that benefits to children continue beyond the official time allocated to the celebration. The series *Child Nurturance* is one response to this concern. The first five volumes of *Child Nurturance* reflect directly the activities held on the Michigan State University campus and consist of original contributions from guest speakers and invited contributors. Subsequent biennial volumes will present original contributions from individuals representing such fields as anthropology, biology, education, human ecology, psychology, philosophy, sociology, and medicine. We hope the material presented in these volumes will promote greater understanding of children and encourage interdisciplinary inquiry into the individual, family, societal and cultural variables which influence their welfare and development.

We would like to express both our thanks and our admiration for Margaret Burritt who not only typed the camera-ready copy for each of the volumes, but also served as general manager of the entire project. Although her contribution to the production of these volumes will not be noted in any chapter headings or indexes, each page reflects her devotion, care, and hard work. We also thank Mary Ann Reinhart for her careful and scholarly preparation of the subject index. Finally, we thank the editors and authors for their cooperation and for their concern for children and their families.

Marjorie J. Kostelnik
Hiram E. Fitzgerald
East Lansing, MI

v

CHILD NURTURANCE

VOLUME 1
Philosophy, Children, and the Family

CHILD NURTURANCE

Series Editors

MARJORIE J. KOSTELNIK
Department of Family and Child Ecology
Michigan State University, East Lansing, Michigan

and

HIRAM E. FITZGERALD
Department of Psychology
Michigan State University, East Lansing, Michigan

A Continuation Order Plan is available for this series. A continuation order will bring delivery of
each new volume immediately upon publication. Volumes are billed only upon actual shipment.
For further information please contact the publisher.

CHILD NURTURANCE

VOLUME 1
Philosophy, Children, and the Family

Edited by

Albert C. Cafagna,
Richard T. Peterson, and
Craig A. Staudenbaur

Michigan State University
East Lansing, Michigan

PLENUM PRESS • NEW YORK AND LONDON

Library of Congress Cataloging in Publication Data

Main entry under title:

Philosophy, children, and the family.

   (Child nurturance; v. 1)
   "Revised versions of selected papers and commentaries on papers delivered at
the Conference on Philosophy, Children, and the Family, held at Michigan State
University in March 1980"—Pref.
   Includes bibliographical references and indexes.
   1. Family—Congresses. 2. Mothers—Congresses. 3. Children's rights
—Congresses. 4. Moral education—Congresses. 5. Infant health services—Moral
and ethical aspects—Congresses I. Cafagna, Albert C. II. Peterson, Richard T. III.
Staudenbaur, Craig A. IV. Conference on Philosophy, Children, and the Family
(1980: Michigan State University) V. Series.
HQ518.P48   306.8'5   82-3701
ISBN 0-306-41003-6   AACR2

© 1982 Plenum Press, New York
A Division of Plenum Publishing Corporation
233 Spring Street, New York, N.Y. 10013

Printed in the United States of America

PREFACE

The present volume contains revised versions of selected papers and commentaries on papers delivered at the Conference on Philosophy, Children, and the Family, held at Michigan State University in March, 1980. In addition, the editors have provided introductory discussions to the sections into which these papers have been organized.

As with the conference itself, the aim here is to contribute to the articulation and debate of issues about the family and childhood. In a period of important changes in attitudes toward children and family life, there is no need to argue that these are significant issues. Nor is there any need here to describe the broad range of academic, professional and directly political contexts in which the family is presently discussed, any more than there is a need to survey the range of perspectives brought to these questions. That the range is broad and filled with conflict reflects not only the intrinsic interest and difficulty of issues about family life, but also the fact that these touch on spheres of social activity which in recent years have been sites of conflict over racial, sexual, generational and other forms of inequality.

If emotions run high over questions of family, then, this is not only because of time-honored beliefs about the sacredness of family life, or even because of the genuine importance of family life in human experience. In fact, these are questions that intersect with challenges about the very directions our society might take. They raise, for example, basic theoretical and practical questions about the definition of personhood and the variety of ways it may be cultivated, about power and authority relations between sexes and generations, about family and broader economic realities, about the relations between families and various state institutions. To be sure, despite their fundamental character, many questions bearing on the family are urgently practical as well, touching as they do on such concrete matters as educational policy, social welfare programs, judicial practice, the use of medical technology, and so on. Nevertheless, because these questions cannot be resolved in a way that is innocent of fundamental conceptual and normative commitments, they retain a distinctively philosophical character. Amidst all the contemporary discussions of children and the family, the specific aim of the present volume, as of the conference on which it is based, is to emphasize this philosophical dimension and to promote the exploration of the issues it involves.

Given the fact that family issues touch on disputed ethical and political questions as well as on unresolved issues about method and theory in the understanding of social phenomena, the philosophical approach to the family cannot be one of simply applying general and noncontroversial truths established by philosophers elsewhere. These problems do not raise questions for some 'applied philosophy' so much as they pose a specific context that embodies broader social dilemmas in addition to presenting quandries of its own. In light of the fundamental disagreements that prevail here, there was no effort to restrict the discussion in the conference to the standpoint or methods of a single philosophical school. The organizers of the conference did, however, proceed with the conviction that inclusion of participants from a number of fields other than philosophy would be fruitful not only for identifying and discussing philosophical issues as they arise in these fields, but also for lending a helpful concreteness to the considerations of philosophers themselves.

Thus it is hoped that the present collection will be of use to students of the family and childhood in a variety of disciplines. As such, its aims are in keeping with the increasingly widespread determination to counter-act the fragmented understanding of social phenomena to which the prevailing academic division of labor so often leads. In general, such a multidisciplinary emphasis can hope to contribute to a process of fruitful mutual learning among diverse fields of study and practice. This is all the more necessary for considering philosophical issues, since reflection on fundamental questions must be as inclusive in its vision as possible if it is to contribute to the advance of concrete research and social action. As part of the program of including a range of disciplines and viewpoints as broad as possible, effort has been made here to maintain a level of discourse that avoids the confines imposed by academic jargon and that remains accessible to readers from a variety of backgrounds and concerns.

With commitments like these, no doubt certain limitations follow regarding what a collection like this can accomplish. In drawing as broadly as possible from contemporary work, its multidisciplinary emphasis should not be confused with the formulation of an integrated multidisciplinary program of research. It would have been futile and self-defeating to pretend to follow some rigorously systematic conceptual framework, or to try to achieve completeness in covering even the most general philosophical questions about children and the family. For the most part, fruitful work today seems to proceed in a relatively piecemeal fashion, with great uncertainty prevailing about general questions of theory and social vision. A collection such as the one now offered the reader can perhaps best hope to provide an index of the kind of work that is today being done. At the same time, it may hope to supply some basis for further discussion among those concerned with these questions.

A word may be in order about the genesis of the present collection. Once the decision was reached to sponsor a conference of the sort described above, a call for papers was sent to all departments of philosophy in the United States (and much of Canada) as well as to philosophy journals and newsletters. In addition, the call for papers was sent to journals and newsletters of disciplines concerned in one way or another with childhood and family. More than 70 papers were received, and of these, 28 were included in the conference held March 28-30, 1980. Once it became clear that there was interest in publication of the proceedings, a further selection was made to form the basis for a suitable volume. The editors have tried to prepare a manuscript that is consistent with the general aims of the conference, and, in the same spirit, have written introductions to the various sections of the volume.

The editors are indebted to many people for their contributions to the conference and this resulting volume. First, we wish to thank our colleagues in the Department of Philosophy at Michigan State University; they all supported the conference in various ways. In particular, Martin Benjamin, Marilyn Frye, Bruce Miller, James Roper, Ronald Suter, Thomas Tomlinson, John Taylor and Winston Wilkinson helped with planning, commenting on papers, or chairing sessions at the conference. Albert Cafagna and Richard Peterson co-chaired the committee which planned and organized the conference. The Department of Philosophy also received the assistance of the Department of Family and Child Ecology in sponsoring the conference. The members of that department who helped in various ways include Barbara Ames, Margaret Bubolz, Beatrice Paolucci, Lawrence Schiamberg, and Alice Whiren; Professor Paolucci assisted the editors with the preparation of this volume as well. Barrie Thorne of the Department of Sociology also helped both with the conference and with this volume. Craig Staudenbaur, Chairperson of the Department of Philosophy, and Eileen Earhart, Chairperson of the Department of Family and Child Ecology, gave their active support to the conference. Funding for the conference was provided by the Department of Philosophy, with additional funds from the College of Human Ecology. We wish to acknowledge the helpful support of the Dean of the College of Arts and Letters, Alan Hollingsworth, and the Dean of the College of Human Ecology, Lois Lund. We are grateful to the diligent work of Mrs. Vera Jacob and Mrs. Marie Drane in typing this manuscript, and to Michigan State University All-University Research grants for aid in preparing the typescript. And finally we wish to thank the general editors of this series, Hiram Fitzgerald and Marjorie Kostelnik, for their help and encouragement in getting this volume ready for press.

Albert C. Cafagna
Richard T. Peterson
Craig A. Staudenbaur
East Lansing, MI 1981

CONTENTS

CONTENTS

PART I

CONCEPTUALIZING THE FAMILY

CONCEPTUALIZING THE FAMILY: INTRODUCTION

Richard T. Peterson

Department of Philosophy
Michigan State University
East Lansing, MI 48824

Family life poses some of the most difficult and disputed questions taken up in contemporary social thought and politics. Often these are issues about which major thinkers of the past have little to offer us: issues about power relations in the family, about the impact of public agencies and mass culture on family life, political issues about school curricula, about biological engineering, and so on. As these examples suggest, if earlier theorists did not speak to *our* questions about family, this is not--entirely--a matter of their having rested, so to speak, on patriarchal privilege. Nor is it because they ignored family issues: Plato, Rousseau, Hegel all gave thought to questions about family and household as part of their larger considerations of rational social life. But it is true that family was not a matter of primary concern for them: they did not see it as an end in itself. Its importance was more in preparing individuals for participation in the political and cultural spheres in which genuine human experience and achievement were thought to be possible. Reference to outstanding questions of our day suggests that it is no longer so easy to separate family (and economic) concerns from political and cultural questions. Issues raised by the women's movement are evidence of this, but so are questions of education, welfare, healthcare, and housing. And, as the sphere that fundamentally shapes the individual's habits of consumption and definition of needs, the family will play a major role in society's response to the deepening ecological crisis and the dwindling supply of its nonrenewable resources.

If family questions have come to play a more central role in our political life, this does not mean that we have a shared understanding of the importance of family life or of what should be considered appropriate family ideals. On the contrary, family is conceived and experienced with a great deal of uncertainty and ambivalence. An individual may experi-

ence family at one time as the anchor of his or her existence, at another
as a crippling fetter that must be torn off, even if at great personal cost.
Some theorists may treat family life as having an all-determining effect
on personality (for example, in questionable uses of Freud), while others
treat family as wholly subject to the play of extra-familial forces (for
example, in questionable uses of Marx). If such basic conflicts characterize our feelings and theories about family, it should not be surprising
that ideas and claims about family play the most disparate roles in our
political life as well. Of late, family slogans figure prominently on the
banners of the 'New Right,' with its opposition to abortion and resistance
to feminism generally. And family matters have been raised in debates
over the causes and remedies of racism in our society. But these have by
no means been the first interjections of family-related questions into
national politics. To take another example close at hand, support for the
civil rights movement and opposition to the Vietnam War not so many
years ago seemed to many to go naturally with a liberalization of
sexuality and a search for new family forms. In sum, our feelings about
family are deeply ambivalent, our attempts to understand it are pulled in
conflicting directions, and our political uses of family questions seem as
confused as they are pervasive.

We speak of "the family." But to what extent may we presuppose a
unique family essence, shared throughout society and persisting over
time? We must guard against the illusion that the modern nuclear
family--working husband, housewife, and children--provides a model of
all family structures, either in the past or in our own society. If there are
universal family functions (for example, cultivating and sustaining the
capacities of persons; organizing household production and consumption),
it is also beyond dispute that family structures have undergone vast transformations in the course of humanity's experience. Changing relations
between families and the spheres of political and economic life attest to
this. We may imagine a historical continuum whose beginning point
corresponds to those earliest societies whose activities are organized
wholly within kinship structures. This social primacy of kinship relations
breaks up with the emergence of civilization and its attendant differentiation of social classes and the appearance of an independent political
organization--the state. The other terminus on this continuum is the
nightmare vision entertained by many today: a society in which meaningful family and kinship ties have given way to a universal atomization of
individuals dominated by large-scale economic and political institutions.
Of course, such a continuum is an intellectual construction to which no
linear historical process corresponds. It is true that the "great transformation" (Polanyi, 1944) brought about by capitalism has fragmented
social life to an unprecedented degree, destroying many of the forms of
community existence that once sustained individuals. On the other hand,
there is some reason to think this process resulted in a relatively greater
reliance on family relations, for material survival in the case of the poor,
and for the cultivation of personality in the case of the middle classes.
At the very least, this larger historical process involved a far greater

preoccupation with family life (Flandrin, 1979, ch. 1). And, in any event, today the family may well be the only context in which many individuals can find personal recognition and emotional commitment.

If the belief, indeed the experience, that "the family" is somehow fundamentally threatened makes family issues emotionally charged (and contributes to their use in the demagogy of racisms, sexisms, and nationalisms), we may doubt whether this is sufficient to explain the unprecedented place family questions have in major social issues of the day. Perhaps these beliefs and experiences figure more as reactions to the striking transformation of the interconnection of family life and economic and political activity in recent decades. While these are not wholly novel trends, since the second world war, state and corporate penetration of the family sphere have accelerated and proliferated in unique and unprecedented ways. Compulsory mass education is an innovation of an earlier phase of capitalist development, but standardized testing, tracking, psychological observation and control, vocational planning, and so on represent new forms of state organization and regulation of what once was a largely parental responsibility for developing children's capacities. And this is only one aspect of increased state activity in family matters: welfare, social work, public health, community planning, etc., all represent ways political institutions shape the experience and functioning of families, tending to leave the immediate family members as reactors to external interventions--in those cases where family functions have not been lost altogether. 'Experts' from a variety of fields, including the 'helping professions,' play an important role in this multifaceted intervention of institutions in family life. Often the result is increased and ongoing dependence on such outside agencies. On the economic side, we have only to consider the various dimensions of the 'sales effort' of consumerist capitalism to appreciate the profound effects on families of economic institutions today. One's emotions are manipulated, sensations assaulted, psychological associations reconstructed by marketing strategies that draw on psychological theories and employ advanced forms of electronic communication. In the case of television, culture itself has become the vehicle of an onslaught of messages about our needs, ideals, and possibilities. These are messages, moreover, whose senders are not constrained by any obligation to inform their hearers of the full costs, implications or even practicability of what they advocate.

Not only does this represent an intrusion in the household as a unit of consumption; the targeting and content of messages cannot help but have a subversive impact on lines of family authority and interdependence. It is not too much to speak of a virtual conspiracy against parental authority when children are invited to contemplate and demand a vast array of commodities without regard to parental ideas about children's real needs or to the family's economic situation. In such ways modern communication technology allows corporations to have their say about genuine needs and practical ideals within the household itself.

All this suggests that conceptualizing the family today means coming to terms with historical developments that have altered the fabric of social life as a whole. If family issues are inseparable from larger political and economic concerns, then we may expect that the conceptual problems in understanding family will be such as to elude the grasp of traditional modes of social thought. In any event, a reflection on the status of received ways of thinking is a necessary part of our coming to terms with family issues. Paul Santilli's paper, "The family and social contract theory," contributes to this task.

Some theorists have conceptualized family in terms developed for understanding other institutions, particularly the state. Santilli examines such a strategy in the works of classical representatives of liberal political theory, Hobbes, Locke, and Rousseau. Their concerns are both normative and structural: they want to know both what kinds of political and family arrangements can be justified, and what is required to hold a political and family community together. Their responses to both kinds of questions begin from a largely individualist conception of human nature, and proceed with the idea that the social bond can be understood as a contractural relation entered into by individuals from considerations of their own advantage.

In Santilli's view, such an approach fails because neither the commitments nor the obligations of family life can be grounded in individual interest. In addition to these shortcomings, liberal thought can be faulted for encouraging ways of thinking that counteract family solidarity in favor of a narrow egoism. In this light, one might wish to challenge the conception of human nature that is at work in such treatments of family bonds. In fact, recent scholarship suggests that the self-interested individual of liberal thought is based less on universal human traits than on the self-interested rationality appropriate to competitive market behavior (MacPherson, 1962). If this is so, then a critique of liberal thought like Santilli's may be taken as a warning about the dangers that follow from the extension of market rationality to the family sphere. It is not surprising that historically the consolidation of market oriented society was accompanied by an intensification of family as an intimate, private sphere, ideologically understood as a 'haven' from the competitive world outside (Shorter, 1975; Lasch, 1977). This experience provides historical support for Santilli's misgivings about the helpfulness of liberal thought for conceiving family relations.

With such considerations in mind, Santilli turns to Aristotle's conception of the family, not so much for a viable alternative to liberalism as for an indication of some of the qualities such an alternative might possess. In particular, this involves finding a way to ground family values in a common good that transcends individual self-interest. According to Aristotle, a child's duty is based on respect for parental virtue, and this is not as much a matter of what the parent does for the child as it is of what the parent does in the larger community. In Santilli's account, Aristotle sees the values of family life and the rights and duties of family members in connection with participation in community life for which family existence is a precondition. Aristotle understands such participation as political activity, the pursuit of the collective good. In this pursuit one may find the dignity and fulfillment that is distinctively human. How far this is from grounding family values in the self-interest of the individuals concerned may be seen not only in the primacy of the collective good, but also in the fact that the political life in which this good is actively pursued is open only to male citizens, that is, only to those who are not slaves, women, children, or foreigners--effectively, a small minority.

This may remind us, not just of the limits of Greek democracy, but also that the community ideal we find in Aristotle involves a hierarchical society of a sort that was unacceptable, in principle, to liberal thought with its formal egalitarianism. Capitalism's rise meant the doom of traditional class societies and the cultures that went with them. In particular, this included the qualitative value schemes that permitted a more positive consensus over communal goals than has been possible since. Liberal utilitarian thought, precisely with its calculating reduction of qualitative values to quantities of interest, provided a modern alternative to traditional cultural frameworks. In a relativistically minded age like our own, Santilli's use of the Aristotelian model may well appear an anachronism. In the hands of relativists, the existing lack of consensus on values tends to be given the elevated status of a philosophical principle to the effect that rational consensus is impossible in any case. But we need not accept relativism to note that the problem posed here is not so much, or primarily, a theoretical one as a practical one: namely, one of finding social conditions and tendencies that at least make the shaping of a consensus a feasible project. And we could certainly think of this as a political project, though it would differ from politics as Aristotle understood it. It would be more like a politics in search of politics of the Aristotelian sort. Reference to such a hypothetical practice has the merit, if none other, of suggesting that Santilli's reference to Aristotle may be fruitful; but finding precisely how it is demands a new conceptualization of the various terms of the problem. If it is fruitful in suggesting the need for broader community values in any attempt to understand families in adequately normative terms, the fact remains that the structural relations of family and state no longer allow for family values (and family life) to stand in a secondary relation to politics as they did in the classical setting. However these issues are to be resolved, they require that our understanding of the political be rethought along with our understanding of family.

Whatever the dangers in using past political theory for thinking about family, it is easy to see why the political model has been an attractive one. Relations between parents and children seem inevitably to involve the exercise of power, and political theory traditionally has been concerned to determine under what conditions the exercise of power is legitimate. Patriarchal right, as an absolute and unquestionable basis for the authority of parents (or of men over women), no longer seems adequate to us even if a few centuries ago political authority itself was construed in patriarchal terms.   In "Authority and the family: some considerations," Frederick Struckmeyer suggests that by now patriarchy in the family may have been dealt a fatal blow, regardless of its theoretical justification.   Though he makes no case for patriarchy, Struckmeyer regards this development with a certain ambivalence since he thinks family coherence requires some viable establishment of authority. But he is reluctant to draw from the political tradition in considering how a justifiable family authority is to be understood.

Struckmeyer follows Karl Popper's argument that it is misleading even to try to justify authority, at least as traditional theorists have done. The proper question is not so much one of justifying the authority of specific individuals as one about the structure of authority that best contributes to the development and happiness of all family members. In a sense, this is to replace a positive question (who ought to rule?) with a negative one (how do we minimize the harm those who have power may inflict?).   It is not clear to what extent these are entirely different questions, since they both refer us to issues of substantive value. If this is chiefly a matter of emphasis, for Struckmeyer it is an emphasis that makes a real difference if it directs our attention to the family as a whole, and makes us consider the complex impact uses of power may have on all famiy members. To this point, Struckmeyer and Popper's emphasis is similar to that of liberalism with its concern for the individual. But Struckmeyer wants to combine a concern for the individual with an understanding that the individual in the family exists essentially as a member of a collectivity. He suggests that it is precisely the failure of political theory to think in adequately systemic terms that has caused its treatments of power and authority to become one-sided, both in its treatment of the family and of the larger political community.

In order to establish a proper sense of the family's group being, Struckmeyer turns to systems theory as a source of concepts for under-standing the family.   In his usage, systems theory provides a way of conceiving an organic unity of family life. He employs the metaphor of health to characterize a family system in which respect for the needs and experiences of all members combines with a harmonious working of the whole. The health metaphor as well as the notion of organic unity clearly involve normative content. If liberalism relied on an assumed naturalness of individualism, systems theory, in Struckmeyer's hands, seems to assume the naturalness of an integrated system.   As a challenge to such an argument one might question the naturalness of any distinctively human organization. In any event, a reliance on such ideas must come to terms with the historical variability of structures of family authority, as Naomi Griffiths points out in her commentary on Struckmeyer's paper.   More-over, if there is some natural order on which family life should be (even if it is in fact rarely) patterned, it is not obvious that such an order is one of harmony.   Indeed, appeals to nature for justifying social arrangements often stress the naturalness of conflict and competition.

These are issues of which Struckmeyer is hardly ignorant. Indeed, he has posed his problem in the context of an appreciation of the historical changes that make appropriate authority relations in families a pressing concern. It is truer to his argument to see the introduction of a systems approach as a proposal for the beginning point of reflections on these issues, not the conclusion of them. Indeed, his recognition of the limits inherent in such an appeal to some natural order is tacit in his concluding statement that normative issues remain open, and that, for him, these can best be resolved theologically.

Struckmeyer's argument is cautionary in tone. The decline of patriarchal authority may be welcomed, since the family, as a system, does not function best under the unilateral rule of any member. Nevertheless, authority does have a place within family relationships. If the integrity of the family depends upon its appropriate systematic functioning, then we should be as concerned about unneeded outside interventions into family life as we are about its internal fragmentation, because both threaten viable family relations, including appropriate kinds of authority.

Determining what counts as unnecessary and damaging external intervention into family is clearly no easy matter, requiring, as it does, both some normative concept of family and an understanding of the complex social forces that today affect families. In "The voluntary one-parent family--some qualms," John Hoaglund considers an example of the technological developments that increasingly affect the very structure of possible families. Though he is concerned specifically with some implications of advances in artificial insemination, similar issues are raised by a variety of projected bioengineering capacities that may fundamentally affect not just family life but social reproduction as a whole (genetic engineering is such a capacity that has received some attention recently).

Hoaglund questions the viability of some family forms which techniques of artificial insemination have made increasingly feasible. His stated focus is the question of planned single parent families, but he discusses families with homosexual parents as well. In either case, the emergence of new techniques of reproduction raises the desirability of these non-conventional family forms as a question of social policy. This is an unavoidable question, since the commercial availability of such techniques ensures that the failure to formulate an explicit policy (or to reach a social consensus about these matters) amounts, in our society, to the unstated policy that market forces shall decide how individuals make use of this new social capacity. More precisely, this would be a policy that makes the use of such methods a matter of personal choice--for those who can afford them. Hoaglund has little confidence that market constraints provide sufficient guarantee that wisdom will prevail in these matters. Nor is he reassured by the fact that in these circumstances medical doctors are the primary vendors of this reproductive technology.

In part, Hoaglund's misgivings follow from doubts he has about the motives of those who embark on single parent or homosexual alternatives to what he calls the 'normal' family. He understands these motives in terms of a misguided individualism, the self-indulgence of contemporary narcissism. In this he agrees with Santilli and Struckmeyer in their criticisms of individualism as destructive to adequate family life. For Hoaglund, individualism lies behind the social fragmentation that results in families where children lack the kinds of relationships with both mothers and fathers needed for development of coherent and socially responsible personalities. He cites evidence that the offspring of such families lead lives that are neither fulfilling nor in harmony with the rest of society.

In her response to Hoaglund, Barbara Ames expresses misgivings about the way he has made his argument. For example, in his use of evidence showing a higher rate of delinquency among the children of single parent families, Hoaglund makes no effort to distinguish between cases where single parenting is voluntary from those where it is not. Without such a distinction we cannot begin to decide whether single parentage as such is the source of the social problem Hoaglund cites. We need to know about the impact of other social factors, for example, the poverty that Ames refers to as plaguing many single-parent families. In numerous cases, poverty has been a factor in the breaking up of families into single-parent households. And with divorce the problem may only deepen as the single parent--usually a woman--is then faced with the dual task of both raising children and earning an income. In contexts such as these, to attribute family problems to individualism is to hold the individual parent responsible for developments that are in fact quite beyond her or his control.

Ames also questions Hoaglund's appeal to the idea of a 'normal' family as a standard by which to judge the prospects of families with single or homosexual parents. Human experience presents no single family model and, in any case, we should hesitate to use models from the past when social circumstances have undergone important change. Of course, this is not to say that one types of family is as good as another, or that change may not be for the worse. But it is to suggest that justified concerns about developments in family life may be misled if they presuppose some lost family ideal that may have been as illusory in the past as it is today. Without committing herself to a specific family model, Ames attempts to restate some of Hoaglund's concerns by refer-ring to the need for a 'caring relation' between parents in a viable family. Such conditions of a coherent family community may be considered crucial for children's development as well as for parental happiness. Other conditions could be cited, not the least of which, as we have seen, are economic.

The point of listing such conditions, presumably, is to consider meaningful family ideals in a context where conventional models are not to be taken for granted. It may be doubted whether such a list makes much sense except in connection with actual family experience. Hoaglund's tendency to treat experiments with family arrangements as corruptions instigated by individualism precludes a searching consideration of their strengths and weaknesses *as* experiments. Even when justified by the rhetoric of individualism (virtually unavoidable in our liberal society), attempts at alternatives to conventional family forms cannot be dismissed simply as exercises in individual willfulness. The social dynamics here are too complex and uncertain for that. As an instance, we may take the emergence of lesbian households (or, at least, their greater visibility), which can hardly be separated from resistence to the complex forms of male domination. Given the many forms of violence and other kinds of domination women have suffered in heterosexual relationships, attempts at alternative arrangements must be granted respect as honest attempts to make humane households, and should be examined as such.

Such considerations suggest that it is misleading to treat the emergence of unconventional family forms as mainly the result of the reproductive techniques that have made them more feasible. While the availability of such techniques may permit wider experimentation with family relations, it does not explain why individuals are ready to make these experiments in the first place. Hoaglund approaches these developments as matters of individual choice, and engages in an essentially moral criticism based on his projection of likely consequences of the spread of single- and homosexual-parented families. His emphasis on the need to look to likely consequences as a condition for responsible action can hardly be faulted, but it leaves aside the question of the social processes that have put individuals in the position of considering alternatives to received family structures. These questions must be posed if we are to arrive at a reasoned social policy regarding the use of new technologies of reproduction. Indeed, such reflection on social processes might well extend to the question of the emergence of these technologies as well.

New technologies do not rise spontaneously from random experimentation, even if we rarely experience technical innovation as the outcome of a planned social effort. But prior to questions of the use of new techniques are, or should be, questions about the kinds of techniques that are most desirable. So long as resources are scarce, one technical innovation will come at the expense of another. Or, the concentration on highly specialized and expensive techniques, as in the case of artificial insemination, may proceed at the same time as the distribution of simpler but more widely needed techniques, for example, of hygiene and nutrition, are neglected. Questions of individual choice and responsibility must be set within the broader framework of social choices which are not the less important for our ignoring them.

Of course this requires that we have available the means for conceptualizing the social processes within which family-related questions arise. In "Family, class and school: the capitalist evolution," Marvin

Grandstaff reflects on some of the elements of such a conceptualization as it bears on the interrelations of family, school, and social class. For Grandstaff, the tensions that so often exist between working class families and schools are more than matters of individual maladjustment. Instead they reflect the socially imposed mission of schools in contributing to the formation of members of different classes. According to Grandstaff, the system of mass education we have today emerged with capitalism, and its functioning must be understood as bound up with the characteristic social relationships of the capitalist economy. He accepts Marx's analysis of capitalism as a system that is divided into opposing classes of workers and owners of capital. While the school system, like the state as a whole, may profess to function for the good of all, in reality it has quite different roles to play in relation to members of the different classes. For the middle classes, schools prepare children for higher education, and cultivate the skills and social graces of individuals who will occupy positions of privilege and influence. Schools here complement middle class home life, with its cultivation of personalities suited to the prerogatives of power and wealth and the pleasures of higher culture. On the other hand, the functions of schools for children of working classes are quite different. For these children, schools in the same systems, or tracks within the same schools, are designed for vocational training and cultural preparation for the discipline of industrial work. In differential ways, then, schools contribute to the shaping of identities, expectations, and capacities appropriate to the social tasks and prospects of various class situations. Though he does not explore the subject in any detail, Grandstaff suggests that the different relations between schools and families of different classes corresponds to different kinds of family existence as well.

Apart from the requirement that claims like Grandstaff's be backed up by far more research and argumentation than he has provided, there are important conceptual issues that such a historical treatment of family and schools must face. How, for example, are we to understand precisely the ways economic divisions lead to class differentiations in school and family? Are economic factors alone the determinant force here? Further, is not the content of education broader than an account that stresses class functions would suggest? As Joseph Flay points out in his comments on Grandstaff's paper, there is sharp division on these questions even among thinkers influenced by Marx. Grandstaff's language is that of functionalism: schools work in ways that serve purposes of the dominant classes. Are we to assume that they are consciously designed to do this? No doubt such institutions have been planned and are managed to meet requirements of the society as it is, but whether such planning and management is successful, and whether 'society as it is' can be understood solely in terms of dominant class interests are matters needing further consideration. Caution in the use of functionalist analysis is needed especially in the context of activities like education which may be doing a number of things (not necessarly consistent) at the same time, and may be doing so under the pressure of a number of social forces (whose demands are not necessarily in harmony with one another). Thus, schools may both be adapting students to the demands of an economic system and, at the same time, be cultivating their abilities to question aspects of that system. Besides responding to the requirements of economic and political institutions, the schools may be forced to bend to the demands of parents, and so on. Rather than excluding analysis of school and family in terms of social class, considerations like these point to the complexity of the processes that such analysis must illuminate. Indeed, a class analysis that looks forward to alternative forms of education must find conflicting tendencies within the material it studies if it is to argue that there is any real basis for the changes it seeks. A rigid functionalism, whether as a 'conspiracy theory' about the ruling class or conceived more mechanistically, runs the risk of affirming that things must remain as they are.

The shortcomings of functionalism as a conceptual strategy does not compromise Grandstaff's point that institutions like the schools tend to functionalize persons to the requirements of predominant tendencies of the society as a whole. This claim, which has to do with a specific way individuals are socialized, does not require that persons or institutions be in fact functional in any rigid way, but that *trying to make them functional* is a characteristic strategy of contemporary forms of socialization. Thus, while it may be inappropriate to view humans as cogs in a machine, this does not prevent them from being viewed and acted upon as such. Existentialists like Heidegger and Sartre have been sensitive to this 'instrumentalization' of modern social life, as have Critical Theorists like Marcuse and Habermas. Recent works by Christopher Lasch (1977) and Jacques Donzelot (1979) have discussed how families have been subjected to such strategies in the practices of the 'helping professions.'

In his discussion of Grandstaff's paper, Flay emphasizes the dangers of forgetting that social structures are effective only as integrated into the experience and activity of individuals. His point is that social thought must preserve the level of individual experience if it is to understand how society occurs as a human process. This is a caution not only against the mechanistic tendencies of functionalist thought, but against any effort to think about society in exclusively structural terms. Flay speaks of 'indexicality' and 'the this-here-nowness' to characterize the individual as the locus of experience and agency. Notions of social structure are, in this view, derivative abstractions of the theorist, and will impede understanding if not referred back to the touchstone of individual experience. One might wonder if this use of phenomenological thinking does not revive the individualism that other authors have treated as an impediment to understanding the family. But Flay's argument is not so much a retreat to the abstract individual of liberal thought as it is a reminder that even if humans are inherently social beings, their sociality is lived as that of specific individuals. Far from recapitulating the retreat from historical conditions characteristic of so much liberal thought, Flay's argument points to the possibility that individuality may be enhanced or diminished depending on prevailing social practices. In this way, Flay points to another reason why Grandstaff's emphasis on historical conditions of family life points to fruitful lines for further study and conceptualization.

Reference to the family's interrelations with institutions of power and wealth reminds us that the course of family life cannot be separated from the dynamics of power. And, we have already referred to ways that the family itself is a framework of power relations, in most human settings a framework of patriarchal domination. Insofar as traditional societies were organized around kinship relations, the power structure of patriarchy organized relations of economic and political dominance as well. Today the situation is virtually reversed: Patriarchy directly organizes power only within the family (and there its role is perhaps declining, given the penetration of outside powers and the impact of the feminist critique of male domination). If forms of patriarchal domination persist outside the family, they seem to have become intermeshed with larger configurations of power and wealth. This is not to say that male dominance is unimportant in these spheres: such phenomena as wage differentials and occupational typing along sex lines, the use of sexist imagery in advertising, and so forth testify to the contrary. Whether sexism is intrinsic to extra-familial structures of inequality is a debated point, but there is little room for doubt that it functions significantly in such structures today.

The question of specifically patriarchal relations and their bearing on family life is not addressed directly in the papers in this section, though related issues do receive treatment here and elsewhere in the present volume. A prior commitment prevented Barrie Thorne from including here her paper on "Feminist Rethinking of the Family" (Thorne, 1981). She argues that feminist analyses of patriarchy have made more visible the patriarchal legacy to family life as well as to our thinking about it. Such analyses have contributed to an understanding of the manifold workings of male domination and they have challenged justifications of this domination as being somehow intrinsic to the working of things. A more historical and a more differentiated understanding of family life has resulted from feminist attempts to demystify the ideology of a timeless, monolithic family--the heterosexual couple with children, with the adult male as breadwinner and authority, and the adult female as nurturing wife and mother. In addition, feminist scholars have explored forms of conflict within family life, thus contesting the functionalist image of family as a homogeneous unit working smoothly on behalf of the larger society.

On the contrary, within the partriarchal family, love does not prove to be exclusive of domination, family unity is not achieved without the suppression of women's and children's individuality, work does not proceed without exploitation. Such relationships and conflicts can no more be analyzed independently of the economic and political context than they can be reduced to it. Thorne argues that our understanding of the dynamics and organization of sexual oppression has been enhanced by conceptions of gender and the sexual division of labor as historically shaped and socially reproduced ways men and women live and act together. In Thorne's view, recent feminist work on gender has done much to clarify the interconnections of patriarchal and class relations.

This summary account of the following papers suggests that basic theoretical and historical questions about families remain unresolved. Today our society's capacity to respond to the associated practical questions remains an open question as well. Family issues will no doubt remain prominent in our political debates and all the rhetoric that goes with them. As units of work, and consumption, of personality formation and social reproduction, families will no doubt continue in the foreseeable future to be the target and instrument of policies of corporations and states alike. Perhaps what seems a steady and growing stream of studies on questions of family gives us reason to hope that such developments will be accompanied by analysis and discussion that will work to overcome old stereotypes and new illusions.

REFERENCES

Donzelot, J. *The policing of families.* New York: Pantheon, 1979.

Flandrin, J. *Families in former times.* Cambridge: Cambridge University Press, 1979.

Lasch, C. *Haven in a heartless world.* New York: Harper, 1977.

Macpherson, C. B. *The political theory of possessive individualism.* London: Oxford University Press, 1962.

Polanyi , K. *The great transformation.* Boston: Beacon Press, 1957.

Shorter, E. *The making of the modern family.* New York: Harper, 1975.

Thorne, B. Feminist rethinking of the family. In B. Thorne (Ed.), *Rethinking the family: Some feminist questions.* New York: Longman, 1981.

THE FAMILY AND SOCIAL CONTRACT THEORY

Paul C. Santilli

Department of Philosophy
Rivier College
Nashua, NH 03060

INTRODUCTION

In this paper I would like to explore the conceptual links between the family union and political society in so far as both are treated by the philosophers who are generally acknowledged to belong to the social contract tradition of modern moral and political philosophy, particularly Thomas Hobbes, John Locke, and Jean-Jacques Rousseau.

The social contract tradition has exerted a tremendous influence on the legal, political, economic, and social institutions of the liberal democratic state. It still plays an important role in contemporary moral philosophy as evidenced by the prominence given it by John Rawl's book, *A Theory of Justice.* Despite great differences between Locke, Rousseau, and Hobbes, at least three crucial points are held in common by all social contract theorists. They believe first, that legitimate political society is formed by the mutual consent or contract of individuals. Second, prior to coming together in a community these individuals are all free and equal with respect to one another. Third, these individuals enter into political society and agree to government only because they expect their rights and liberties to be safeguarded by the state. From these points it follows that these theorists think that the political community is a man-made, artificial thing and that the natural state of man is one of a free-wheeling individualism with only a tenuous connection to one's fellow man.

In today's democratic societies many people in fact take exactly the same view of the individual in the arena of politics or in the marketplace. On the other hand, however, many of these same people hold the opposite view of the individual in the context of more intimate social institutions such as the family. Many of us believe that the family, unlike the state,

17

is not artificial but is natural to man and may indeed be a creation of God. Thus, while we may appreciate unlimited freedom, individuality, and the pursuit of self-interest in matters of politics and economics we hold to loyalty, self-restriction, and obedience in family life.

And yet, as I hope to make clear in this paper, if we go back to the philosophical texts that were among the most important documents for the founding of modern liberal democracies, we shall find that the contractarian philosophers so developed the premises of their political philosophy as to define the family as a contractual institution like the state. This should raise the question of whether or not it is possible to be consistently libertarian in one's political philosophy and traditional in one's attitude toward the family, given the assumptions about man and nature found in contractarian liberalism. An examination of the texts also ought to bring out a second point, namely that when the family comes to be seen as a contractual unit, an intellectual climate is prepared for the dissolution of the family. And this should raise the question to those who adhere to traditional liberal ideals and at the same time deplore the breakdown of the family and other social bonds as to whether or not they are being entirely consistent in this matter.

By introducing the issue of the breakdown of the family I do not mean to imply that I shall point to social contract theory as being in some way causally responsible for the formation of, changes in, or breakdowns of family groups. In fact, the core of the paper is not at all concerned with the actual history or empirical realities of the family. My intent is to work within a limited range of theory, and my main question is whether social contract theory serves intellectually to defend or undermine the integrity of the family unit.

The historical background to this discussion has been nicely summarized by the eminent nineteenth century jurist, Sir Henry Maine:

> The movement of progressive societies has been uniform in one respect. Through all its course it has been distinguished by the gradual dissolution of family dependency and the growth of individual obligation in its place. The individual is steadily substituted for the Family, as the unit of which civil laws take account... Nor is it difficult to see what is the tie between man and man which replaces by degrees those forms of reciprocity in rights and duties which have their origin in the Family. It is Contract (p. 162).

This was written in 1861. Later, in 1879, Ibsen creates this dialogue between the character Torvald Helmer and his wife, Nora, in "A Doll's House";

> Nora: What do you consider my most sacred duties?
> Torvald: Do I need to tell you that? Are they not your
> duties to your husband and your children?
> Nora: I have other duties just as sacred.
> Torvald: That you have not. What duties could those
> be?
> Nora: Duties to my self.
> Torvald: Before all else you are a wife and a mother.
> Nora: I don't believe that any longer. I believe that
> before all else I am a reasonable human being just as you
> are--or, at all events, that I must try and become one.

What Maine and Ibsen have described is a shift in the perception of the
family which develops in western history, from the traditional sense of it
as a unity founded upon divine, moral, or natural law, to the modern view
of it as a legal union founded on contract. Where traditional thought of
ancient and medieval times binds and subordinates individuals to duties
corresponding to their status in the family, modern notions release
individuals from the obligations of any union to which they, as free and
equal persons, have not consented or in which their rightful claims and
interests are not fulfilled. In practice it has been difficult for the state
and individuals to treat the family association as a contractual and,
hence, artificial union. But modern custom and legislation in the areas of
divorce, property rights of married and unmarried couples, child abuse,
and child rights make it easier to do so. The view of the family as a union
which one may willingly enter but also willingly break is made strikingly
clear by Ibsen when Nora, about to leave her husband says:

> Listen Torvald. I have heard that when a wife deserts
> her husband's house, as I am doing now, he is legally
> freed from all obligations toward her. In any case I set
> you free from all your obligations. You are not to feel
> yourself bound in the slightest way, any more than I
> shall. There must be perfect freedom on both sides.

Nora and Torvald then give up their wedding rings, signifying that it is not
God or nature that binds men to and frees them from their duties, but the
acts of individuals.

PART I

Let us begin with Hobbes and Rousseau, who explicitly express the
interconnection between the political and familial contract.

The social contract theory of government has had a long history. It
was known to Plato and probably advocated by the Sophists. It is an
important part of much medieval political thought (Barker, 1960). But not
until Hobbes was it conceived that society itself needed to be framed
according to contractual principles. Hobbes believes that man by nature

is driven by desire and aversion, primarily the desire for self-preservation
and the fear of death. By nature also he is equal to every other man and
has the right to take and hold whatever contributes to the maintenance of
his existence. This state of affairs, known as the state of nature, consists
of a war of all against all, and leads man through fear for his life and
property to place himself under the protection of the Commonwealth and
the Sovereign. The political union exists only because men are by nature
estranged from and fearful of one another; so, to secure their lives they
mutually contract to give up their freedoms and powers to the Sovereign,
whose subsequent power forms the single rational basis for the political
community.

Given this picture of human nature, it is not surprising that Hobbes
(1968) thinks that even a basic social unit like the family must be
fashioned by appetite, fear, and expediency. In the state of nature, he
says in the *Leviathan*, "there are supposed no lawes of Matrimony; no
lawes for the Education of Children; but the Law of Nature, and the
natural inclinations of the Sexes, one to another and to their children" (p.
253). Thus the family is founded on two principles, the law of nature and
mutual desire and affection. The law of nature is not a moral law but the
psychological law that each person is governed chiefly by the urge of self-
preservation and seeks means to satisfy that urge. The basis of parental
authority is simply the *power* of parents to secure the life of the child,
and this power is the reason why an offspring owes anything to its
progenitors: "it ought to obey him by whom it is preserved; because the
preservation of life being the end, for which one man becomes subject to
another, every man is supposed to promise obedience to him in whose
power it is to save or destroy him" (p. 254). The motive which binds the
child to the family is the same as that which binds him to the
commonwealth, the fear of annihilation at the hands of a superior power.
Likewise, the mechanism uniting a child with his parents is the same as
that which joins the individual to the political community, namely mutual
promises or contractual exchanges, which are essentially reduced to
obedience for the preservation of life.

Mutual desire, rather than fear, brings the mother and father
together. But Hobbes recognizes that a stable conjugal union needs more
than natural inclinations, which are notoriously fickle. What it needs, he
claims, is contract: in the condition of nature, "Parents between
themselves dispose of the dominion over Child by Contract..." (p. 253).
Without such contract authority over the child, Hobbes reasons, it belongs
naturally to the mother, since only she can know who the father is. It is
not clear, however, why this knowledge should be grounds for maternal
dominion; and, in fact, Hobbes thinks that the true ground for authority,
paternal or maternal, is power and fear, as we have discovered.

Two problems remain unsolved in Hobbes' view of the family as a
contractual union. Nothing more than self-interest ties each family
member to the other, just as nothing more than self-interest ties each

member of a commonwealth to the other. How, then, is the self-interest of the parents served by the toil of caring for their children? What, so to speak, do they get out of the bargain? A second problem is closely related to the first: What obliges a father to care for his spouse and his children? This can be answered by pointing to the duties undertaken and promised in the marital contract. But that simply pushes the problem further back, for now the question is, Why should the father fulfill the terms of the contract? If no natural obligation precedes the establishment of the familial contract and if there is no supreme power like the sovereign of the Commonwealth enforcing the terms of the contract--as Hobbes says there must be if the contract is to be a contract--there are no rational motives, not self-interest, not morality, not fear, to bind the father to his family. And, ultimately, the same could be said for the mother.

Rousseau, like Hobbes, explicitly defines the family as a contractual association, analogous to political society, and he also tries to supply the father with a rational motive missing in Hobbes for joining and remaining in the contract. Rousseau (1967) states that the family is "the primitive model of political societies; the chief is the analogue of the father, while the people represent the children; and all being free and equal alienate their liberty only for their own advantage" (p. 8). Like Hobbes he believes that the first natural law of a man's being is "to attend to his own preservation." This law compels the individual to leave the state of nature where he is continuously subject to the threat of war and destruction and to enter into a political society. The political state is made when individuals by mutual consent and contract alienate their natural rights and liberties to the whole community, gaining thereby security and moral freedom (pp. 17-19, 23). Similarly, children oblige themselves to their father "only so long as they have need of him for their own preservation." "As soon as this need ceases, the natural bond dissolves" (p. 8). What makes the bond of child and father natural, for Rousseau, is certainly not the tie of blood or the commands of morality, but rather the natural desire to keep one's self from death. The family is a convenient, but also conventional instrument for achieving this end for a child; it should not be supposed that it is a necessary or the sole instrument. When the child is old enough to take care of himself any pretense that the family union is natural and enduring is dissolved; if the family continues at all, it is, to quote Rousseau, "kept together only by convention." This convention, however, is merely the explicit expression of the convention at the heart of family relationships which had been present from the beginning. The child is conceived as having from the start tacitly agreed to family membership and obedience to its rules in exchange for the advantages received from that relationship. In turn, the father obligates himself to care for the child because his love for her "repays him for the care he bestows." According to Rousseau, therefore, the family becomes a means by which the father fulfills his self-interest, namely by gratifying paternal desires; and as long as the father feels

affections for his children the exchange can be said to be equitable--
affection in payment for life.

The problem with this, however, is that fatherly love, like familial
love in general, is not natural to man, but is artificially induced.
Rousseau tells us this in the *Discourse on the Origin and Foundation of
Inequality Among Mankind.* In that work he hypothesizes that man in the
original state of nature does not have families, and is a rather uncom-
plicated creature, living for no purpose, moved by simple unaffected
appetites, sympathetic but not especially moral, without reason and
language. His desires push him to join with the other sex, but in a
haphazard and temporary way only: "Their need once gratified the sexes
took no further notice of each other, and even the child was nothing to his
mother the moment he could do without her" (pp. 208, 212). The father
"did not even know his children." Paternal, as indeed conjugal, love begins
rather by accident, from the fact that people happen to find themselves
living together in the same shelters and buildings and begin to take
affectionate notice of one another. Love is not the basis for family union
so much as it is the *result* of accidental cohabitation. Rousseau explains
the origins of romantic love among the young: "By seeing each other
often they *contract* (emphasis added) a habit which makes it painful not to
see each other always" (p. 218). Rousseau insists that the emotional bond
of family life is in truth an artificial need which has become a habit of
such compulsion that it has degenerated into a real need.

For both Hobbes and Rousseau, then, the family is no more natural
to man than the state; or rather we should say that they are equally
natural because they both result from a logic of private desires which
drives the individual to family and state in order to satisfy those desires.
These institutions will be stable and enduring as long as the proper desires
are present and as long as restrictions on liberty are seen to be
advantageous to the individual. Otherwise, reversion to a more primitive,
freer state is likely.

Part II

At first glance, Locke's (1924) view of the family seems quite
different from that of Hobbes and Rousseau, especially as he writes of it
in the first of the *Two Treatises of Civil Government.* His avowed
purpose in writing the *Treatises* is to show, against Sir Robert Filmer's
Patriarcha, that patriarchal and civil authority and the unions which they
govern are based on two, incompatible types of power. Civil authority is
determined by a contract wherein each individual gives up to the state the
power he had in the state of nature of defining and executing moral law in
protection of his rights (II, sections 6, 7, 87-89). Prior to the civil
contract there are rights and duties defined by the natural law known to
reason. This natural law, in accordance with tradition, obliges parents to
care for their children and children to obey and honor their parents. This
law also defines the divine nature of the marital relationship, and Locke

cites with approval the command of the New Testament, "for whom God hath joined together let no man put asunder" (I, section 63). Whereas a political association can be broken upon the failure of the contracting parties to carry out the terms of the contract, no power, including magisterial authority, can release a child from the duty to honor his parents: "the title to this 'honour' is vested in the parents by nature, and is a right which accrues to them by their having begotten their children, and God by many positive declarations has confirmed it to them" (I, section 63).

Does Locke's liberal political philosophy affect only the state, leaving matters of family life untouched? It would be strange if Locke did not see the consequences of his contract doctrine which others of his generation saw almost immediately. Locke's remodelling of the political theory of state power brought with it, according to the historian, Lawrence Stone (1977), "a severe modification of theories about patriarchal power within the family and the rights of the individual" (p. 240). In 1697, seven years after the publication of the *Treatises*, a character, Lady Brute, in Vanburgh's play, *The Provoked Wife*, declares, "The argument's good between the King and the people, why not between the husband and the wife" (Stone, p. 240). As a matter of fact, if we read Locke carefully, especially the second of the *Treatises*, we find that he too is engaged in the overthrow of tradition's concept of the family in the name of individual rights and contract.

First of all, in the second *Treatise* Locke explicitly defines conjugal society as one "made by a voluntary compact between man and woman," whose chief end is procreation and the continuation of the species, and which is responsible for the nourishment and support of the young until they are able to take care of themselves. When the end for which the union is made is achieved the marriage may be ended "either by consent, or at a certain time, or upon certain conditions, as well as nay other voluntary compacts, there being no necessity in the nature of the thing, nor to the ends of it, that it should always be for life..." (II, section 81). Marriages by this view, needless to say, are not made in heaven but in the same earthly nature where civil society is begotten. No moral grounds for divorce, other than not meeting contracted promises, need be present; dissolution comes through the consent of autonomous and free partners.

Secondly, there is evidence to suggest that Locke thought the society between parents and children to be contractual also. The child, he believes, has essentially two obligations to his parents, that of obedience and that of honor. Obedience is owed because the parents rear, educate, and otherwise provide for the preservation and nurture of the child; and it is owed only so long as the parents carry out these functions. When the child is able to reason for himself, he is able to will for himself and look out for his own interests. He does not then owe obedience to his parents unless he consents to follow their will in exchange for an inheritance or for lodging (II, sections 72, 73). Family bonds upon the maturity of the children are thoroughly contractual, and are mediated by the promise of property.   Strictly speaking, there is nothing natural about paternal authority at any point in the child's development, for the father exists as the representative of the child's interests, earning obedience if he satisfies those interests, forfeiting obedience if he fails.   The family is merely a temporary representative of the child's interests, but nothing in Locke demonstrates that it is the *best* representative. It happens to be a prevalent social group, but other persons or communities, like foster parents or state workers, could speak for the child's interests equally well, and hence earn his obedience (I, section 100; II, section 65).   Parental authority is much like the authority of a lawyer, whose *authorization* to act in the individual's interest comes from the individual himself.   Just as Locke needs the concept of tacit consent to explain how persons born into a state subject themselves freely to the laws of the state, he needs it also to explain why children must submit to the rules of their parents.   As long as their interests are being met by their parents, their consent to be governed by authority is presumed, although mute.

The second duty a child owes his parent is that of honor, which demands acts of respect, deference, and care.   A child must honor his parents, even when he has reached the age of reason, claims Locke, for this is commanded by natural and divine laws.   Honor, then, seems to be the source of a natural bond within the family and is immune from considerations of contract.   And yet, despite many passages affirming this to be the case, one has grounds to be suspicious of Locke here.   For instance, notice how contractualistic concepts invade the meaning of honor in the following text from the second *Treatise*: "the honour due from a child places in the parents a perpetual right to respect, reverence, support and compliance, too, more or less, as the father's care, cost, and kindness in his education have been more or less" (II, section 67).   The language of reciprocal agreements is present in Locke's version of honor, as has been well brought out by Leo Strauss (1953):

> It follows from this that if the father's care, cost, and
> kindness have been zero, his right to honor will become
> zero too. The categorical imperative Honour thy father
> and thy mother becomes the hypothetical imperative
> Honour thy father and thy mother if they have deserved
> it of you (p. 219).

Thus Locke has revealed that even the deepest duty of family life, honor, is not immune from the reciprocal bargains and exchanges that characterize the civil contract, and in this he is one with Hobbes and Rousseau.

Part III

This review of Hobbes, Locke, and Rousseau will suffice to show that for them the model of family life has been assimilated to the contractual model of political life. I would now like to offer reasons why I think this assimilation to be inhospitable to the survival of the family group.   To bring out these reasons I shall look briefly at a traditional model of the family as drawn by Aristotle. My purpose in using Aristotle is not to defend the traditional model of the family but rather to emphasize by way of contrast those moral, political, and economic principles of contract theory which render family bonds fragile.

Aristotle thinks the natural drive of man is not simply to self-preservation but rather to self-sufficiency.   Self-sufficiency requires economic self-sufficiency and the satisfaction of basic needs, and for this reason the family (or household) exists.   But the economic mode of existence is merely a foundation for man's true end of moral self-sufficiency and happiness, which is fully attainable only in the political association or *polis*.   Aristotle says that man *by nature* is a political animal.   By this he does not mean that man finds it convenient to satisfy his egoistic desires or to preserve his life and property by political contrivances.   He defines nature to be "whatever is the end-product of the perfecting process," and that "can only be that which is best, perfection" (1962a, p. 28).   Therefore, man by nature is political because the political association is the best form of life for him, providing the self-sufficiency, happiness and moral perfection which are his proper ends as a human being.   A man, of course, could actually not live in a city or could seek merely to gratify private desires, but that would make him in Aristotle's mind decidedly unnatural.   A person who is by nature not disposed to live in a community is either a sub-human beast or a superhuman god, with the sub-human being "mad on war"--a type elevated to human status by Hobbes.   For Aristotle, then, the economic self-sufficiency of the household is not complete in itself, but is organically linked to the full end or perfection of man.   What draws an individual both to the family and to the civic community is not the push of private desires, as it is for Hobbes, Locke, and Rousseau, and many others in modern philosophy, but rather the pull of the final good for which he lives.

The knowledge of this final good and the love or friendship (*philia*) based on this knowledge form the substrate of family unity.   What makes a family is the sharing of a common perception of good and evil, right and wrong, just and unjust, which human virtue and reasoned speech (*logos*) make possible.   The essence of friendship holding between equals in a *polis* or between members of a family stems from the perception of mutual virtue and a common good.   Family members do not love one another simply because they are useful or pleasureable to each other, as is the case with lesser types of human bonds, but because each has and sees in the other the virtue needed for the achievement of the good of family life, and ultimately of political life.   The affection in family relationships corresponds to the proportion of moral excellence possessed by each family member; moral excellence determines the amount of affection one person owes to another.   For example, children *owe* more honor and affection to their father in respect of his moral superiority than he to them.   With the passage of time family bonds become stronger, since everyone, but especially children, comes to perceive the good more thoroughly and clearly by gaining in reason and insight (1962b, Bk. VIII, chs. 3, 7, 12).

In contrast, the passage of time for Hobbes, Locke, and Rousseau weakens the bonds of family unity by rendering them even more conventional than they were in the beginning, because with the maturing of the child the need of the family to secure its preservation diminishes. No common good can be said to hold men together either in the state or in the family except the primitive and minimal good of preservation and security of property, which is actually a collective good, established by the summary of private urges, rather than a genuine common good. The theory of nature informing contract philosophies makes all goods personal and private, and inaccessible to rational definition. For example, Hobbes states "For these words of Good, Evill, and Contemptible, are ever used with relation to the person that useth them: There being nothing simply and absolutely so; nor any common Rule of Good and Evill, to be taken from the nature of the objects themselves" (p. 120). Unless the family is to be kept together by power alone, the legitimacy of the family, in the absence of final common goods, must be explained by the fact that it serves the private interests of its members. Those interests are usually reduced to sexual pleasure, affection, property, and life. In this case, family bonds in contract theory are rooted in what Aristotle called usefulness and pleasure, which when compared to bonds based on goodness are the most fragile and unstable of ties. For instance, the family may or may not be a particularly useful means of realizing one's property interests. It may be profitable to adhere to the family if a son, daughter, or wife expects an inheritance on the death of the father. (Notice that the grounds of family unity are the expectations of the death of one of its members.) But given a modern market economy it is highly unlikely that the family will be a means for the achievement of economic self-sufficiency, and it is likely to be the case that individuals, following the pull of the market, will desert the family, propelled by their insatiable desires for more and more economic goods. Even when we consider the family before the children are grown it is often dubious as to whether or not the child's interests are best served by the family. Since there is no objectively rational definition of the good, any such definition of a child's good by the parents is likely to be seen either by the child or by the state or by the relevant social agencies as alienating, irrational, mistaken, harmful, *etc*. Parents are no more privileged than anyone else under a contractual model of family life to know what is best for the child. Since, finally, the sheer fact that people share the same blood or the same abode does not ensure that they will have the same desires and interests, the family must be seen as a highly artificial and often arbitrary instrument for realizing private interests; and exists only as long as individuals, believing that their interests are being met by it, consent to its existence.

What may be said, however, of the love which family members are supposed to feel for one another? Does affection in Hobbes, Locke, and Rousseau serve to hold persons together even in the absense of contract or mutual self-interest?   According to Marx and Engels (1964), the bourgeosie has torn away from the family its sentimental veil (p. 62). Social contract theory with its concepts of individual liberties and rights, natural self-interests, and contract itself provided a needed social-political ideology for the growing bourgeois class of entrepreneurs and capitalists in the seventeenth and eighteenth centuries. One could argue that on an ideological level it also served to de-sentimentalize the family by turning it into a contractual relationship. The actual intensification of sentiment among family members in the form of romantic love and devotion to children which occurs in modern well-to-do families, as described for instance by Aries (1962) in *Centuries of Childhood,* does not demonstrate that families have been strengthened by an increase in love. On the contrary, it shows that the moral grounds of love and friendship have decayed with the loss of a conception of the good, and mere sentiment in detachment from virtue takes on the burden of holding the family group together because nothing else is left to do it.   Without rational foundations in virtue, merit, excellence, and common ends sentiment is adrift, cut off from everything but the highly accidental, arbitrary, and irrational stimulations of desire. To put it as directly as possible, that family members should love each other in social contract theory is a matter of luck. Moreover, affection without natural duty or virtue blurs the boundaries between the family and the rest of society. If affection is what Rousseau says it is, namely either a generalized feeling of sympathy for all men or a spontaneous product of circumstances, such as the sharing of living quarters, then there is no reason to suppose that a person will have an inclination or an obligation to love a blood relative more than any other person, or the family more than any other group. Affection is uprooted from the no-longer-natural bonds of family life, able to settle on anything from cults to corporations, unable, perhaps, to focus on anything but the self. We should remember that fathers and mothers are not naturally more loveable than anyone else; indeed, for part of life one is much more inclined to hate them.

A possible product of social contract theory, then, is the *molecular* family, a highly unstable, radioactive molecule, whose atomistic members, ever seeking their self-interest, in the absence of counteracting force or economic sanctions, must disperse.

REFERENCES

Aries, P. *Centuries of childhood: A social history of family life* (trans. R. Baldick). New York: Vintage Books, 1962.

Aristotle.   *Politics* (trans. T. A. Sinclair).   Harmondsworth, England: Penguin, 1962. (a)

Aristotle.   *Nicomachean ethics* (trans. M. Ostwald). New York: Bobbs-Merrill, 1962. (b)

Barker, E. *Social contract.* London: Oxford University Press, 1960.

Hobbes, T. *Leviathan.* Harmondsworth, England: Penguin, 1968.

Locke, J. *Two treatises of civil government.* London: J. M. Dent and Sons, Every Man's Library, 1924.

Maine, H. S. *Ancient law.* Boston: Beacon Press, 1963.

Marx, K., and Engels, F. *The Communist Manifesto* (trans. S. Moore). New York: Washington Square Press, 1964.

Rousseau, J. J. *The social contract and discourse on the origin of inequality*, L. G. Crocker (Ed.). New York: Washington Square Press, 1967.

Stone, L. *The family, sex and marriage in England 1500-1800.* New York: Harper and Row, 1977.

Strauss, L. *Natural right and history.* Chicago: University of Chicago Press, 1953.

AUTHORITY AND THE FAMILY: SOME CONSIDERATIONS

Frederick R. Struckmeyer

Department of Philosophy
West Chester State College
West Chester, PA 19380

Until fairly recently, in the West, the supremacy of the father in the home was taken for granted. Even though philosophers as far apart historically as John Locke and Karl Marx had protested against the abuses of paternal authoritarianism (Marx in particular calling for the total elimination of the patriarchal, bourgeois family), it has not been until this century that patriarchal thinking seems to have been fatally undermined. Today the role of the father has changed to such an extent that the question of who ought to be considered the highest authority in the nuclear family may be considered open. Gregory Bateson in fact asserts candidly that "the American family is a unit with imperfectly defined leadership and a spectrum of opinions. Neither parent is in a position of recognized final authority." Indeed, he continues, the "outstanding parent" in a given family

> ...must overtly act as though he or she were orches-
> trating a diversity of opinions--and must perform this
> function not with a silent baton, but playing actually in
> the orchestra, exerting an integrating influence only by
> his or her contribution to the total sequence of sound
> (Bateson and Ruesch, p. 162).

It is not my purpose in this paper to discuss whether the demise of patriarchal thinking, if not always patriarchal practice, represents a healthy change (it has certainly not made the father's role any easier), or whether it is merely one further stage in the decline of the West. I wish instead to discuss certain aspects of "authority" as this concept bears upon the family.

John Locke, I think, would have been surprised to discover what has happened to patriarchy. He found it necessary, in 1690, to point out that neither political nor domestic absolutism is justified, no matter what basis of argumentation--scripture, history, or logic--is used. "We are born free as we are born rational," he insists, and while children are properly in subjection to their parents during the early years, parental jurisdiction is strictly temporary and, hopefully, benevolent (Locke, Bk. II, Ch. VI, Section 61).

The relationship between parents themselves, Locke thinks, ought to be similarly benevolent and non-dictorial. Husbands clearly have no monopoly on parental authority, wives having what he calls "an equal title" (Section 52). Does Locke then think that men and women are *equal* in every fundamental respect, and that there is no natural hierarchy in the family? He does speak, in a famous paragraph, of the "equal right, that every man [i.e. person] hath, to his natural freedom, without being subjected to the will or authority of any other man" (Section 54). But if a person is part of civil society, he is no longer in the state of nature. So his natural freedom is necessarily restricted to some degree. In the family, Locke argues, husbands and wives *share* parental authority. But if there is a disagreement, for instance concerning matters of policy, the paternal view should prevail. His reasoning is as follows:

> It therefore being necessary that the last determination, i.e. the rule, should be placed somewhere, it naturally falls to the man's share, as the abler and the stronger. But this reaching but to the things of their common interest and property, leaves the wife in the full and free possession of what by contract is her peculiar right, and gives the husband no more right over her life than she has over his; the power of the husband being so far from that of an absolute monarch, that the wife has in many cases a liberty to separate from him, where natural right or their contract allows it...(Section 82).

The residual sexism of Locke's thinking, if I may call it that, is evident in his assumption that males are naturally "abler and stronger" than females. But considering the date at which he wrote, his views are on the whole a remarkably prescient anticipation of attitudes long since taken for granted.

But has equlitarianism come of age? Are we *now* absolutely clear about how the politics of the contemporary, rapidly changing family ought to be structured?

Hardly. Equalitarian considerations have admittedly made a strong case for the view that there should be no hierarchical decision-making procedures in the family, and in the American family at least--as the sociologists Bennis and Slater (1968) point out--a democratizing tendency has been underway for some time. While I am inclined to concede the merits of equalitarianism as a moral or social doctrine, it should be remarked that philosophers are divided on precisely what it means to speak of equality in a normative way.

This difficulty stems partly from the fact that, in a family contest we surely are not talking about merely legal rights. If we are, then the problem diminishes considerably, since it is arguable that children below a certain age or in special circumstances do not yet possess such rights--for example, the right to decide whether they shall attend school. Everyone does *not* concede, unfortunately, that women ought to be treated as men's equals in every important respect, and in a way that the law (Locke's "contract") minimally recognizes. Delayed ratification of the Equal Rights Amendment provides some evidence of this.

But equalitarianism is not my major concern. It is the issue of *control* within the family--taking this momentarily as *descriptive* rather than as a normative issue--that I find more perplexing. Who controls whom, and how? Which parent is dominant, assuming a two-parent family, and how does the other respond to this dominance--with self-effacing submissiveness or with bitterness and ill-concealed hostility? And what are the effects upon all concerned of the power relationships that hold between the parents themselves as well as between parents and children?

"Human relationships," says Dr. Hedy Porteous (1972) in her book *Sex and Identity*, "remain, under all circumstances, power politics." The difference between the "meek and mild," on the one hand, and the "vigorous," on the other, is *not* one of strength, but of methods of attack. "Where the confident will attack directly, the weak use underhand methods of attack."

Political philosophers as well as psychologists have been concerned with power relationships. Bertrand Russell, Santayana and others have in fact argued--erroneously, as Herbert Schneider and others have pointed out--that power is *the* fundamental political concept.   The classic doctrine of *realpolitik* insists that raw power (by which *force* or might, technically a different concept, is usually meant) is the one constant in human affairs. The stronger party prevails, and ought to prevail, simply because it *is* stronger.   And the weak ought to submit to the strong because they have no other rational choice.

Most political thinkers in both East and West have been dissatisfied with the doctrine of *realpolitik*, despite its recurrence in various forms over a period of several millennia; these thinkers have instead tried to *legitimize* power in some way, the most prevalent means in modern times being the contract: one party agrees to defer to the other provided both parties live up to the terms of the contract between them. Each side stands to gain something from the contract, and it is rational for each to observe its terms carefully.

Some of the pitfalls of contractualism--as a basis for genuine family solidarity, that is, and not merely as a foundation for legal guarantees--have been pointed out by Sorokin in his *Social and Cultural Dynamics* (1937); the chief of these, perhaps, is its *egoistic* character. I merely point out here that in family politics as actually practiced a contractarian flavor is often apparent. No matter *who* is dominant, the others must consent to his (or her) authority. But they may well chafe under an unjust or emotionally ambivalent administration of executive power, and a price in personal health may have to be paid for the maintenance of apparent order. Whether sick or healthy, then, the family exhibits power relationships analogous to those found in the state. (This is true of non-nuclear families as well, I believe.) If the mother is dominant and the father weak and submissive, this fact is mirrored in the children's personalities. If the father is harsh and distant, or absent, this too has its pernicious effects (some of which have been documented at length by researchers). But in all cases the relationships of power have their emotional, if sometimes hidden, components as well as their long-term consequences. Thus Dr. Porteous, a child psychiatrist, is able to assert flatly that it may take twenty years for the adult to begin bearing the emotional fruit of his own childhood experiences, the time lag between "sowing" and "reaping" being frequently that long.

Sometimes those consequences, when they do appear, lead to the breakup of the nuclear unit. In many other cases, the family does not disintegrate as a social entity, but one or more of its members suffers a neurotic or even psychotic disorder; a split takes place within the personality itself. (R. D. Laing (1964) documented some of these cases.) The psychiatrist or family therapist sees a few of these troubled individuals, especially the more serious cases, but many others he does not see. Yet the social and personal consequences are just as real (and tragic) in the one case as in the other.

If alienation is a noteworthy phenomenon in our culture, then, we should perhaps seek the root causes in the family--as well as in political and social structures of a larger sort--since the family both mirrors society and acts causally upon it. More than one "true believer" (in Eric Hoffer's sense) has come from precisely the sort of family that might be expected to produced such an individual. Some evidence exists, for example, that a person with Fascist inclinations is more likely to come from a home where authoritarianism has been the rule than from a different sort of family. Max Horkheimer, the German social philosopher of the so-called Frankfurt School, believes this to be the case. "The family in crisis produces the attitude which predisposes men to blind submission," he states. "As the family has largely ceased to exercise specific authority over its members, it has become a training ground for authority as such" (p. 388). In saying this, Horkheimer (who has recently been echoed by Christopher Lasch in his book, *Haven in a Heartless World*) notes particularly the fact that potential Fascists have no "psychological shelter," coming as they often do from homes where "protection" has not

been adequately provided. They learn to fend for themselves, and as adolescents or adults incline toward an ideology which exalts "repressive
authoritarianism" (Horkheimer, p. 398). The pre-World War II German
family may have had a tendency to produce such individuals, as Eric
Erikson also thinks (1963). But Horkheimer wonders if "mass society" may
not pose a totalitarian threat to the family on a world-wide scale.

Philosophers who have no particular ideological axe to grind--
Horkheimer and the Frankfurt School having a Marxist orientation--may
at this point wish to interject a normative question: granted that the
issue of *de facto* authority in the home is frequently ambiguous, who in
principle *ought* to exercise dominance? Where, in the two-parent family,
does the buck properly stop?

It is significant here that Sir Karl Popper (1945), writing as a
political theorist in criticism of Plato, Hegel and Marx, takes the question
about who ought to rule (in the state) to be misleading. The central
question, he insists, is rather this: How can we organize political
institutions so that bad or incompetent rulers are prevented from doing
too much damage? The question as originally put ("Who ought to rule?")
gets us into immediate difficulties and tends naturally, Popper says, to
lead to the wrong answers--specifically, to the sort of "closed society"
advocated by Plato in both the *Republic* and the *Laws*. Phrasing this key
question of political philosophy in the alternative way, however, enables
us to see that another possibility exists. The emphasis now is upon the
minimization of harm to, and thus the maximized freedom of individual
persons. The danger of excessive social control is to that extent lessened.

Transposing Popper's insights to the context of the family, it would
seem that here too we have possibly gone about our inquiry in the wrong
way. Perhaps a better way of stating the key issue is this: What sort of
political structure for a given family will do the least (emotional) harm to
the members of that family? In other words, what sort of relation-
ship--one which certainly will not be based essentially on naked force but
not on a mere contract either --ought to obtain among the members of a
family so that there is the least likelihood of anyone's emotional "space"
being violated? How, in short, can families be deterred from contributing
to mental illness as well as social pathology?

These are hard questions, made all the harder by the state of crisis
many families are presently experiencing. Moreover, philosophers are
notorious for asking rather than answering questions. Yet on the level of
theory, at least, perhaps Popper's question is the correct one. To the
wrong question ("Whose will should prevail in the family?") we naturally
tend to get the wrong answer ("the father" or "the parents"). These
answers are wrong because each tends to generate its own practical if not
theoretical difficulties: the mother is likely to resent the father's
authority, or at any rate the manner in which it is imposed, and the
children may refuse to accept the authority of either parent. The *de*

facto authority that the dominant figure has may easily tend to be abused, though this seems (perhaps *only* seems) to be much less a danger now than in former centuries. Moreover, many families now have only a single parent, or a combination of natural parent and step-parent.

There is also, of course, the further difficulty of justifying paternal or parental authority. Scriptural or historical arguments, such as Locke encountered from Sir Robert Filmer, would not be thought convincing by many today. But Locke's appeal to the "law of nature" is equally unpalatable to many philosophers.

Perhaps the problem of *justifying* authority, in a family context, is less crucial than the problem of avoiding injury to persons. And possibly the issue of who ought to run the family pales in comparison with the observed fact that healthy families seem not to stress the matter of authority at all (Lewis, et al., 1976). Those kinds of families embody what has been called a 'polycentric' order (Wilczak, 1975) as opposed to a 'pyramidal' sort; decisions are not made unilaterally and uncontestably, but involve everyone who has a stake in them.

The pyramidal model, so prevalent in the past, is severely handicapped by its reliance on political ideas--most notably that of the kingship--which are largely obsolete. The monarchical model is not *totally* without value, for of course *someone*--in the family as in the state--must make certain decisions binding on everyone, decisions which may benefit certain parties more than others. But to stress the *right* of particular parties (say, the male) to make arbitrary final decisions overlooks the practical necessity for mutual give and take as well as the serious emotional consequences of treating some persons in the family as though their input did not count at all or counted less than that of others.

Political metaphors and analogies are of limited worth in family contexts not only because they don't work very well, but also because they overlook the part-and-whole, systemic structure of family functioning. Systems theory, as applied to the family (Bateson, 1971; Lewis, et al., 1976; Satir, 1972), emphasizes the holistic self-corrective tendency in any system so that questions of authority are properly peripheral to the larger alternatives of health versus illness, growth versus decay. The family, as a whole, cannot be emotionally healthy if the constituent members are not healthy, and to help one of the parts is to help the whole. If the family does indeed constitute a kind of natural system, then the political question as posed by Popper in its revised form does possibly suggest, if not the right answer, then at least some of the wrong answers to the problem of domestic authority. Perhaps it is upon the *mutually* beneficial or *mutually* harmful purposes of a family's members that the well being of the whole *and* its parts depends. As one practitioner of "family therapy" who is also committed to the systems approach puts it, in a healthy family "...children and parents control and accommodate to each other, and the hierarchical issues are more differentiated" (Minuchin and Minuchin, 1974,

p. 132, my italics). Unlike what might be done on a more traditional model of the family, intervention here--for instance, in the case of a battered child--involves "all parts of the system". On this model, there can be no simple cause and effect explanation that will account for the complexity of interpersonal relationships in the family, and therefore trying to help a family by identifying some one individual or factor as the cause of its woes is both stupid and counter-productive.

It is also harmful, however, for individuals *within the family* to act on purposes which are "anti-systemic". Aristotle, we remember, defined the family as "the association established by nature for the supply of men's everyday wants..." (*Politics*, I, 2). Let us assume that "everyday wants" certainly refers to more than food, clothing and shelter, and that it at least includes emotional needs as well. If this is so, then such popular options as divorce may be interpreted in many cases (but certainly not in all) as working against a child's basic "wants". It is a form of "interference with nature", as Bateson might put it, since one-parent families often deprive the child of something which "by nature" he would normally have--that is, the regular care of *both* a male and female adult.

This example may be argued with. It may be insisted that the high incidence of one-parent families is a sociological fact with which we must simply reckon. It may also be pointed out (in fact, it *has* been pointed out by the historian, Lawrence Stone (1977) that, in the early modern period, most or many children were denied satisfaction of their basic emotional needs *despite* having two natural parents--even though one of those parents had often died before the child reached adulthood. And the high death rate among children themselves tended to insulate parents against an excessive emotional involvement with their offspring.

These considerations notwithstanding, I am convinced that the systems approach to the family is more adequate as a theoretical model than are more traditional models based on obsolete political assumptions and misguided political metaphors. "Lack of systemic wisdom is always punished", as Bateson says (1972, p. 434). (Conscious malice need not be presupposed.) Families, like eco-systems, may be seriously harmed or even destroyed by what the ancient Chinese would call "actions contrary to Tao", the cosmic flow. And they may be *helped*, as family therapists have found, by evaluating both child and parent *in context*, and as having a relationship of *complementarity* to one another--*not* a relationship based on competition or dominance.

Negatively stated, then, families ought to be so structured as to minimize that colision of purposes which is a main obstacle to emotional well-being and growth, though clearly not *all* conflict can or ought to be removed. Authoritarian families perhaps tend to maximize such goal-related conflicts, but this does not seem to be necessarily the case; patriarchy was not *entirely* bad. It would seem that it must at least be possible to have families in which the uncoerced recognition of adult authority--though not an inflexible authority--does not by itself make it impossible to have healthy, supportive relationships among the various family members. If the family--*any* family--is a type of natural system, then what Wilczak (1975) calls a "poly-centric" order may in fact be its desirable characteristic form and its structural ideal. On this view, there will be as many "centers" in the system as there are persons, and the emotional health of each will be considered as important as that of all the rest. The rights of one are no more (but no less) important than those of everyone else. Moreover, the family will be flexible enough to "shift centers", as Wilczak puts it, depending on whose needs are greatest or most critical at a particular time.

The troubled family, so visible today and experienced by so many of us, reflects a lack of the systemic wisdom necessary to maintain and enhance the personal well-being of family members. The sickness of the modern Western family does not necessarily mean its death (as David Cooper thinks), but it does indicate that something is in need of correction. Sickness is always a warning.

One's metaphysical view concerning the nature of man and his purpose on earth is relevant here in clarifying the ultimate issues involved. On my view, which is theistic, the family should ideally be a means to the realization of God's purposes--chief of which, perhaps, is that every individual is to become a loving person in harmony with himself, others, and the Creator.

While family forms have varied in the past and are still changing in the present, there is no evidence that the emotional, moral and spiritual nature of many has changed. The need for *parenting* continues, psychia-trists assure us, no matter who does the parenting. The need for healthy adult relationships continues. The need to be loved, to be unconditionally accepted as a human being, also continues. Christian theism asserts that, in the family where genuine love and trust are learned, where what Fromm calls the "art of loving" is taught, something of the nature of God has been communicated. "You are accepted", as Paul Tillich has put it, is a fundamental truth, perhaps the most basic truth of the universe. And this sense of acceptance need not be merely a childish, mother-centered "oceanic feeling", but a recognition that an accepting and forgiving love is what we were made to receive as well as to give. Personhood is more fundamental than gender, and love is stronger than legal guarantees and even stronger than death. The idea of the Kingdom of God, as Tolstoy realized, is not primarily political but spiritual and moral; it involves, as Bateson recognized, *service*. "Familism", to borrow Sorokin's apt term, may and must be nourished not only within our varied families, but also among nations and races.

REFERENCES

Bateson, G., and Ruesch, J. *Communication: The social matrix of psychiatry.* New York: Norton, 1968; Orig. ed. 1951.

Bateson, G. *Steps to an ecology of the mind.* New York: Ballantine, 1975. Orig. ed. 1972.

Bennis, W. G., and Slater, P. E. *The temporary society.* New York: Harper and Row, 1968.

Erickson, E. *Childhood and society,* 2nd rev. ed. New York: Norton, 1963.

Horkheimer, M. Authoritarianism and the family. In R. Nanda Anshen (Ed.), *The family: Its function and destiny.* New York: Harper, 1959. Orig. ed. 1949.

Laing, R. D. *Sanity, madness and the family,* 2nd ed. New York: Basic Books, 1971. Orig. ed. 1964.

Lasch, C. *Haven in the heartless world.* New York: Basic Books, 1977.

Lewis, J. M., Beaver, W. R., Gossett, J. T., and Phillips, V. A. (Eds.) *No single thread: Psychological health in family systems.* New York: Brunner-Mazel, 1976.

Locke, J. *Two treatise of civil government.* London: J. M. Dent and Sons, 1924.

Minuchin, S., and Minuchin, P. The child in context: A systems approach to growth and treatment. In N. B. Talbot (Ed.), *Raising children in modern America.* Boston: Little, Brown and Co., 1974.

Popper, K. *The open society and its enemies,* 4th rev. ed. Princeton: Princeton University Press, 1966. Orig. ed. 1945.

Porteous, H. *Sex and identity.* Indianapolis and New York: Bobbs-Merrill, 1972.

Satir, V. *People making.* Palo Alto: Science and Behavior Books, 1972.

Sorokin, P. A. *Social and cultural dynamics,* 4 Vols. New York: Bedminster Press, 1962. Orig. ed. 1937.

Stone, L. *The family, sex and marriage in England, 1500-1800.* New York: Harper and Row, 1977.

Wilczak, P. F. Indwelling as a method of family research and therapy: A perspective on the human suggested by the thought of Michael Polanyi. *Zygon,* 1975, *10*, 175-190.

COMMENT:

Family Relations: Response to "Authority and the Family:

Some Considerations"

Naomi E. S. Griffiths

Faculty of Arts
Carleton University
Northfield, MN 55057

I would like to open the published version of my remarks on the papers given in this section of the conference by congratulating Drs. Cafagna and Peterson. The need for communication between the various fiefdoms of intellectual life, the entrenched disciplines of our universities is, at the moment, so urgent that any attempt to help in this area is welcome. When the attempt is made with hard work and intelligence, and the result the level of scholarship achieved at the conference in 1980, then the organizers must be encouraged in the hope that others will emulate them. Those of us who have been engaged in the organization of conferences of scholars from a single discipline can only marvel at the dilligence that has been the obvious order of the day for the hosts: congratulations.

My consideration of the paper by Professor Struckmeyer has obviously been governed by my own professional formation, that of a historian. The basis for my remarks is "the state of the art" in history today as regards the study of the child, both as an individual and as member of the family. Work in this area has been greatly influenced by the development of the "Annales" school of history, established in France by Lucien Febvre and Marc Bloch in 1929, by the traditions of the demographic studies begun at the University of Cambridge at much the same time, and by the fruitful impact of sociology on historians generally during the past thirty years. In recent decades, particularly in the United States, works using the ideas of psychology for the analysis of the past have further influenced the nature of studies in history about the child.

The contribution of the "Annales" school has been to alter the very basic concept of what history as a discipline involves. Once the first issues of the journal, whose short title the word is, had been published, the idea that accounts of the past should be limited to the inter-relationship of "maps, chaps, and flaps, organized by the incidence of death" was ended. Past societies were recognized as being like those of the present: complex, fragmented and multivarious, presenting any scholar attempting their analysis with a need to understand both the static factors of the time in question as well as particular processes moving events. The Oxford historian Hugh Trevor-Roper has called its philosophy "social determinism limited and qualified by recognition of independent human vitality" (1972, p. 469). Works such as Ferdinand Brandel's monumental study of the Mediterranean world, published in 1949, stand out as massive efforts of synthesis in this tradition but works such as the collection of essays published in 1971 by the journal under the title *Crimes et criminalité en France--17e-18e siècles* (Cahiers des Annales 33) or Yvon Castan's *Honnêteté et relations sociales en Languedoc* 1715-1780, published by PLON in 1974 make my point here more clearly. In the first work, for example, evidence concerning youthful criminals is found throughout. As well, there is a particularly good essay devoted to juvenile delinquency and the legal responsibilities of the under-age in eighteenth century France. Similarly, Caston takes account of the process of the human aging cycle throughout his work and devotes complete sections to the questions of the training and behaviour of children. It is not surprising that one of the first attempts to present a history of western European childhood was written by a French scholar: Philippe Aries published his *L'Enfant et la Vie Familiale sous l'Ancien Régime* in Paris in 1960.

The work of the Cambridge scholars has been above all statistical, based in the first instance upon medieval parish records, and so building the picture of what the households of the communities are about. Peter Laslett's work is typical of this school, both his book *The World We Have Lost*, published in 1965, and his organization of the conference held in 1969 on the theme of the household and the family, proceedings of which were published as *Household and Family in Past Time*, published by Cambridge University Press in 1972. In both these publications the history of the child is given as that of a member of a greater whole, not yet of individual importance but very definitely as a relevant topic of historical research. By 1971 the development of interest in the family had reached a level of such consequence that *The Journal of Interdisciplinary History* published a complete issue on the matter, which was later re-issued in book form, editors Rabb and Rotberg: *The Family in History* (Interdisciplinary Essays, Harper Torchbooks, 1973). Once more the child was both an integral part of essays such as Robert Wells' "Demographic Change and the Life Cycle of American Families", and the centre of attraction in others, such as David Rothman's "Documents in Search of a Historian: Toward a History of Children and Youth in America".

Time and space preclude any real discussion of the way in which the impact of sociology on history during the last decade has led to support for studies of the child.   Suffice it to underline the importance of the *Journal of Interdisciplinary Studies*, published by the Massachusetts Institute of Technology, and of a similar journal, the *Comparative Studies in Society and History*, published by Cambridge University Press.

The work in psycho-history is, as has been suggested, the most recent development in attempts to relate the history of the child. One of the very best examples is the short essay by the American historian John Demos entitled "Demography and psychology in the historical study of family life: a personal report", published as part of the edition of essays edited by Laslett and Wall (1972). Briefly, Demos wonders what the cramped space of the average late seventeenth century houses of Puritan families meant for the ethics of the individuals, and suggests that since "the family had to maintain a smooth kind of operational equilibrium.... What this probably meant in practice was a strong unconscious restraint on the expression of hostile impulses against the members of one's own household" (p. 563). He goes on to suggest that Puritan upbringing in this area would result in anxieties about aggression being the root of childhood training rather than anxieties about sexual conduct. Consideration of this paper makes an excellent introduction to the specific comments I wish to make on the ideas of Professor Struckmeyer, for Dr. Demos is quintessentially the historian at work, concerned with how matters are translated into action. Authority is taken for granted, the control of parent over child is seen as there, present. What is at issue are the matters for which control is used and the methods by which control is put into practice.

For Professor Struckmeyer, while such questions have an importance, the thrust of his paper is not on the use of authority for well-defined aims, and only marginally upon the way in which authority is exercised. His concern is the existence of authority as an element in the organization of the family and, the family being the social unit which molds its members, the probably neurotic or psychotic consequences which will result from authority ill-established. I found the argument presented interesting and pleasantly discussed. The use of arguments from Bateson's work *Communication: The Social Matrix of Psychology*, 1961, and of Porteus on psychology, *Sex and Identity*, 1972, as well as points taken from Karl Popper and Pitirim Sorokin made for an elegant theory, based, if I have understood it correctly, on a belief in the natural strength of the family unit.

I would like to see Professor Struckmeyer's ideas examined in much more detail, and given a historical context. As has been suggested, there does exist the type of evidence in published works which would provide for this possibility in terms of European and North American households for almost any period after the Renaissance. It would be most interesting to discuss the way in which authority was made manifest and whether there was any variation in obedience codes according to the situation of the families, possible variables being rural/urban, religious belief, poverty or wealth, etc. Was there significant difference in the authority patterns of the wealthy Catholic Italian families of the late Renaissance, whose marriage contracts provided considerable protection for women, and the Dutch bourgeoisie who favoured educated women as marriage partners because of their value as secretaries in business? Are there major differences in family behaviour shown by families of the Protestant fisherfolk from the British West country, off to the Grand Banks of Newfoundland, and families of Basque fishermen, who were similarly employed?

I would like to conclude by reiterating my opening point: the necessity for such communications as these between scholars. My own interests at the moment include the history of women and the history of the Acadians. I would like now to have time to set about a consideration of Dr. Struckmeyer's theories on the influence of particular divisions of authority within the family in the specific context of seventeenth century Europe, the Europe that spawned North American colonies. Roger Thompson's *Women in Stuart England and American--A Comparative Study*; (Routledge Keegan Paul, 1974) and Carlyn Lougee's *Le Paradis des Femmes--Women, salons and social stratification in seventeenth century France* (Princeton, 1976) would provide a base for such an enterprise. Questions about the variation between family authority in Royalist or Roundhead groupings, the difference between elite family behaviour in the society of the rigid manners produced by Court of Louis XIV and that of the families of the court of Charles II--these are the questions which I would not have considered in any depth before this conference.

REFERENCES

Demos, J. Demography and psychology in the historical study of family life: A personal report. In P. Laslett and R. Wall (Eds.), *Household and family in past time.* Cambridge: Cambridge University Press, 1972.

Trevor-Roper, H. Ferdinand Braudel, The *Annales,* and the Mediterranean. *The Journal of Modern History,* 1972, 44.

THE VOLUNTARY ONE-PARENT FAMILY--SOME QUALMS

John Hoaglund

Department of Philosophy
Christopher Newport College
Newport News, VA 23606

PART I

A salient development in the U. S. today that bears on value questions about the family and children is the trend toward more freedom in sexual matters. At a time one perceptive journalist (Wolfe, 1976) has cleverly analyzed as the 'Me Decade', even more stress is being put on individual autonomy and choice, perhaps even whim. Some social psychologists and sociologists have held that we are already the most individualistic of peoples, and they view our individualism as too extreme (Slater, 1970; Lasch, 1979). Many are claiming today that they should be free to use their sexual organs as they choose. Sexual relations between and among consenting adults appear to occur more frequently today, that is with fewer legal and moral restraints than in the past. People are less reluctant to discuss their sex lives publicly. Sexual relations between teenagers of ever tenderer years seem also on the increase.

No doubt the aim of much of this sexual activity is sensual gratification. *But a highly significant and as yet little noticed concomitant of this sexual freedom for sensual gratification is a parallel claim of sexual freedom for the individual in matters of reproduction or procreation.* Indeed there is an even further claim on access to whatever aids to reproduction modern medical technology can provide. Here is an instructive example of such a claim on artificial insemination with donor sperm (AID). The February 12, 1979 issue of *Newsweek* carries under the caption 'Life/Style' an article entitled 'Lesbian Mothers'. (The maturing generation, I might interject for anyone who has failed to notice this, prefers to view value questions, questions of good or bad and right or wrong, as questions of more or less acceptable lifestyles.) We are told that some lesbians are using AID to satisfy their maternal desires. One

43

unmarried lesbian waits apprehensively in the office of a Santa Monica gynecologist, hoping he will provide her with AID without asking for a husband's consent.

'Just because I'm gay,' she says, 'doesn't mean I don't want to experience pregnancy and parenting. I've made my sexual decision, now I should have the right to decide if I should bear children. Heterosexual women have the right. Why shouldn't I have it too?'

This case raises a number of value questions. Are there pregnancy and parenting experiences to which everyone has rights? Do all hetero-sexual women have a right to bear children? Can heterosexual women be granted such a right and homosexual women denied a similar one without discrimination against the latter? Does every woman have a right to any medical technique which might enable her to experience the pregnancy and parenting which congenital defect, illness, or disinclination to engage in procreative sexual relations has otherwise denied her? Or (which may be the same question put a different way) should the free-market forces of supply and demand be the only check on the public's access to medicine's new fertility techniques?

What about men? Traditionally they have played a role in pregnancy and parenting. Until relatively recent times their role was an indis-pensible one. The above questions arise in part because man's role in procreation, except as an anonymous donor of sperm, is now a dispensible one. Parthenogenesis, or shock stimulation of cell division in the ovum, may in the future dispense with even the sperm. But further refinements of *in vitro* fertilization (TVF) and gestation of the embryo and fetus outside the uterus (ectogenesis) may also render women's role in pro-creation dispensable, except as an anonymous donor of ova. Here are some questions that arise in part because of this. Do men have a right to experience parenting? Do they have a right to experience pregnancy to the extent that they are able, for example, with the artificial womb? Or as Joseph Fletcher envisages (Pratt, 1980), with IVF and the embryo transferred to a uterus that has been implanted in the male abdominal cavity? Do men have a right to any new medical tachniques that might gain them greater access to these experiences? Can women be granted such a right and men be denied a similar one without discrimination against the latter?

These questions are at once important and difficult ones. I do not have the answers. But I hope that my groping efforts may spur others on to find them.

First of all, a right (whatever else it may be) is a legitimate claim. There is no doubt that some people are making a claim to experience pregnancy and parenting. Is this claim legitimate? The more basic question seems to be: Do people have a right to reproduce? The Universal Declaration of Human Rights adopted by the United Nations in

1948 does recognize that 'Men and women of full age, without any limitation due to race, nationality, or religion, have the right to marry and to found a family' (Article 16.1). A reasonable interpretation of this would encompass a right to procreate, at least in the context of a family. Cultural anthropology also yields evidence of such a right: 'Every culture legalizes an enduring union between two or more persons of the two sexes explicitly for purposes of parenthood' (Kluckhorn, 1971).

There also is ample evidence in the Bible of a right to procreate, again in the context of a family. If it is a duty of the faithful to be fruitful and multiply, then surely they have the right to do so. Having many children was regarded as a blessing of the Lord (Genesis 17:6; 22:17-24; 29:31), barrenness a curse (Genesis 20:18; 29:31). No right to procreate is mentioned explicitly in the U. S. Constitution or the Declaration of Independence. But in a Chinese-box sort of arrangement, a series of decisions of the U. S. Supreme Court have identified a right of privacy protected by several of the Amendments (Griswold vs. Connecticut, 1965 in Wasserstrom). Within this zone of privacy, the Court in Meyer vs. Nebraska further specifies a right 'to marry, establish a home and bring up children'. The right to marry then encompasses the right to procreate. Existing legal requirements for marriage, such as minimum age, freedom from venereal disease, are readily understood as calculated to protect the health and well being of children expected to result from the union.

All of this evidence points to the existence of a right to procreate. None of it, however, suggests that this right belongs to the individual as an atomistic entity, so that it might directly extend to cover pregnancy and parenting experiences. All of it suggests that the right to procreate is restricted to a couple or a small group comprising both sexes and united for the purpose of procreation by social, moral, legal, or religious sanctions. Vesting procreation in this unit appears to have the health and welfare of the offspring as a goal.

PART II

Does the child of a single-parent family or of homosexual parents fare as well as the child of normal parents? This would be important to know. The *Newsweek* article mentioned above tells of one British lesbian couple who informed their son of his AID provenance as soon as he was able to appreciate that even though he didn't have a father, he *did* have a sort of a father. His mother did not intend to influence his sex life, nor would she be upset if he manifested heterosexual tendencies. The *Newsweek* reporters urge that no evidence has yet turned up of it being harmful for such children to be raised in lesbian homes. And they advise us further that 'whatever the findings of such studies, the result will surely be the same. Women who want to have babies will have them--one way or the other'.

The rearing of AID children by single parents or by homosexual couples stands on a quite different footing from the use of artificial insemination for married couples. The latter are cases of a therapy intended to overcome infertility. The former do not involve infertility and are not therapeutic in the usual senses of the term. They are clearly social experiments. A reasonable attitude toward them would be to keep an open mind. If they turn out well, they should be encouraged. If they turn out poorly, they should be discouraged.

But up to now the matter has been botched. The use of AID to promote new and untested forms of the family has been quite mislocated conceptually. There is no precedent for individuals having rights to do as they please with their resulting offspring. If we insist on discussing this in the framework of individual rights, then there has been no effective recognition up to now that we are *dealing with a new human being who also has rights.* The discussion is mislocated as one concerned with an alleged right to experience pregnancy and parenting, or as one asserting that homosexuals are being denied rights granted to heterosexuals. Legitimate claims of this type stop where the rights of the new human being start. The salient right of the new human can be identified provisionally as the right of an infant or child to the optimal conditions of nurture and development that the state can provide (consistent with its other obligations) or encourage by its laws and policies. Much evidence indicates that these conditions comprise male and female parents bound for a long term. Their care and concern is needed for the extended period of relative physical, social, and economic helplessness of human offspring.

We cannot allow the burden of proof to shift onto the person who opposes this social experiment to show what ill it might bring. The experiment is already underway, and if it turns out poorly, many lives can be blighted. The burden of proof should lie on the advocates of the experiment to show how it promises *positive benefits* to the child over what he would receive from a normal family, or at least to show that the child will be no worse off in the experimental situation. For an intriguing reason (to be mentioned below) such evidence in the case of AID children will be quite difficult to come by. To my knowledge, no one is even attempting to gather it.

To hold that it is useless to consider the pros and cons of a practice because some people are going to do it anyway is not to exercise moral responsibility but to abdicate it. It is probably true, for instance, that some women will do virtually anything to have a baby--be it clearly wrong, strongly disapproved, or even a felony--though I doubt that this is true of most or even many women. Even so, this would not constitute weighty evidence for a practice pernicious in other important respects. It is probably true, by way of comparison, that U. S. citizens are the most murderous of those of the world's advanced industrial nations. But have you heard anyone argue that because some people are going to murder anyway, we should remove the statutes against homicide from the criminal codes, or cease to enforce them?

PART III

What about the medical professionals? They are the custodians of current and soon-to-be medical techniques which can vastly extend the availability of experiencing parenting. What stand do they take on the value questions involved? Opinion is divided. Some fertility specialists will provide AID only to married couples. Yet according to the most extensive survey of AID as currently practiced in the U. S. (Curie-Cohen, et al., 1979), the third most common reason for administering AID (after infertility and fear of transmitting a husband's genetic disease) is to provide children for single women. The reasoning of at least one physician (in Decker and Loebl, 1979) who approves this practice is of interest. He indicates changing lifestyles, and finds that single women are suitable candidates for AID if they are aware of what parenthood involves. They should also have an accepting extended family, a secure social position, and the means to provide for the child economically. 'Under such circumstances,' he continues, 'there is no reason to assume that the offspring will fare worse than if the mother were divorced, widowed, or had opted for bringing up her out-of-wedlock child.'

This liberal stance seems unwise until we have more evidence on the welfare of AID children of single parents. To my knowledge no one is disputing that the optimal chances for a child's nurture and development, all other factors being equal, are in a family where he has the care of both a mother and a father. Yet all of the situations cited above as comparable to that of the single AID mother are in fact *breakdowns* of the family structure most conducive to the child's development. The divorcee has lost her husband due to a broken marriage, the widow has lost hers to death, and frequently the unwed mother is not unwed by choice. *Choice* is the key idea. Given her choice, the widow would probably prefer to have her husband alive, the unwed mother would probably prefer to be wed, and the divorcee would probably prefer to be a partner in a well functioning marriage. In this sense all of the above are cases of *involuntary* single-parent families. The single woman who chooses to have a child (whatever the insemination) without a social father is different. She *voluntarily* opts for the single-parent family that appears to offer less to the child.

It is difficult to square this sanguine approach to single parenthood with what psychology and sociology teach us about personality development, the internalization of values, and the plight of children from homes that lack either a mother or a father. The interaction of mother-infant, mother-child, father-child, and mother-father relative to and perceived by the child is the basic source of the new and unique person who develops out of the helpless newborn infant. Personality develops as the child models itself on the parents and its behavior receives their approval or disapproval. The characteristics and features acquired in the early years persist as the basic personality structure. This structure is adapted, built on, and added to by later experiences with peers, but it is not changed fundamentally (Brophy, 1977).

Because our one-parent families are either mother-absent or father-absent families, it is useful to distinguish the roles of mother and father. Talcott Parsons' distinction of the two correlates with a dual perspective toward the family, which takes the family as itself a system and then also as a part of the larger system of society. Keeping the family itself functioning smoothly as a unit is the role of the mother. Her role is expressive, integrative, and supportive. She copes with stresses and strains, regulates tensions, gives emotional support, buffers father-child tensions, and allays sibling rivalries. 'These activities perpetuate family solidarity and sustain the children's emotional security.' Relating the family to the larger surrounding social configuration is the instrumental role of the father. He directs the family toward distant goals, and imparts the discipline and self-control that the children must acquire to function on their own effectively in society (Lynn, 1974; Parsons and Bales, 1955). These contributions are not biologically sex-specific, and in any given family the mother may perform aspects of the father role and vice versa.

Unfortunately we have no space here to explore the manifold ways in which each parent influences a child. We want to know specifically how the child fares in the father-absent home. Investigators do not identify AID children of single mothers as a separate group, and they fall into this more general class. There does exist a strong correlation between the father-absent home and juvenile delinquency, attested to by evidence too vast and too well known to need citing here (Lynn, 1974; White House Conference, 1934; Cortes and Gatti, 1972). It is of special interest that the father-son relation looms so prominent in statistical surveys and causal explanations. One study shows that if the father is warm and helpful the boy can then take him as a model, and this in turn enhances his moral development. On the other hand, many delinquents report that a severe breech had occurred in the father-son relation. The availability of the father in the earlier years seems especially important. A cross-cultural study comprising 48 pre-literate societies showed that 'Both theft and personal crime increased in relation to lack of availability of Father in the living arrangement of the society' (Lynn, 1974, pp. 200, 211f.). Interaction with the father from the 4th to the 7th year seems crucial in distinguishing the delinquent from the non-delinquent. Studies show also that the delinquency rate is higher for boys living with the mother alone after the loss of the father to death, separation or divorce than for boys living with the father alone after the loss of the mother.

A number of factors can be isolated in boys from father-absent homes. Early father absence diminishes aggression, competition, and physical activity. The development of mathematical and analytical reasoning skills is adversely affected by absence of the father. Poorer adjustment and slower development are typical features that show up in the school situation also. Some investigators stress how absence of the father reduces the number of parents to one, which often bears on the quantity and quality of supervision, education, and recreation available to the boy. Other investigators lay emphasis on how the absent father would have represented the rules and principles of the society for the children, and also the delay of immediate gratification in the interest of greater future rewards (Lynn, 1974, pp. 255, 279 f.).

One suggestive model of the delinquent boy from the father-absent home puts forward inadequate sex-role identification as an important factor. Interacting at home only with his mother, the boy never develops a satisfactory and secure masculine identification. He rejects adult masculine models and seeks to compensate for his deficiency as perceived by himself with crudely 'masculine' behavior:

> He may adopt immature peer-culture standards of mas-
> culinity, which stress aggression and daring but lack the
> modulating ingredients of protection, providing for
> others, social responsibility, and tenderness that come
> with adulthood. Since tenderness and mannerliness are
> virtues taught by mother and teachers, the boy may
> come to believe that masculinity is toughness, brutality,
> and crudeness (Lynn, 1974, p. 210).

Our investigator points out further how in some neighborhoods "there is enormous pressure to conform to gang standards...The child is daily confronted with violence, sexual promiscuity, and the sale and use of hard drugs" (Lynn, 1974, pp.206, 255). How great must the lure of the streets be for the fatherless boy who is at a disadvantage in many or all of these respects!

In view of these factors, the prudent course of action would be to study the welfare of the AID children of single parents that we already have before we put medical techniques in the service of creating more such families. One commercial sperm bank is preparing a home insemi- nation kit, complete with sperm and instructions, to market directly to the customer (Annas, 1979). So it is imperative for us to deliberate and decide now whether such techniques as they are developed should be given over to the free-market forces of supply and demand. We will also be deciding whether or not to approve a process best called 'baby-making', subject only to the whim of the paying customer.

Why is it that we have neither short-range nor long-range studies of the welfare of AID children of a type that might justify or condemn the voluntary one-parent AID family? The startling reason emerges from the extensive study of AID in the U. S. mentioned earlier (Curie-Cohen et al., 1979): Records are simply not being kept. The main reason appears to be not so much enhancing the chances of the child as protecting the semen donor from liability. About one-third of the responding AID practitioners do not follow up their patients systematically once pregnancy is achieved. Only slightly more than a third keep permanent records on AID children, and somewhat fewer than a third keep permanent records on donors. The extent of obscurantism in this area of medical practice boggles the mind:

Some respondents asked patients to conceal the donor insemination from their obstetricians, thus allowing the obstetrician to place the husband's name on the birth certificate in good faith. Respondents usually guaranteed donor anonymity by intentionally keeping inadequate records or by inseminating patients with multiple donors in a single cycle, making the identity of the genetic father uncertain.

Obviously much work remains to be done here. Legitimate claims to confidentiality must be separated from spurious, and ways must be found to protect legitimate confidentiality yet enable scientific studies of AID families and children to be carried out. The necessary value judgments cannot be made in a vacuum. It is interesting to note how Edwards and Steptoe were criticized by the medical and scientific communities for making a publicity circus of the birth of the first 'test-tube' baby, Louise Brown. Yet the publicity they allowed seems healthy by contrast with the calculated obscurantism engulfing the practice of AID. The counsel of the stoic sage, Epictetus, seems not wholly out of place here: If what you are doing is morally acceptable, then do it openly. If it is not, then instead of doing it secretly, don't do it at all.

REFERENCES

Annas, G. Artificial insemination: Beyond the best interests of the donor. *Hastings Center Report*, 1979, *9*, 14-43.

Cortes, J. B., and Gatti, F. M. *Delinquency and crime.* New York: Academic Press, 1972.

Curie-Cohen, M., Luttrell, L., and Shapiro, S. Current practice of artificial insemination by donor in the United States. *New England Journal of Medicine*, 1979, *300*, 585-590.

Decker, A., and Loebl, S. *Why can't we have a baby?* New York: Warner Books, 1979.

Kluckhorn, C. Variations in the human family. In *Community Service Society of New York, the family in a democratic society.* Freeport, N.Y.: Arno Press, 1971.

Lynn, D. *The father: His role in child development.* Belmont Calif.: Brooks Cole, 1974.

Parsons, T., and Bales, R. F. *Family, socialization and interaction process.* New York: Free Press, 1955.

Pratt, L. Memorandum on Bill to Prohibit Experimentation with a Human Conceptus. Unpublished, 1980.

Slater, P. *The pursuit of loneliness.* Boston: Beacon Press, 1970.

Wasserstrom, R. *Today's moral problems.* New York: MacMillan, 1975.

White House Conference on Child Health and Protection. *The adolescent in the family.* New York: Arno Press, 1975; reprint of original, 1934.

Wolfe, T. The Me Decade and the Third Great Awakening. In T. Wolfe (Ed.), *Mauve gloves and madmen, clutter and vine, and other stories, sketches and essays.* New York: Bantam, 1976, pp. 126-168.

COMMENT:

Response to "The Voluntary One-Parent Family--Some Qualms"

Barbara D. Ames

Department of Family and Child Ecology
Michigan State University
East Lansing, MI 48824

Hoaglund identifies bioethical dilemmas which concern all of us. Using medical technology to create voluntary single parent families is indeed awesome. Regardless of recipient, custom ordering our children through AID has frightening implications on both the micro and macro levels. These implications are humorously illustrated in a story of Bernard Shaw and Isadora Duncan (Anderson, 1977, p. 41). Duncan suggested that they should have a child since her body and Shaw's brain would be such a marvelous combination. To this Shaw replied, "Yes, madam, the snag would be if it had your brain and my body!" Indeed, there are many and much more serious potential snags.

Hoaglund presents a myriad of very complex issues. The scope of this paper shall be to examine the ideas relative to family and parenting. The issues cluster around three questions, and each question becomes increasingly difficult and complex. The first question is, "Is pregnancy and parenting a basic human right of all couples?" The second question is, "Is pregnancy and parenting a basic right of all single heterosexuals?" The final and most complex question is, "Is pregnancy and parenting a basic right of all homosexual persons?"

Let us begin with the first question concerning the basic right of all couples to pregnancy and parenting. As Hoaglund states, there is ample indirect evidence of the right of U. S. citizens to procreate. Speaking more globally, Article 16 of the International Bill of Human Rights states that "men and women of full age have the right to marry and found a family" (O'Neill and Ruddick, 1979, p. 26). Most claims of rights to procreate, however, are ambiguous and assume that those with the right are married heterosexual couples. A second underlying assumption is that

51

children will come as a natural product of the union, not a result of advanced and perhaps extreme medical and technological intervention.

These underlying assumptions raise a number of issues concerning a couple's right to bear children and the cost to society. Should public funds be used to finance such procedures as AID? Is it fair for members of a group health insurance program for infertile couples to take extreme and expensive measures to conceive? Even in dealing with heterosexual married couples, the issues are complex.

The second question which evolves from the Hoaglund paper concerns the right of single heterosexuals to experience pregnancy and parenting. Since we are discussing pregnancy as well as parenting, we will set aside the notion of adoption. Most of us would agree that a child would be better off in a single parent home than in an institution. Our concern is whether we should create, through artificial means, single parent families. It is on the issue of single parent families that I become very concerned with the reasoning in the Hoaglund paper.

Bothersome generalizations and stereotypes are used throughout the paper. For example, "The burden of truth should be on the advocates of the experiment to show how it promises positive benefits to the child over what he would receive from a *normal* family..." What is a normal family? Scholars in family studies no longer discuss *the* family. There are several optimal ways of living, and there are many more variables to optimal growth and development than having a heterosexual married couple in the home. The traditional family, composed of father-breadwinner, mother-homemaker, and children, now represents less than 30% of families. If we consider families with dual working parents and offspring, the figure is 45%. Clearly, "traditional" families represent less than half of all families. If we define "normal" as "the norm", it is a meaningless concept. "Normal family" simply perpetuates sterotypes about families.

A second, and very serious, reasoning dilemma in the Hoaglund paper is the cause and effect relationship drawn between single parent families and maladjusted or delinquent children. Based on the assumption that more maladjusted children come from broken homes than "normal" homes, Hoaglund implies that AID for single parents is a disservice to the potential children and to society.

Hoaglund sees the AID single parent family as comparable to the mother who is divorced, widowed, or raising an out-of-wedlock child. He refers to these family forms as breakdowns in the family structure most conducive to the child's development. There are some very important differences, however, between the AID parent and the divorced, widowed or out-of-wedlock parent.

First, family relationships prior to single parent status must be considered. In a study of aspects of divorce which affect children,

Lupnitz (1979, p. 84) learned that marital conflict *before* the divorce produced much stress for the children. It was stress before the divorce rather than the divorce itself or the single parent status of the family which had significant impact on many of the children. We cannot draw parallels between single parent families which have been strongly influenced by the trauma of death, divorce, or unwanted out-of-wedlock pregnancy and AID single parent families.

Second, the socio-economic position of single parents must be considered. Most single parents are women, and many are black women. Whereas female-headed families comprise nearly 15% of all families, they account for almost half (49.1%) of families in poverty (Espenshade, 1979, p. 16). The inverse relationships between socio-economic status and the probability of marital dissolution demonstrates that divorce is initially selective of less well off families. Many forced single parent families are victims of poverty, discrimination, frustration, and powerlessness. We may predict that the socio-economic position of the AID parent will be better than the average single parent.

Third, unlike most other single parent family forms, AID parents are parents by *choice*. Their active seeking of AID would suggest a high motivation to parent and a strong commitment to the potential child. Although Hoaglund reviews literature which shows correlations between father-absent families and maladjustment in children, the correlation could well be attributed to the trauma experienced before or during divorce or death or the social and economic differences between single and two-parent families. Hoaglund implies that single parent familes are responsible for social ills when, in fact, they are often the victims of social ills. I do agree with Hoaglund that research is needed in this area, but meaningful research involving single parent families must control for such variables as prior trauma, age of children, income, education, time spent with children, desire to parent, and reasons for single parent status.

The final question we must ask is whether a homosexual single person has the right to pregnancy and parenting. I have attempted to dispel the idea that single parent families, *per se*, are necessarily detrimental environments for children. But what of the homosexual single parent? As mentioned previously, homosexuals who seek out AID may be in a better financial situation than many single parents. Also, we can be somewhat assured that the potential parent will be highly motivated to nurture a child. On a negative note, we can be nearly certain that the child will experience some ridicule and discrimination if his parent is identified as a homosexual.

Just as we do not know the long range effect of single parent families on child development, we do not know the effect of homosexual parenting on the sexual orientation of children. Recent studies of gay parents find no disproportionate amount of homosexuality among offspring (Miller, 1979). The jury is definitely still out on this issue, and there is a great need for longitudinal research and nonstereotypic reasoning. Because we have no definitive answers, we cannot address the issue of children's rights. We do not know if nurturance in a homosexual family interferes with or contributes to a child's normal course of development. There are many styles of parenting within heterosexual families. There also must be as many styles of gay parenting as there are heterosexual parenting. Can we justify evaluating parenting on the basis of sexuality alone?

Given adequate resources and opportunities, single parent families can be a viable family form. My concern about single parent families, whether voluntary or involuntary, heterosexual or homosexual, is the lack of a role model of a loving, caring relationship between two parents. AID children do not even have the sense of being conceived as a result of an interpersonal relationship. The implications of this void in a child's development are many and beyond the scope of this paper. Again, we cannot generalize or stereotype, as some single parent families may interact with very effective surrogate models.

We have raised many issues of rights at the child, parental, and societal level. However, any time we raise questions of rights we must raise questions of responsibilities. Is it a single parent's responsibility to see that adequate role models are provided for a child? Is it a homosexual parent's responsibility to raise a child to be heterosexual? Is this valuable or even possible to control? Is it the responsibility of the practitioner who performs AID to assure optimal conditions for the potential child? Could an unhappy AID child sue a practitioner for malpractice?

In a discussion of begetting, bearing, and rearing children, Onora O'Neill (1979) argues that the right to beget or bear a child is not unrestricted, but contingent upon begetters and bearers having or making some feasible plan for their child to be adequately reared. But what is adequate? In this case, is adequate being reared in a heterosexual orientation? O'Neill postulates that when persons foresee that they cannot or will not be minimally adequate parents, they should not merely avoid procreating, but they have no right to do so. Perhaps there should be stringent requirements for AID parents. But *who decides* what the requirements should be?

As with many other moral and ethical dilemmas, the law will be of little use in addressing this issue. Our hope is an extreme sense of responsibility on the part of AID practitioner and recipients. Each case must be judged individually--persons cannot be denied parenthood on the basis of stereotypes alone.

As Toffler (1970) said, "the more transcient and novel the environment, the more important the family....Families won't either die or have a golden era, but will recreate themselves in weird and novel ways." We must accept the tremendous challenge of simultaneously providing for children the optimal conditions for development and accepting new, yet viable, family forms without interjecting conventional wisdom and stereotypic attitudes.

REFERENCES

Anderson, N. *Issues of life and death.* Downers Grove, IL: Intervarsity Press, 1977.

Espenshade, T. The economic consequences of divorce. *Journal of Marriage and the Family,* 1979, *41(3)*, 615-625.

Luepnitz, D. Which aspects of divorce affect children? *The Family Coordinator,* 1979, *28(1),* 79-85.

Miller, B. Gay fathers and their children. *The Family Coordinator,* 1979, *28(4),* 544-552.

O'Neill, O. Begetting, bearing and rearing. In O. O'Neill and W. Ruddick (Eds.), *Having children.* New York: Oxford University Press, 1979, pp. 25-38.

O'Neill, O., and Ruddick, W. (Eds.) *Having children.* New York: Oxford University Press, 1979.

Toffler, A. *Future shock.* New York: Random House, 1970.

FAMILY, CLASS AND SCHOOL: THE CAPITALIST EVOLUTION

Marvin Grandstaff

College of Education
Michigan State University
East Lansing, MI 48824

The history of modern society, from one point of view, is the assertion of social control over activities once left to individuals and their families.

--Christopher Lasch
Haven in a Heartless World

PART I

To paraphrase Marx, people raise their own children, but they do not raise them just as they please; they do not raise them under circumstances chosen by themselves, but under circumstances directly encountered, given and transmitted from the past. We cannot comprehend the condition of the child in the family fully without also attending to other elements of the society that share directly or indirectly in child-rearing.

With this notion in mind, let me state briefly the program and contention of this paper. First, I intend to explore the role of social class as a contextual influence on the shape and character of family life. My notion of class is marxian, centering upon the conventional distinction between bourgeois ("middle-class") and proletarian ("working class") culture. Second, I wish to examine the formative effect on family life of the institution that most generally and decisively "interpenetrates" the family--the school. Finally, I will examine the class-related aspects of schooling in the historical context in which they first emerged--the transition from feudalism to capitalism that culminated in the eighteenth century industrial revolution in England and, in France, in the Revolution of 1789. That historical epoch displays clearly the impact of the primary economic dynamics of emergent capitalism on culture and social arrangements--an impact that has since been obscured by two centuries of ideological snow. I will argue that from the outset of the idea and practice of mass schooling, schools have had quite different purposes for bourgeois children than for working class children and that the roots of those differences can be found in the class relationships generated by capitalism. In simple, I will suggest that the relationship between the school and the bourgeois family has been basically a complementary one in which, despite frequent and sometimes heated disagreements, home and school have represented two aspects of a single agenda of socialization. To the children of the proletariat the school turns a different face--one of hostility, competition and conflict, of quite dramatically differing hopes and intentions for the young. For the bourgeois child, the "heartless world" of the school from which the home may be a "haven," is, nonetheless, one whose ultimate goals are consonant with those of the family. For working class children, it is just heartless. A great many problems of both home and school arise from the Janus nature of schooling and our understanding of those problems is contingent upon our recognition of the bifurcated and contradictory mission of mass schooling in capitalist society.

PART II

In 787, Charlemagne issued a proclamation exhorting all Christian parishes in the Empire to establish free schools for the children of the laity. Charlemagne was reported to have had great respect for education and learning and did, indeed, do a great deal to foster the learning of the nobility. However, his vision--if he had such--of an educated populace went aglimmering, as his vision of a European empire was shattered by feudalism. Feudalism evidenced no major imperatives to which mass schooling appeared as a response. There was, to be sure, some need for higher learning, especially for the church and "learned professions," and the great medieval universities arose to meet those needs. But the boundary relations between serf and lord and between town and countryside were so narrowly defined, so parochial and so heavily dependent on the ascription of birth, that the basic functions of schooling were pretty much irrelevant to the social equation.(1) The nobility made do with "chivalry" as a means of reproducing the social order and the peasantry made do with family and village life. The monasteries remained under some pressure to "school" the rural boys, primarily, as Phillipe Aries suggests, "to satisfy the requirements of ecclesiastical recruiting" (Aries, 1962, p. 137). But this was mainly professional or technical training, rather than anything approximating mass education. The mandate to provide free, general schooling for all the children of the laity was not taken seriously and atrophied.

> With few exceptions the monasteries were astounding depositories of ignorance, enamoured of the easy, slothful life, recoiling from any hint of secular learning as from the very devil. The legend of the exterior school also dies

hard. It was the exceptional monastery, like that of St. Gall, which provided for lay pupils some modicum of religious instruction, and to counterbalance this, there were many cloisters that disdained any form of school even for their own novices (Schachner, 1938, p. 7).

There was no general mass schooling as a preparation for the universitites. That office was filled by the cathedral and grammar schools and, later, by the colleges which were immediate adjuncts to the universities (Aries, 1962, pp. 141-159). The idea of mass schooling, venerable as it was, had to await, for its fruition, the appearance of a social and economic system in which its capabilities could be usefully employed. That situation obtained with the "breakthrough" of capitalism as the dominant economic system of Western Europe. And, by the mid-nineteenth century, mass education was a stable feature of practice and social policy throughout Western Europe, the U.S. and Canada.

Capitalism did not just erupt spontaneously in the Western world. It developed over the course of several centuries, with a number of false starts and remissions. Nor did it develop uniformly across the face of the West. Furthermore, it appeared in conjunction with a great many other profound changes--science, the philosophy of the Enlightment, the Reformation, technology, republican democracy and class society were major facets of Western development from the sixteenth through the eighteenth centuries. Because the transitional phase was long and uneven and because nearly the entire shape of the Western world was transformed, it has been extraordinarily difficult for historians to forge any clear concensus on the chief dynamics--the "prime movers"--of the transition.(2) Among the rather bewildering array of explanations and "causal arrows" contained in historical scholarship on the transition, however, three developments can be identified that have both wide acceptance among historians and particular significance for the emergence and career of mass schooling: (1) the appearance of a class system based on economic attainment rather than hereditary right; (2) the extension and diversification of the arena of public life through the inclusion of production in the public realm; and (3) the rise of the factory system as the dominant mode of production. Let us inspect these developments in brief detail.

PART III

Even simple societies have systems of social stratification by means of which some members have more favored positions than others. The emergence of capitalism did not produce social stratification as such, but, rather, it generated a class system based on new criteria. Instead of stratification based on position of birth and legitimated by recourse to divine ordination, capitalism evolved a class system based on material success and legitimated by the concept of "talent" (Hobsbawn, 1962, pp. 218-223). In specific, the new capitalist elite consisted of those who, through one means or another, were able to amass sufficient money to enter profitably into commerce or the ownership of production facilities. In some cases the new capitalists sprang from the old aristocracy, but many others attained their stock of capital from commerce in the towns, from control of manufacturing, trade, transportation and so on. Access to the privileged status was seen to depend as much on enterprise, luck and ability, as on the accident of birth. Class status now shifted from being a given of social life to being problematic, open to contention and change.

As capitalism created a new basis of status and wealth for the bourgeoisie, it also transformed the economic situation of the masses. The power of capital resided in the ability of the capitalist to purchase labor power from workers and to sell their product for more than the wages given to the workers. This required that labor be "free" and available to purchase, rather than bound to a particular landowner. This resulted in the appearance of the second new class of the capitalist revolution, the wage worker or "proletarian." The economic status of capitalists and workers is interrelated. The more "labor value" the capitalist retains as "profits," the less there is for the worker and vice versa. Hence, the bourgeoisie and the proletariat are locked in unremitting competition over the fruits of the worker's labor--the "class struggle" in Marx's terms. The class struggle defines the political and social character of capitalism, as the two great classes employ social and political means in their efforts each to protect and enhance its own interests. This is, of course, an oversimplified exposition. It does, however, indicate the central character of social class in capitalist society--an "open" bourgeoisie and an "exploited" proletariat.(3) The emergence of the class structure of capitalism had profound consequences for family life and for schooling.

First, and most obviously, the validation of claim to bourgeois status, while initially rooted in economic success, quickly developed supplementary trappings. While the early capitalists were not disturbed by their crude origins--indeed, prided themselves on them--it was not sufficient, for long-term familial interests, to simply be a new capitalist. The status had to be expressed in other areas, such as consumption, place of residence, "etiquette" and so on. The school developed, in part, in response to the need for an agency to provide the new bourgeoisie with a patina of "culture" which could serve to reinforce its class status. "The advance guard of middle class nationalism fought its battle along the line which marked the educational progress of large numbers of 'new men' into areas hitherto occupied by a small elite" (Hobsbawn, 1962, p. 166). This form of status allocation was initially carried out through private means, particularly the secondary school. As Aries (1962, p. 313) puts it, "secondary education became a class monopoly, the symbol of a social status and the means of its selection." Through most of the eighteenth century, class-validating schooling was guarded fairly jealously by the emerging bourgeoisie. When the educational "needs" of the proletariat were considered at all, it was under the assumption that working class children would become working class adults.

We are accustomed to think of "elementary schooling" in a unitary way--as a single school serving all classes in more or less the same way. The historical picture, however, is quite different. As the two great classes emerged, two distinct patterns of early education developed. For the old aristocracy and the new bourgeoisie, the organizing center of educational practice remained the university and its subsidiary, secondary education. The primary schools that began to appear in the sixteenth century were for poor children, concerned mostly with discipline-- especially moral and religious discipline--with no anticipation that the children would go on to secondary education or college. Aries (1962, p. 309) notes that in 1543 the city council of Rouen resolved to support schools for the children of the poor, so that "they shall be prepared for service at an earlier age and in a more agreeable manner." In seventeenth century England, the Society for Promoting Christian Knowledge estab- lished charity schools to teach working class children religion and "some other things which are useful in their station in life" (Aries, p. 309). Similar sentiments were expressed in nineteenth century New York by the Free School Society, an organization of bourgeois leaders (Ravitch, 1974, p. 39). Meanwhile, the children of the elite were given their early tuition at home or at grammar schools, where the specific expectation was that they would progress on to the secondary schools and, perhaps, university. Aries concludes that early elementary education possessed a "lower-class character" and, "far from being one step in a hierarchy in which all children climbed at least the first steps together, it strikes us as a specifically lower-class education, as opposed to secondary education, the monopoly of the middle class" (p. 306).

Aries regards these early elementary schools as the true progenitors of primary education. While they reached only a small fraction of the children of the poor, they did express the class character of emerging capitalist society. They also indicated quite clearly that the schooling of the poor was defined in terms of the interests of the elite. The standard division of elementary-secondary schooling was not, then, at the outset, a division of sequence or age, but one of class.

As the class character of schooling crystallized, the interest of the new bourgeoisie in public support for early schooling waned rather quickly. A "conservative backlash" of opinion appeared which was overtly hostile to schooling for working class children (Aries, 1962, pp. 311-313). Elementary schooling for the proletariat declined, even as secondary schooling for the bourgeoisie expanded. As the children of the poor were edged out of early schooling, it became possible to divert the primary schools increasingly to the purposes of the bourgeoisie--to remove early education from the home and to translate the primary school into a preparatory institution for secondary, then higher, education. Schooling was adapted to the problem of the new relationship between the family and the dramatically enlarged and somewhat frightening domain of public life.

PART IV

Capitalism, as Richard Sennett suggests, substantially altered the scope and texture of public life. Getting the means of everyday living became a matter of daily exchange in the market of goods, labor and money, necessitating an enormous increase in just the number of social interactions taking place in an arena populated by "strangers" (Sennett, 1978, pp. 16-19). The expansion of public life institutionalized the distinction between "public life"--the life of the streets, the market and the factory--and "private life"--the life of the closed community of family, neighbors and friends. For the bourgeoisie, the private world was the place where one could be "as he really was," while the public sphere called for the submergence of personal idiosyncrasies in conventionalized behavior.*(4)*

It was, plausibly, the capitalist transformation of public life that produced what Aries (1962) has characterized as the invention of child-hood. As the public and private realms solidified, the "natural" world of the child--the family--became increasingly distinct from the "civil" world of public behavior. The child--at least the bourgeois child--was seen to move from one world to another. "Henceforth it was recognized that the child was not ready for life, and that he had to be subjected to a special treatment, a sort of quarantine, before he was allowed to join the adults" (p. 412). The school formed the mechanism for that "quarantine,"--the place where the rather difficult transition from the bourgeois family to the rigors of public life might be worked. The home and the school entered into a sort of symbiotic relationship, neither one a whole agent of social reproduction, each dependent on the other for the performance of discrete tasks.

> The family ceased to be simply an institution for the transmission of a name and estate--it assumed a moral and spiritual function, it moulded bodies and souls. The care expended on children inspired new feelings, a new emotional attitude...the modern concept of the family (pp. 412-413).

Thus evolved the historic "bargain" between the school and the bourgeoisie--a bargain in which the responsibility for reproducing the social order from one generation to the next was divided up, with that part of it having to do with what we would now call "role" socialized and vested in the school. The bourgeois family was not, in these terms, ever a "total" institution, but a partial one, nearly inconceivable in the absence of the attendant school.

The sharing of responsibility for reproduction between the private realm of the family and the public realm of the school constitutes the spine of the "modern" mass primary school. The "moral ascendency of the family was originally a middle-class phenomenon: The nobility and the low class...retained the old idea of etiquette much longer and remained more indifferent to outside pressures" (Aries, pp. 413-414). When a renewed impetus for the schooling of the working class appeared, the problem was defined in terms of bourgeois, not proletarian, interests, and the vehicle that was adopted was the thoroughly bourgeois primary school.

PART V

As public life in general was qualitatively transformed by the capitalist breakthrough, so too was work life. Specifically, the achievement of capitalism moved productive labor from the private to the public arena. In feudal society, production took place within the community of life on the landed estates. Production was primarily in agriculture where, until recently, a community-based mode of production has always been the norm. But manufacturing, either in support of agriculture or for (limited) trade was also "embedded" in a small, privatized community life and was, itself, subject to the rhythms and patterns of agricultural production. The first movement away from feudal production took the form of "cottage industry" or the "putting-out system," in which an entrepreneur sold raw materials to independent producers--still, mostly farmers--and bought finished products from them. In the putting-out system, the home and village remained the primary locations of production and the producer retained control over rates and times of production (though not over costs and prices). As production for exchange grew, so did the activity of the cottager as industrial producer. Several factors--the hope of the worker to improve his situation by becoming an active seller of his labor, the contradictory hope of entrepreneurs to lower wage rates and increase profits by bidding for labor with no alternative save wage labor, the desire of owners to break production free from the cyclic and seasonal rhythms of agricultural production, to achieve greater control over work forces and to centralize production geographically--operated to replace the putting-out system with factory production. The factory was production in public and, as such, required a different kind of worker. As Hobsbawm (1962) puts it:

> To acquire a sufficient number of labourers was one thing; to acquire sufficient labour of the right qualifications and skills was another...In the first place *all* labour had to learn how to work in a manner suited to industry, i.e., in a rhythm of regular unbroken daily work which is entirely different from the seasonal ups and downs of the farm, or the self-controlled patchiness of the independent craftsman. It had also to learn to be responsive to monetary incentives (p. 70).

A number of practices developed to "socialize" the new factory work force. Hobsbawm mentions "the practice, where possible, of paying labour so little that it would have to work steadily all through the week in order to make a minimum income," the employment of "tractable (and cheaper) women and children," and the subcontracting of production to skilled workers, making them, and not the capitalist responsible for worker discipline (p. 70). As several recent studies in the history of education have demonstrated, slowly, over a century and a half, a substantial part of this burden was shifted to schooling. The schools, for the children of the new industrial working class, took on the special responsibility of reproducing the culture of industrial work--its habits, attitudes and "values".(5) Socialization to the harsh and oppressive life of wage labor was not, nor was it perceived as, a benefit to the children of the working class. Despite the prevalence of the myth of the "common school," it is clear that the proletariat was initially hostile to compulsory schooling (at least until recently) (Bowles and Gintis, 1976, pp. 158-159). The family-centered hope for improvement of position and the worth-affirming dimensions of family life were patently contrary to the disciplining thrust of primary schooling. As David Nasaw (1979) has commented:

> The spread of indiscipline among the working people--
> their refusal to accept their place within the established
> social hierarchy, their continued agitation at workplace
> and poll--were traced back to the households in which
> they had been (improperly) raised...it was the poor and
> working families that were considered the problem (p. 17).

At this point, the elements of "common" mass education are in place: for the bourgeoisie, the reproduction of public life in general, providing a transition from privileged homes to privileged positions in capitalist society; for the proletariat, the reproduction of industrial modes of production (supplemented by the very restricted possibility of access to bourgeois society)--a transition from the gemeinschaft of family life to the lowest and most miserable stations in the rampant gesellschaft of industrial capitalism. It is of utmost importance to realize that mass schooling has been, from the beginning, an institution with two distinct functions, despite the placement, in many countries, of those two functions under a single roof. Later "innovations," such as the use of standardized tests and "tracking," vocational education, selective admissions to higher education and "compensatory education for cultural deprivation"--all of which call attention to the "class bias" of schooling--were not new inventions, but were built on the base of a functional distinction that had been there all along.

In summary, for bourgeois society, the schools emerged as a congruent appendage to family life. School and family were intermeshed and reciprocally dependent, and remain so at the present. For the proletariat, schooling was more limited and partial. The range of reproduction remaining in the family was much larger, the aims of schooling narrower and not integral to the "values" and aspirations of working class family life. As factory labor was exploitative and "alienated," so too was the schooling of the working class, as it aimed to

accustom working class children to behavioral forms that were contradictory to those of family and community life. And that condition, too,
prevails.

We cannot comprehend the family in capitalist society fully or
adequately unless we realize that the bourgeois family receives significant assistance from the school, while working class and poor families
encounter the school as an agency intent upon perpetuating what Sennett
(1978) has aptly called the "hidden injuries of class." We must not forget
that beneath the veneer of concern for all children that is the official
rhetoric of schooling lies a system born in class conflict and nurtured for
the benefit of the ruling class.

REFERENCES

Aries, P. *Centuries of childhood: A social history of family life.* Tr.
    Robert Baldick. New York: Vintage Books, 1962.
Bowles, S., and Gintis, H. *Schooling in capitalist America.* New York:
    Basic Books, 1976.
Hobsbawn, E. J. *The age of revolution.* New York: Mentor, 1962.
Nasaw, D. *Schooled to order.* New York: Oxford University Press, 1979.
Ravitch, D. *The great school wars.* New York: Basic Books, 1974.
Schachner, N. *The medieval universities.* New York: Frederick A.
    Stokes, 1938.
Sennett, R. *The fall of public man.* New York: Vintage Books, 1978.

FOOTNOTES

(1) For a discussion of the general economic and cultural conditions
that provide the genetic impulse for the establishment of schools, see
Yehudi Cohen, Schools and Civilizational States. In John Fisher (Ed.),
Social Science and the Comparative Study of Educational Systems,
Scranton, Pa: International Textbooks, 1970, pp. 55-147.

(2) For general treatment of the capitalist transition that gives
primary emphasis to capital itself as the central dynamic, see: Carlo M.
Cipolla, *Before the Industrial Revolution,* New York: W. W. Norton,
1976; E. J. Hobsbawm, *The Age of Revolution,* New York: Mentor, 1962;
Paul Sweezy, et al., *The Transition from Feudalism to Capitalism,*
London: Verso, 1978; Carlo M. Cipolla, ed. *The Fontana Economic History
of Europe: The Emergence of Industrial Societies,* London:
Fontana/Collins, 1976; and *The Fontana Economic History of Europe: The
16th and 17th Centuries,* London: Fontana/Collins, 1974.

(3) The two-class construction omits, specifically, the old aristocracy, the (marxian) "middle classes"--groups which, while owning or
controlling the means of production, do not buy the labor of others (i.e.,
small farmers and merchants)--the permanently unemployed ("lumpen-
proletariat") and (a point of major contention in recent marxian analysis)
public employees and bureaucrats.

(4) On Sennett's (1978) view, "the line drawn between public and private was essentially one in which the claims of civility--epitomized by cosmopolitan, public behavior--were balanced against the claims in conflict, and the complexity of their vision lay in that they refused to prefer the one over the other, but held the two in a state of equilibrium. Behaving with strangers in an emotionally satisfying way and yet remaining aloof from them was seen to the mid-18th century as the means by which the human animal was transformed into a social being. The capacities for parenthood and deep friendship were seen in turn to be natural potentialities, rather than human creations; while *made* himself in public, he *realized* his nature in the private realm, above all in his experiences within the family" (p. 6, italics in original).

(5) See, for example, Samuel Bowles and Herbert Gintis, *Schooling in Capitalist America*, New York: Basic Books, 1976; Colin Greer, *The Great School Legend*, New York: Basic Books, 1972; Michael Katz, *The Irony of Early School Reform*, Boston: Beacon Press, 1968; and David Nasaw, *Schooled to Order*, New York: Oxford University Press, 1979.

COMMENT: Historical Concreteness in Family/Society Studies:

Response to "Family, Class and School: The Capitalist Evolution"

Joseph C. Flay

Department of Philosophy
The Pennsylvania State University
University Park, PA 16802

There are at least two senses of historical concreteness when one is engaged in studies of the family in relation to the individuals who typically comprise it and to the society in which the family is found. The first sense is a rather obvious sense and has to do with a clear specification of what historical milieu it is in which the family to be studied is found. It is clear that it is not possible, in any but the vaguest terms, to propose to talk about "the family." The family is not something which has a single structure or significance over historical time, nor even within one specific historical epoch and within one specific society in that epoch. The structure and significance of the family always to some degree differs from epoch to epoch and from socio-economic class to socio-economic class. The family of a patrician in ancient Rome and of a street-beggar in that same time and place, and, in contrast to each of these, the family of the bourgeois in suburbia and the family in a black ghetto in the inner city are all markedly different one from the other. There is not even one sort of "nuclear" family or one sort of "extended" family to which one can point and say that that is the paradigm of a family. Whether or not the family can be described as a "haven" or in any other way depends upon which kind of family and in which time and place that family exists.

To be "historically concrete" in this sense means, then, to specify clearly the historical boundaries of one's discussion. And since within one historical time and place there is also a relative difference between classes of one sort or another, one must also be historically concrete in specifying the socio-economic, political, and general cultural structures within which the family one wants to discuss is to be found. Furthermore, if one proposes to discuss the several kinds of families found in a given society, that concreteness must involve also a clarification of the intrasocietal relations which occur between the different types and affect, in turn, those societal structures supporting and being supported by the family. Finally, since it is individuals, after all, who comprise families and societies, the psychological and psycho-social relations, significations, and structures cannot be overlooked.   What are the psychological structures operative, and what is the nature of the relationship between psychological and social factors? What conception of the human individual is presupposed in the discussion of individuals? This opens up also onto the questions of what sort of and to what degree is there independence between family and society and between individuals, on the one hand, and family and society on the other? That is to say, to what degree if any?

The essay by Marvin Grandstaff goes far in heeding the demands made for historical concreteness in this sense. Grandstaff announces and articulates a Marxist view, thereby making clear the grounds on which his argument is being made and the view of the socio-economic, political, and cultural matrix underlying that argument. I do think that some of the historical facts and analyses that he gives us are questionable or at least still open to further inquiry. But that happens to be "the state of the art"; for the whole project of really inquiring into the family in a concrete historical and theoretically sound way is rather young. So anything I might say in that respect would probably reflect no particular soundness on *my* part which would surpass the degree attributable to *his* facts and statistics. At any rate, the analysis of the school as inextricably bound up with the other societal components should be heeded by any who would attempt to see the school as *the* place to acquire leverage for societal change as Dewey, for instance, was too ready to do. And the same must be said for the family *per se*; for it cannot be discussed without a discussion of the concrete structures and significances "outside" of it which have a profound effect upon it and its formation and development.

So my remarks here are not so much oriented toward criticism of Grandstaff's concreteness in this respect. Nevertheless, one would like to know to just what sort of Marxian analysis we are being treated here. All but the most doctrinaire Marxist or individuals with only the most superficial knowledge of Marxism know that both historically and in terms of our own contemporary times there exist differences within the Marxian tradition which at times separate some marxists from others to a greater degree than any Marxist position is separated from non-Marxist theory and practice. From crude Stalinism to the Marxism of the Frankfurt School--and with a great variety between and beyond these designated formations--what is meant by "Marxism" is multiform. Thus, it would further his analysis if we knew just what is intended here by the class analyses offered.

But regardless of what the answer would be to that question, there is a danger which I see in his essay which seems to remain whatever the answer to the "which Marxian" question. The danger and consequent problems lie with the common Marxist practice of understanding as something purely objective the contradictions and tensions which underlie and constitute the social formations. That is to say, contradictions are something originating in and constituted by socio-economic and cultural structures themselves. This is not to say that all Marxists are structuralist in orientation; it is only to say that the socio-economic and/or political are understood as the real locus of contradiction. But it seems to me that the contradictions and tensions are in those structures only as possibilities and not as actualities. They become actual only in the experience of real individuals who live their lives in that society, and interact and form, and either perpetuate or revolt against those socio-economic and cultural institutions. The nature of the values inherent in the schools, the families, and civil society in general can be adequately understood only if they are encountered in the lived indexicality of the experience of those engaged with them. The world in which I or anyone else lives--and lives in the concrete sense of that term--is not that world abstracted by social scientists and abstractly discussed by them; it is the lived world of the constant "this-here-now" in which I am faced with the values for the bourgeoisie as they conflict with the values for the proletariat, or the world in which I must try to live through the negative experience of what is supposed to be positive. Life as lived through is not *just* a set of relations; for the self is not just a set of relations. Life in a concrete sense is *also* the "living-through" of those relations, a center in which and through which those relations come from abstract possiblity and are transformed into a reality and a problem.

No relation or problem of relations concretely exist "in society"; they exist only in the experience of the individuals who live in that society, if they exist at all. It is not enough, therefore, to give an "objective" analysis of school, family, and individuals-in-relation; one must also turn to concrete experiential consequences of the values and demands which lie potentially in the relations and institutions of society. Those relations and institutions become problematic only within the experience of each individual, as do also the various social roles which one has been "trained" to take on. Each individual is a unique index, a unique "place" where the givens of society and its structures, and the developed roles or comportments coalesce and form a confluence. *What* is indexed and the way it is indexed is public in character, common to all of the individuals who participate in the set of institutions and relations and who share the roles. But the "this-here-now-for-me" is not public or common and can never be. The indexical component of experience is what gives location to experience and to reality; and in so far as we discuss the structure of our lives without reference to it, to that extent we can say only the most abstract and thus in the end misleading things about it. If, on the other hand, we are to come to an adequate understanding, then we must always take into account that which constitutes experience and life in the concrete as personal, private. In other words, it is certainly possible to discuss roles, institutional structures, social formations, etc.

as constituents of life; but without connection to the indexicality of individual experience these are empty schemata.

This is not to dismiss Grandstaff's analysis; on the contrary, it is a request that it be made more concrete. What makes it abstract is that it seems that socialization is taken to be the crux and standard of the development of the self and that objective contradictions exist at the heart of society itself. And this is true of much or even most of what is presented not only by Marxists but by others as well. My criticism has been that when this is done, the indexical as such is ignored, and that the effect of this is reductionism of one sort or another; for totality is reduced to the abstract schemata of a sociology, a political theory, or an ontology. The element of uniqueness, however troublesome it might be, cannot be dismissed. What is necessary, I suggest, is the development of a sense of the indexical nature of experience and its relation to the social formations and roles. This will give us a way of understanding how, in a concrete way, the type of contradiction which Grandstaff has so well indicated actually comes to be a lived contradiction which demands our attention and cries for solution.

PART II

WOMEN AND FAMILY LIFE

WOMEN AND FAMILY LIFE: INTRODUCTION

Richard T. Peterson

Department of Philosophy
Michigan State University
East Lansing, MI 48824

Understanding motherhood--the shared concern of the papers that follow--hardly exhausts the theme of Women and Family Life, but it raises a complex of issues that are crucial to the future of women and families in our society. These are not narrowly "women's issues" (as if there were such a thing), since they affect all family members; and they are not issues whose significance ends at the borders of the family, since they concern the capacities and possible forms of fulfillment of women (and, indirectly, of men) in general. Nevertheless, the context of motherhood is surely an appropriate point at which to consider aspects of these larger issues, since, given our patriarchal inheritance, this has been the point of much debate and struggle over the proper roles of women in society and the forms family life should take.

With the exception of racial issues, perhaps no contemporary social question has stimulated as much controversy over the relation between the natural order and our social practices. No doubt this is tied to women's biological role in reproduction, but it also reflects a longstanding cultural assumption that women are somehow more responsive to natural impulses, dominated by feeling, and less given to disciplined thought or universally significant social achievement. Of course it is not only in these contexts that thinkers have appealed to what they considered a natural order in trying to understand and prescribe forms of social life. Appeals to laws of nature have figured prominently in ancient as well as modern social thought and played an important part in the thinking behind the American Revolution and the formulation of the U.S. Constitution. Today, however, a greater appreciation of the broad diversity of human social arrangements and of the logical difficulties of deriving values from objective regularities has made the defense of social norms by arguments from natural law much less popular. Rather than eliminating dependence on ideas of what is natural in discussions of social policy, this has instead prompted adoption of an alternative strategy, one that many writers take to be more in tune with scientific thinking.   Rather than justifying specific values by appeals to philosophical conceptions of nature, some recent thinkers rely on biology to establish that certain social patterns are more or less inescapable, given our genetic inheritance. Though the argument is primarily negative, seeking to show what cannot be done (e.g., arguments that compensatory education cannot improve the educational performance of blacks or the mathematical abilities of females), there are definite normative implications nonetheless.   In the recent context, these implications have been mainly conservative, though this may not be intrinsic to appeals to biology as such.   Perhaps the most popular contemporary expression of such views has been that of sociobiology (which argues that many social practices are shaped or constrained by genetic factors), but this is only one episode in a long line of attempts to draw from biology in the defense of political and social views. In the late 19th century Social Darwinism relied on evolutionary thought to justify the competitive market economy and the individualism that goes with it.

Obviously, the mere appeal to science is no guarantee of the rigor of the ideas employed, particularly when it is a matter of a relatively undeveloped science, as biology is in the context of social studies. Given the prestige of science in our society, there is always the danger that the aura of scientificity may be used to cloak preconceptions that serve partisan ends.   The reality of the danger is clear from historical experience: we need only cite the apparent manipulation of data on I.Q. by Cyril Burt--a case in which evidence was shaped to fit racist preconceptions (Wade, 1976).

The effort to explain social processes by biological factors denies what has seemed evident to many thinkers, namely, that humanity's distinctiveness lies in its active differentiation of itself from the natural order.   Certainly many philosophers have held this view, whether in theories of the mind, of freedom, of culture or of politics.   Family processes themselves seem to testify to this: not only is the initiation of the human child into human culture a process different from what we find in nature, it seems to be one that has the precise function of extricating the individual from the play of natural drives and forming distinctively human ways of experiencing and acting. Even in the context of play, the child masters physical and conceptual abilities that in the sphere of labor are turned to the task of subduing the forces of nature and turning them to human purposes. Considerations of this sort may impress the advocate of sociobiology very little.   After all, it is just such seemingly evident claims about our world that have repeatedly fallen before the advance of scientific theory in the past. In any event, it is clear that such issues cannot be resolved by purely philosophical means.   A merit of the following papers is that they help us to see what some of the conceptual and empirical issues here are.

In "Mother/nature: a skeptical look at the unique naturalness of maternal parenting," Hugh Wilder critically analyzes one attempt to use biological considerations to show that women are inherently more disposed than men to raise children. His target is an argument by Alice Rossi, who believes social scientists tend mistakenly to seek accounts of social behavior in exclusively social terms. By neglecting the findings of biology, social scientists have, in her view, contributed to a misplaced 'egalitarianism' that assumes sex role differences can be approached solely as a matter of social convention. From this perspective, the sex-differentiation of social roles becomes a political question: if these are oppressive, then efforts should be made to shape new social arrangements. Conversely, if Rossi's belief in the biological conditioning of social roles can be supported, then political energies aimed at changing such roles might well be misdirected.

Rossi clearly cannot--and does not--argue that biological factors make it impossible for men to raise children. But she can point to the overwhelmingly preponderant place of women in child-rearing roles. The issue, then, is whether women or mothers are somehow more disposed biologically to engage in these activities, and whether, accordingly, men would need what she calls "compensatory socialization" were they to play an equal role. The first of Rossi's arguments that Wilder considers has to do with the relation, if any, between physiological differences between men and women and the ability to learn to care for infants or to prepare food for them. Rossi postulates a connection between specific hormonal processes and their different effects on the development of the brains of men and women with the observed fact that women more often carry out these domestic tasks. The point at issue is not whether there are such differences in physiological development, nor is it whether biological processes affect the ability to learn. As Wilder sees it, the issue is whether the existing patterns of sex-differentiated learning can be traced to physiologically determined differences in the ability to learn *these specific tasks*. For Rossi, the rejection of such a connection betrays an egalitarian dogma that all sex-related differences in skill are socially determined. Wilder's argument does not rule out the possibility of such differences. He suggests, however, that consideration of the skills at issue shows that the ability to learn *these* cannot be biologically determined because, rather than being unique and irreducible kinds of activity, these skills are combinations of more general capacities that are exercised in a variety of contexts, including some where skills do not follow the same sex-related patterns they do in the family. Thus, he suggests that food preparation skills can be analyzed into more general cognitive and manual abilities and these are used in a variety of social contexts. If this argument holds, then no physiological account will be able to explain the existing sex-related differences in the learning and use of the maternal skills referred to by Rossi.

Wilder does not provide the analysis of the skills Rossi discusses that would be needed to show that these are indeed combinations of more general capacities. This may seem intuitively plausible in the case of food preparation, but one need not be a biological determinist to wonder if there is not something qualitatively distinct about caring for an infant that the technocratic-sounding analysis into 'skills' might miss. In any event, it appears that both theorists are engaging in a certain amount of speculation in fields (e.g., learning theory) where research and theorization are still relatively undeveloped.

A second kind of argument taken up by Wilder has to do with a more direct connection between biological factors and maternal behavior. Here it is a question of responses which are not learned abilities, but seemingly direct physiological responses of mothers, for example, those bound up with nursing infants. Clearly, here is an ability that Wilder must concede is biologically determined, but in admitting this he does argue that a biological account of *maternal* responses is not thereby established, since *any* lactating woman may respond in the relevant ways to a given child. Nevertheless, in such cases, biological factors do have a role in differentiating skills by sex, assuming that 'skill' is an appropriate term here. The question remains, however, whether this is not a relatively trivial matter since it leaves open the question of a host of other maternal activities that do not obviously require a female anatomy, and since even many mothers use other means for feeding their infants.

The last of Rossi's arguments considered by Wilder asserts that evolutionary theory makes it plausible to think that sex-differentiated roles have a biological basis. Along with their specific anatomy, women are said to have distinctively maternal dispositions for their roles in the sexual division of labor: Rossi speaks of an 'innate orientation' to their young. This she takes to include a specific disposition to learn the requisite maternal skills, and in this respect her claim is open to the same objections Wilder made of the earlier argument about the ability to learn such skills. Wilder is also critical of the idea of innate sex-related orientations. On Rossi's view, each sex has such an orientation toward the other (thus accounting for heterosexual attraction), but only women have an innate orientation to the young, a kind of maternal instinct. Wilder objects to this claim on the grounds of the notorious ambiguity of the relevant terms, and he points out that the existence of even an inherently heterosexual orientation is a matter of much debate.

Wilder's argument is largely a negative one, seeking to indicate the weaknesses of Rossi's case for the naturalness of maternal childrearing. At the same time, his discussion indicates some of the important conceptual and empirical questions that any attempt to understand motherhood in sociobiological terms must answer. Wilder also advances some general considerations for a more traditional humanist approach to motherhood. He argues that biological determinism should be rejected because of the undesirable consequences of such a position. He does not say whether he takes this to be in general a sound way of approaching the truth or falsity of theses about social life. Wilder claims further that the sociobiological view ignores those respects in which to be human is precisely to break from the natural order. He appeals to the development of such views by Freud, Marx, and Sartre, but does not offer a position of his own. No doubt sociobiologists would regard such a humanism as idealistic and reactionary in theoretical terms just as Wilder considers their position to be conservative in social terms.

The conservatism in Rossi's use of sociobiological thinking reflects her fear that reactions against the oppression of women bound up with their relegation to housework may result in the devaluing and abandonment of crucial social practices that are not to be so easily replaced along egalitarian lines. But one need not accept the sociobiological argument to recognize this, any more than one need identify resistance to sexism as the source of the devaluation of family tasks. The recognition that exclusive concentration on such tasks may result in a one-sided existence need hardly involve rejection of their importance for social life as a whole or for the identity and dignity of mothers in particular. Indeed, too casual a treatment of these activities, as Marilyn Frye notes in her commentary on Wilder, simply extends the devaluation of women. Our society's devaluation of housework may tell us more about the quality of its social relationships as a whole than it does about housework itself.

Sara Ruddick's conception of "Maternal thinking" seeks to develop a feminist understanding of motherhood that respects the dignity and lasting values of maternal activity while refusing to treat these as biologically determined. Her use of the term 'thinking' is perhaps misleading, since she is concerned with more than thoughts. Rather she is placing characteristic patterns of thought, attitude, and emotion within a distinctively maternal practice. As a sphere of intentional and rational activity, maternal thinking cannot be understood as biologically conditioned behavior. Rather than 'pushed' by biological causes, maternal activity directs itself by distinctively human interests. Ruddick borrows from the West German theorist, Jürgen Habermas, in conceptualizing such a rational practice as oriented to, indeed constituted by, interests that are both practical and rational. Unlike Habermas, who thinks of such interests as organizing forms of activity and thought universal to all human societies, Ruddick suggests that there may be interest-organized practices that emerge within human history and structure the activity of only a section of humanity. Maternal practice is guided by interests in the preservation, growth, and acceptability of the child--interests that thus organize the maternal task of raising a vulnerable organism into membership in a specific human society. Contrary to Wilder's assumption that maternal skills are analyzable into elements of more general capacities, Ruddick's view seems to be that however much mothering may rely on skills applicable elsewhere, it still retains a distinctiveness in its guiding and organizing concerns. Thus it is a rational framework of thought, emotion, and activity whose techniques are animated more by a preservative spirit of 'holding' rather than by acquisitiveness or instrumental manipulation. It involves a maternal assertiveness that is to be distinguished from aggressiveness, and a 'resilient cheerfulness' that is distinguishable from either mindless optimism or manic resignation.

Such a framework of dispositions and attitudes amounts to a distinctive maternal rationality involving characteristic normative claims. With it, Ruddick can hope to illuminate both how maternal practices are effectively organized and how they are rational. As she acknowledges, her present work does not yet represent a complete analysis of maternal thinking, nor does it provide a developed assessment of the extent to which it is an idealization of existing practices. She does not claim that her conception can be applied to all societies, but she has not established what the limits to its applicability may be. Because Habermas treats rational interests as inherent in human activity as such, he can defend their universality on these grounds. Since Ruddick's interests take shape within history, her account leaves open the question of how we are to understand their validity.

Were one to treat maternal thinking as having application to all childrearing, the way might seem open to a sophisticated sociobiological use of these themes. But this would be incompatible with Ruddick's historical emphasis, which is reflected in her identification of contradictory features of maternal practices as well as with her proposal that such features be modified through a feminist critique. To be sure, the contradictions Ruddick criticizes in existing maternal practices do not bring the organizing interests of maternal thinking into question. On the contrary, it is because she presupposes these interests that the contradictions emerge at all: they consist of the ways mothers in effect betray the principles of maternity by readying their children for participation in a society organized by the hierarchies and oppressions of sexism, domination, and exploitation. In such a context, for example, the maternal interest in cultivating a child's acceptability threatens to become a training in the acceptance of and adaptation to these kinds of social relationships. What the larger society regards as a 'good mother' may be one who has compromised the normative principles of maternal thinking in preparing her children to meet the demands of institutions beyond the family. Ruddick's point seems to be that when the extra-familial social relationships for which children are being educated themselves violate the ethical character of the relationship between mother and child, then maternal practice is at odds with its own maternal thinking. What is more, such a contradiction threatens to corrupt the quality of the mother-child relationship itself. In a society where this happens, it would not be surprising if maternal activities were themselves devalued. According to Ruddick, it is in this context that feminist critiques of the family have something important to say about existing practices of mothering. By defining and contesting the organization of women's oppression—both within and without the family—feminists locate forces that compromise women's maternal potentialities. By confronting such forces, the feminism that Ruddick has in mind helps to preserve and more fully realize the promise of maternal thinking. Because she treats maternal thinking as a cultural achievement and not the expression of biological forces, Ruddick can find in it an expression of the strength and dignity of women.   Since it is an achievement within history, it is open to modification--for better or for worse.

Though maternal thinking is a kind of women's culture, it is by no means open exclusively to women, and Ruddick looks forward to the day when men might as 'naturally' adopt its perspective and commitments as women.   In the absence of larger social changes that would challenge sexist practices in our society, however, the integration of men into maternal practices might well further compromise maternal practices by bringing into them more directly forms of male domination that women's predominant role in parenting has minimized.

All the same, maternal thinking provides a norm for parenting in general, just as it suggests standards to guide the larger society's policies toward children and family life. But whether this norm will be respected by larger social institutions, and whether maternal thinking can avoid the compromises Ruddick describes, is clearly bound up with the forces that shape economic and political life. In general, our understanding of the conditions which make maternal thinking possible, and therefore our understanding of its range of application as an analytical and normative model of mothering, requires a broader historical and structural analysis than Ruddick so far has provided. For example, such study might explore whether Ruddick is right to see maternal thinking as essentially at odds with the forms of domination characteristic of political and economic institutions or whether instead there might be a more complementary and functional relation with them. Are the values of preserving and 'holding' peculiarly appropriate in the family 'haven' within societies organized by competition and scarcity? Or does the maternal sphere betoken a quality of social relations that a pacified world might generalize?   Because housework has for the most part stayed outside the sphere of paid work, does it recall and preserve qualities of social life before the proliferation of market relations? Is Ruddick's analysis already backward looking, as women increasingly find jobs outside the home and rely more on baby-sitters, day care, and the schools? Such questions cannot be answered independently of historical research and social experience.

However they are answered, it seems clear that questions about motherhood, like those about family more generally, will continue to raise social and moral issues that have an inescapably political dimension. These will remain political not least because they are tied to the direction other social institutions will take. Given the ongoing resistance to sexual, racial, and economic inequalities, it is evident that this cannot be a politics based on nostalgia.   At the same time, as Ruddick's argument testifies, our approach to the future will be impoverished if it does not draw creatively from the culture and experience of past family life.

REFERENCE

Wade, N.   I.Q. and heredity: Suspicion of fraud beclouds classic experiment. *Science*, 1976, *194*, 916-919.

MOTHER/NATURE

A SKEPTICAL LOOK AT THE UNIQUE NATURALNESS

OF MATERNAL PARENTING

Hugh T. Wilder

Department of Philosophy
Miami University
Oxford, OH 45056

1. INTRODUCTION

"Is it more natural for mothers to parent than it is for fathers or anyone else?" Although this is an ill-defined question, in several respects, Rossi (1977) offers a sophisticated defense of the traditional affirmative answer to it. Rossi argues that not only is it more natural for mothers to parent than for fathers or anyone else, but it is also natural that mothers will be in certain respects better parents than anyone else. Rossi's thesis is that mothers have natural, unique and superior parental abilities and responsibilities, especially toward their infants and very young children. Rossi phrases her thesis in terms of what her "biosocial perspective" suggests rather than what nature dictates, but her point is clear:

> It is...likely that the emotional ties to the children are more important to the mothers than to the fathers....(T)he predisposition to respond to the child may be much greater on the part of the mother than the father....If a society wishes to create shared parental roles, it must either accept the high probability that the mother-infant relationship will continue to have greater emotional depth than the father-infant relationship, or institutionalize the means for providing men with compensatory exposure and training in infant and child care in order to close the gap provided by the physiological experience of pregnancy, birth, and nursing (Rossi, 1977, p. 18).

81

> A biosocial perspective on parenting...cautions against the
> view that equity of affect between mothers and fathers in
> their relationship to the very young infant and toddler is
> easily attainable (Rossi, 1977, p. 24).

> There may be a biologically based potential for heighten-
> ed maternal investment in the child, at least through the
> first months of life, that exceeds the potential for invest-
> ment by men in fatherhood (Rossi, 1977, p. 24).

Rossi's defense of the unique natural superiority of maternal child-rearing
is based on what she claims is an overdue recognition of "some fundamental human characteristics rooted in our biological heritage" (1977, p.
2).   She also embeds her thesis about the naturalness of maternal
childrearing in what she calls a "radical vision" of a family life "more
attuned to the natural environment, in touch with, and respectful of, the
rhythm of our own body processes" (1977, p. 25).

Rossi's thesis about the unique naturalness of maternal child-rearing
is important and provocative, for several reasons. First, the topic is of
both theoretical and practical importance. We think it matters whether it
is more natural for mothers to parent than for fathers or anyone else to
parent, and also whether it is natural that mothers will be better parents
than will anyone else. Theoreticians as well as policy-makers, not to
mention parents and children, think these questions matter. I will argue
that in interesting ways it does *not* in fact matter very much to humans
whether mothers are more natural, or naturally better, parents than is
anyone else. But Rossi's thesis is important simply because we *think* these
things matter.

Second, Rossi's thesis is important because it confirms the intuitions
and theories of an enormous range of people. Many people's intuitions tell
them that a woman's experiences of pregnancy, birth and nursing create a
special, unique bond between mother and child. This bond is thought to
involve unique parental abilities and responsibilities in the mother, which
cannot be matched by the father, or anyone else. Philosophers and theo-
logians have often told these people that, according to several well known
laws of nature, these intuitions about the special parenting abilities and
responsibilities of mothers are correct. And now Rossi re-confirms these
intuitions, appealing to the latest findings of endocrinology and bio-
evolutionary theory. It is as we always thought, Rossi assures us: a
woman's hormones and evolutionary niche make her especially good at and
responsible for bringing up children.

Rossi's thesis about the naturalness of maternal parenting is also
provocative. It is provocative in its own right, and because Rossi argues
for it in the context of a larger argument against what she calls the
"egalitarian ideology," and for a "post-feminist" vision of the family
which, as we have already noted, she sees as a "radical" vision of the

family finally in tune with the rhythms of nature. The "egalitarian ideology" is identified by Rossi with particular claims about sexual equality in the workplace, in home maintenance, and in child-rearing. It also urges, Rossi says, "a reduction of maternal investment in children," "an increased investment by men in their fathering roles," "supplementation of parental care by institutional care," and an "emphasis on the autonomy and the 'rights' of the child" (Rossi, 1977, p. 1).   This "egalitarian ideology" is today taken for granted, in whole or in large part, by liberal philosophers, social scientists, and policy-makers, as Rossi points out, as well as by many feminists. Rossi has been in the past a defender of liberal feminism, and yet she is now arguing against the "egalitarian ideology," particularly as it applies to child-rearing. The problem is acute: Rossi, herself, was an early and ardent proponent of a version of the "egalitarian ideology" in her landmark defense of "Equality Between the Sexes: An Immodest Proposal," in *Daedalus* in 1964 (Rossi, 1964);*(1)* in 1977, Rossi is attacking the "ideology" of sexual equality in the pages of the same journal. The issues are provocative, to say the least.*(2)*

In this paper, I will do three things. First, I will situate Rossi's thesis in the context of the development of sociobiology, and will review her arguments for the naturalness of maternal parenting. Rossi's arguments are usually, but not always, directed toward the unique naturalness of maternal abilities and responsibilities toward infants and very young children; "maternal parenting" will refer here to these abilities and responsibilities and will occasionally be extended to cover parenting of older children. Second, I will point out the fallaciousness of each of Rossi's arguments for her thesis. (These two projects are completed in sections 2 through 5 below.) And third, I will argue for the general irrelevancy of the naturalness issue in the context of theorizing about human parenting (section 6). Therefore, I will be arguing that Rossi's thesis is not only unsupported by her arguments, but is incorrect because it rests on the mistaken assumption that it makes sense to try to understand human parenting in terms of what is natural and what is not. My paper concludes with a brief sketch of the view that the only natural way for humans to be is unnatural.*(3)*

2. THE "BIOSOCIAL PERSPECTIVE" AND SOCIOBIOLOGY

Rossi's "biosocial perspective" is best understood as a version of the perhaps more familiar sociobiological perspective. Sociobiology is "the systematic study of the biological basis of all forms of social behavior in all kinds of organism" (Wilson, 1977, p. xiii); more specifically, it is "the application of evolutionary biology to the social behavior of animals" (Barash, 1977, p. 2).*(4)* Rossi's "biosocial perspective" likewise assumes that certain biological factors are particularly important in determining human social behavior. Since these biological factors are "natural," the biosocial perspective reveals that social behavior is natural just when its strongest determinants are these particular biological factors. Specifically, Rossi argues that two different kinds of biological factors are particularly important in determining human maternal parenting behavior: factors concerning human endocrine functioning and evolutionary history.

Rossi explicitly situates her discussion of these biological determinants of parenting behavior in the context of "the nature-nurture debate" (Rossi, 1977, p. 6). Rossi understands "the nature-nurture debate" as a debate about the relevance of biology to the explanation of human social behavior and psychological states. Defenders of "nature" in this debate are defenders of biological determinism: "common to many social scientists who draw heavily on biology is a belief in biologically rooted hormonal (and/or genetic) differentiation between the sexes as being a basic determinant of sex-linked psychological characteristics and sex-differentiated social organizations" (Rossi, 1977, p. 6).(5) Defenders of "nurture," according to Rossi, are defenders of the irrelevance or unimportance of biology to explanations of social behavior and psychological states (Rossi, 1977, p. 8), and of the explanatory sufficiency in these areas of "cultural determinism" (Rossi, 1977, p. 24).

A substantial part of Rossi's article consists of what amounts to an intellectual history of sociobiology: a description and explanation of the pendulum swings in opinion about the relevance of biology to social science, especially to social scientific explanations of issues concerning sex and gender differences. Rossi explicitly addresses both the theoretical and political implications of this debate: she points out that her article "brings up many important questions for future investigation, debate, and policy formulation" (1977, p. 25). Rossi claims that there has been a recent alliance formed between political "activists" in the "egalitarian movement" and academic social scientists, on the "nurture" side of the "nature-nurture debate" (1977, p. 2). These activist defenders of sexual, racial, and cultural egalitarianism and academic social scientists have generally been vigorous defenders of "a strong cultural-determinist perspective" (Rossi, 1977, p. 2), as well as vigorous opponents of nativistic or biological explanations of social behavior and psychological states.

Rossi notes that current social scientific suspicion of biological explanations of social behavior and psychological states is particularly strong in the area of sex and gender-linked behavior (1977, p. 8). She explains the suspicion in this area as stemming from a well-justified general suspicion among social scientists of the outmoded biological theories usually appealed to in defenses of the relevance of biology to social science.

Rossi believes that this general social scientific rejection of biology is a case of the baby being thrown out with the bathwater, however. She places herself firmly in the "nature" camp of the "nature-nurture debate," and argues that the "nature" position ought not be rejected simply because it has heretofore relied on outmoded theories of "nature." Rather, she claims that recent developments in biology--especially in endocrinology and evolutionary theory--confirm the importance of "nature" in the explanation of learning and behavior in the area of sex and gender. Rossi states that her "application of a biosocial perspective to current explorations of marriage and parenthood puts serious questions to the cultural determinism to which the social sciences have long adhered" (1977, p. 24). Rossi sees her own project as illustrating the biosocial or sociobiological revitalization of the "nature" side of the "nature-nurture debate": her approach illustrates, she claims several times, the "great promise for joint research by social and biological scientists that would enrich our understanding of both psychological and social processes" (1977, p. 24; see also pp. 2, 9, 10, 13).

Rossi is not only defending "nature" in the "nature-nurture debate" in the explanation of sex-linked characteristics; she is also criticizing the egalitarian views often associated with the "nurture" side of the debate. She links these two points explicitly when she writes, for example, that "the particular version of egalitarianism underlying current sociological research on, and advocacy of, 'variant' marriage and family forms is inadequate and misleading because it neglects some fundamental human characteristics rooted in our biological heritage" (Rossi, 1977, p. 2). Thus, the traditional polarization of views, pitting "nativist" (biological) defenses of "non-egalitarianism" against "environmentalist" (cultural) defenses of "egalitarianism" is continued and encouraged in Rossi's recent work.

This polarization of views is unfortunate, I believe, for several reasons. First, the "nativist/environmentalist" as well as the "egalitarian/non-egalitarian" distinctions as discussed by Rossi are misleading and simplistic. Second, the association of "nativism" with "non-egalitarianism" and "environmentalism" with "egalitarianism" is also misleading and simplistic. Third, Rossi labels her encouragement of this polarization and defense of the nativist, non-egalitarian position as a "more radical vision" of the family based on a reassessment of her early feminism. This label does an injustice, I believe, to accounts of the family which are truly radical and progressive. The first two points just made about the "nature/nurture" and "egalitarian/non-egalitarian" distinctions have been amply demonstrated by others,(6) and are not addressed directly here. The third point is defended in the conclusion of this paper.

3. ENDOCRINOLOGY AND LEARNED PARENTING BEHAVIOR

Rossi criticizes traditional appeals to the relevance of biology in the "nature-nurture" debate on two grounds: on their inadequate model of endocrine functioning, and on their ignorance of relevant parts of evolutionary theory. Rossi proceeds to supplement the traditional defense of biology in these two areas: she argues that recent developments in endocrinology and evolutionary theory support her thesis that mothers are more natural--and in certain respects naturally superior--parents than fathers or anyone else. I will evaluate her arguments in these two areas.

Rossi's general position in both areas is the same: she argues that endocrinology and evolutionary theory both demonstrate that certain *"biological contributions shape what is learned, and that there are differences in the ease with which the sexes can learn certain things"* (1977, p. 4; italics Rossi's). Thus, Rossi is not arguing for direct biological determination of sex-differentiated behavior, nor for biological determination of sex-differentiated abilities to perform. Rather, she is arguing for the biological determination of sex-differentiated abilities to learn or acquire behavior.

The two examples she cites of biologically determined sex-differentiated abilities to learn are the skills of "care for the newborn" and "food preparation for household consumption" (Rossi, 1977, p. 4). She asserts that "men can learn such skills, but as a group they are less apt to show ease in infant handling and food preparation than women are" (1977, p. 4), and also that the differing abilities of men and women to acquire such skills are biologically determined. Rossi has spared us any specific arguments supporting her assertion that men are biologically determined to be less adept at learning the skill of "food preparation for household consumption" than are women. The assertion is *prima facie* implausible, and the source of its implausibility is also a main source of the problems in her arguments concerning infant care. The source of the implausibility of her claim that men are biologically determined to be relatively inept at learning the skill of "food preparation for household consumption" is that "biology" determines nothing like such specific learning abilities. The skills involved in preparing food for household consumption are general skills, and the abilities to learn these skills are also general. There is no isolable ability to learn such specific behavior as "food preparation for household consumption" which might or might not be biologically determined.

Sociobiologists (and bio-sociologists) often cite the universality or near-universality of behavior types in support of their claims that abilities to learn these behaviors are biologically determined. This appeal is of no help, however, in supporting claims about the biological determination of abilities to learn highly specific behavior types. On such grounds, one could as plausibly claim that *men* are biologically determined to have superior abilities in learning the skill of "food preparation for consumption in five-star restaurants"--as plausibly, that is, as Rossi claims that women are biologically determined to have superior abilities in learning the skill of "food preparation for household consumption."

Rossi does provide supporting argument, however, for her claim that there are biologically determined differences in the ease with which men and women can learn the skill of infant care. One sort of biological determinant is "hormonal differentiation between the sexes": differential hormonal functioning is alleged to be a basic determinant "of sex-linked psychological characteristics and sex-differentiated social organizations" (Rossi, 1977, p. 6). These hormonal differences are claimed to determine specifically that men will be relatively inept at learning the skill of infant care.

The model of the endocrine system appealed to by Rossi pictures the endocrine system as open to the influence of external social stimuli through the nervous system, and in particular through the hypothalamus (Rossi, 1977, pp. 9-10). The hypothalamus receives input from the hormonal signals in the bloodstream as well as from the rest of the brain and nervous system; glands secrete hormones on the basis of information received from the hypothalamus.

This model of the endocrine system suggests that there is not a simple one-way causal connection between hormones and behavior. Rather, behavior and any kind of stimulus in the external world may causally influence hormonal secretion, and hormonal secretion may in turn influence behavior (Rossi, 1977, p. 10). Applied to sex-linked behavior and psychological characteristics, Rossi argues that this model implies that exposure of the fetal brain to particular hormones lays down "propensities for male, as opposed to female, behavior after birth." And, Rossi claims, *"such propensities shape the parameters within which learning takes place and affect the ease with which males and females learn (or unlearn) socially defined appropriate gender behavior"* (1977, p. 12; italics Rossi's).

One example of this influence of fetal hormonal secretion on future sex-linked behavior concerns what is known as "testicular feminizing syndrome." In this syndrome, fetal androgen secretion at a crucial time is inadequate, and a genetic male fetus develops, with the internal gonads of a male but with external genitalia more closely resembling those of a female. It has been found that "if the infant is defined at birth as, and reared as, a female, the individual shows a relative ease of gender identification as a female" (Rossi, 1977, p. 12).(7) Rossi hypothesizes that this relative ease in learning "feminine behavior" may be due not to culture overriding genetics and internal physiology, but to the inadequate exposure of the fetal brain to androgen, this inadequacy heightening "the brain's capacity to comply with the demands of female sex assignment and rearing" (1977, p. 12).

What Rossi is claiming is that exposure of the brain to hormones at times crucial in the learning of particular skills will have an influence on one's abilities to learn those skills. In particular, the implication is that exposure of one's brain at crucial times to adequate levels of androgen will determine that that person will be relatively adept (other things being equal) at learning "male behavior." Exposure of one's brain at these crucial times to different, lower levels of androgen will determine that that person will be relatively adept (again, other things being equal) at learning "female behavior." Infant care is, for Rossi, "female behavior" *par excellence* ("socially defined appropriate female behavior"). Therefore, Rossi is arguing that prenatal hormonal secretions determine that females will and males will not be adept at learning the skill of infant care.

Unfortunately for Rossi's thesis, this argument fails, for two reasons which I shall explain. First, there is no evidence given for thinking that prenatal hormonal secretions determine propensities to learn the skill of infant care. We grant Rossi the point that hormonal secretions causally influence the brain and nervous system, *via* the hypothalamus. We also grant that brain states as affected at crucial times by hormonal secretions have an effect on learning abilities. What we do not grant, and what there is no reason to grant, is that there is any causal connection between any specific prenatal hormonal secretions and the specific ability to learn the skill of infant care.

The reason why there is no reason to grant this connection is simply because there is no such thing as an ability to learn the skill of infant care. Therefore, it makes no sense to either assert or deny that such abilities are causally influenced by hormonal secretions. This is the second reason for the failure of Rossi's endocrinology-based defense of her thesis about the naturalness of maternal parenting.

Learning abilities are general, and in no case are they as specific as "the ability to learn the skill of infant care" needs to be for Rossi's argument to be valid. General learning abilities depend on such factors as perceptual and motor response capacities, intelligence and motivation. These factors contribute to the development of general multipurpose learning strategies: strategies which allow for the acquisition of whole new repertoires of behavior, as well as for specific responses. The details of these general multipurpose learning strategies remain largely unknown, but they are usually explained in terms of more basic concepts such as reasoning, coherence, explanation, simplicity, evidence, hypothesis, and selection. Plausible candidates for these learning strategies include such simple principles as trial and error reasoning and association and generalization, as well as more complex principles of "conjecture and refutation" and "inference to the most coherent explanatory account."

Whatever the exact principles turn out to be, they will be general enough to account for the learning of such diverse abilities as talking, reading, writing, adding, subtracting, cooking, cleaning, and loving, *as well as* talking in English with Mother, reading a textbook in German, writing a letter in French, balancing a checkbook, cooking chicken Kiev, and caring for one's infant daughter. It should be noted that even if it should turn out that humans have various "faculties" or "organs" which underlie our abilities to learn, say, first languages and mathematics, it will not necessarily follow that these faculties do not use the same multipurpose learning strategies that other faculties use. There is simply no reason to believe that these general multipurpose learning strategies are as specific as they need to be in order for Rossi's argument about "the ability to learn the skill of infant care" to be valid.

A further problem with Rossi's argument is that "the skill of infant care" is not a specific skill. The plural skills involved in infant care include complex skills such as feeding, cleaning, soothing and cuddling an infant, playing and establishing eye and body contact with the infant, etc. While in some cultures some non-mothers may not often display these particular "skills," there is reason to believe (based on the related skills these and all people do display) that all people (as always, other things being equal) have the *abilities to learn* these skills. These abilities to learn are precisely the general multipurpose learning strategies just described; these strategies must be very general in order to account for our acquisition of the variety of skills involved in infant care, as well as the countless other skills acquired by humans on the basis of these strategies. General multipurpose learning strategies are widely distributed in the human population, and are not distributed in humans by sex. The fact that these very general learning abilities underlying our acquisition of the skills of infant care are not distributed in humans by sex is sufficient to refute Rossi's claim that sex-differentiated prenatal hormonal secretions determine the occurrence of abilities to learn the skills of infant care in females and the non-occurrence of these abilities in males.

4. ENDOCRINOLOGY AND UNLEARNED PARENTING BEHAVIOR

Rossi offers a second argument based on endocrinology, however, for her thesis about the naturalness of maternal parenting. We have dispensed with the argument that specific hormones determine specific abilities to learn specific parenting behavior. Rossi claims, however, that some parenting behavior may be unlearned. And, she suggests that at least some of these unlearned parenting behaviors may be direct responses to hormonal secretions associated with pregnancy, birth, and lactation: experiences unique to women. The specific parenting behaviors which Rossi suggests are unlearned include: "uterine contractions and nipple erection preparatory to nursing"; women cradling their infants most often in their left arm (where the infant can hear and be soothed by the maternal heartbeat); common approaches taken by mothers to their newborn infants (involving *en face* eye contact, etc.); common sets of behaviors when mothers talk to their infants (including, for example, wide-open eyes, raised eyebrows, vowel elongation in speech, etc.) (1977, p. 6).

Rossi is making two claims about these behaviors: that these behaviors are unlearned only in the case of a mother responding to her biological infant offspring, and that at least one--uterine contraction and nipple erection preparatory to nursing--is a direct response to maternal hormonal secretions. The naturalness of these maternal parenting behaviors is equated here with the unlearned quality of these behaviors. Rossi's defense of the unique naturalness of maternal parenting depends on the claim that these behaviors are unlearned *only* in the case of a mother responding to her own biological baby.

In evaluating this argument, let us note first that Rossi's equation of the naturalness of these behaviors with their unlearned quality is at odds with her general view that biological contributions shape sex-differentiated propensities to *learn* behavior rather than sex-differentiated behavior itself. Here, Rossi is claiming that several unlearned responses of mothers toward their babies establish the unique natural abilities and responsibiities in mothers to parent their babies.

This general view about unlearned maternal responses is widely held, and we may grant Rossi's shift of focus, away from the learning of parenting skills and to these unlearned maternal responses. For the sake of argument, we will also grant that these responses are unlearned; if they should turn out to be learned, then anyone could learn them, according to the arguments just given. However, even if these responses are unlearned, they do not seem to be uniquely *maternal* responses.

There is simply no reason to think that each of the respnses listed occurs only in mothers in their interactions with their biological babies, as Rossi's argument demands. Further, it is common knowledge that some of the responses listed occur as widely, as early, and as spontaneously in others besides the biological mother. For example, fathers and others show consistent approach and speech patterns with infants, which are similar to the patterns shown by the mothers. And, right-handed people generally, not only mothers, regularly cradle infants in their left arms; this practice offers infants the soothing sounds of the cradler's heartbeat, and also, not coincidentally, offers the cradler use of his or her dominant hand.

Some of the unlearned maternal responses cited by Rossi may be triggered by early postpartum maternal-infant bonding. The crucial importance of such bonding for future mother-child relations is well established.(8) In criticizing Rossi's use of maternal-infant bonding, we are not denying the existence and importance of this phenomenon. However, the triggering of maternal responses by early maternal-infant bonding does not preclude the existence of (say) paternal responses by early paternal-infant bonding. In fact, there is simply no research on paternal (or other)-infant bonding, due to the childbirth practices in societies in which such research might be conducted.(9) It is possible that, were childbirth practices different, allowing for early paternal as well as maternal-infant bonding, both fathers and mothers would exhibit unlearned parenting responses which, if not identical for each sex, would be functionally equivalent.

It is often replied that one response which occurs in no one but mothers toward their biological offspring is "uterine contraction and nipple erection preparatory to nursing"; and it is also claimed that this response alone is sufficient to establish the unique infant care abilities and responsibilities of mothers. This argument is popular enough to deserve a name; we will refer to it as the "let-down argument," (partly) with reference to the maternal response to which it appeals. Rossi is offering a version of this "let-down argument" in her inclusion of uterine contractions and nipple erection in her list of unlearned maternal behaviors. Specifically, Rossi claims that "infant crying stimulates the secretion of oxytocin in the mother"; this "triggers uterine contractions and nipple erection preparatory to nursing" (1977, p. 6); and it is alleged to follow that mothers have a unique ability and responsibility to care for their babies.

Now, it is true that only women can lactate. This fact is irrelevant, however, to the "let-down argument," when this argument is used in defense of the unique naturalness of maternal (vs. female) parenting. Infant crying can trigger the let-down reflex in any lactating woman within earshot. Further, the "let-down argument" does not even establish the unique naturalness of female parenting. Infant crying also regularly triggers a response in fathers and others within earshot. When these people are those responsible for feeding the infant, this response regularly includes behavior preparatory to feeding the baby--as regularly, that is, as infant crying triggers in nursing mothers behavior preparatory to feeding. Therefore, while the let-down reflex occurs only in lactating women, functionally similar responses occur in others who are responsible for infant care. The "let-down argument" does not establish the unique naturalness of maternal parenting abilities and responsibilities.

5. THE ARGUMENT FROM EVOLUTION

Rossi offers one other argument for the natural, unique, and superior abilities of mothers to parent. This argument is based on evolutionary theory rather than endocrine functioning, and is presented as a case of Rossi's general view that "biological contributions shape what is learned, and that there are differences in the ease with which the sexes can learn certain things." Rossi argues here that "species survival has been facilitated by physiological factors in the bonding of the mother and the newborn" (1977, p. 24). Maternal parenting has contributed essentially to the survival of the human species, and will continue to do so. Any trend away from maternal parenting is an attempt to deny our evolutionary heritage, and, Rossi claims, is doomed to failure unless extraordinary compensatory adjustments are made.

More specifically, Rossi claims that sexual dimorphism and sexual division of labor are characteristics of the human species which have been determined by forces of adaptation and selection in our evolutionary history. The division of labor has not always been the same, but trends may be discerned. According to Rossi, from the evolutionary point of view, "reproductive success went to those females capable of two conjoint activities: the bearing and rearing of their young and the hunting of small game and gathering of food" (1977, p. 4). Reproductive success similarly went to those males who possessed "the body stature, shoulder strength, and visual acuity required for skill in big-game hunting with spears and for group defense" (Rossi, 1977, p. 4).

Further, Rossi argues that "residues of these selective processes can be seen among contemporary men and women" (1977, p. 4). Rossi mentions as examples of these evolutionary residues the relatively obvious cases of male height, shoulder strength and "precise spatial perception," and female "manual dexterity and emotional stamina" (1977, p. 4). She also mentions as evolutionary residues the rather surprising cases of female predominance as workers in electronic-equipment firms and male predominance in construction work and military combat. We may pass over these cases, and consider Rossi's crucial example of an evolutionary residue: maternal parenting.

Rossi argues that the contemporary predominance and near universality of maternal parenting is a result of innate factors in female physiology and psychology. These innate factors are contributions of our evolutionary heritage, and determine that mothers will have a propensity to learn parenting skills more easily than men. Rossi's argument depends on a general principle: "the more critical the behavior is to species survival through reproduction, the more apt these innate features are to be present" (Rossi, 1977, p. 5). Rossi proceeds to assert that, for two reasons, a superior ability to learn parenting skills is apt to be an innate feature of women (1977, p. 5). Rossi concludes from the general principle and its application that the mother-infant relationship has a fundamental and unique evolutionary salience: that mothers are innately better fit to parent, other things being equal, than are others.

The first reason given by Rossi for expecting women to possess innately superior abilities to learn parenting skills is as follows:

> ...the female is more closely involved in the reproductive process than the male. Biologically males have only one innate orientation, a sexual one that draws them to women, while women have two such orientations: a sexual one toward men and a reproductive one toward the young (1977, p. 5).

These "orientations" of males and females are alleged to be innate because they are "critical for species survival."

The second reason given by Rossi for expecting women--specifically, here, mothers--to possess innately superior abilities to learn parenting skills is that "there is even greater need for close bonding of the human infant to its mother than there is in other species" (1977, p. 5). This need is derived from the specific "prematurity" of humans at birth. Thus, the uniquely close mother-infant bond is also alleged to be innate because it is "critical for species survival."

Unfortunately for Rossi's argument, neither of these reasons for expecting women to possess innately superior abilities to learn parenting skills is known to be true. There is no reason to suppose that men have only one "innate orientation," a "sexual one toward women," while women have two "innate orientations," a sexual one toward men" and a "reproductive one toward the young." And there are also reasons to deny it. First, the terms are too ill-defined to even permit evaluation: What is an "innate orientation"? When is an "innate orientation" a "sexual one"? When is an "innate orientation" a "reproductive one"? Who are "the young"? None of these questions is answered in Rossi's account. Second, even assuming that a clear definition of "innate orientation" is forthcoming, it seems safe to say that there will (still) be no agreement as to how many "innate orientations" humans have. Many claim that humans have no "innate orientation"; on other accounts both men and women are alleged to have innate bisexual orientations; both men and women are also alleged to have innate self-preservative orientations (e.g., to eat, eliminate wastes, etc.); both men and women are alleged to have innate species-preservative orientations (e.g., to copulate); both men and women are alleged to have innate death orientations; and so on. My point is that there is wide disagreement on what an "innate orientation" is, on whether humans have *any* innate orientations, and, if we do, on which ones. Rossi presents no evidence for thinking that males possess only one, a sexual one toward women, and that women possess two toward men and the young.

Notice, also, that these alleged "innate orientations" of men and women are said by Rossi to determine the heightened ability in women to learn parenting skills. To repeat a point made earlier in this paper, there is no such ability. Therefore, there is no reason to believe that this putative ability is or is not determined by any putative innate orientation. There is no ability to learn parenting skills, because parenting skills are incredibly diverse and because the abilities to learn these skills are also diverse and generally applicable to the learning of other skills. Anyone who can learn anything of sufficient complexity can learn to parent.

Rossi's second point mentioned earlier, that "there is even greater need for close bonding of the human infant to its mother than there is in other species," is not known to be true either. There is no evidence establishing in human infants a uniquely great need for *maternal* bonding; and, what anecdotal evidence there is, suggests that a bond with *any* sensitive provider of food, care and love is sufficient for establishing a basis for healthy and happy human growth and development. It is true that humans are born uniquely premature, with greater specific needs than those of other species. It is also true in many cultures that there is a uniquely close bond between a mother and her child, due, no doubt, to the nearly exclusive maternal care children, in fact, receive in those cultures. It is not known, however, that the great needs of human infants can only or even best be satisfied by this close bonding of the infant to his or her mother. Others besides the biological mother regularly satisfy fully the needs of human infants. And special bonds, filled with love and hate and gratitude and envy--i.e., bonds closely resembling those between mother and infant--grow between these providers and the infants provided for.

Therefore, Rossi's appeal to the allegedly great need in humans for mother-infant bonding does not support her claim that mothers possess innately superior abilities or responsibilities to learn parenting skills.

6. GOING BEYOND NATURE

What we have just argued is that each of Rossi's arguments for her thesis that mothers have natural, unique and superior parental abilities and responsibilities is fallacious. Rossi's thesis is widely believed, and her arguments are worth refuting because they capture the intuitions and theories of so many believers in the traditional parental role of mothers. All we have shown so far, however, is that Rossi's thesis is unsupported by her arguments; the thesis may well be true.

I believe the thesis is false, and will conclude this paper with a sketch of why I believe it is false. There are two main reasons for believing Rossi's thesis to be false. The first reason is relatively superficial, and is, in effect, a *reductio ad absurdum* refutation of Rossi's thesis in the mode of practical reason. The reason is that actions based on the perceived truth of the thesis that mothers have natural, unique and superior parental abilities and responsibilities have such disastrous consequences that the thesis cannot possibly be true. Actions based on the perceived truth of Rossi's thesis center on the continuation of the predominance of exclusively maternal care for the very young. Of course, maternal infant care has many benefits and is a source of great joy for both mothers and children. But these benefits of maternal infant care must not blind one to the *disadvantages* of the practice of nearly exclusive maternal infant care.

This practice has disadvantages for the infant: he or she is deprived of contact with others, including peers, father, other adults, and often even siblings. Infantile dependence on one person, the mother, is enforced. The practice has disadvantages for the father and other adults: they are deprived of contact with infants. And, the practice has other disadvantages, for the mother: she often is deprived of contact with all but her own young children. And again, while caring for her children can be a mother's greatest source of joy, her children's *exclusive* dependence on her for this care can also be, on a day-to-day basis, a great burden and instrument of maternal oppression. It is particularly ironic that Rossi and other social scientists(10) are *now* reminding mothers of their superior parental abilities and responsibilities, at a time when economic realities virtually guarantee that few mothers can afford to invest very much of their energy in the non-remunerative labor of parenting.

The practice of nearly exclusive maternal care for the very young also has unfortunate consequences for a culture as a whole; Dinnerstein (1976) contains analyses of several of these consequences. Among the cultural consequences analyzed by Dinnerstein are: several problematic areas of adult sexuality, including a pernicious sexual double-standard for men and women; a tendency to infantilize ourselves, and to perceive ourselves and others as children; our tendency to hold rapacious and destructive views toward both women and nature; our destructive association of women with death; and our tendency to view men as the makers and masters of history. Dinnerstein's analyses of these consequences of nearly exclusive maternal infant care are controversial. They are cited, not in defense of Dinnerstein's specific analyses, but as illustrations of the problematic nature of exclusive maternal infant care.

In citing these problems, I am in no way denying the values and benefits of maternal parenting. The problems just cited do not stem from maternal parenting. Rather, according to Dinnerstein, they stem from the practice of nearly exclusive maternal parenting. The value of maternal parenting will not be lost in a world in which parenting is shared; and the children in this world will experience the values of parenting by fathers and others as well. My point, then, is that to put Rossi's thesis into practice, or more precisely, to continue to act as if it were true, is to continue the practice of mother-dominated child-rearing. And continuation of this practice means continuation and exacerbation of ways of life which are harmful, unjust, and avoidable.

The second reason for believing that Rossi's thesis is false is deeper than the first, and in a way undercuts the first, even though this second reason is also found in Dinnerstein (1976, pp. 18-22). Rossi has argued that it is only natural that human mothers should raise their young. Our first counter-argument to this was to say, in effect, that if this is what is natural, then nature is cruel. My final point will be a recommendation to go beyond the issue of what is or is not natural in the issue of human parenting.*(11)*

My point is that humans are not "natural beings" in the sense required for any argument about the "naturalness" of various family forms and parenting patterns. As we have noted, Rossi explicitly embeds her defense of maternal parenting abilities and responsibilities in a defense of what many see as "traditional family and work roles for men and women" (1977, p. 25), and which Rossi herself presents as "a society more attuned to the natural environment, in touch with, and respectful of, the rhythm of our own body processes." In defending institutions tied to nature in this way, I suggest that Rossi is defending particularly non-human institutions of the family and parenting.

Humans, to an extent greater than any other species, need not be slaves to nature. We are an intelligent and a creative species. This means that neither nature nor we ourselves are given as fixed entities which must be pushed and pulled into some grudging alignment. Rather, humans create much of what others call both "nature" and "human nature." We create much of what we see as nature around us when we domesticate animals, practice agriculture, harvest and transform natural resources, live in social groups, and--more to the point--form families.

And we create our own "human nature" when we identify these projects as our own. Therefore, we create what we see as the relationship between ourselves and nature. It is up to us to create a good relationsip. In this creative condition, it is ironic and even cruel to recommend to humans that we follow "biologically determined" parenting patterns, when we alone have the creative abilities to adopt new ones.

Of course, Rossi is calling for a family pattern "attuned to," "in touch with," and "respectful of" nature, not enslaved to it. And she does not argue that fathers and other non-mothers cannot or should not parent. She admits that fathers and others *can* parent. But she also thinks that serious programs of compensatory training are necessary if men and non-mothers are expected to be good at caring for young infants (Rossi, 1977, pp. 4, 18). And, "since evolutionary changes take place at an infinitely slow pace through long stretches of time, each generation of males and females would require compensatory training," for many generations to come, if any long-lasting gains in non-maternal parenting abilities are to be made (Rossi, 1977, p. 5).

Rossi may not be asking us to willingly enslave ourselves to nature; but she is certainly counseling us to be cautious in our expectations of the gains we can make over nature, i.e., over our hormonal secretions and evolutionary heritage. And I am saying that to counsel such caution, especially on the basis of such empty arguments as Rossi has done, is to deny human intelligence and creativity. The corrective to Rossi's "biosocial perspective" is not, of course, to fly to the opposite extreme of a technological flaunting of our human supremacy over nature. The view of society and family life which I am sketching is based on the belief that we humans create our own natures, our own societies, and our own families. Our creations may be monstrous or they may be good, but they are ours. To worry about whether they are natural is beside the point.

Human beings live for a while, and die. That much is natural. Everything else is "aberration," if one is a Freudian, "creation," if one is a Marxist, "freedom," if one is a Sartrean. Parenting, no matter who does it, is something else.*(12)*

REFERENCES

Bane, M. J. *Here to stay.* New York: Basic Books, 1976.
Barash, D. P. *Sociobiology and behavior.* New York: Elsevier, 1977.
Block, N. J., and Dworkin, G.   I.Q.:   Heritability and inequality. *Philosophy and Public Affairs*, 1974, *3*, 331-409.
Block, N. J., and Dworkin, G.   I.Q.:   Heritability and inequality. *Philosophy and Public Affairs*, 1974, *4*, 40-99.
Bracken, H. M. Philosophy and racism. *Philosophia*, 1978, *8*, 241-260.
Cerullo, M., Stacey, J., and Breines, W.   Alice Rossi's sociobiology and anti-feminist backlash. *Berkeley Journal of Sociology*, 1977-78a, *22*, 167-177; excerpted from Cerullo, Stacey, and Breines (1977-78b).

Cerullo, M., Stacey, J., and Breines, W. Social biology, family studies, and anti-feminist backlash. *Feminist Studies*, 1977-78b, *4*, 43-67.

Chodorow, N. Considerations on a biosocial perspective on parenting. *Berkeley Journal of Sociology*, 1977-78, *22*, 179-197; excerpted from Chodorow (1979).

Chodorow, N. *The reproduction of mothering.* Berkeley: University of California Press, 1979.

Chomsky, N. Linguistics and politics. *New Left Review*, 1969, 57, 21-34.

Chomsky, N. Language and freedom. *Abraxas*, 1970, *1*, 9-24.

Chomsky, N. Psychology and ideology. *Cognition*, 1972, *1*, 11-46.

Chomsky, N. *Reflections on language.* New York: Pantheon, 1974.

Cohen, M. Nagel, T., and Scanlon, T. (Ed.) *Equality and preferential treatment.* Princeton: Princeton University Press, 1977.

Dinnerstein, D. *The mermaid and the minotaur.* New York: Harper, 1976.

Gartner, A., Greer, C., and Riessman, F. (Ed.) *The new assault on equality: I.Q. and social stratification.* New York: Harper and Row, 1974.

Gornick, V., and Moran, B. K. (Eds.) *Woman in sexist society.* New York: Basic Books, 1971.

Gross, B. R. *Reverse discrimination.* Buffalo: Prometheus, 1977.

Kamin, L. J. *The science and politics of I.Q.* Potomac, MD: Lawrence Erlbaum, 1974.

Karier, C. J. (Ed.) *Shaping the American educational state.* New York: Free Press, 1975.

Klaus, M. H., and Kennell, J. H. *Maternal-infant bonding: The impact of early separation or loss on family development.* St. Louis: C. V. Mosby Co., 1976.

Marks, R. Politics and the nature-nurture question. In C. J. Karier (Ed.), *Shaping the American educational state.* New York: Free Press, 1975, pp. 316-342.

Money, J., and Ehrhardt, A. *Man and woman, boy and girl.* Baltimore: Johns Hopkins University Press, 1972.

Pierce, C. Natural law, language and women. In V. Gornick and B. K. Moran (Eds.), *Woman in sexist society.* New York: Basic Books, 1971, pp. 242-258.

Rossi, A. S. Equality between the sexes: An immodest proposal. *Daedalus*, 1964, *93*, 607-652.

Rossi, A. S. (Ed.) *Essays on sex equality.* Chicago: University of Chicago Press, 1970.

Rossi, A. S. (Ed.) *The feminist papers.* New York: Bantam, 1973.

Rossi, A. S. A biosocial perspective on parenting. *Daedalus*, 1977, *106*, 1-31; reprinted in Rossi, Kagan and Harevan (1978).

Rossi, A. S., Kagan, J., and Harevan, T. K. (Eds.) *The family.* New York: Norton, 1978.

Symons, D. *The evolution of human sexuality.* London: Oxford University Press, 1979.

Trebilcot, J. Sex roles: The argument from nature. *Ethics*, 1975, *85*, 249-255.

Wilson, E. O. *Sociobiology: The new synthesis.* Cambridge: Belknap, 1975.
Wilson, E. O. Forward. See Barash (1977), xiii-xv.
Wilson, E. O. *On human nature.* Cambridge: Harvard University Press, 1978.

FOOTNOTES

(1) See also Rossi (1970) and Rossi (1973).

(2) Rossi (1977) has already provoked several responses in print. See, for example, Cerullo, Stacey and Breines (1977-78a), and Chodorow (1977-78). To the author's knowledge, however, no one else has developed a philosophical critique of Rossi's appeal to "nature," which is the focus of the present paper.

(3) This phrase is adapted from Dinnerstein (1976), p. 21. The view is adapted from Freud and Marx, as well as from Dinnerstein.

(4) Reviews of the literature on the application of sociobiology to the study of human sexuality are given in Barash (1977), Wilson (1975), and Wilson (1978). See also Symons (1979).

(5) Rossi cites Goldberg, Gilder, Fox and Tiger as social scientists aligned on this "nature" side of the debate.

(6) On the complexity of the "nature-nurture" issue, see, for example, some of the recent literature on I.Q. testing. Especially helpful are: Gartner, Greer and Riessman (1974), Kamin (1974), and Block and Dworkin (1974).

On the complexity of the "egalitarianism/non-egalitarianism" issue, see, for example, some of the recent literature on affirmative action policies. Two useful sources are: Cohen, Nagel and Scanlon (1977), and Gross (1977).

Finally, on Rossi's simplistic association of biological nativism with non-egalitarianism and cultural environmentalism with egalitarianism, see, for example, the literature inspired by Chomsky's theory of language: Chomsky (1969, 1970, 1972, and 1974), Bracken (1978), and Marks (1975).

(7) See also Money and Ehrhardt (1972).

(8) See Klaus and Kennell (1976).

(9) I owe this point to Adele Laslie.

(10) See, for example, Bane (1976).

(11) Trebilcot (1975) offers several different arguments for the related thesis that various appeals to "nature" do not support the claim that gender-determined social roles should be encouraged in a society. See also Pierce (1971) for arguments for the further thesis that from "X is a natural human practice" one cannot, in general, infer that "X is good or valuable."

(12) Earlier versions of this paper were read at Miami University and at the Michigan State University Conference on Philosophy, Children, and the Family, March 28-30, 1980. I wish to thank Judith de Luce, Richard Momeyer, Peter Rose, Iris Young, and Adele Laslie for their helpful comments. For lively debate about Rossi's article, I am also indebted to students in my classes at Miami University on "Philosophy of Love, Sexuality and the Family."

MATERNAL THINKING

Sara Ruddick (1)

Seminar College
Department of Philosophy
New School for Social Research
New York, NY 10011

INTRODUCTION

We are familiar with Victorian renditions of Ideal Maternal Love. My own favorite, like so many of these poems, was written by a son.

> There was a young man loved a maid
> Who taunted him. "Are you afraid,"
> She asked, "to bring me today
> Your mother's heart upon a tray?"
>
> He went and slew his mother dead,
> Tore from her breast her heart so red,
> Then towards his lady love he raced,
> But tripped and fell in all his haste.
>
> As the heart rolled on the ground
> It gave forth a plaintive sound.
> And it spoke, in accents mild:
> "Did you hurt yourself, my child?"
> (J. Echergray, in Bernard)

Many of this story's wishes and fantasies are familiar. Our love for our sons is said to be dangerous to the "maid" who seeks to take him from us. Like the first mother, a mother-in-law is a maid's rival for the sexual possession of a man. We too were maids and lovers before we were mothers; we understand. We understand too that our love may jeopardize our sons' manhood. As "good" mothers we allow our sons contempt for our feelings ("the normal male contempt for women") (Brunswick, quoted in

Chodorow, 1978), if not for our lives, so that they may guiltlessly "separate themselves" from us. There is, however, an unfamiliar twist to the poem. The lady asked for our head, the son brought our heart. She feared and respected our thoughts. He believes only our feelings are powerful. Again we are not surprised. The passions of maternity are so sudden, intense, and confusing that we ourselves often remain ignorant of the perspective, the *thought* that has developed from our mothering. Lacking pride, we have failed to deepen or to articulate that thought. This is a paper about the head of the mother.

***

Central to our experience of our mothers and our mothering is a poignant conjunction of power and powerlessness. In any society a mother is unavoidably powerless. Nature's indifference--illness, death, and damage to the child or its closest loved ones--can frustrate the best maternal efforts. To unavoidable powerlessness is added avoidable social powerlessness. Almost everywhere the practices of mothering take place in societies in which women of all classes have less domestic and social power than men of their class. In addition, most mothers (and fathers) are powerless to change, economic, military and cultural policies which are detrimental to their children.

Powerless mothers are also powerful. "Most of us first know both love and disappointment, power and tenderness, in the person of a woman" (Rich, 1976, p. 11). For a child, a mother is the primary, uncontrollable source of the world's goods; a witness and judge whose will must be placated, whose approval must be secured.(2) Some of a mother's power is avoidable if childcare is shared, from infancy on, with other adults and older children. However, a mother has a residual power acruing from her capacity to bear and nurse infants. So long as she is able and chooses to utilize her reproductive body in her own and her children's interest, she will, in the predictable technological future, have power to give or deny children to men as well as to maintain some irreducible power over her children by dint of her unique and extraordinary physical intimacy with them.

In most societies, however, women are socially powerless in respect to the very reproductive capacities that might make them powerful. The primary bodily experience of mothers is a poignant reminder that to think of maternal power is immediately to recall maternal powerlessness--and conversely. Freudians and feminists have made us aware of the unfortunate consequences of this lethal conjunction. Children confront and rely upon a powerful maternal presence only to watch her become the powerless woman in front of the father, the teacher, the doctor, the judge, the landlord--the world. A child's rageful disappointment in its powerless mother, combined with resentment and fear of her powerful will, may account for the matriphobia so widespread in our society as to seem normal. For whatever reasons, it seems almost impossible for older children or adults to construct a coherent, let alone a benign, account of maternal power.*(3)*

The conjunction of maternal power and powerlessness makes maternal practices oppressive to mothers and children alike. The oppression is real; much more could be said about it. However, to suggest that mothers are principally victims of a kind of crippling work is an egregiously inaccurate account of women's own experience as mothers and daughters. Although one can sympathize with the anger that insists upon and emphasizes the oppressive nature of maternal practices, an account that describes only exploitation and pain is itself oppressive to women.*(4)* Mothers, despite the inevitable trials and social conditions of motherhood, are often effective in their work.

In articulating those conditions of mothering that allow for happiness and efficacy, we need to remember some simple facts. Maternal practices begin in love, a love which for most mothers is as intense, confusing, ambivalent, and poignantly sweet as any they will experience. Although economic and social conditions, such as the poverty that is widespread and the isolation that is typical in America, may make that love frantic, they do not kill the love. For whatever reasons, mothers typically find it not only natural but compelling to protect and foster the growth of their children. Relatedly, mothers, especially those who have chosen or come to welcome parenthood, experience a social-biological pride in the function of their reproductive processes, a sense of the activation of maternal power. In addition to a sense of maternal competence, a sense that they *are* able to protect and foster the growth of their children.

That maternal love, pleasure in reproductive powers, and a sense of maternal competence survive in a patriarchal society where women are routinely derogated, makes one wonder at the further possibilities for maternal happiness in decent societies. Even in this relatively indecent society, mothers are usually socially rewarded for their work by the shared pleasure and confirmation of other women, by the gratitude and pride of grandparents, and frequently by the intense, appreciative paternal love of their mates. Moreover, mothers who work primarily at home frequently have more control over the details of their working day than is available to other workers.*(5)* Many mothers, whatever their work in the public world, feel part of a community of co-mothers whose warmth and support is rarely equaled in other working relationships. Loving, competent, and appreciated, a mother need not experience her work as oppressive. When their children flourish, mothers have a sense of well-being.

On the other hand, no children flourish all of the time. The emotional and physical pains of their children are anguishing for mothers, inducing a sense of helplessness and guilt. Isolation, restricted options, and social devaluation can make mothering grim even for economically privileged women.   It is difficult when writing about motherhood--or experiencing it--to be balanced about both its grim and its satisfying aspects.

Yet loving, competent well-being is an important element in our (my) memories of our mothers and mothering. We must bear these memories in mind if we are to understand that neither the world's misogyny nor our own related psychic dramas have totally prevented us from acquiring an image of benign maternal power. Whatever their scientific status, persistent interest in and positive response to myths of matriarchy show how avidly women search for a society in which mothers are powerful. Feminist utopias are apt to assign government to mothers. "You see we are *mothers*," their authors seem to say, as if in saying that they have said it all.*(6)* Cultural myths and our own dreams tell of us a connection we would wish to make with a mother who is socially as well as personally powerful, powerful in adult as well as in infants' eyes. The construction of matriarchal pasts and futures signal longing and regret; longing for a powerful mother we remember and wish we could recognize; regret, often resentful and blaming, that she does not come again after the years of childhood.

> My mama moved among the days
> like a dreamwalker in a field;
> seemed like what she touched was hers
> seemed like what touched her couldn't hold,
> she got us almost through the high grass
> then seemed like she turned around and ran
> right back in
> right back on in (Clifton, 1969).

It is enormously difficult to come by an image of maternal power that is even coherent, let alone benign: it is easy to come by images of powerlessness and malign power. I consider my attempt to express and respect maternal thought one contribution to an ongoing shared, feminist project: the construction of an image of maternal power which is benign, accurate, sturdy, and sane.

My particular project, the expression of maternal thought, connects to a general question. Do women, who now rightfully claim the instruments of public power, have cultures, traditions, and inquiries which we should insist upon bringing to the public world? If the "womanly" can be identified, should we respect it or attempt to surpass it? These questions divide feminists. The ideology of womanhood has been invented by men. It confines as it exalts us. On the other hand, the ideology of androgyny is often a disguised ideology of manhood that continues the disrespect for women shared by both sexes.

I am aware of the oppressive uses to which any identification of the "womanly" can be put. Our current gender dichotomies are rigid and damaging.   Praising cultures of oppression comes close to praising oppression itself. Often we celebrate our mothers' lives only because we are afraid to confront the damage our past wreaked upon them and us. Despite these doubts, I am increasingly convinced that there are female traditions and practices out of which a distinctive kind of thinking has developed.

Maternal thinking is only one example of "womanly" thinking.(7) In articulating and respecting the maternal I do not underwrite the still current, false, and pernicious identification of womanhood with biological or adoptive mothering of particular children in families.(8) For me, "maternal" is a social category: although maternal thinking arises out of actual child-caring practices, biological parenting is neither necessary nor sufficient. Many women and some men express maternal thinking in various kinds of working and caring with others. And some biological mothers, especially in misogynistic societies, take a fearful, defensive distance from their own mothering and the maternal lives of any women.

Maternal thought does, I believe, exist for all women in a radically different way than for men. It is because we are *daughters* that we early receive maternal love with special attention to its implications for our bodies, our passions, and our ambitions. We are alert to the values and costs of maternal practices whether we are determined to engage in them or to avoid them. Although some men do, and more men should, acquire maternal thinking, their ways of acquisition are necessarily different from ours.(9)

I do not wish to deny any more than I wish to affirm some biological bases of maternal thinking. The "biological body" (in part a cultural artifact) *may* foster certain features of maternal practice, sensibility, and thought. Neither our own ambivalence to our women's bodies nor the bigoted, repressive uses which many men, colonizers, and racists have made of biology, should blind us to our body's possibilities. In concentrating on what mothers do rather than upon what we are, I postpone biological questions until we have the moral and political perceptions to answer them justly.(10)

Along with biology, I put aside all accounts of gender difference or maternal nature which would claim an essential and ineradicable difference between female and male parents. However, I do believe that there are features of mothering experience which are invariant and nearly unchangeable, and others which, though changeable, are nearly universal.(11) It is therefore possible to identify interests that appear to govern maternal practice throughout the species. However, it is impossible even to begin to specify those interests without importing features specific to the class, ethnic group, and particular sex-gender system in which those interests are realized. I will be drawing upon my knowledge of the institutions of motherhood in middle-class, white, Protestant, capitalist, patriarchal America as these have expressed themselves in the heterosexual nuclear family in which I mother and was mothered. Although I have tried to compensate for the limits of my particular social and sexual history, I principally depend upon others to correct my interpretaions and to translate across cultures.*(12)*

I speak about a mother's *thought*--the intellectual capacities she develops, the judgments she makes, the metaphysical attitudes she assumes, the values she affirms. A mother engages in a discipline. That is, she asks certain questions rather than others; establishes and cares about the findings she makes and can act upon. Like any discipline, hers has *characteristic* errors, temptations, and goals. The discipline of maternal thought consists in establishing criteria for determining failure and success, in setting the priorities, and in identifying the virtues and liabilities which the criteria presume. To describe the capacities, judgments, metaphysical attitudes, and values of maternal thought does not presume maternal achievement. It is to describe a *conception* of achievement, the end to which maternal efforts are directed, conceptions and ends quite different from dominant public ones.*(13)*

In stating my claims about maternal thinking, I use a vocabulary developed in formulating theories about the general nature of thought.*(14)* According to these theories, *all* thought arises out of social practice. In their practices, people respond to a reality that appears to them as given, as presenting certain *demands.* The response to demands is shaped by *interests* which are generally interests in preserving, reproducing, directing, and understanding individual and group life. These four interests are general in the sense that they arise out of the conditions of humans-in-nature and characterize us as a species. However, these interests are always and only expressed as interests of people in particular cultures and classes of their cultures, living in specific geographical, technological, and historical settings. They are always and only responses to some realities--human and nonhuman, natural and supranatural--which present themselves to particular interested people as given. Thinking is governed by the interests of the practice out of which it arises. Thinking names and elaborates the "given" reality to whose demands practice is responding. It expresses, refines, and executes the interests of the practice in a way that is disciplined, directive, and communicable.

Maternal practice responds to the historical reality of a biological child in a particular social world. The agents of maternal practice, acting in response to the demands of their children, acquire a conceptual scheme--a vocabulary and logic of connections--through which they order and express the facts and values of their practice. In judgments and self-reflection, they refine and concretize this scheme. Intellectual activities are distinguishable, but not separable from disciplines of feeling. There is a unity of reflection, judgment, and emotion. It is this unity I call "maternal thinking." Although I will not digress to argue the point here, it is important that maternal thinking is no more interest governed, no more emotional, no more relative to its particular reality (the growing child) than the thinking that arises from scientific, religious, or any other practice.

Children, "demand" that their lives be preserved and their growth be fostered. Their social group "demands" that their growth be shaped in a way acceptable to the next generation. Maternal practice is governed by (at least) three interests in satisfying these demands for preservation, growth, and acceptability. Preservation is the most invariant and primary of the three. Because a caretaking mother typically bears her own children, preservation begins when conception is recognized and accepted. Although the form of preservation depends upon widely variant beliefs about the fragility and care of the fetus, women have always had a lore in which they recorded their concerns for the baby they "carried." Once born, a child is physically vulnerable for many years. Even when she lives with the father of her child or other female adults, even when she has money to purchase or finds available supportive health and welfare services, a mother typically considers herself and is considered by others to be responsible for the maintenance of the life of her child.

Interest in fostering the physical, emotional, and intellectual growth of her child soon supplements a mother's interest in its preservation. The human child is typically capable of complicated emotional and intellectual development; the human adult is radically different in kind from the child it once was. A women who mothers may be aided or assaulted by the help and advice of fathers, teachers, doctors, moralists, therapists, and others who have an interest in fostering and shaping the growth of her child. Although rarely given primary credit, a mother typically holds herself and is held by others to be responsible for the malfunction of the growth process.

From early on, certainly by the middle years of childhood, a mother is governed by a third interest. She must shape natural growth in such a way that her child becomes the sort of adult that she can appreciate and others can accept. Mothers will vary enormously, individually and socially, in the traits and lives that they will appreciate in their children. However, a mother typically takes as the criterion of her success the production of a young adult acceptable to her group.

These three interests in preservation, growth, and acceptability of the child govern maternal practices in general. However, not all mothers are as individuals, governed by these interests. Some mothers are incapable of interested participation in the practices of mothering because of emotional, intellectual, or physical disability. Severe poverty may make interested maternal practice and therefore maternal thinking nearly impossible. Then, of course, mothers engage in practices other than and often conflicting with mothering. Some mothers, aware of the derogation and confinement of women in maternal practice, may be disaffected. In short, actual mothers have the same sort of relation to maternal practice as actual scientists have to scientific practice, or actual believers have to religious practices. As mothers, they are governed by the interests of their respective practices. But the style, skill, commitment, integrity, with which they engage in these practices, differ widely from individual to individual.

The interest in preservation, growth, and the acceptability of the child are frequently and unavoidably in conflict. A mother who watches a child eagerly push a friend aside as she or he climbs a tree will be torn between preserving the child from danger, encouraging the child's physical skills and courage, and shaping a child according to moral restraints-- which might, for example, inhibit the child's joy in competitive climbing. Although some mothers will deny or be insensitive to the conflict and others will be clear about which interest should take precedence, mothers typically will know that they cannot secure each interest, will know that goods conflict, will know that unqualified success in realizing interests is an illusion. This unavoidable conflict of basic interests is one objective basis for the maternal humility which I will shortly describe.

A mother, acting in the interest of preserving and maintaining life, is in a peculiar relation to "nature." As a childbearer, she often takes herself and is taken by others to be an especially "natural" member of her culture. As a childtender, she must respect nature's limits and court its favor with foresighted actions ranging from immunizations; to caps on household poisons; to magical imprecations, warnings, and prayers. "Nature" with its unpredictable varieties of dirt and disease, is her enemy as much as her ally. Her children themselves are natural creatures, often unable to understand or abet her efforts to protect them. Because they frequently find her necessary direction constraining, a mother can experience her children's own liveliness as another enemy of the life she is preserving.

It is no wonder then that as she engages in preservation, a mother is liable to the temptations of fearfulness and excessive control. If she is alone with two or more young children as she tries to carry out her responsibilities, then control of herself, her children, and her physical environment is her only option, however rigid or excessive she looks to outsiders. Though necessarily controlling in their acts, reflecting mothers themselves identify rigid or excessive control as the likely defects of the very virtues they are required to practice. It is the identification of liability as such, with its implication of the will to overcome, which characterizes this aspect of maternal thought. The epithet "controlling mother" is often unsympathetic, even matriphobic. On the other hand, it may, in line with the insights of maternal thought, remind us of what maternal thinking counts as failure. To recognize excessive control as a liability sharply distinguishes maternal from scientific practice.(15)

To a mother, "life" may well seem "terrible, hostile, and quick to pounce on you if you give it a chance."(16) In response, she develops a metaphysical attitude toward "Being as such," an attitude which I call "holding," an attitude which is governed by the priority of keeping over acquiring, of conserving the fragile, of maintaining whatever is at hand and necessary to the child's life. It is an attitude elicited by the work of "world-protection, world-preservation, world-repair...the invisible weaving of a frayed and threadbare family" (Rich, 1977).

The priority of holding over acquiring distinguishes maternal thinking from scientific thinking and from the instrumentalism of technocracy. To be sure, under the pressures of consumerism, holding may become frantic accumulating and storing. More seriously, a parent may feel compelled to preserve her *own* children whatever befalls most other children. The more competitive and heirarchical the society, the more thwarted a mother's individual pursuits, the more likely that holding will become egocentric, frantic, and cruel. Mothers themselves recognize the pitfalls to which holding is liable, and fight to avoid them.

Holding, preserving mothers have distinctive ways of seeing and being in the world which are worth considering. For example, faced with the fragility of the lives it seeks to preserve, maternal thinking recognizes humility and resilient cheerfulness as virtues of its practice. In so doing, it takes issue both with contemporary moral theory and with popular moralities of assertiveness.(17) Humility is a metaphysical attitude one takes toward a world beyond one's control. One might conceive of the world as governed by necessity and chance (as I do) or by supernatural forces that cannot be comprehended. In either case, humility implies a profound sense of the limits of one's actions and of the unpredictability of the consequences of one's work. As the philosopher Iris Murdoch puts it: "Every 'natural' thing, including one's own mind, is subject to chance....One might say that chance is a subdivision of death....We cannot dominate the world" (Murdoch, p. 99). Humility which emerges from maternal practices accepts not only the facts of damage and death, but also the facts of the independent and uncontrollable, developing and increasingly separate existence of the lives its seeks to preserve. "Humility is not a peculiar habit of self-effacement, rather like having an inaudible voice, it is selfless respect for reality and one of the most difficult and central of virtues" (p. 95).

If in the face of danger, disappointment, and unpredictability, mothers are liable to melancholy, they are also aware that a kind, resilient good humor is a virtue. This good humor must not be confused with the cheery denial which is both a liability and, unfortunately, a characteristic of maternal practice. Mothers are tempted to denial simply by the insupportable difficulty of passionately loving a fragile creature in a physically threatening, socially violent, pervasively uncaring, competitive world. Defensive denial is exacerbated as it is officially encouraged, when we must defend against perceptions of our own subordination. Our cheery denials are cruel to our children and demoralizing to ourselves.

Clear-sighted cheerfulness is the virtue of which denial is the degenerative form. It is clear-sighted cheerfulness that Spinoza must have had in mind when he said: "Cheerfulness is always a good thing and never excessive"; it "increases and assists the power of action."*(18)* Denying cheeriness drains intellectual energy and befuddles the will; the cheerfulness honored in maternal thought increases and assists the power of maternal action.

In a daily way, cheerfulness is a matter-of-fact willingness to continue, to give birth and to accept having given birth, to welcome life despite its conditions. When things fall apart, maternal cheerfulness becomes evident courage. There are many stories of mothers who, with resourcefulness and restraint, help their children to die well. The most common but disturbing stories concern mothers who accept their sons' wartime deaths, the most affecting, those which involve the deaths of small children in families.*(19)* These visible and accessible examples are but the manifestation of psychic strengths that have been developed in conditions of mothering which are invisible and frequently denied. Resilient good humor is a style of mothering "in the deepest sense of 'style' in which to discover the right style is to discover what you are really trying to do" (Williams, p. 11).

Because in the dominant society "humility" and "cheerfulness" name virtues of subordinates, and because these virtues have in fact developed in conditions of subordination, it is difficult to credit them, easy to confuse them with the self-effacement and cheery denial which are their degenerative forms. Again and again, in attempting to articulate maternal thought, language is sicklied o'er by the pale cast of sentimentality and thought itself takes on a greeting card quality. Yet literature shows us many mothers who in their "holding" actions value the humility and resilient good humor I have described. One can meet such mothers, recognize their thought, any day one learns to listen. One can appreciate the effects of their discipline and perserverance in the unnecessarily beautiful artifacts of the culture they created. "I made my quilt to keep my family warm. I made it beautiful so my heart would not break."*(20)*

Mothers not only must preserve fragile, existing life. They must also foster growth and welcome change. If the "being" which is preserved seems always to be endangered, undone, slipping away, the "being" which changes is always developing, building, purposely moving away. The "holding," preserving mother must, in response to change, be simultaneously a changing mother. Her conceptual scheme in terms of which she makes sense of herself, her child, and their common world will be more the Aristotelian biologist's than the Platonic mathematician's. Innovation takes precedence over permanence, disclosure, and responsiveness over clarity and certainty. The idea of "objective reality" itself "undergoes important modification when it is to be understood, not in relation to "the world described by science," but in relation to the progressing life of a person" (Murdoch, p. 26).

Women are said to value open over closed structure, to eschew the clear-cut and unambiguous, to refuse a sharp division between inner and outer or self and other. We are also said to depend upon and to prize our private inner lives of the mind.*(21)* If these facets of the "female mind" are elicited by maternal practices, they may well be interwoven responses to the changeability of a growing child. A child is itself an "open structure" whose acts are irregular, unpredictable, often mysterious. A mother, in order to understand her child, must assume the existence of a conscious continuing person whose acts make sense in terms of percep- tions and responses to a meaning-filled world. She knows that her child's fantasies and thoughts are not only connected to the child's power to act, but often the only basis of her understanding of the child and for the child's self-understanding.*(22)*

A mother, in short, is committed to two philosophical positions: She is a mentalist rather than a behaviorist, and she assumes the priority of personhood over action. Moreover, if her "mentalism" is to enable her to understand and to love, she must be realistic about the psyche whose growth she fosters. All psyches are moved by fear, lust, anger, pride, and defenses against them, by what Simone Weil called "natural movements of the soul" and likened to laws of physical gravity (Weil, 1947). This is not to deny that the soul is also blessed by "grace," "light," and erotic hungering for goodness.*(23)* However, mothers cannot take grace for granted, nor force nor deny the less flattering aggrandizing and consola- tory operations of childhood psychic life. A mother must again and again "regain the sense of the complexity and the reality and the struggle...with some pity, some envy and much good will."*(24)*

Her realistic appreciation of a person's continuous mental life allows a mother to expect change, to change with change. As psychologist Jean Baker Miller puts it: "In a very immediate and day to day way women live for change" (Miller, 1973, p. 54). Change requires a kind of learning in which what one learns cannot be applied exactly, and often not even by analogy, to a new situation. If science agrees to take as real the reliable results of repeatable experiments,*(25)* its learning will be quite different in kind from maternal learning. Miller is hopeful that if we attend to maternal practices, we can develop new ways of studying learning appropriate to the changing natures of all peoples and communities, for it is not only children who change, grow, and need help in growing. Most obviously those who care for children must change in response to changing reality. And we all might grow--as opposed to aging--if we could learn how. For everyone's benefit, "women must now face the task of putting their vast unrecognized experience with change into a new and broader level of operation.*(26)*

Miller writes of achievement, of women who have learned to change and respond to change. But she admits:

> Tragically in our society, women are prevented from fully enjoying these pleasures (of growth) themselves by being made to feel that fostering them in others is the only valid role of all women and by the loneliness, drudgery and isolated non-cooperative household setting in which they work (Miller, p. 40).

Similarly, in delineating maternal thought, I do not claim that mothers realize in themselves, the capacities and virtues which we learn to value as we care for others. Rather, mothers develop conceptions of abilities and virtues according to which they measure themselves and interpret their actions. It is no great sorrow that some mothers never acquire humility, resilient good humor, realism, respect for persons, and responsiveness to growth, that all of us fail often in many kinds of ways. What is great sorrow is to find the task itself misdescribed, sentimentalized, and devalued.

The third demand that governs maternal practice is the demand, at once social and personal, that the child's growth be shaped in a manner which makes its life acceptable. 'Acceptability' is defined in terms of the values of a mother's social group-whatever of its values she has internalized as her own, plus values of group members whom she feels she must please or is fearful of displeasing. Society demands that a mother produce an adult acceptable to the next generation. Mothers, roughly half of society, have an interest in meeting that demand. They also are governed by a more stringent form of acceptability. They want the child they produce to be a person that they themselves, and those closest to them, can appreciate. From early on, the demand of appreciability gives an urgency, sometimes exhilarating, sometimes anguishing, to maternal practice.

The task of producing an appreciable child gives a mother a unique opportunity to explore, create and insist upon her own values, to train her children simultaneously for strength and virtue, and ultimately to develop openness and reciprocity in regard to her child's most threatening changes and differences from her, namely moral ones. As a mother thinks upon the appreciability of her child, her maternal practice becomes a self-conscious, reflective discipline and expression of conscience.

In response to the demand of appreciability, maternal thinking is apt to become contradictory--that is, it betrays its own interest in the growth of children. Almost everywhere, the practices of mothering take place in societies where women of all classes are less powerful than men of their class to determine the conditions in which their children grow. Throughout history, most women have mothered in conditions of military and social violence, often of extreme poverty. They have been governed by men and increasingly by managers and experts of both sexes whose policies mothers neither shape nor control. Out of maternal powerlessness, in response to a society whose values it doesn't determine, maternal thinking is distorted in both style and content. Acting so as to produce an appreciable child, a mother's thinking is liable to become rigid in form, as she becomes fearful, moralistic rather than moral. Acting out of powerlessness, maternal thinking has often and largely opted for inauthenticity and the "good" of others.

By "inauthenticity" I designate a double willingness--first a willingness to *travailler pour l'armee,(27)* to accept the uses to which others will put one's children; second a willingness to remain blind to the implications of those uses for the actual lives of women and children. Maternal thought embodies inauthenticity by taking on the values of the dominant culture. Like the "holding" of preservation, "inauthenticity" is a mostly nonconscious response to Being as Such. Only this attitude is not a caretaker's response to the natural exigencies of childtending, but a subordinate's reaction to a social reality essentially characterized by the domination and subordination of persons. Inauthenticity constructs and then assumes a world in which one's own values don't count. It is allied to fatalism and to some religious thought, some versions of Christianity, for example. As inauthenticity is lived out in maternal practice, it gives rise to the values of obedience and "being good"; that is, it is taken as an achievement to fulfill the values of the dominant culture. Obedience is related to indifferent nature, the incomprehensible supernature, and human fallibility, obedience respects the actual control and preferences of dominant people.

Individual mothers, living out maternal thought, take on the values of the families and subcultures to which they belong and of the men with whom they are allied. Because some groups and many men are vibrantly moral, these values are not necessarily inadequate. However, even moral groups and men almost always accept the relative subordination of women, whatever other ideals of equality and autonomy they may hold. A "good" mother may well be praised for colluding in her own subordination with the destructive consequences to herself and her children that I've described. Moreover, most groups and men impose at least some values that are psychologically and physically damaging to children. A mother practiced in fostering growth will be able to "see" the effects of, for example, injurious stratification, competitiveness, gender stereotyping, hypocrisy, and conscription to war. Damage to a child is as clear to her as the effect of a hurricane on a young tree. Yet to be "good," a mother may be expected to endorse and execute inimical commands. She is also the person principally responsible for training her children in the ways and desires of obedience. This may mean training her daughters for powerlessness, her sons for war, and both for crippling work in dehumanizing factories, businesses, and professions. It may mean training both daughters and sons for defensive or arrogant power over others in sexual, economic, or political life. A mother who trains either for powerlessness or abusive power over others betrays the very life she has preserved, whose growth she has fostered. She denies children even the possibility of being both strong and good.

The strain of colluding in one's own powerlessness, coupled with the frequent and much greater strain of betraying the children one has tended, would be insupportable if conscious. A mother under strain may internalize as her own values those values which are clearly inimical to her children. She has, after all, usually been rewarded for just such protective albeit destructive internalization. Additionally, she may blind herself to the implications of her obedience, a blindness which is excused and exacerbated by the cheeriness of denial. For precariously but deeply protected mothers, feminist accounts of power relations and their cost call into question the worthiness of maternal work and the genuiness of maternal love. Such women, understandably, fight insight as others fight bodily assault, revealing in their struggles a commitment to their own sufferings which may look "neurotic" but is in fact, given their options, realistic.

When I described maternal thought arising out of the interests in growth and preservation, I was not speaking of the actual achievement of mothers, but of a conception of achievement. Similarly, in describing the thought arising out of the interest in acceptability, I am not speaking of actual mothers' adherence to dominant values, but of a conception of their relation to those values in which obedience and "being good" is considered an achievement. There are many individual mothers who "fail," that is who insist on their own values, who will not remain blind to the implications of dominant values for the lives of children. Moreover, I hope I have said enough about the damaging effects of the prevailing sexual arrangements and social hierarchies on maternal lives to make it clear that I do not blame mothers for their (our) obedience. Obedience is largely a function of social powerlessness. Maternal work is done according to the Law of Symbolic Father and under His Watchful Eye, as well as, typically, according to the desires, even whims, of the father's house. "This is my Father's world/Oh let me ne'er forget/that though the wrong be oft so strong,/He is the ruler yet." In these conditions of work, inauthentic obedience to dominant patriarchal values is as plausible a maternal response as respect for the results of experiment is in scientific work.

As I have said, the work of mothering can become a disciplined, rewarding work of conscience. In order for this opportunity to be realized, either collectively or by individual mothers, maternal thought will have to be transformed by feminist consciousness.

> Coming to have a feminist consciousness is the experience of coming to know the truth about oneself and one's society....The very meaning of what the feminist apprehends is illuminated by the light of what ought to be ....The feminist apprehends certain features of social reality as intolerable, as to be rejected in behalf of a transforming project for the future....Social reality is revealed as deceptive....What is really happening is quite

different from what appears to be happening (Bartky, pp. 22-34, 33, 25, 28-29).

Feminist consciousness will first transform inauthentic obedience into wariness, uncertain reflection, at times, anguished confusion. The feminist becomes "marked by the experience of moral ambiguity" as she learns new ways of living without betraying her women's past, without denying her obligations to others. "She no longer knows what sort of person she ought to be, and therefore she does not know what she ought to do. One moral paradigm is called into question by the laborious and often obscure emergence of another."(28)

Out of confusion, new voices will arise, voices recognized not so much by the content of the truths they enunciate as by the honesty and courage of enunciation. They will be at once familiar and original, these voices arising out of maternal practice, affirming its own criteria of acceptability, insisting that the dominant values are unacceptable and need not be accepted.

> How *does* the male child differentiate himself from his mother, and does this mean inevitably that he must "join the army," that is, internalize patriarchal values? Can the mother, in patriarchy, represent culture, and if so, what does this require of her?....What do we want for our sons?....We want them to remain in the deepest sense, sons of the mother, yet also to grow into themselves, to discover new ways of being men as we are discovering new ways of being women.

> What do we mean by the nurture of daughters? The most notable fact that the culture imprints on women is the sense of our limits. The most important thing one woman can do for another is to illuminate and expand her sense of actual possibilities....The quality of the mother's life ....however embattled and unprotected--is her primary bequest to her daughter (Rich, 1976, pp. 198, 211, 246, 247).

I have been arguing that maternal thought as it is governed by the interest in acceptablility is clear and distinct enough to be expressed, but is not yet worthy of respect. The interest in acceptability will always shape maternal practices and provoke mothers to affirm and announce some values, their own or others.(29) The production of a child worthy of appreciation is a *real* demand which a mother would impose on herself even if it were not demanded of her by her community. The only question is whether that demand is met by acquiescence or the struggles of a conscience attending clearly to the good of children. When mothers insist upon the inclusion of their values and experiences in the public world which children enter, when they determine what makes their children acceptable, the work of growth and preservation will acquire a new gaiety and joyfulness.

Finally, I would like to discuss a capacity--"Attention"--and a virtue--love--which are central to the conception of achievement that maternal thought as a whole articulates. This capacity and virtue, when realized, invigorate preservation and enable growth. Attention and love again and again undermine a mother's inauthentic obedience as she perceives and endorses a child's experience though society finds it intolerable. The identification of the capacity of attention and the virtue of love is at once the foundation and the corrective of maternal thought.

The notion of "attention" is central to the philosophy of Simone Weil and is developed, along with the related notion of "love" by Iris Murdoch, who was profoundly influenced by Weil. Attention and love are fundamental to the construction of "objective reality" understood "in relation to the progressing life of a person," a "reality which is revealed to the patient eye of love" (Murdoch, p. 40). Attention is an *intellectual* capacity connected even by definition with love, a special kind of "knowledge of the individual" (p. 28). The name of this intense, pure, disinterested, gratuitous, generous attention is love" (Weil, 1962). Weil thinks that the capacity for attention is a "miracle," Murdoch ties it more closely to familiar achievement. "The task of attention goes on all the time and at apparently empty and everyday moments we are 'looking,' making those little peering efforts of imagination which have such important cumulative results" (Murdoch, p. 43).

For both Weil and Murdoch, the enemy of attention is what they call "fantasy," defined not as rich imaginative play, which does have a central role in maternal thinking, but as the "proliferation of blinding self-centered aims and images" (Murdoch, p. 67). Fantasy, according to their original conception, is intellectual and imaginative activity in the service of consolation, domination, anxiety, and aggrandizement. It is reverie designed to protect the psyche from pain, self-induced blindness designed to protect it from insight. Fantasy, so defined, works in the service of inauthenticity. "The difficulty is to keep the attention fixed on the real situation" (Murdoch, p. 91)--or, as I would say, on the real children. Attention to real children, children seen by the "patient eye of love" "teaches us how real things (real children) can be looked at and loved without being seized and used, without being appropriated into the greedy organism of the self" (Murdoch, p. 65).

Much in maternal practices work against attentive love: intensity of identification, vicarious living through a child, daily wear of maternal work, harassment and indignities of an indifferent social order, the clamor of children themselves. Although attention is elicited by the very reality it reveals--the reality of a growing person--it is a discipline that requires effort and self-training. Love, the love of children at any rate, is not only the most intense of attachments; it is also a detachment, a giving up, a letting grow. To love a child without seizing or using it, to see *the child's* reality with the patient, loving eye of attention--such loving and attending might well describe the separation of mother and child from the mother's point of view. Of course, many of us who are mothers fail much of the time in attentive love and loving attention. Many mothers also train themselves in the looking, self-restraining, and empathy that is loving attention. They can be heard doing so in any playground or coffee klatch.

I am not saying that mothers, individually or collectively, are (or are not) especially wonderful people. My point is that out of maternal practices distinctive ways of conceptualizing, ordering, and valuing arise. We *think* differently about what it *means* and what it takes to be "wonderful," to be a person, to be real.

Murdoch and Weil, neither mothers themselves nor especially concerned with mothers, are clear about the absolute value of attentive love and the reality it reveals. Weil writes:

> In the first legend of the Grail, it is said that the Grail...belongs to the first comer who asks the guardian of the vessel, a king three quarters paralyzed by the most painful wound, "What are you going through?"
>
> The love of our neighbor in all its fullness simply means being able to say to him: "What are you going through?" ...Only he who is capable of attention can do this (Weil, 1951, p. 115).

I do not claim absolute value but only that attentive love, the training to ask, "What are you going through?" is central to maternal practices. If I am right about its place in maternal thought, and if Weil and Murdock are right about its absolute value, the self-conscious inclusion of maternal thought in the dominant culture will be of general intellectual and moral benefit.

I have described a "thought" arising out of maternal practices organized by the interests of preservation, growth, and acceptability. Although in some respects the thought is "contradictory," that is it betrays its own values and must be transformed by feminist consciousness, the thought as a whole, with its fulcrum and correction in attentive love, is worthy of being expressed and respected. This thought has emerged out of maternal practices that are oppressive to women and children. I believe that it has emerged largely in response to the relatively invariable requirements of children and despite oppressive circumstances. As in all women's thought, some worthy aspects of maternal thought may arise out of identification with the powerless and excluded. However, oppression is largely responsible for the defects rather than the strengths of maternal thought, as in the obedient goodness to which mothers find themselves "naturally" subscribing. When the oppressiveness of gender arrangements is combined with race, poverty, or the multiple injuries of class, it is a miracle that maternal thought can arise at all. On the other hand, that it does indeed arise, miraculously, is clear both from literature (Alice Walker, Tillie Olsen, Maya Angelou, Agnes Smedley, Lucille Clifton, Louisa May Alcott, Audre Lorde, Marilyn French, Grace Paley, countless others) and from daily experience. Maternal thought *identifies* priorities, attitudes, and virtues, *conceives* of achievement. The more oppressive the institutions of motherhood, the greater the pain and struggle in living out the worthy and transforming the damaging aspects of thought.

It is now widely argued that the most liberating change we can make in institutions of motherhood is to include men equally in every aspect of maternal care. I am heartened to read that "societies that do not elaborate the opposition of male and female and place positive value on the conjugal relationship and involvement of both men and women in the home seem to be most egalitarian in terms of sex role" (Rosaldo, 1974). To prevent or excuse men from maternal practice is to encourage them to separate public action from private affection. Moreover, men's domination is present when their absence from the nursery is combined with their domination of every other room. To familiarize children with "natural" domination at their earliest age in a context of primitive love, assertion, and sexual passion is to prepare them to find equally "natural" and exhaustive the division between exploiter and exploited which pervades the world. Although daughter and son alike may internalize "natural" domination, neither, typically, can live with it easily. Identifying with and imitating exploiters, we are overcome with self-hate; aligning ourselves with the exploited, we are fearful and manipulative. Again and again, family power dramas are repeated in psychic, interpersonal and professional dramas, while they are institutionalized in economic, political, and international life. Radically recasting the power-gender roles in those dramas just might revolutionize social conscience (Rich, 1976; Dinnerstein, 1976).

Assimilating men into childcare both inside and outside the home would also be conducive to serious social reform. Responsible, equal childcaring would require men to relinquish power and their own favorable position in the division between intellectual/professional and service labor as that division expresses itself domestically. Loss of preferred status at home might make socially privileged men more suspicious of unnecessary divisions of labor and damaging hierarchies in the public world. Moreover, if men were emotionally and practically committed to childcare, they would reform the work world in parents' interests. Once no one "else" was minding the child, there would be good daycare centers with flexible hours, daycare centers to which parents could trust their children from infancy on. These daycare centers, like the work week itself, would be managed "flexibly," in response to human needs as well as "productivity," with an eye to growth, rather than measurable "profit." Such moral reforms of economic life would probably begin with professionals and managers servicing themselves. However, even in nonsocialist countries, their benefits could be unpredictably extensive.

I would not argue, however, that the assimilation of men into childcare is the primary social goal for mothers to set themselves. Rather, we must work to bring a *transformed* maternal thought into the public realm, to make the preservation and growth of *all* children a work of public conscience and legislation. This will not be easy. Mothers are no less corrupted than anyone else by concerns of status and class. Often our misguided efforts on behalf of the success and purity of our children frighten them and everyone else around them. As we increase and enjoy our public effectiveness, we will have less reason to live vicariously through our children. We may then begin to learn to sustain a creative tension between our inevitable and fierce desire to foster our own children and the less compulsive desire that all children grow and flourish.

Nonetheless, it would be foolish to believe that mothers, just because they are mothers, can transcend class interest and implement principles of justice. All feminists must join in articulating a theory of justice shaped by and incorporating maternal thinking. Moreover, the generalization of attentive love to *all* children requires politics. The most enlightened thought is not enough.

Closer to home again, we must refashion our domestic life in the hope that the personal will in fact betoken the political. We must begin by resisting the temptation to construe "home" simplemindedly, as a matter of justice between mothers and fathers. Single parents, lesbian mothers, and co-parenting women remind us that there are many ways to provide children with examples of caring which do not incorporate sexual inequalities of power and privilege. Those of us who do live with the fathers of our children will eagerly welcome shared parenthood--for overwhelming practical as well as ideological reasons. But in our eagerness, we mustn't forget that so long as a mother is not effective publicly and self-respecting privately, male presence can be harmful as well beneficial. It does a woman no good to have the power of the Symbolic Father brought right into the nursery, often despite the deep affectionate egalitarianism of an individual man. It takes a strong mother and father to resist the temptations to domination and subordination for which they have been trained and are socially rewarded. And whatever the hard-won equality and mutual respect an individual couple may achieve, so long as a mother--even if she is no more parent than father--is derogated and subordinate outside the home, children will feel angry, confused, and "wildly unmothered" (Rich, 1976, p. 225).

Despite these reservations, I look forward to the day when men are willing and able to share equally and actively in transformed maternal practices. When that day comes, will we still identify some thought as maternal rather than merely parental? Might we echo the cry of some feminists--there shall be no more "women"--with our own--there shall be no more "mothers," only people engaging in childcare. To keep matters clear I would put the point differently. On that day, there will be no more "Fathers," no more people of either sex who have power over their children's lives and moral authority in their children's world, though they do not do the work of attentive love. There will be mothers of both sexes who live out a transformed maternal thought in communities that share parental care--practically, emotionally, economically, and socially. Such communities will have learned from their mothers how to value children's lives.

REFERENCES

Bartky, S. L. Toward a phenomenology of feminist consciousness. In M. Vetteeling-Braggin, F. A. Elliston, and J. English (Eds.), *Feminism and philosophy.* Towata, N.J.: Littlefield Adams, 1977.

Bernard, J. *The future of motherhood.* New York: Deal, 1974.

Chodorow, N. *The reproduction of mothering.* Berkeley: University of California Press, 1978.

Clifton, L. My mama moved among the days. In *Good times.* New York: Random House, 1969, p. 2.

Dinnerstein, D. *The mermaid and the minotaur: Sexual arrangements and human malaise.* New York: Harper and Row, 1976.

Miller, J. B. *Toward a new psychology of women.* Boston: Beacon Press, 1973.

Murdoch, I. *The sovereignty of good.* New York: Schocken, 1971.

Rich, A. *Of woman born.* New York: Norton, 1976.

Rich, A. Conditions for work: The common world of women. In S. Ruddick and P. Daniels (Eds.), *Working it out.* New York: Pantheon, 1977.

Rosaldo, M. Z. Women, culture and society: A theoretical overview. In M. Z. Rosaldo and L. Lamphere (Eds.), *Women, culture and society.* Stanford: Stanford University Press, 1974.

Weil, S. Reflections of the right use of school studies with a view to the love of God. In *Waiting for God.* New York: G. P. Putnam's Sons, 1951.

Weil, S. Gravity and grace. In *Gravity and grace.* London: Routledge and Kegan Paul, 1952. First French edition, 1947.

Weil, S. Human personality. In *Collected essays.* London: Oxford University Press, 1962.

Williams, B. *Morality.* New York: Harper and Row, 1972.

FOOTNOTES

(1) This article is reprinted from *Feminist Studies*, Volume 6, Number 2 (summer 1980): pp. 342-367 by permission of the publisher *Feminist Studies*, Inc., c/o Women's Studies Program, University of Maryland, College Park, D 40742.

I began circulating an early draft of this paper in the fall of 1978. Since then, the constructive criticism and warm response of readers has led me to believe that this draft is truly a collective endeavor. I would like especially to thank Sandra Bartky, Gail Bragg, Bell Chevigny, Nancy Chodorow, Margaret Comstock, Mary Felstiner, Berenice Fisher, Marilyn Frye, Susan Harding, Evelyn Fox Keller, Jane Lilienfeld, Jane Marcus, Adrienne Rich, Amelie Rorty, William Ruddick, Barrie Thorne, Marilyn Blatt Young, reader for *Feminist Studies*, and Rayna Rapp.

(2) For an extensive discussion of the power of mothers, see Dorothy Dinnerstein, 1976. In expressing our fears of maternal power Dinnerstein sometimes, unfortunately and unwittingly, gives voice to the very matriphobia she decries.

(3) In traditional heterosexual parenting, a returning father may distract even the nursing mother from her child, demanding attention and service which is frequently more alienating, more threatening to a mother's self-possession than children's demands. To the extent that the infant is sensitive to the gender of the mother, as Dinnerstein and others claim, to that extent it would be dimly aware of the gender-linked character of the interruption. In any case, the child will soon become aware that females are caretakers whose work and caring is endlessly interruptible.

On the politics of interruption, see Michelle Cliff. The Resonance of Interruption. *Chrysalis*, no. 8. Summer 1979; Pamela Fishman. Interaction: The Work Women Do. *Social Problems 25*, no. 4. April 1978; and Don Zimmerman and Candace West. Sex Roles, Interruptions and Silences in Conversations. In *Language and Sex: Difference and Dominance*, eds. Barrie Thorne and Nancy Henley. Rowley, Mass.: Newbury House, 1975.

Many fathers are of course, socially unappreciated. Poor, declassed, or "failing" fathers know the pain of introducing their children to a world in which they do not figure. Sometimes their powerlessness is visited directly upon the mothers. Even when it is not, mothers suffer a double powerlessness when the "fathers" of her kin and cultural group are degraded by the Laws of the Ruling Fathers; the "world of the fathers" belongs neither to her sons nor to the men her daughters will live among.

(4) I am indebted to Susan Harding for this point (personal conversation and lecture notes from the Residential College, University of Michigan).

(5) For an analysis of the evil of factory work which emphasizes workers' loss of control of their time, see Simone Weil. Factory Work. In *Simone Weil Reader*, ed. George A. Panichas. New York: McKay, 1977. For a similar comparison of mothers' control over time compared with that of other workers, see Barbara Garson. Clerical. In *All the Livelong*

Day. New York: Penguin Books, 1975. Of course, many mothers also work in factories, stores, and fields; and some mothers work in managerial, professional, and executive positions. The issue is whether mothers have more control over time and order of their work (in the Weil sense) in their maternal than in their other working hours. Mothers do not have control over their *lives,* and this relative absence of self-determination has consequences which I will specify.

(6) Carol Pearson. Women's Fantasies and Feminist Utopias. Makes the general point that in several feminist utopias, "human kinship procedures can govern an entire society because the people in the society are mothers." See *Frontiers 2,* no. 3. Fall, 1977. Pearson quotes extensively from *Herland* by Charlotte Perkins Gilman. "You see we are *mothers"* is taken from *Herland.* New York: Pantheon, 1979. For a clear discussion of the significance of matriarchy, see Paula Webster. Matriarchy: A Vision of Power. In *Toward an Anthropology of Women,* ed. Rayna R. Reiter. New York and London: Monthly Review Press, 1975. pp. 141-156.

(7) Among other possible aspects of women's thought are those that might arise from our sexual lives, from our "homemaking," from the special conflict women feel between allegiance on the one hand and their world, and on the other hand, to all people of their kin and culture. Any identifiable aspect of women's thought will be inter-related to all of the others. Because women almost everywhere are relatively powerless in relation to men of their class, all aspects of women's thought will be affected by powerlessness. Whether we are discussing the thought arising from women's bodily, sexual, maternal, homemaking, linguistic, or any other experience, we are faced with a confluence of powerlessness and the "womanly" whatever that might be.

(8) The pervasive and false identification of womanhood and biological or adoptive motherhood injures both mothers and nonmothers. The identification obscures the many kinds of mothering performed by those who do not parent particular children in families. It frequently forces those labeled "nonmothers" to take a distance from their own mothers and the maternal lives of all women. Out of justified fear and resentment of the obligation to mother, these "nonmothers" may become caught up in socially induced but politically myopic efforts to divorce female identity from any connection with maternal practices. Meanwhile, mothers engage in parallel self-destructive efforts which further divide women from each other. In their fight to preserve their nonmaternal aspirations and projects, mothers may belittle the importance of maternal experience in their lives. Or out of fear of their own anger at a limiting social identity as well as out of legitimate fury at the devaluation of mothers and motherliness, they may overidentify with the maternal identification foisted upon them, letting their nonmaternal working and loving selves die. Whichever we mothers do, and frequently we do both, the cost to our maternal and nonmaternal works and loves is enormous.

(9) For the most complete and sensitive account of girl's special relation to mothers' mothering, see Chodorow. *The Reproduction of Mothering.* See also Jane Flax. The Conflict Between Nurturance and Autonomy in Mother-Daughter Relationships and Within Feminism. *Feminist Studies 4*, no. 2. June, 1978. pp. 171-189.

(10) See Nancy Chodorow. Feminism and Difference: Gender, Relation, and Difference in Psychoanalytic Perspective. *Socialist Review,* no. 46. July-August, 1979. "We cannot know what children would make of their bodies in a nongender or nonsexually organized social world....It is not obvious that there would be major significance to biological sex differences, to gender difference or to different sexualities" (p. 66).

(11) Examples of the invariant and *nearly* unchangeable include: long gestation inside the mother's body; prolonged infant and childhood dependence; physical fragility of infancy; radical qualitative change ("growth") in emotional and intellectual capacities from infancy to adulthood; long development and psychological complexity of human sexual desire, of memory and other cognitive capacities, and of "object relations." Features which are *nearly* universal and certainly changeable include: the identification of childbearing and childcaring, the consequent delegation of childcare to natural mothers and other women, the relative subordination of women in any social class to men of that class.

(12) To see the universal in particulars, to assimilate differences and extend kinship is a legacy of the ecumenical Protestantism in which I was raised. I am well aware that even nonviolent, well-meaning Protestant assimilations can be obtuse and cruel for others. Therefore I am dependent on others, morally as well as intellectually, for the statement of differences, the assessment of their effects on every aspect of maternal lives, and finally for radical correction as well as for expansion of any general theory I would offer. However, I do not *believe* that the thinking I describe is limited only to "privileged white women" as one reader put it. I first came to the notion of "maternal thinking" and the virtues of maternal practices through person exchange with Tillie Olsen and then through reading her fiction. My debt to her is pervasive. Similarly, I believe that "Man Child: A Black Lesbian Feminist's Response" by Audre Lorde. *Conditions,* no. 4. Winter, 1979. pp. 30-36, is an excellent example of what I call "maternal thinking transformed by feminist consciousness." My "assimilation" of Olsen's and Lorde's work in no way denies the differences which separate us nor the biases that those differences may introduce into my account. These are only two of many examples of writers in quite different social circumstances who express what I take to be "maternal thinking."

(13) Nothing I say about maternal thought suggests that the women who engage in it cannot engage in other types of intellectual discourse. A maternal thinker may also be an experimental psychologist, a poet, a mathematician, an architect, a physicist. I believe that because most

thinkers have been men, most disciplines are partly shaped by "male" concepts, values, styles, and strategies.   However, unless we have identified "male" and "female" aspects of thought, the claim of gender bias is an empty one.   I do not doubt that disciplines are also shaped by transgender interests, values, and concepts, which women, whether or not they engage in maternal practices, may fully share.   To the extent that the disciplines are shaped by "male" thought, mothers and other women may feel alienated by the practices and thinking of their own discipline. Correlatively, when thinkers are as apt to be women as men, thought itself may change.

(14) I derive the vocabulary most specifically from Jürgen Habermas. *Knowledge and Human Interest.* Boston: Beacon Press, 1971. However, I have been equally influenced by other philosophical relativists, most notably by Peter Winch, Ludwig Wittgenstein, and Suzanne Kessler and Wendy McKenna. See Winch. Understanding a Primitive Society. And other papers, in *Ethics and Action.* London: Routledge and Kegan Paul, 1972; Wittgenstein. *Philosophical Investigations, Remarks on the Foundations of Mathematics, Zettel,* and *On Certainty.* Oxford: Blackwell, 1953, 1956, 1967, 1969.   Kessler and McKenna.   *Gender.* New York: Wiley, 1978.   I am also indebted to the writings of Evelyn Keller. Especially, Feminist Critique of Science: A Forward or Backward Move, He, She and Id in Scientific Discourse (unpublished manuscripts); and Gender and Science. *Psychoanalysis and Contemporary Thought 1,* no. 3. 1978.

(15) See Habermas.   *Knowledge and Human Interests* for the view that scientific knowledge is organized by its interests in control.

(16) The words are Mrs. Ramsay's in Virginia Woolf.   *To the Lighthouse.* New York: Harcourt Brace and World, 1927, p. 92.

(17) For the comparison, see Murdoch.   Popular moralities as well as contemporary moral theory tend to emphasize decision, assertion, happiness, authenticity, and justification by principle.

(18) Spinoza.   *Ethics,* Book 3, Proposition 42, demonstration.   See also Proposition 40, Note and Proposition 45, both in Book 3.

(19) For example of the first, see Virginia Woolf.   *Mrs. Dalloway.* New York: Harcourt, Brace and World, 1925.   In which Lady Bexborough opens a bazaar holding the telegram announcing her son's death.   Her action is simultaneously admirable, repellent, and politically disturbing as I hope to show in the section on acceptability.

(20) The words are a Texas farmwoman's who quilted as she huddled with her family in a shelter as, above them, a tornado destroyed their home.   The story was told to me by Miriam Schapiro.

(21) These are differences often attributed to women both by themselves and by psychologists. For a critical review of the literature see Eleanor Maccoby and Carol Jacklin. *The Psychology of Sex Differences.* Stanford, Calif.: Stanford University Press, 1974. For a plausible account of women's valuing of inner life, see Patricia Meyer Spacks. *The Female Imagination.* New York: Knopf, 1975. Maccoby and Jacklin are critical both of the findings I mentioned and of adequacy of the psychological experiments they survey for testing or discovering these kinds of differences. I make little use of psychology, more of literature, in thinking about the kinds of cognitive sex differences I discuss. Psychologists are not, so far as I know, talking about women who have empathically identified with and assimilated maternal practices, either by engaging in them or by identifying with their own or other mothers. It would be hard to identify such a subgroup of women without circularity. But even if one could make the identification, tests would have to be devised that did not measure achievement, but conception of achievement. Mothers, to take one example, may well prize the inner life, but have so little time for it or be so self-protectively defended against their own insights (as I will discuss shortly) that they gradually lose the capacity for inner life. Or again, a mother may not maintain sharp boundaries between herself and her child or between her child's "outer" action and inner life. However, she *must* maintain some boundaries. We value what we are in danger of losing (e.g., inner life); we identify virtues because we recognize temptations to vice (e.g., openness because we are tempted to rigid control); we refuse what we fear giving way to (e.g., either pathological symbiotic identification *or* an unworkable division between our own and our children's interests). It is difficult to imagine tests sophisticated and sensitive enough to measure such conceptions, priorities, and values. I have found psychoanalytic theory the most useful of psychologies and Chodorow. *The Reproduction of Mothering.* The most helpful in applying psychoanalytic theory to maternal practices.

(22) One reader has suggested that my account of a mother attuned to her own child's thoughts and fantasies is biased by my white, middle-class experience. By appreciation of a person's continuous mental life, I do not mean only the leisurely (and frequently intrusive) hovering over the child's psyche, hovering which is often the product of powerlessness and enforced idleness. The appreciation I think of is often a kind of pained groping for the meanings that a child is giving to its own experiences, including to its own sufferings. I believe I have heard these gropings both first-hand and in literary reflections of mothers who are not white and/or middle class. For two of many examples, see Tillie Olsen. I Stand Here Ironing. From *Tell Me a Riddle.* New York: Delacorte Press, 1956. And Audre Lorde. Man Child. If my interpretation of others' experiences is wrong, other women with different lives will correct me. Expressing maternal thinking is necessarily a collective project.

(23) Weil. Gravity and Grace. And other essays in *Gravity and Grace.* Both the language and concepts are indebted to Plato.

(24) Bernard's words in the summing up of Virginia Woolf. *The Waves*. New York: Harcourt, Brace and World, 1931, p. 294.

(25) As Habermas argues, *Knowledge and Human Interest*.

(26) This vast experience is unrecognized partly because psychologists assume that while mothers are responsible for preservation, fathers are responsible for growth. This view of psychologists "denies the possibility of a maternal nurturance which actually encourages autonomy. But what is nurturance if not the pleasure in the other's growth? If not the desire to satisfy the other's needs whether it be the need to cling or the need to be independent?" Jessica Benjamin. Authority and the Family Revisited: or, A World Without Fathers? *New German Critique*, no. 13. Winter 1978, pp. 35-57.

(27) I am indebted to Rich. *Of Woman Born*. Especially chapter 8, both for this phrase and for the working out of the idea of inauthenticity.

(28) On the riskiness of authenticity and the courage it requires of women, see also Miller. *Toward a New Psychology of Women*. Chapter 9.

(29) For a discussion of the relative weight of parents' and children's values in determining children's lives, see William Ruddick. Parents and Life Prospects. In *Having Children*, eds. Onora O'Neill and William Ruddick. New York: Oxford University Press, 1979.

COMMENT:

Response to Wilder's "Mother/Nature,"

and Ruddick's "Maternal Thinking"

Marilyn Frye

Department of Philosophy
Michigan State University
East Lansing, MI 48824

I very much welcome Professor Wilder's debunking of Rossi's theses and arguments and I wholeheartedly share his rejection of that sort of biological determinism and his recognition of the unnaturalness of all human behavior. That last is, I think, an essential first step toward our assuming responsibility for how things are. However, I am not as comfortable as he seems to be with the liberal anyone-can-parent line of thought. What gives me pause about that may be some of the same experience and observations that make the Rossi sort of view so plausible to so many people. That is, regardless of my clear knowledge that an ability to acquire facility in the home kitchen or with infant care is not biologically determined, and also my knowledge that ability to become competent in the maintenance of the common automobile is not biologically determined either, I see many such propensities and abilities as being hardly less difficult to acquire or to lose as a gendered adult than if they had been biologically determined. In other words, the tracking into gender-correlated competencies creates a "second-nature"--each individual seems to take to some activities and practices naturally. It feels natural, one is "a natural" as a mother or as a businessman; it seems natural to all those around, as well. And, learned and human-created though it may be, it is not therefore easy to undo. Furthermore, a similar point arises on the more general level of inherited cultural patterns, myths, images. Humans, indeed, invented the patriarchal family and the myths around it. It seems clearly not to be a natural thing. But the partriarchal family as an institution, an idea, a guiding myth, does not lose its power to shape our lives, to contribute mightily to our abilities to learn and to determine what we learn. Just because it is "manmade" and not "natural" does not mean it is significantly easier to change than the weather.

127

I take mothering to be an enterprise or practice of great complexity and one which cannot be summarized in some rules of thumb in a handbook, nor done well by just anybody who sets her or his mind to it. I also see it as coming more naturally to those with certain sorts of upbringings than to those with others. Those brought up in musical families would usually be better set to develop into fine composers than those raised where nobody plays any instruments or loves to listen to music. The good, the very good, and the great practitioners of most complex and subtle arts or practices tend to be those who start absorbing the art young, are encouraged into it by the structure of the social and material environment of their childhood and youth, and are rewarded for their budding competence, skill and artistry. I submit that for the same sorts of reasons males will constitute a dismaying majority of the competent, good, or great scientists in this country for rather a long time to come, and females will constitute a great majority of the competent, good or great mothers--the currently fashionable liberal egalitarianism notwithstanding.

There is another source of my discomfort with the egalitarianism that Wilder defends against the attack by the biological determinist, and this is a political one. What we may have here is another case of a trick which is becoming all too familiar--an "integration" which rides under the banner of Equality but is really an invasion and pillage. If men move into mothering, they are, among other things, moving in on territory which has belonged to women. It is one of the few areas in which women have func- tioned autonomously and sometimes with some respect. The strong and special association of mothering with women has also been a source of power for women. Breaking that association is breaking the mythic power of the Mother. Women claim choice, and claim the value and honorable- ness of this Women's Work. In response (it almost seems, in retaliation) the work is quickly re-conceived as gender-neutral. The history of mothering as something done by generations of *women* is assumed irrelevant, and women's only deep source of power is appropriated as a "human" project. It seems politically wise to be cautious about strategies for change which involve dissolution of what power the subordinate group has.

This quick excision of the concept of women from the concept of mothering is of a piece with an erasure of the woman and the experience of women in some of the talk that gets bandied about on the subject of birthing. In writing and discussion by people who clearly mean to be liberal on issues about birthing, it is quite common to find women erased from the birthing scene. The person whose body is utterly and over- whelmingly involved in the physiological process of birthing is swallowed up in *the couple*. There is much talk about the couple seeking this, needing that, advocating the other, in these times of changing views about birthing. And this supports an abstraction of the birthing process into an entity called "the birth," which is claimed and squabbled over like a piece of property. One hears from the mouths of liberals such things as "Who does the birth belong to?" and "The couple asserts its right to its own birth."

While it seems morally and politically wrong thus to erase a major agent in the birthing process, it can also lead to error. For instance, it supports the appearance of plausibility of a currently fashionable thesis which is that any birthing procedure any culture ever uses will make for "healthy childbirth" just so long as everybody in the scene perceives the procedure as a good one.(1) I think that this can only seem plausible if you do not really think about the lived experience of the woman and the baby. Think of your own body, female or male--of your own bodily experiences of radical changes in your environment or of the bodily experience of strong physiological processes and of extremely strenuous muscular work. Surely gross differences in blood levels of powerful drugs make a real difference to the health of babies. Surely gross differences in the amounts of light and sound and rough handling of the newborn make a difference to the health of the baby. Surely laboring against gravity on one's back versus laboring with gravity from an upright position makes a difference to the damage done to mother or baby, or the suffering incurred.

One does not have to have actually given birth to notice and appreciate these things. One needs only to *pay attention* to the experiencer, the woman, and what is going on with her. The erasure which displaces attention and encourages poor judgment in this matter is a consequence of the relatively unthinking liberal assumption that men and women are, or somehow should be, *equally involved* in birthing...as though this followed from the fact that they should be equally involved in government. Busy with including considerations of the father, parents, the state, the "deliverers of medical services," etc., one overlooks the information available through attention to the birthing process itself-- that is, to something that is both happening to and being done by a living woman.

The kind of analysis that Sara Ruddick is doing seems to me to be half of the necessary prolegemenon to developing a clear picture of the politics of dissociation of motherhood and womanhood. The other half is the sort of analysis of the patriarchal political institution of motherhood that Adrienne Rich did in *Of Woman Born*. Ruddick analyzes mothering as done by a living woman mother in a real present cultural milieu--an analysis of a practice *as seen by the practitioner*. This analysis is a part of the project of understanding mothering which must be well underway *before* we will be able to comprehend the personal and political meaning of a fairly general moving of men into mothering.

As Ruddick has said, the practice of mothering as it is now lived has been developed by a subordinated, and enslaved, caste; the practice is furthermore guided by conceptions of success or accomplishment which are in many ways inimical to the welfare of the practitioners and to the children. It is rather easy to suppose that a solution to the compulsory confinement of one group to this practice would be the introduction of others from other groups.   But those others who are suggested are members of a *dominant* group. The difference is enormous.   There is no reason to think they would carry out the practice similarly, or with the same orientation to the same conceptions of success and achievement. And it is not necessarily so easy to see what it will mean for women, for whom this has historically been *the* permitted and honored vocation, to have it not only integrated and universalized (so it is not *theirs* anymore) but also so greatly altered as a practice. I do not claim that males doing more and better parenting cannot be part of short-term survival strategy for some women and children, nor that we will necessarily always have and always want a division of childrearing involvement by gender. But the association of motherhood and womanhood has deep roots in our mythic structure, our political structure, and, for women, in our senses of ourselves. If the dissociation of these is a desideratum, it can only be so if it is not to be accomplished by the premature dissolution of "Woman."

Images of "mothers of both sexes," presented as progressive or utopian, are perplexing and problematic, and should not be embraced hastily.   The image of woman as mother works to bind women in opposition, but it also connects to women an image of strength, ingenuity, endurance, wisdom and grace.   Dissociation of womanhood and motherhood suggests liberation from compulsory motherhood, compulsory heterosexuality and compulsory monogamy for women; but it also suggests yet another rape and robbery and yet another betrayal of our women's past.

FOOTNOTE

(1) This seems to be a standard understanding of the conclusions of the anthropological work of Brigitte Jordan, but I do not claim here that this is in fact, or exactly, what Jordan argues.

PART III

CHILDREN'S RIGHTS

CHILDREN'S RIGHTS: INTRODUCTION

Albert C. Cafagna

Department of Philosophy
Michigan State University
East Lansing, MI 48824

My aim in this introduction is to provide a framework which will help to characterize and critically evaluate the contributions in Part III. The authors and commentators all seem to agree that there is an urgent need to improve our understanding and treatment of children. They also agree that this may require some alteration in the ways we conceptualize, talk, and think about children. However, they do not agree about how we should go about such reconceptualizing. In particular, they are divided over whether it would be helpful to talk and think about children as rights-holders on a par with adults. Some see the extension of equal rights to children as a natural development of the civil rights, women's rights and gay rights movements. They feel that to reserve certain rights for adults would uphold an unjustifiable double-standard. We might coin the term "ageism" to point to the implied analogy with racism and sexism. Others feel just as strongly that emphasis upon children as rights-holders could be harmful to children by casting them as adversaries of the very adults upon whom they must depend. Still other writers insist that the entire children's rights controversy is largely irrelevant since most children lack the interests or capacities which our cherished adult rights are designed to protect or further. Instead, the critical agenda calls for an articulation of the unmet needs of children, a strengthening of parental skills, and an enrichment of the special relationships between children and adults.

As might have been expected when philosophers entered the children's rights debate, they have brought an ever-increasing number of important distinctions into the arena. However, due partly to diversity in terminology, the debate has not yet fully benefitted from their conceptual insights. For example, what one writer refers to as "liberty rights," as distinguished from "claim rights," another refers to as "negative claim-rights," as distinguished from "positive claim-rights." Whereas one author distinguishes "active" from "passive" rights on the basis of the powers they confer upon their holders, another distinguishes "performance" from "non-interference" interpretations, based on the duties they impose on others. So a discussion of some central concepts should be helpful.

Anyone who enters the domain of "rights talk" does so with trepidation. The issues are complex and subtle; the literature prolific and confusing. I will try to say just enough to guide the reader through the essays which follow. Generally, when we say that someone has a right, we mean: (1) that some person (e.g., a lender) has a justifiable claim to something (repayment of a loan) against someone (the borrower); (2) that the claim is recognized by some legal or moral code. The party or parties against whom the right is held owes a duty to the right-holder. Every right involves a corresponding duty (though some duties, such as to contribute to charity or to cultivate our talents correspond to no rights). An employee has a duty to perform the services for which he was hired and to which his employer has a valid claim. Some rights do not entitle their holders to goods or services, but rather require the non-interference of others. For example, my rights to freedom of speech or movement impose upon others only the duty of tolerance. The term 'positive rights' (which some call 'claim rights' or 'entitlements') refers to the rights which empower us to claim the goods or services of others. 'Negative rights' (which some call 'liberty rights') refers to those which impose the duty of forebearance on others. Rights such as those of lenders and employers are recognized, and their correlative duties enforced, by law. Other rights, such as having our interests taken into account, or being free from needless harm, rest upon the moral code of the community.

Besides positive versus negative, and legal versus moral, it will prove useful to introduce some further distinctions. Joel Feinberg (1973, p. 59) refers to rights which are held against determinate individuals, such as a lender against his borrower, as 'in personam rights'; rights which are held against everyone in general, such as a homeowner's right to the peaceful private occupancy of his home, are called 'in rem rights.' Most often, in personam rights are positive and in rem rights are negative. My in personam right against my mechanic is a claim for positive action (the auto repairs I contracted for); whereas my in rem rights to the contents of my locked glove-compartment is a claim against everyone to refrain from taking them.

Another distinction introduced by Feinberg (1973, pp. 59-60) cuts across the in personam/in rem division within (but not, as we shall see, completely within) the class of negative rights: "Active rights are rights to act or not to act as one chooses; passive rights are rights not to be done to by others in certain ways." My rights to freedom of inquiry, association, and religion illustrate the former; my rights not to be harmed, cheated, or made to suffer needlessly illustrate the latter. Whereas the positive/negative distinction is based upon the kind of correlative duties, and the *in personam/in rem* upon the particularity of the parties against whom rights are held, the active/passive distinction rests upon the way the rights themselves are exercised.

Before turning to the essays and the application of our three sets of rights distinctions, two further preliminary matters should be addressed. With what are rights meaningfully compared and contrasted? With what is the adoption of a children's rights strategy meaningfully compared and contrasted? Rights can be compared with needs and values, on the one hand, as alternative grounds for duties and obligations, and with privileges, on the other, as the bases for powers or liberties. The former comparison relates to moral strategies, to be taken up next. At this point, our interest is rights versus privileges.

Though 'privilege' has had many, sometimes inconsistent uses, two are relevant to this discussion. The first is analyzed by Wesley Hohfeld (Benn, 1968, p. 196) along the following lines. Whereas, as we have seen, X's right to Y is correlated with Z's duty (to either provide Y or not interfere with X's relation to Y), X's *privilege* with regard to Y is merely correlated with Z's having no right to interfere with X's pursuit or enjoyment of Y. Examples might be X's privilege to run for public office or to apply for a job. Here, Z has no right to interfere with X's pursuit of Y. By the same token, X's privilege does not keep Z from competing for Y himself, or from otherwise interfering with X's pursuit of Y; he merely has no right to do so. The second sort of use is analyzed by Feinberg (1973, pp. 56-58; 1970, pp. 249-250): privileges (sometimes called 'liberties') are a variety of absences of duty; they license us, or they exempt us from customary restrictions. Examples of this are the privilege to drive a motor vehicle, to reveal confidential information (as a witness), to carry a master key, or to kill in self-defense. Privileges empower their holders, but, unlike rights, they impose no correlative duties. They are also discretionary and revocable. In *both* of these uses, an individual can have a privilege which is not also a right, but cannot have a right which is not also a privilege. If X has a right to do Y, then he cannot have a duty to refrain from Y; but if X has no duty to refrain from Y, then X has a privilege to do Y. What the right adds to the privilege is the duty of others to aid or to not interfere.

As a final preliminary matter, let us briefly compare (children's) rights as a moral strategy with paternalism and moral obligation. First of all, it is important to point out, though this point is often overlooked in the literature, that paternalism is not the only alternative to children's rights. Children's needs can come to be met, even reliably and predictably, through adult love, compassion, obedience to divine authority, intuition of self-evident principles, noblesse oblige, recognition of their intrinsic value, or commitment to general utility. Accordingly, a program for furthering child welfare can be based upon any of these sources of obligation. Let's say that any such proposal follows a need/obligation-strategy. By contrast, a rights-strategy seeks to ensure the decent

treatment of children, not as a means to good or cost-efficient consequences, but as the fulfillment of rightful claims. The rights-holder is a
dignified object of respect who stands on his authoritative demands. He
asks only his just deserts, not gifts or favors. Far from feeling gratitude
when his rights are met, the rights-holder feels indignation when they are
not. Since his rightful claims entail their duties, the rights-holder stands
in a theoretically adversarial relationship with others. Not only are the
correlative duties enforceable (morally or legally), but their fulfillment is
justifiable independently of the nature of their probable or actual
consequences.

Paternalism is a very confusing notion in this context. Typically,
when it is used pejoratively, paternalism refers to the treatment of adults
(college students, women, minorities, handicappers, gays, etc.) as if they
were mere children--unable to determine what is in their own best
interest, unable to postpone immediate gratification in the interest of
long-term benefits, irrational, etc. How can one treat *children* paternal-
istically? As a neutral term, paternalism refers to any interference with
a person's actions done in his own best or real interest. It would seem to
be in this latter sense that paternalism is an alternative to children's
rights. For, particularly negative rights (e.g., to choose one's own diet,
wardrobe, abode) impose duties of *non*-interference upon others. Even
positive rights (e.g., to medical care, food, shelter) call for others to
provide goods and services only upon the holder's demand. So for our
purposes, paternalism is any normative theory which calls for the withholding of any (negative or liberty) or all types of rights from children
with the aim of furthering their welfare. Since such strategies see
children's best interests served by adult, typically parental, control, they
seek to strengthen parental childrearing capacities or to deepen or enrich
parent-child relationships. In this respect, paternalism is compatible with
a wide variety of moral theories--teleological, deontological, hedonistic,
etc. It should not be overlooked, finally, that some thinkers might oppose
children's rights because they subscribe to a holistic or organic view of
social institutions such as the family, and reject the atomistic, egoistic
ontology that underlies all rights philosophy.

Other rights distinctions abound, such as those based on the classes
who hold them (e.g., child-rights, adult-rights, adult-child rights, family
rights), contingent versus non-contingent rights, those based on the kind
of interest protected, those based upon the grounding principle (e.g.,
justice, benevolence, equality), etc., which are relevant to the area
covered in Part III, but not directly to the essays. However, the foregoing
(incomplete) discussion should be sufficient to help the reader compare
the essays and commentaries and evaluate their conflicting claims.
Sometimes a dispute can be resolved by a terminological clarification.
For example, an advocate of children's rights may be thinking of an *in rem*
right against society in general, whereas a rights opponent, fearing an
adversarial parent-child relationship, is thinking of the right as *in*
personam against parents. Other disagreements might be expected to

dissolve if their rights descriptions were more complete, including answers to such questions as: against whom is it held, how is it exercised, and/or what duties does it impose? Let us turn now to a consideration of our essays.

While the children's rights controversy has not yet arrived at a central question or issue, or a fixed set of positions, our contributors focus on three representative topics: (1) Whether we should ascribe equal rights, particularly "liberty rights," to children; (2) Whether, or how, parent's and children's rights actually or potentially conflict with one another; and (3) What are the outstanding unmet needs or unrecognized rights of children? Let us treat these issues as our authors and others in the field address them, and summarize their positions.

1. *Equal Rights for Children*

What is our fundamental obligation to children? Advocates of equal rights for children suspect that the traditional answer--*to protect them*, from nature, from others, from themselves--may well reflect an under-lying cause of the current crisis in childrearing. That is, they believe that our very conception of children and of the nature of our relationship to them may serve to harm rather than protect children. Thus John Holt says, "...I have come to feel that the fact of being a 'child,' of being wholly subservient and dependent, of being seen by older people as a mixture of expensive nuisance, slave, and superpet, does most young people more harm than good" (1974, p. 84). Convinced that this "paternal-istic" attitude is demeaning and self-perpetuating, even unjust, Holt continues, "I propose instead that the rights, privileges, duties, responsi-bilities of adult citizens be made *available* to any young person, of whatever age, who wants to make use of them" (1974, pp. 84-85).

In "Ending the double standard: Equal rights for children," Howard Cohen notes that the understanding of our principal obligation to children has shifted from protecting them to protecting their rights. He shares the conviction of other equal rights advocates that children should be accorded any and all rights available to adults (including "liberty rights"), subject only to the restrictions imposed upon adults. Though he is convinced that such fundamental changes in adult-child relationships would be beneficial to family life and society in general, he does not, as others have, argue for them on utilitarian grounds. He argues instead that advocates of the double standard have failed to justify unequal treatment as they have not shown that children and adults are relevantly dissimilar, thus violating the formal principle of social justice.

Calling the current appeal for children's rights--thinking of children as miniature adults--a kind of conceptual child abuse, William Ruddick, in "Children's rights and parents' virtues," sharply objects to the extension of adult liberty-rights to children. He contends that those who believe that the children's rights movement is a natural development from the black, women, gay and handicapper rights movements are making a fundamental mistake. Children are not mistreated when they are treated as immature. Though paternalism (restriction of one's freedom on his own behalf) is demeaning to adults, it is not necessarily demeaning to children. Given the unavoidable special vulnerability of children, we could either disallow the extension of liberty rights to children altogether (Ruddick's option), or modify them so that they are appropriately strengthened or weakened when they apply to children. In either case, it would be clear that we were not ascribing equal rights to children. Ruddick's reasoning is easily understood given his conception of a 'liberty right': the very point of a liberty right is to secure the freedom to control one's actions, free from the interference of others. Obviously J. S. Mill is thinking along the same line when he says: "The only freedom which deserves the name, is that of pursuing our own goal in our own way..." (1947, p. 12). Or again: "All that makes existence valuable to any one, depends on the enforcement of restraints upon the actions of other people" (1947, p. 5). It would, of course, be pointless to have such liberty if, in the absence of interference, one were not capable of independently pursuing one's own goal in one's own way. Thus Ruddick completely agrees with Mill's explanation: "It is perhaps, hardly necessary to say that...we are not speaking of children, or of young persons...who are still in a state to require being taken care of by others (and) must be protected against their own actions as well as against external injury" (1947, p. 10).

Ruddick's objective in dispensing with the current preoccupation with liberty rights is to emphasize that children do have two unique claim rights (child-rights): to become adults and to have an adequate parent. The fulfillment of these rights and the proper object of child-rearing reform call for a program to cultivate and strengthen the parental virtues of attentiveness, patience, self-love, forethought, and flexibility.

How would Howard Cohen reply to challenges, such as Ruddick's, to his proposal that children be accorded equal rights (including liberty rights)? Cohen insists that such challenges must do more than undermine the equal rights proposal--they must justify the double standard proposal. This they fail to do. Cohen adopts Joel Feinberg's formulation of the necessary condition of the formal principle for social justice: "Treat people equally unless and until there is a justification for treating them unequally." As this formula makes plain, the burden of proof rests with those who oppose equal rights. Cohen notes that people have attempted to justify withholding certain rights on the grounds that children lack certain capacities (e.g., to be appealed to by reason, to pursue self-interest, to accept social responsibility, etc.) which adults have and which are alleged to be necessary to exercise the rights in question.

Though he is convinced that a "slippery slope" argument defeats any attempt to draw a non-arbitrary line between the capacities of all adults and all children, Cohen concedes that there are expressible differences in capacity between some adults (say, over eighteen) and some children (say, four and under). But this does not yet win the case for the double standard. Even granting that some liberty rights (e.g., to hold or to buy and sell property) require the use of certain capacities (such as to manage financial accounts) to be exercised meaningfully, and further, that many children (say, six and under) lack these capacities, it does not follow that the right must be withheld from all who lack the requisite capacity. Cohen insists that a person without the relevant capacities may still have certain rights as long as someone who has the capacities can be obligated (via the interpretation of rights as claims on the performance of others) to help the person with the right. Rights interpreted in terms of the principle of performance allow children to *borrow* the capacities of others to secure whatever they are entitled to. Cohen points out that children are not alone in their need to borrow the capacities of others in order to enjoy their rights. Adults regularly borrow the capacities of attorneys and doctors when they exercise their rights to due process or health care.

Cohen's proposal calls for the establishment of a practice of child-agency (or proxies). He is aware, however, that many practical and theoretical problems await such a practice. For example, how could we prevent the role of an agent from degenerating into that of a paternalistic protector? But, at a time when our child-rearing practice is already in such deep trouble, and social justice is at issue, Cohen asks: How can we continue to deny children their equal rights?

The following queries might be kept in mind while reading the Cohen and Ruddick essays and their commentaries: How might Ruddick reply to Wade Robison's charge that he has only offered premises for claiming that children have no *privileges*, but concludes that children have no (liberty or negative) rights? Ruddick might take his cue from Feinberg and follow the analysis presented in the discussion of rights concepts at the beginning of this introduction. He could reply that since privileges are necessary components of rights, and if he has shown that there is no privilege to Y, he has *a fortiori* shown that there is no right to Y.

What are we to make of Robison's criticism that Ruddick has confused being able to independently *exercise* a right with *having* the right itself? It is interesting that although they come to opposite conclusions about whether children have equal rights, Cohen and Ruddick agree that unless we can furnish some way for children to exercise them, we cannot ascribe rights to them. This is the whole point of Cohen's essay--that children can exercise negative rights if they can borrow the capacities of their agents. Cohen and Ruddick seem to be on firm ground here. Rights are always held against someone; where the right is negative, say, the right to choose one's own diet, the correlative duty of the parents is to not interfere. But unless the parent's "interfere" by providing the variety of food from which to choose, the child can hardly be said to have the right to select his own diet, except in a trivial Pickwickian sense. Yet, surely Robison is right--children do have the negative right not to be harmed. We seem to have arrived at an impasse. However, here is a case where a fuller description of a putative right can resolve a dispute. Ruddick's examples (leaving home, working) are *active* negative rights (i.e., rights to act free from interference); whereas Robison's right not to be harmed is a *passive* negative right (i.e., a right not to be done to in a certain way). Both are correct; they are simply talking about different kinds of rights. Passive negative rights seem to apply to children and adults alike; whereas active negative rights apply only to those with the capacity to exercise them independently of the parties against whom they are held *in personam*. It is also interesting that adult active *negative* rights *in rem* (e.g., life, liberty and the pursuit of happiness) are applicable to children only as passive *positive* rights *in personam* (e.g., the rights to food, clothing, shelter, childcare, etc.).

It should be clear that though Ruddick has some reservations about it, Cohen and Ruddick are using 'liberty rights' interchangeably with the more standard use, 'negative rights,' discussed earlier. Ruddick's child-rights (to become adults, and to have an adequate parent) would seem to be a complex of two rights; as held against one's parents, they are *in personam* passive positive rights, claims that parents cultivate the parental virtues which will improve their nurturing skills. As against society in general, they are both *in rem* passive negative and positive rights. Other adults, and even the state, are charged with the duty of taking actions or adopting policies which will maximize complete maturation and minimize threats to the survival of children.

Cohen may be hard put to effectively reply to Allen Verhey's excellent comment. Verhey's sensitive treatment of negative and positive rights as qualified by varying justifying moral principles is especially worthy of attention. However, his most telling point pertains to the "Catch-22" in Cohen's borrowed capacity solution to the exercise of negative rights. The child needs to borrow the agent's capacities because he lacks the capacity to enter into contractual relationships. Yet unless the agent stands in a contractual relationship to the child, he will be a paternalistic protector. But if the child has the capacity to enter a contractual relationship with his agent, then he doesn't need the agent.

2. *Do Parent's and Children's Rights Conflict?*

In "Children's needs and parental liberty: a liberal contradiction and how to escape from it," Susan Perkins goes to the heart of a striking phenomenon receiving widespread attention today, namely, an increasing number of young married couples choosing to remain childless in order to avoid restriction of their freedom. In the past it was not unusual for couples to postpone 'having a family,' or to never have children at all, under the guise of 'postponement.' But only recently have adults openly avowed their permanent rejection of parenthood. Since this has occurred contemporaneously with women's liberation, it has naturally been viewed as a spin-off from that movement. But Perkins maintains that this phenomenon has deeper and less contingent roots. The source of this perception that children's needs are irreconcilable with parental liberty is traditional liberalism--specifically, the liberal conception of humans as atomistic beings whose subjective primary goals are in conflict with the goals of others. Wedded to this atomistic conception is the assumption that the primary goal is liberty or freedom from constraint. Thus, though they pursue incompatible ends, individuals must tolerate one another to achieve peaceful coexistence. Liberalism, then, recommends a trade-off of interests in order to maximize individual liberty. Here the problem arises, for, unlike that which occurs between adults, the conflict between adult and child provides no non-contingent reciprocally beneficial trade-off. For, while the child essentially makes prodigious demands on adults, parents only *contingently* desire a child's love, feel contractually obliged to provide child care, acknowledge child care as a divine duty, or are committed to maximize general utility. Wherever any of these well-springs of nurturing is in a weakened state, as they all seem to be today, we are faced with a forced option between parental freedom and child care as a "zero sum game." This impasse is especially ironic from the liberal perspective because individual freedom is sacrificed by either option. A child may gain a chance to enjoy freedom only in cases where parents decide to limit their own.

According to Perkins, the way out of this dilemma is to excise the atomistic conception from traditional liberalism and/or to elevate equality from a means to an end, on a par with liberty. According to this conception, we abandon the understanding of humans as isolated entities pursuing ends separate from all others, including our children. Instead, we are invited to see families as organic unities whose members give, as well as receive, nurturing. It must be recognized that parents' liberty, properly understood, cannot be inversely proportional to that of their children. On this view, one's freedom is enhanced by the equality of its distribution. According to Perkins, then, the conflict between parents' and children's rights rests upon a deeply entrenched but eradicable misunderstanding of human nature.

The reader is invited to consider whether commentator William Dibrell is right in claiming that Perkins has confused the issue--whether, on the liberal view, parents have good reason (i.e., justification) to nurture children--with the issue of whether parents, on the liberal view, are sufficiently motivated (i.e., are apt to be caused) to nurture children. For clearly, if this charge is correct, Perkins can only claim to have shown that the liberal conception is incapable of *motivating* parenthood. But while all philosophers agree that giving reasons is, most insist that furnishing incentives is not, the business of philosophy. Perhaps even more potentially damaging is Dibrell's suggestion that rather than resolve the liberal's dilemma (parental liberty vs. children's needs), Perkins has merely paraphrased it. Would Perkins have an effective reply to these criticisms?

A right to liberty to which Perkins refers can be analyzed as a complex of several rights. As an adult active right it would be negative *in rem*--a claim that all others refrain from confining me or erecting barriers to my possible actions. For children it is describable as an *in personam* passive positive as well as negative right. As positive, it is a claim upon parents that they encourage the development of the child's capacity to be able to exercise active liberty rights. As negative, it is a claim that a child's parents not treat the child in a manner apt to delay or preclude the development of the child's capacity to be able to exercise active liberty rights.

In "Rights of children, rights of parents, and the moral basis of the family," Ferdinand Schoeman has a twofold aim: first, to provide a moral basis for thinking that biological parents have a presumptive right to keep their children under their care in the setting of privacy, autonomy, and responsibility which is usually accorded the family; second, to make clear that such a defense of family autonomy need not, and indeed had best not, rest upon the cost/benefit-to-children approach found in much of the literature.

In adopting the parents' perspective, Schoeman allows for potential conflict between parents' and children's rights, for he argues that a biological parent has such a presumptive right "even when recognition of this right involves some comparative cost to the child." What could justify parents' rights to their children even when children could benefit more by living outside their biological parents' domain? Schoeman dismisses such accounts as: children are property of their parents; parents have met the minimal standards of child care and prefer to have their children; and nuclear families perform certain vital functions. Instead, Schoeman argues that the parents' right to raise their children "stems naturally from the right to engage in intimate relationships (i.e., relationships which involve sharing ourselves with others and which are crucial to the self-image and meaningful existence of most people)."

Since intimate relationships are mutually beneficial and children share their parents' needs for and rights to such relationships, it would seem that, on this account, parents' and children's rights could not really conflict after all. To uncover the source of the potential conflict and to gain a fuller understanding of Schoeman's view, we must grasp the connection between intimacy and family autonomy. Though intimate relationships obtain outside the family, our culture has conventionally vested the biological relationships within the family as the primary locus of intimacy. Since outside interference is inimical to the cultivation and preservation of intimacy, family autonomy is essential. But parents have a greater stake in family autonomy than children. First of all, children do not consent to become members of the family. Secondly, children depend upon the state to guarantee their rights to minimal child care. Schoeman finally contends that in cases of a conflict of interest between the rights of parent and child, the state should favor the parent, because parents "can be seen as representing the interests of the family as an integrated whole in addition to representing their own particular interests." The state must, however, observe the strictest circumspection before breeching family autonomy, for "important ends are served by relegating to parents the right to decide important issues for the family even when what is at issue is a conflict in interests between the parent as individual and the child as individual." So, at least within the family, conflict between the rights of parent and child must be seen as a continuous possibility.

In reading the Schoeman essay, the following questions or concerns might be kept in mind: commentator Joyce Pillote calls attention to the fact (acknowledged by Schoeman) that many thinkers are currently debating the very value of the family as an institution and whether it should be preserved. In defining the family as an "intimate organization" or as an institution "involving an intimate relationship" between at least one adult and child, hasn't Schoeman begged the question as to whether the family is the most appropriate setting in which to cultivate intimate relationships? Enormous differences in spiritual and material resources exist in different families. By "making children depend on the spiritual and material resources of the family they happen to be born into," isn't Schoeman helping to perpetuate such socio-economic inequalities? As Pillote asks, if this is a consequence, shouldn't we "examine more seriously alternatives to the family?" As these problems suggest, a link in Schoeman's argument which needs strengthening is the connection between the right to intimacy and the right to intimacy within the family.

A final observation about Schoeman's right to intimacy: it is analyzable as a complex of two rights. As directed against and between specifiable members of a family, it is an *in personam* active positive right. That is, it is a right to make claims on other family members to open themselves to us as we share ourselves with them. As directed against the extra-familial world, it is an *in rem* passive negative right that others abstain from breeching our family's privacy and security.

3. Some Unrecognized Rights or Needs of Children

Some writers have been concerned with children's rights not in order to discuss whether they are identical or in conflict with the rights of adults. Rather, some have sought to bring to light certain rights which, though very important to child welfare, have not received the attention they warrant. A case in point is Joseph Evans who contends, in "The identity of the child and the right to integration," that our misconceived ideal for the socialization and identity development of children has caused us to overlook one of our most basic rights, the "right to integration." Evans claims that not only is he promulgating a little known basic right, but he has uncovered both the cause of and the cure for the "destructive state of mind" in children today: "Children have become too undisciplined, too resistant to authority, too interested in their own personal preferences, too disinterested in the world around them, too selective in their personal interests, and, in the last analysis, too indifferent to their own overall human welfare. The reason for this is that their own basic right to integrate themselves is consistently and systematically ignored."

Evans reconstructs our current crisis as the convergence of two developments. The first, a causal sequence blending recent social scientific concepts from several disciplines, runs as follows: the child who grows up in a pluralistic non-authoritarian society internalizes (i.e., takes into his memory and imagination) divergent cultural ideals (e.g., equality, independence and rationality from the schools; dependence, uniqueness and inequality in the home; competiveness, dominance and stoicism from peer groups, etc.) from which he constitutes himself divisively (i.e., adopts divergent and apparently incompatible bases for his priorities, commitments, projects and intentions). Evans theorizes that "the young person becomes several different persons instead of a single, unified person, and he becomes divided against himself...and proceeds to act in dubious and destructive ways. He has a fundamental right to overcome this division and to integrate himself." That is, the child has the right to be assisted in developing the capacity to frankly confront the unpleasant fact of the division of his personality and to constructively unite the opposing self-images. The second sequence is a dialectical process by which one conception of the identity or the ideal-type for childhood (which reflects a stage in societal development) persists, even though it has become obsolete, until it is displaced by a more appropriate ideal-type. The prevailing ideal-type, which displaced the older conception of the child as "someone to be disciplined, ordered about, and made into a physical laborer at a fairly early age," seeks to shield the child from all negative experience. By amassing exclusively positive experience (according to the prevailing concept), the ideal person who emerges is as complete a human being as possible--"competent to function in a variety of settings and be comfortable in each...able...to exercise all of the talents and abilities he possesses. He will find the whole world open to him and suffer no fears or inhibitions...in his personal and public life." Unfortunately, this ideal-type which was well-adapted to the slower-paced simpler social life of an earlier time has become obsolete.

Not only is this ideal-type ill-adapted to the diversity and complexity of current social and family life, but its artificial emphasis on positive experience and memory almost precludes the inculcation of integrative processes and skills. For, according to Evans, "in play, through stories, in conversation, in classroom themes and exercises a child can be encouraged to identify his own multiple self-images, how they compete or threaten to compete with each other..." This learning process inevitably involves uncomfortable memories and unpleasant and ambivalent feelings. But if integration is to become a realistic possibility for all children, we must abandon the notion that children can develop into whole persons only through positive experience, and evolve a conception of childhood compatible with the realities of current social life.

Evans' right to integration is a complex of two rights. Insofar as it is a right against a child's parents, teachers, or other personally identifiable individuals, it is an *in personam* active positive right. That is, it is a claim that a child's responsible elders take certain positive steps to help him develop his integrative skills. As it is directed against all others, it is an *in rem* passive negative right that others refrain from treating him in a way which produces divisive self-images and self-destructive narcissistic behavior.

Though it deals in an interesting way with important issues, the reader may find it hard to evaluate Evans' essay. What kind of thesis is it? Commentator Lawrence Schiamberg objects that no empirical evidence is presented for what appear to be controversial factual claims. If it is an empirical hypothesis, do concepts such as 'identity' and 'integration' lend themselves to operational definition? How many independent cases exist which could be tested to verify whether it is true that cultural diversity together with the sheltering of children from negative experience cause the self-destructive narcissism of a "me generation?" Is Evans claiming that a more realistic, less artificially positive childrearing practice would be sufficient or merely necessary for the effective development of integrative techniques? It is not very helpful when Evans says he is proposing a 'philosophical principle,' but offers no proper arguments for it. Perhaps Evans is making the normative recommendation that we ought to recognize a right to integration for children who are exposed to very divergent cultural stimuli. But the only case he seems to make is a utilitarian one that depends upon probable factual consequences. So we are forced to return to the question of how to evaluate Evans' thesis.

Though David Black is primarily concerned with a "phenomenological" treatment of such questions as, 'What does it mean to play?' and 'How is it possible to recognize an act of play?', his article, "The rhetoric of toys," contains an implicit claim that a child has a right to have his toys taken seriously and selected with sensitivity and care. For, as Black argues, toys are "a part of the very essence of play." Toys have a 'normative value' or 'rhetorical form'--they open a perceptual world to the child. The concrete sensuous character of a toy partly determines the games that can be played with it. As the child touches the toy, the toy touches the child, and as toys shape play they "provide means for the child to explore his powers of imagination by serving as a link to the external world." So, as an intrinsic part of play, toys exert a vital influence on the perceptual, imaginative, and creative potential of the child.

Yet, there is a danger that in our efficiency-conscious world, we may ignore or underestimate the importance of play and misunderstand the role of toys. A case in point is the so-called educational toy. To our cost/benefit mentalities, these seem to be double-bargains. But, according to Black, while an educational toy undoubtedly has a normative value, "it is not properly a toy. An educational toy is didactic; a toy is fun-loving...An educational toy...puts play to work...is no longer self-justifying; it...has a job to do." To take another example, the Barbie doll is an impersonal, lifeless replica: "She is the paragon of dollhood. Barbie is not a toy; she is a concept."

What, then, are the criteria for a toy? Black suggests a fourfold perceptual or rhetorical schema: a toy ought to display mutability, uselessness, rhythm, and a sense of hyperbole. Kaleidoscopes, tinker-toys, spinning tops, swing sets, circus wagons and clowns are mentioned as examples of toys. We may deduce, then, that Black is calling our attention to an unrecognized right of children. It would be an *in personam* passive positive right, i.e., a claim on the parent or responsible adult that when toys are bought, care be taken to select toys which will encourage and enrich (not stultify or stereotype) the child's play, imagination, and perceptual growth.

The reader may wish to consider commentator Alice Whiren's worthy challenge: How would Black classify pantomime? Though it is purposive, especially in its theatrical uses, it is a common form of play even in terms of Black's description, yet involves no toys (or artifacts). When Black says that toys are "part and parcel" or "part of the very essence of play," does he mean that toys are necessary for play? Some jumping and running games involve no toys. On the other hand, much of Marcel Marceau's genius lies in his uncanny reproduction of every kinesthetic nuance of turning doorknobs, climbing stairs, leaning on furniture, etc. So we might suggest that even pantomime is parasitic on artifacts. Whiren raises another interesting point in her distinction between playthings, as natural objects, and toys, as artifacts. How would Black treat playthings? It would seem odd to impute a rhetorical function to natural objects, yet some stones, fruits and sticks, for example, have many of the same attributes as some toys. We also wonder how culture-specific the rhetoric of toys is. While it is a virtue for an essay to provoke further thought, these questions contain a hint of peril to Black's thesis. For if, in answering them, he must unload more and more of the meaning of a toy from the artifact to the player and the cultural context, there remains less and less to the rhetoric of the toy. But, then, according to the widely held anthropological principle--that the meaning of all artifacts is independent of their form--(White, 1949, pp. 22-39) that is just what we should expect.

Now that we have roughly charted the landscape of rights-discourse, summarized our contributor's essays and their respective commentaries, and suggested guidelines for evaluation, it's time to see whether we have (as we set out to do) helped the reader, by allowing him to get on with the reading that lies ahead.

REFERENCES

Benn, S. I. Rights. In P. Edwards (Ed.), *The encyclopedia of philosophy*, 1978, 7, 195-199.

Feinberg, J. The nature and value of rights. *Journal of Value Inquiry*, 1970, 4, 245-257.

Feinberg, J. *Social philosophy*. Englewood Cliffs, NJ: Prentice-Hall, 1973.

Holt, J. Liberate children. In W. Aiken and H. LaFollette (Eds.), *Whose child? Children's rights, parental authority, and state power.* Totowa, NJ: Littlefield, Adams and Company, 1980.

Mill, J. S. *On liberty.* New York: Appleton Century Crofts, 1947.

White, L. A. *The science of culture.* New York: Farrar, Straus and Company, 1949.

ENDING THE DOUBLE STANDARD: EQUAL RIGHTS FOR CHILDREN

Howard Cohen

Philosophy Department
University of Massachusetts
Boston, MA 02125

The family, its internal relations and its place in society, is presently an object of great interest to American academia. Philosophers, too, for perhaps the first time, have taken it as a subject in its own right--rather than an incidental example within some more general investigation. This new and vigorous interest is not entirely a happy one, for the dominant theme of recent family studies is that the family is in trouble--perhaps in crisis. Even the most optimistic scholars are unwilling to say that everything is fine.

Much of the trouble with the family, of course, is trouble for children. Scholars disagree as to whether child abuse and child neglect are on the increase or on the decline, but nearly all agree that there is much too much of it. Most also think that the data under-represents the problem. If we add to the dramatic evidence of abuse and neglect the more mundane problems (youth disaffection in the schools, the frustration with high youth unemployment, and the use of the courts to deal with what are essentially family relations issues--truancy, incorrigibility, custody), it is fairly easy to understand that children bear a substantial burden in the struggle to carry out a sane and sensible family life in America.

Historically, Americans have not been insensitive to the problems of children in families. Child-saving and child-protection have been our standard ideological posture toward children since the middle of the nineteenth century. The development of a highly protective *parens patriae* doctrine in *ex parte Crouse* (1834) gave the courts control over parental treatment of children. Thereafter, private efforts, such as the establishment of the many Societies for the Prevention of Cruelty to Children, and public efforts, such as the creation of juvenile courts and

149

the U.S. Children's Bureau, signaled society's expectation that parents be their children's care-takers or others would take on this role should the parents prove unwilling or unable.

All of this care and protection, however, cannot change the facts of family trouble or family crisis. The problems with our relations to children seem to be a normal part of family life rather than occasional deviances or freak occurrences. If this is so, then it is likely that the problems are structural--that is, are consequences of the internal structure of family relations or the structure of relations between the family and other social institutions. The belief that these problems are structural and that the solution to them does not lie in identifying the deviant cases and protecting the children in those abnormal situations, has led a number of recent writers on this topic toward an alternative to child protection. As Richard Farson (1974, p. 9) puts it in *Birthrights*: "On the one hand there are those who are interested in protecting children, and on the other those who are interested in protecting children's rights."

Protecting children's rights is, at present, more of a slogan than an activity, for children in our society do not really have the rights which Farson has in mind. Farson is not talking about those claims to special protection which are sometimes called rights, but about the liberties which most adults in our society enjoy. With Farson, I want to argue for equal rights for children. Children, in my view, should be entitled to all of the rights adults are entitled to in law and in custom (subject only to the same kinds of restrictions and limits imposed on adults). In short, it is time to end the double standard of rights for children and adults.

Farson and others have argued for children's rights on the grounds that children would be better off were they granted these rights. Children do not grow best under the domination of paternalist adults. Advocates of children's rights often add that society would be better off in the long run if children were treated more like adults with the dignity that comes with being a right-holder. I believe that the assessment that this structural change in adult-child relationships (equal rights for children) would be of benefit to family life is essentially correct, but I cannot prove it. Rather, I intend to make the case on less speculative and more immediately compelling grounds: the grounds of social justice.

The denial of equal rights for children has created an unjustifiable and, hence, unjust double standard. Now, of course, not all double standards are unjust. Social justice requires that we treat similar cases similarly and different cases differently. This is what is usually termed the formal principle of justice; it is a necessary (but not a sufficient) condition of just treatment. A somewhat stronger necessary condition which will make the issue even more perspicuous has been articulated by Joel Feinberg (1973, p.99): "Treat people equally unless and until there is a justification for treating them unequally." If there is such a justification, or if children and adults are relevantly dissimilar, then the double

standard is benign. The burden of proof, however, as Feinberg's formulation makes clear, is squarely with those who would maintain the double
standard. In the absence of established reasons to treat adults and
children differently, the denial of equal rights for children is unjust. This
is as it should be, for the use of double standards in the service of
oppression has been common practice--as the struggles by Blacks and
women for political rights indicate.

The fact that the burden of proof falls this way is no small matter.
Adult intuitions that children would be better off with paternal protection
or claims that all of the evidence about the potential of children to handle
equal rights is not in yet are too weak to justify a double standard.
Opponents of children's rights must be able to point to differences
between adults and children (as groups) which are both demonstrable and
relevant. Anything less is a grave injustice.

The difference which most advocates of the double standard cite to
justify denial of many adult rights to children is a difference in capacities. Adults are said to have certain capacities which children lack.
Which capacities? The answer is usually given in general, and the
relevant capacity is expressed variously: the capacity to make reasoned
choices, the capacity to be persuaded by reason, the capacity to pursue
one's own self-interest, the capacity to accept social responsibility, the
capacity to see and understand the consequences of one's action, and so
on. On occasion, the capacity in question is more specific and tied to a
specific right. One writer argues that the right to vote requires the
"capacity to recognize which candidate will pursue policies in your
interest" (Schrag, 1975, p. 449). Whether general or specific, though,
these capacities must differentiate children from adults, and they must be
relevant to having the rights in question.

Establishing differences between adults as a group and children as a
group is notoriously difficult. The problem is that acquiring a capacity,
particularly any of the capacities mentioned above, is a developmental
process--it does not happen all at once and there is no single moment at
which one can say: "Now she has it." Furthermore, individuals develop
their capacities at different rates of speed and at different times in their
maturation process. No sharp line drawn on the basis of a capacity will
sort all adults on one side and all children on the other. A sharp line is
necessary because our rights are not developmental: we either have them
or we do not. Consequently, any attempt to demonstrate a difference
between adults as a group and children as a group is subject to a slippery
slope argument. A slippery slope argument tries to show that presumed
differences in cases cannot be defended by showing the similarities that
exist through a range of intermediate steps. If a person with a single hair
is bald, and if there is no significant difference between having one hair
or two, than a person with two hairs is bald. If a person with two hairs is
bald.... This may go on as long as you please. No capacity which is
relevant to the granting of liberty rights will be able to distinguish the
eighteen year old from the seventeen year and eleven month old.

The slippery slope argument exposes the arbitrariness of drawing lines between adults and chldren, but it can be pushed too far. There may be no expressible differences between an eighteen year old and a seventeen year and eleven month old, or between a seventeen year eleven month old and a seventeen year ten month old. However, there are expressible differences in capacity between eighteen year olds and four year olds. We may make our cuts too fine, but only a fool would argue differences in capacity could not be demonstrated at some level. This does not eliminate the arbitrariness and injustice (to some) of drawing precise lines for right-holders, but it does ease the criticism somewhat. Line-drawing becomes a practical political problem rather than a refusal to recognize an injustice at the level of theory.

Nevertheless, to grant that this critique of attempts to demonstrate differences in capacity between adults and children is not conclusive is not to accept the double standard. The differences in capacities, such as they are, must also be shown to be relevant. That is, the fact that an individual lacks a particular capacity must be a sufficient reason to withhold a particular right from an individual. The assumption that *if* children lacked certain capacities, they could justifiably be denied certain rights is usually left unexamined. But when we look at it closely, we shall see that it is a false assumption.

Let us assume that some liberty rights, anyhow, require the use of certain capacities if they are to be exercised in a meaningful way. Does that mean that the person who has the right must also have the relevant capacities? At first glance, it may seem obvious that the person must have these capacities; yet I would argue it is far from obvious. What makes it seem so unproblematic is that we typically think of rights in terms of non-interference: If a person has a right to something, then everyone else has an obligation not to interfere with that person's having or doing that thing. A person is pretty much left alone with rights understood in this way. Lacking the capacities, the person lacks what is needed to exercise the right. But rights need not be understood in this way. Often rights are better expressed in terms of a principle of performance: If a person has a right to something, then someone has an obligation to help that person have or do that thing. When we think of rights in this way, we can see that a person without the relevant capacities may still have certain rights as long as someone who has the capacities can be obligated to help the person with the right. In other words, the principle of performance allows us to *borrow* the capacities of others in order to secure whatever it is we are entitled to.

I want to explain the idea of borrowed capacities more fully, but it is important, first, to notice its significance. We began considering the possibility that the double standard of rights for children and adults was unjust. Those who would say that it is not, must show a relevant difference between children and adults, relevant to granting rights to one group which are denied to the other. The difference most commonly cited is the difference in capacities. Although this difference does not correspond very precisely to the difference between children and adults, we conceded that the imprecision was not a decisive criticism. However, we noticed that defenders of the double standard also assume that a person must be able to initiate the exercise of the right on her or his own in order to have it. But this does not seem to be so. What is true is that a person who is incapable of initiating certain kinds of actions misses out on the joys of doing those things for herself. While there is undeniably joy in self-reliance, it does not provide life's only satisfactions; and a person who misses out on it should not also have to forfeit her rights, for she can still have those rights as long as she is in a position of demanding performance from others who do have the relevant capacities. So if children can borrow the capacities of those who have them, then the fact that some children do not have full capacities is not a relevant reason to impose a double standard of rights.

Borrowing the capacities of others is not at all unusual; we all do it at one time or another. None of us is so multi-talented that we can shape our lives without relying on the abilities and skills of others. I would not defend myself in court or remove a growth from my leg. And it is not just that I do not have the time or the interest in doing so; I could not do either job because I am incapable. I do not have the training of a lawyer or a doctor; I do not have their experience or their skills. I have these capacities as potentials, I suppose, but it would take time and effort to develop them. In this respect, my position is quite analogous to the child's. And I certainly do not forfeit my rights to a lawyer or to medical attention because of my incapacity to attend to these things myself.

For some of our rights, the relative incapacities of children and adults are basically a matter of degree. Adults have the right to information about themselves which they may be incapable of under-standing. Medical or psychiatric reports are most likely to fit into this category, but some financial information could be of this sort as well. When we cannot understand this information, we have the right to seek out someone--a doctor, a psychologist, an accountant, a knowledgeable friend--who can interpret it for us. Children have a similar problem--or they would if they had the right to access to information about them-selves. They may well be incapable of understanding medical reports that find their way into a child's school file. But if this difference is one of degree, then the lack of capacity should not be used as an excuse to deny them the right to information, for children, too, could find someone who had the capacity to understand these things and make them accessible.

To be sure, with some other rights children would need to borrow capacities which most adults actually have. The rights related to running one's own financial affairs are rights which most adults are capable of exercising on their own. What I have in mind here are the rights to hold property, enter contracts, have an independent source of income (the right to work or receive welfare payments), receive credit, and have a bank account. In light of the economic organization of our society, this constellation of rights is necessary in order to maintain an independent financial existence. Such an existence is well within reach of most adults. The fact that they manage--for better or for worse--shows that they have the relevant capacities.

Many children are pretty clearly incapable of doing some of these things. A five year old could not manage a checkbook alone; a seven year old could probably not keep a budget or buy or sell a car without assistance. But this does not mean that these children could not make financial decisions. It means that they could not make them and carry them out on their own. There is no reason to think that they could not make these decisions with the help of a financial advisor. Such an advisor would have to be sufficiently adept at running the economic life of another and at doing so in such a way as to leave the major decisions in the client's hands. As a matter of fact, people of great wealth rely on such advisors all the time, and they do not forego their economic rights. There is no reason why children with financial advisors should have to forego theirs, either.

The point here is that by relying on the capacities of agents children could exercise their rights without doing harm to themselves or to others, without interfering with the obligations their parents or guardians might have to society at large, and without doing much damage to the system of rights and liberties. The role of the child's agent would be to supply information in terms which the child could understand, to make the consequences of the various courses of action a child might take clear to the child, and to do what is necessary to see that the right in question is actually exercised. A sensitive agent would try to do these things in such a way that the child could build on the experience and eventually act on her or his own. Any rights currently enjoyed by adults which children could exercise with the aid of agents are rights which children should have.

The usual arguments for denying rights to children lose most of their force when we entertain the possibility of agents loaning their capacities to children through rights expressing a principle of performance. We can see how these arguments are played out, for example, in Mill's emphatic denial of rights (and with them, civil liberties) for children. In "On Liberty" (Mill, 1962, pp. 135-136), after insisting on the absolute right of the individual to freedom in those areas which concern no one but herself or himself, Mill goes on to remark:

> It is, perhaps, hardly necessary to say that this doctrine is meant to apply only to human beings in the maturity of their faculties. We are not speaking of children, or of young persons below the age which the law may fix as that of manhood or womanhood. Those who are still in a state to be protected against their own actions as well as against external injury.

By way of clarification, Mill (1962, pp. 135-136) says that once people have the relevant capacities to use their liberty ("the capacity of being guided to their own improvement by conviction or persuasion"), "compulsion...is no longer admissible as a means to their own good, and justifiable only for the security of others." When people attain the level at which they can responsibly exercise their liberties, then they ought to have them. But for Mill, this does not generally happen in childhood.

Those who reject equal rights for children offer several reasons for denying certain rights to those without the relevant capacities, and it is time to single them out more explicitly. Mill mentioned two. The first is that children might harm themselves if left to their own devices. The second is that they might be harmed by others when their liberty brings them up against situations for which they are not adequately prepared. These are the concerns of paternalism: "the interference with a person's liberty of action justified by reasons referring exclusively to the welfare, good, happiness, needs, interests or values of the person being coerced" (Dworkin, 1971, p. 108). We can see how paternalism works if we imagine how it would be used to deny a child the right to choose an alternative home environment. (As adults, we are not required by the state to live in any particular place or with any particular group of people.)

Suppose that a child is quite unhappy at home and wishes to live elsewhere. We can imagine that the child is approximately twelve years old, that the parents have done nothing which could legally be described as child abuse or neglect, that they have genuine concern for the child's development, and that they are rather strict disciplinarians. Let us also imagine that the child can stay with the parents of a friend, but it is by no means clear that the arrangement would be permanent. Should the child have the right to choose to leave home? The paternalist would say "no," and offer two kinds of reasons. In the first place, the child may have needs that she or he is not really aware of. Goldstein, Freud, and Solnit, in their book, *Beyond the Best Interest of the Child*, claim that one of the overriding needs of childhood is continuity of a parent-figure. Their motto is leave things as they are unless you can prove that some alternative will be less detrimental to the child. The child may be unhappy, but the child cannot know of the future unhappiness which the lack of continuity at this stage of her or his life would cause. Thus, the child should be coerced into remaining at home in the name of protection against self.

The other version of the paternalist argument is that the child in this example could be quite incapable of recognizing whether an alternative home would be better or worse than the present one. It is quite possible that the child could get into a situation of serious physical or emotional abuse. Owing to the child's lack of experience of the real horrors of an unhappy home, and the child's presumed inability to put long-term interests ahead of present displeasures, it is necessary to sacrifice the child's liberty to her or his welfare, good, happiness, and so on. The right to an alternative home environment is too dangerous to be left to the child on this view.

There are other ways in which children's lack of capacities are used to deny them rights.   John Locke, in *The Second Treatise of Civil Government,* argues that parents have an obligation to God to protect their children. We may prefer to think of the obligation as one we have to our society for the development of its future members. In any event, child-rearing is not exclusively private business.   If parents do have obligations to the society at large, they may not let their children do anything which would cause them to fail to discharge *their own* obligations. Suppose the parents of the twelve year old in our example do have an obligation to raise a productive member of society if they decide to have children. Then they can be held responsible for failures of child-rearing. If the parents of the child's friend do not do an adequate job, the responsiblity is not theirs, since the biological parents should not have relinquished supervision in the first place. The upshot of this is that the child should not have a right to an alternative home environment since that right could interfere with the discharge of prior parental obligations.

A fourth reason for denying the right to those without the relevant capacities is that granting it to them would be frivolous to the point of making a mockery out of the very idea of rights. This is a little hard to see in the case of a twelve year old, but if the right to an alternative home environment is to belong to all children, it becomes quite clear. A one or two year old child barely has a notion of what a home environment is, let alone a concept of "alternatives." In order to actually exercise the right in a meaningful way, the child would have to be able to assess the relative merits of the alternatives, perceive her or his own proper interests, and act on the basis of that understanding. Anything short of this is not a significant exercise of a right--and the two year old child falls considerably short of being able to do this owing to her or his lack of the relevant capacities. Since the child cannot really do anything with the right, it is pointless to bestow it.   And given the seriousness with which we generally treat our rights in this society, extending rights in these situations can only serve to degrade the concept of rights rather than to enhance the status of children.

A final reason for denying this right to children is that in the course of exercising it they could do inadvertent harm to others. I am not speaking here of the harm that would come from acting beyond the limit of the right; everyone, not just children, can abuse their rights. But there are situations falling short of interference with the rights of others in which we may prevent them from doing things they want to do, or in which we cause them to do things which put them out a little. Often it is possible to exercise our rights in ways which lead to minimal disruptions in the lives of others or to exercise them in more intrusive ways. People who recognize the difference and are sensitive to the system try to do as little disrupting as possible. But children who do not have the capacity to see that there are ways to and there are ways *not* to exercise their rights will, as often as not, cause more havoc than is necessary. The system of negative freedoms is sufficiently delicate that it needs a large dose of mutual good will to work really well (to maintain a large area of civil liberty). To admit people to it who do not have the capacities to use their rights as considerately as possible is to unnecessarily jeopardize the system. The child who is changing home environments may not realize the extent of the imposition on her or his friend's parents. They may be willing to put up with a certain amount so as to see that the child does not go rightless in this case, but unless the child is aware of this and treats them accordingly, this sort of alternative home arrangement could come under attack and ultimately limit the options available to others who would exercise this right. In order to protect the right, one could argue that it should be denied to children.

Each of these arguments depends for its plausibility on the assumption that one must have the relevant capacities one's self in order to have the right. Thus, these arguments present us with a cut and dried choice: the child is either left strictly alone to make a decision or the child has no right. But as soon as we entertain a third option--that the child exercise the right by borrowing the capacities of an agent who is specifically obligated to help--these arguments lose most of their force. An agent could certainly inform the child of the advantages and the importance of continuity, just as the agent could see whether the proposed alternative home was likely to be better or worse than the child's present one. While it is true that an agent, as I understand the term, could not absolutely prevent a child from making a particular choice which rested within the rightful range, this possibility should not be blown out of proportion. Agents would probably be trusted advisors, and their views are likely to be respected by children. Furthermore, we are speaking of children who are at least old enough to articulate the desire to change homes, and so are presumably old enough to comprehend something of what would be involved in the move--as long as the agent expressed the situation in an appropriate way (i.e., at the child's level).

In a similar vein, there is no very good reason to think that children would not be able to exercise this meaningfully once we have specified an adult whose obligation it is to assess the relative merits of the child's alternatives, to help the child articulate her or his proper interests, and to lay the groundwork for the child's subsequent action. Far from being frivolous, extending this right to children is likely to have a significant impact on parent-child relationships to the extent that children will be in a position to make good on the threat to leave home. Likewise the agent would be experienced enough and knowledgeable enough to see that the changes of residence which occur do so with a minimal amount of fuss and inconvenience. The sort of diplomacy required here is well within the reach of most people, and we can suppose that agents would be sensitive to it. But even if particular agents are not very smooth about helping out their clients, it would be unfair to paint them as less effective than the average adult would be in exercising a similar right--and that is all I really want to insist on.   Finally, there is the matter of parental responsibility.   While it is true that parents would be irresponsible to society to informally abandon their children to someone else, under a system of agents there would be formalized and traceable transfers of responsibility.   Guardianship, after all, is not an unknown phenomenon in our society, and rights can and do have binding force in law.   In sum, all of the arguments for withholding civil rights from those who lack the relevant capacities are remarkably short-sighted about the kinds of support which might be offered to the potential right-holders instead.

I am not saying that it would be easy to institute the practice of child agency.   There are numerous difficulties both practical and theoretical to overcome.   Theoretically, it will not be easy to keep clear the difference between an agent and a protector.   The distinction is crucial if equal rights for children is not to become a disguised form of paternalism. Practically, we must face the questions of social costs in terms of resources and money.   I have tried to address a number of these issues elsewhere (Cohen, 1980).   They are serious problems for anyone who would take this proposal seriously.   Nevertheless, one must remember that social justice is at issue here.   The difficulty of the task and the cost (within reason) cannot be overriding reasons to maintain the double standard. Given the burden of proof, complaints about the difficulty of this enterprise are not justified until we have tried and failed.   Until then, children are systematically and unjustly being denied their equal rights.

REFERENCES

Cohen, H. *Equal rights for children.* Totowa, NJ: Littlefield, Adams and Company, 1980.

Dworkin, R. "Paternalism." In A. Wasserstrom (Ed.), *Morality and the law.* Belmont, CA: Wadsworth, 1971.

Farson, R. *Birthrights.* New York: Macmillan, 1974.

Feinberg, J. *Social philosophy.* Englewood Cliffs: Prentice-Hall, Inc., 1973.

Mill, J. S. "On liberty." In M. Warnock (Ed.), *John Stuart Mill.* New York: Meridian Books, The New American Library, 1962.

Schrag, F. The child's status in a democratic state. *Political Theory,* 1975, *3(4).*

COMMENT:

Response to "Ending the Double Standard:

Equal Rights for Children"

Allen Verhey

Religion Department
Hope College
Holland, MI 49423

It is probably best that I acknowledge quite candidly at the outset that I am not a philosopher by trade or ambition. Nevertheless, when I first read Mr. Cohen's very interesting paper with some care, I resolved to attempt to prepare the sort of philosophical response his paper warrants. I resolved to attempt to include a number of neat philosophical distinctions and a good bit of sage philosophical advice. Now I mind telling you that my initial attempts to draft such a response always seemed unsatisfactory and incomplete, that the notes on which the distinctions and wisdom began to take shape were often brooded over and discarded, and that the reasons for this frustration were not related to Mr. Cohen's paper as much as to the concrete reality of living with three children. The chores and pleasures of parenting, tucking my five year old into bed, listening to my eight year old rehearse and destroy a little piece for the piano, and talking over a math problem with my twelve year old, seemed constantly to dash to pieces my pretentions about philosophizing about children. I began to realize that I am both jealous and suspicious of my authority as a parent and that neither my jealousies nor my suspicions are easily rendered into logical justifications. I am jealous and suspicious of the authority I exercise *over* them, to distribute snacks, to settle disputes, to punish violence and injustice. And I am even more jealous--and less suspicious--of the authority I exercise *on their behalf,* the authority I use to demand to see their school records, to sign (or not) a surgical consent form, to exercise some control over their social environment. That, of course, is not a response to Mr. Cohen's paper, but it may be important to say as a preface to my response.

159

The first observation I wish to make about Mr. Cohen's paper is an obvious one--he has chosen to frame his argument in terms of the language of "rights." That is understandable, of course, in terms of the emphasis on such language in contemporary moral and legal discourse. Indeed, it sometimes seems presupposed that no argument can be persuasive unless it can invoke the language of rights. The language of rights does have, of course, the obvious advantage of emphasizing the stringency of those obligations which correlate with the right. Obligations imposed by the *rights* of others are ordinarily understood to be *overriding* obligations. But, having chosen to use the language of rights, it would seem that Mr. Cohen owes us some explanations of rights and considerable attention to the kinds of distinctions which may be made with respect to rights.

I understand "rights" to refer to the justified (or justifiable) claims which an individual or a group can make upon others or on society. But if that is the case, then the language of rights always points beyond itself to its justification, a justification offered presumably by certain principles or rules or precedents. The justification is important for distinguishing different kinds of rights and for discerning the proper content and distribution of the right. One might distinguish, for example, *legal* rights from *moral* rights in terms of the kind of justification which would be offered for the claims; legal rights are justified by existing legal principles and rules, and moral rights are justified by moral principles.

For the purposes of my response to Mr. Cohen, however, a more important distinction is the distinction of certain *moral* rights from certain other moral rights on the basis of the *moral* principles by which they would be justified. Mr. Cohen introduced the distinction between *non-interference* and *performance*. That distinction applies, of course, as Mr. Cohen says, to the duties which are correlative to rights. Some rights impose obligations of non-interference. Others impose obligations of performance. The rights themselves are often distinguished in terms of negative rights and positive rights. The distinction is an important one, and Mr. Cohen does not enhance our ability to think clearly about this matter by inviting us to construe all rights as positive rights, as imposing obligations of performance. The abortion controversy is an obvious reminder of the importance of this distinction--and of the fact that the distinction is based on the distinctive principles by which the claims are justified. Attempts to justify a woman's "negative right" to terminate a pregnancy, the right which imposes a duty of non-interference, rely on the principle of autonomy or privacy. Attempts to justify a woman's "positive right" to terminate pregnancy, the right which imposes a duty of performance, of providing medical services, appeal to the principle of equality or justice. Now I am not here interested in the question of whether or not there really is a right, either negative or positive, to terminate a pregnancy, but only in the importance of the distinction between positive and negative rights and in the fact that the distinction is related to the distinctive principles which would be offered in justification.

Some "negative rights," as we have seen, are based on the principle of respect for autonomy. The right not to be operated on without one's informed consent, for example, is surely a negative right based on respect for autonomy. But not all negative rights are based on the principle of respect for autonomy. Some are based on the principle of non-maleficence, or "do no harm." The right to life, for example, is such a negative right based not on respect for autonomy but on non-maleficence.

With respect to positive rights, too, it is important to distinguish the principles in terms of which the claims would be justifiable. Some have argued, for example, that there is a positive right to life as well as a negative right to life, that the right to life imposes an obligation to provide a minimum standard of living, including food, shelter, and medical care. If there is such a right its justification rests neither on the principle of autonomy nor non-maleficence but on the principle of beneficence, either in its weaker sense of avoiding harm or its stronger sense of doing good. Such positive rights are plainly less categorical than negative rights, as the principle of beneficence is less stringent than the principle of non-maleficence. Such claims are merely *ideals* in a number of societies which simply do not have the resources to insure such a standard of living. But such claims are made stringent in those societies with the resources to provide such services by the principle of *equality*, and that principle is almost always invoked along with the principle of beneficence to justify such rights. A society's provision of goods and services for its members should be equitable. That is not to say that the same things must be given to all, but that inequalities must be considered arbitrary unless such inequalities work out to the approximately equal benefit of all (Rawls, 1971). So a right to health care can require that provision be made for the sick. A right to work can demand that jobs be available for those of working age. And a right to an education can demand schooling for children. It is also important to observe, finally, that certain positive rights can belong to individuals because of certain contracts, promises, and role expectations.

With the observations about rights as background, the second set of observations I wish to make about Mr. Cohen's paper respond to his recommendation of "equal rights for children." It depends, I suggest, on the kind of "right" one is talking about, on the distinctive principle by which the right is justifiable. Those negative rights based on the principle of non-maleficence, do no harm, are surely held equally by children and adults. Indeed, because of the relative powerlessness of children, such rights may deserve special protections in their case. But negative rights based on the principle of respect for autonomy are not held equally by children. The right not to be operated on without one's informed consent is an instructive illustration. In the case of adults, that right is based on the respect for autonomy. When my daughter needed surgery, she was incapable of giving her consent, indeed of signing her name at all, much less to a consent form. So, after consultation with the doctor, I signed the form. A form still had to be signed. She was not without rights. But they were not the *same* rights.   The principle which justified my daughter's right not to be operated on without informed parental consent was not respect for autonomy but rather non-maleficence.   It was not simply that she borrowed my capacities, but that the principles protected were different.   The point can be made clearer still if one supposes a medical procedure unrelated to the patient's health, a medical procedure which puts the patient at some risk but promises benefits only to others. As an adult I may consent to such a procedure, indeed I have a right to participate in experimental procedures.   But my daughter has no such right.   Respect for my autonomy justifies my right, not my daughter's. But the principle "do no harm" protects her from anyone's willingness to make of her a "medical heroine."   This is not to say that my twelve year old does not have some rights based on respect for autonomy, more than when he was twelve months old at least, but still less than when he will be eighteen or twenty-one.   As he develops his autonomy (and he's doing a nice job of that), the principle of respect for autonomy makes increasing and more stringent justifiable claims, and so his rights based on that principle increase.   There is necessarily some vagueness and arbitrariness to the notion of developing rights.   Every good parent is sensitive to that problem and the social system should be sensitive to it, too.   But it cannot be moral progress--and may be morally dangerous--to suppose that children have "equal rights" where the claims are justified by the principle of respect for autonomy, an autonomy which simply does not yet exist.

With respect to positive rights, those rights which impose an obligation to provide goods and services, it is again sensible to talk about "equal rights for children."   But it is obvious that "equal rights" does not mean that the same rights always belong to children as to adults.   The right to work for example, is a positive right according to the United Nations Declaration on Human Rights, but it surely does not entail an obligation to provide children with jobs.   The point is obvious when we remember that besides equality the principle which justifies such rights is beneficence, and it is at least questionable whether a job would either avoid harms or promote goods for children.   The inequality can be justified in terms of the equal advantage of all.   On the other hand, another positive right in the United Nations Declaration is the right to an education (which includes the parental right to choose the kind of education).   Here children have special claims, special rights, which are nevertheless "equal" because the inequality can be justified as working out to the approximately equal advantage of all.

With respect to the special relationships which legitimate positive rights for particular individuals, rights legitimated by contracts presuppose again an autonomous individual.   The right to enter into contracts is legitimated by the principle of respect for autonomy.   Children, therefore, have not equal access to the sorts of rights legitimated by their entering into contracts.   They have, however, in role expectations special rights.   Every child has a right to parental care.   The relationship of parent-child gives children certain rights simply by virtue of their being children. The obligations these rights impose fall not on everyone, but on the adult within the role relationship. There are probably a number of chldren whose health has been threatened by dehydration, but only one, my daughter, has a special claim on me to secure care for her.

These last remarks allow, I think, two final observations to be made in response to Mr. Cohen's paper, one concerning the notion of borrowed capacities and one concerning the role of an agent. The most compelling examples of "borrowed capacities" which Mr. Cohen gives are contractual relationships, an adult's borrowing the capacities of a doctor, lawyer, or financial consultant.   But the contractual relationship is itself the problem.   Can children enter contractual relationships as autonomous individuals? *If so,* the argument based on borrowed capacities may stand up. But if they cannot enter contractual relationships as autonomous individuals, then the argument seems to fail. And, of course, it is unsatisfactory to say children can "borrow the capacity" to enter into such contractual relations, for it's like saying they can enter into a contractual relationship which would enable them to enter into a contractual relationship. One might quickly have an infinite regress.

All of this is not to say, of course, that children have *no* rights, or that they are only infrequently violated, or that the role of child advocate or agent or ombudsman ought not be institutionalized, and quickly. On the contrary, they have rights and their rights are sadly often violated. One of their special rights is the right to parental care. Children, just by virtue of their being children, have a right to an advocate, namely a parent. It is the obligation of parents to provide both biased affection and objective standards. Children need both if they are to become autonomous adults respecting as well as enjoying equal rights. (William Golding's *Lord of the Flies* is a literary testimony, urban gangs are a tragic testimony, and Urie Bronfenbrenner's *Two Worlds of Childhood: US and USSR* is social-scientific testimony that a parent-absent peer culture produces social disarray and barbarism.)   It is also the obligation of parents to protect the rights of children. They are obliged to be their child's advocate in the world, to protect their rights and welfare.

Sadly parents sometimes fail. Parental abuse of the power of their role must be acknowledged as an unpleasant and sometimes tragic reality. Parental abuse might be either *negative,* by not providing for them, by abandoning them, by withholding parental support, affection, protection, and supervision, or *positive,* by physical or psychological persecution or attack. Such abuses of parental power violate the rights of children, including the right to parental care. We must find legal and social ways to enhance the capacity of parents to fulfill their role-obligations and to restrain and supplant parental abuse of the powers their role provides. Parent-child relationships may not be broken lightly; but sometimes the protection of the child and his rights and the protection of the parent-child relationship as a morally legitimate social role requires it be broken. In this context the child advocate would have an important and legitimate role.   He or she would be an embodiment not of the principle of *equal rights* for children but of the principle of parens patriae, the recognition that government must protect the rights of children, the at-least-equal negative rights based on "do no harm;" the developing negative rights based on "respect autonomy," the equal but different positive rights based on beneficence and equality, and the special rights to parental care based on the role relation of parent and child.   Children *have* rights.   They *are* sometimes violated.   And a child advocate would be an important step in protecting them.   About those things, Mr. Cohen and I agree.

REFERENCES

Bronfenbrenner, U.   *Two worlds of childhood: US and USSR.*   New York: Russell Sage Foundation, 1970.

Golding, W.   *Lord of the flies.*   New York: Capricorn Books, 1959.

Rawls, J.   *A theory of justice.*   Cambridge, MA: Harvard University Press, 1971.

CHILDREN'S RIGHTS AND PARENTS' VIRTUES

William Ruddick

Department of Philosophy
New York University
New York, NY 10003

INTRODUCTION

Philosophers, by and large, have lacked intimate experience of children. Like Plato and Kant, they have been childfree or, like Socrates and Rousseau, they have left the care of their children to wives or orphanages. This inexperience explains an otherwise puzzling neglect of family matters in our moral and political philosophy. Since Plato, philosophers have concerned themselves with macrolevel political institutions and microlevel individual actions. They have ignored that intermediate context of family life within which most people make their political and personal choices. They have made little attempt to discover and assess whatever principles guide our decisions to form, continue or leave our families.

Without a "philosophy of the family" we are limited in our thinking about children and their welfare. We uncritically apply the categories of adult life to children and thereby distort or ignore morally important aspects of childhood, and of parenthood as well. We thereby think of children as miniature adults--a kind of *conceptual* child abuse of which even child-advocates are guilty. The current panoply of "children's rights" is a case in point.

(Young) children have few if any of the rights adults have. They do, however, as children have at least two distinctive "child-rights": the right to become an adult and the derivative right to have an adequate parent. Were these rights defined and recognized, they would benefit children at least as much as many of the adult-rights claimed for them by child-advocates, particularly adult-rights to liberty in various matters. Yet even fully recognized "child-rights" will be of limited benefit by them-

165

selves. Children's welfare requires rights to be supplemented by certain parental *virtues* and by institutions to foster those virtues.

In trying to make these claims plausible within short order, I shall ignore children over ten years of age in our culture. I mean thereby to focus on children whose need for parents is not yet at issue. The rights of adolescents is a topic too complex to address here.

1. DO CHILDREN HAVE THE SAME RIGHTS AS ADULTS?

In thinking about rights, it is helpful to distinguish liberty-rights from claim-rights. Liberty-rights allow us to control various aspects of our lives--our choices of abode, associates, religion, entertainment, and the like--free from interference by other individuals, public officials, or agencies. By contrast, claim-rights entitle us to the services of certain individuals, officials, or agencies. Examples of alleged claim-rights are rights to medical care, employment, and information.*(1)*

I say *alleged* rights because it is debatable (and hotly debated) whether every adult, or even any adult has such entitlements, except by way of special contracts with those who provide services. Liberty-rights, by contrast, are less controversial, for the duties they impose on others are far less onerous: duties of non-interference usually require only restraint, not assistance. And it is just this difference between assistance and restraint that makes most adult liberty-rights inappropriate, useless, or worse when extended to children.

Suppose, for example, my young daughter were to assert a right to leave home and live elsewhere, and that I (in unsympathetic irony) replied: "I recognize your right to leave and to live elsewhere: I'll not stop you. I'll even see to it that no one else stops you, but that's as far as I will go." She and I both realize *that* is not far enough: without my help in finding and maintaining an apartment and surrogate care-takers, she cannot survive in desirable conditions. My reply in effect treats her assertion of a claim-right as if it were a much less demanding liberty-right, and she can easily appreciate (without terms for the distinction) that an offer of non-interference is useless to someone of her age and unavoidable dependence on adult assistance in living arrangements.

In general, liberty-rights without supporting claim-rights are of no use to children. The same is true for adults, it is said, but this is not so. Liberty-rights per se are of use to *some* adults who have, whether through hard work or good fortune, the capacity to exercise those rights without further demands on the services of others. But liberty-rights by themselves are of no use to any child, no matter how hardworking or fortunate. Given our slow biological and social maturation, childhood is inescapably a period of physical and mental incapacity, hence dependence on the capable. The length and conception of childhood incapacities vary with the definition and demands of maturity in a culture, but only in fiction can children become adult at birth or soon after.*(2)*

Without supportive claim-rights, liberty-rights alone are in practice worse than useless for children: they are dangerous and exploitative. As we now admit, a child's alleged "right to work" was and still is a ruse to provide cheap labor for adult enterprises. A right to work (taken as a right to choose a line of work and a suitable employer) may be of little or no value to unskilled or single-skilled adults. But for young children, such a right would expose them to special harms, including the harm of inter- rupted education and an adulthood with few, if any skills. Grant the right to work too early and you will guarantee its eventual uselessness.

There are three ways we might take account of the special vulnerability of children: 1) We could couple every adult liberty-right with a claim-right to special protection and assistance for children (as in special provisions for the education of child actors). But this coupling would produce an unwelcome hybrid in an already baroque catalogue of rights compiled by legal-minded philosophers; 2) We could allow adult liberty-rights to be more easily overridden by paternalistic considerations in the case of children. But easily overridden liberty-rights are nearly worthless: even if they are not always decisive, liberty-rights should always be weighty obstacles to interference; 3) We could disallow the extension of adult liberty-rights to children altogether. I prefer this option for two reasons. First, it respects the fact that we *do* limit children's choices of abode, work, and the like in their own present and future interest, as well as our own, without the public rituals of rights--namely, justification, reviews and adjudications. We allow young children as much liberty as befits their current capacities, their welfare, and that of the rest of the family (including our own). As parents, we are welfare-providers, not rights-respecters.

Moreover, this third option resists the recent proliferation of rights in moral and political thought. We must beware a Gresham-effect, by which some rights drive out other, more worthy rights. If, as Feinberg (1974, Ch. 4) argues, rights are claims on, or against others for assistance or restraint, then there may be a pragmatic limit on how many rights can be recognized. Even the most conscientious person cannot attend to indefinitely many claims. Better that morality and institutions foster a variety of moral responses: a world of people related primarily by their asserting and recognizing claims would be as uninviting as a Kansas farmer's stereotype of Manhattan. At least some of the welfare of children (like the welfare of animals) should be entrusted to the feelings of affection, protection, and assistance children evoke in parents and other adults. Otherwise, parenthood and family life would become dour, adversarial, and uninvitingly onerous.

But whichever line with liberty rights we take, it should be clear that children's rights are not the same as adult liberty-rights: on option (1) children's liberty-rights would, supported by claim-rights, be stronger than adult analogues; on option (2) they would be weaker, because more easily overridden; on option (3) they would be non-existent.

Let us turn now to children's rights that have no adult analogues, rights they have in virtue of being children. Let us call such distinctive rights "child-rights" and reserve "children's rights" for whatever rights children and adults both may claim.

2. DO CHILDREN HAVE DISTINCTIVE RIGHTS?

Rights are closely tied to avoidable general harms from which they purport to protect us (Scanlon, 1978). Let us then look more closely at the harms to which children are distinctively prone. Certain harms may befall humans at any age or stage of development: physical injury, disease, pain, anxiety, and so on. Such universal harms may be more intensely felt by children and may more easily and frequently befall children. Worse yet, these harms may interfere with a child's growth and development into adulthood. Lack of food, for example, may not only cause more intense pain and anxiety in a child than in an adult; it may also inhibit or permanently impair the child's growth and maturation. Even should some children suffer less pain and anxiety from hunger than do most adults, the harm they would suffer would be greater if malnutrition arrested or stunted their development.

In general, childhood is a preparatory stage in life: hence children are vulnerable to special and severe harms that may prolong immaturity or reduce a child's life possibilities and capacities. I do not think adulthood is preferable in every respect in all circumstances. But in decent societies adults do have a fuller life than children in virtue of those various, developed capacities that make liberty-rights worth having. In Greek terms, an adult's *bios* (*life* in a biographical sense) exhibits a *telos* (completeness) which contrasts with the relatively disordered souls of children. In our terms, a (mature) adult "has it all together." Arrested development of one or more capacities makes the forming and leading of an ordered life more difficult.

These considerations support the need for at least one special child-right, namely the right to mature or to become an adult. Clearly, such a right must be a claim-right, since it requires far more than non-interference with a child's natural growth. "Growing up" requires the assistance of a variety of people over many years, as well as adult restraint and forbearance: it is not a spontaneous, natural process.

On whom should these claims and associated correlative duties of aid (and restraint) fall? That depends on the answers to three more specific questions: Who is most likely to cause a child the kind of harm that can impede its growth? Who is best able to protect a child from such harm and dangers of harm? Who has the most interest in providing protection and support for a child's development toward adulthood?

Standardly, the adults who can be and occasionally are the most arresting are the same people who can be and usually are the most

protective and supportive, and they are also the adults most interested in
a child's development--namely, a child's parents. This complex relationship reflects a basic fact of human existence, namely, the gradual,
uncertain development of a child within the lives of its parents. Physically and otherwise, a child poses what philosophers call problems of
"individuation." During pregnancy, for example, it is hard to say when
there come to be two human bodies rather than just one (the woman's) in
an altered state. Likewise, it is hard to say when after birth a child
comes to have a life distinct from that of its parents, a life as defined not
by birth dates, but by a person's principal concerns, activities, associates,
and projects. In infancy and early childhood, a child's life is in most
respects part of, and determined by its parents' lives: its parents share or
at least decide most of a young child's concerns and activities. Only
gradually does a child come to have capacities and opportunities for
choosing new (or retaining old) associates and projects. A distinct life of
one's own requires those very capacities for self-definition, for relative
self-dependence, and for concern for others that define maturity in our
culture. In short, maturation is increasing individuation from parents,
their delegates and surrogates--a gradual process parents are in a unique
position to foster or hinder, wittingly and otherwise.

Parental efforts and influences depend in part on agencies of state
and other institutions. What role should the state play in this maturation
and individuation process of children? Conservative, anarchist, and
disgruntled critics dismiss any state action as interference likely to hinder
parental efforts. Many critics proclaim *parens patriae* to be an anachro-
nistic legal doctrine: contemporary bureaucratic paternalists, they
charge, can neither judge nor serve the best interests of children. Middle-
class, majority standards of parenthood are imposed on people who, it is
said, either do not share or do not have the means to meet those
standards. And middle-class homes and schools are disrupted by legis-
lators' and judges' conceptions of social justice--a violation, allegedly, of
the rights of majority (white) parents and children.

These objections may presuppose that government agencies are
necessarily like traditional fathers--that is, primarily passive, inattentive
spectators who occasionally rush in when mothers seem unable to cope,
thereby often making matters worse. Now if the state is conceived as
such a father-figure, then state intervention is indeed likely to be
unsatisfactory for many of the same reasons, writ large. To salvage the
doctrine of *parens patriae*, we must reconceive the state as a parental
supplement, not a parental substitute. Rather than a Super-father who
rescues, the state would be a mother's (and father's) daily helper. A
conscientious *parens patriae* would provide child-care assistance as a
matter of course and not just in cases of special need that come to the
attention of the authorities.

There seems to be some movement in this direction. Where
previously courts and child welfare agencies would intervene by removing

a child to a foster home, they are beginning to provide the child's own parents with training and material assistance to improve home conditions. In so doing, courts and agencies are fostering those parental *virtues* on which a child's welfare ultimately rests.

Current developmental theories trace immaturity in adults--overdependence, lack of ego-boundaries or generativity--to conditions of childhood, especially to failures of parental attention and affection. Ideally, state assistance would foster such parental capacities by various forms of relief from continuous child care (babysitters, daycare centers, camps, excursions): parental batteries need recharging by nonparental periods.

State assistance can, we know, become subtle or unwelcome political and cultural control. Visions of Sparta and Nazi Germany haunt us. But it is the state that takes young children from their parents, not the state that enables children to remain with their parents that should worry us. Admittedly, assistance aims at some minimal standard of adequate parenting, and it would be necessary to define that standard. Otherwise parental aid could be withheld from socially eccentric parents whose goals and ways of family life were socially deviant.

There is a further reason for defining adequate parenting. Such definition will not only help set clear minimal conditions for, or goals of, state assistance to parents; it will also allow us to move conceptually beyond the narrow limits of child, parent, and state *rights* to more comprehensive notions of parental virtues and principles.

3. WILL RIGHTS ALONE FOSTER CHILDREN'S WELFARE?

For historical and sociological reasons the notions of *rights* is primary in current moral and political discourse. The U.S. Constitution with its Bill of Rights is now the only commonly shared sacred text in a nation composed of culturally and religiously diverse immigrants. Appeal to these and other rights is a way of transcending that diversity and resolving disputes in the absence of other shared values.(3) Recently such appeals have gained blacks, women and the handicapped somewhat fuller adult status. Each of these groups has complained against being treated like children, thereby being made dependent on whites or males or the able-bodied. Children, however, are not victims of systematic infantilizing and self-serving prejudice of adults. To treat a child as a child is not oppression, but realism. Children's incapacities, hence their dependence on adults, cannot be eliminated by affirmative action or legal extension of adult rights.

Legal recognition of a child's rights to become an adult and to have an adequate parent would be a boon for children and parents. So, too, would a theory and recognized list of parental virtues to coordinate with those child-rights. I have mentioned the virtues of attentiveness and patience--daily parental virtues. In addition, parents need the long-range virtues of forethought and flexibility: parents must take thought for the next century as well as for tomorrow, and they must allow that the world will make unfamiliar demands on them as well as on their children as individuation and maturation proceed.

Given the rapid change in our culture and the difficulty of foresight, it may seem that the good parent is infinitely flexible, preparing a child for as many life-possibilities as resources and talents allow. The ideal parent would, it may seem, set out a smorgasbord from which a child would eventually choose some life or other, according to future desire and circumstances. This spread would, given unpredictable mores and values, have to include dishes parents themselves would not choose. The child's range of choices should not be limited by prior parental preferences.

This smorgasbord principle of parenthood may appeal to libertarians, especially those without children. But it has a serious defect: it requires denial of a common motive for parental efforts, namely, the desire to reproduce certain aspects of the parents' own lives and ideals. Men, for example, have wanted to continue the family name, or genes, or business through their sons. Women have less specific reproductive desires, such as the desire to continue human kind, or a certain moral or social kind of human being.

If parenthood is to continue in an effective contraceptive society, such reproductive motives must be honored, or at least tolerated. It may be objected that such motives place a selfish burden on the children these motives generate. But to the extent that children are, as described earlier, part of their parents' lives and are not fully individuated, parental self-love will encompass, rather than exploit those children. Indeed, children might fare better if parents were more self-loving in the ways psychotherapists often encourage. People who enjoy self-respect and self-acceptance are less likely to force children to live out parental fantasies and unrealized hopes.

There are, of course, limits to efforts at self-reproduction. Some critics think that certain self-isolating religious sects like the Amish exceed those limits and violate their children's rights to become adults. It is true that the Amish go to an extreme opposite that of the Smorgasbordians: they set out only one dish, and a fairly simple one at that. They do prepare their children for adult life--in the very world they have so far managed to preserve. Detractors claim that the Amish world cannot survive and that Amish children are unprepared for any other, hence may be unable to lead self-dependent adult lives in a world their parents reject. Amish parents, it is said, lack the virtue of flexibility necessary for a child's individuation and self-definition.

Let me, without assessing these charges, assume that the principles defining parental virtues will fall somewhere between the smorgasbordian and Amish extremes. We might consider the following a plausible intermediate: So far as resources and prediction allow, an adequate parent fosters 1) life-prospects, any one of which if eventually realized by a child, would be acceptable to both parent and child; 2) life-prospects which jointly encompass the range of likely futures the child may encounter in adult life; and 3) characteristics in a child (and in her- or himself) that make for the child's eventual independence of parents.

The first provision encourages diversity within the scope of parental ideals and motivations.   The second provision encourages a longer perspective than daily family life requires. The third provision reflects the self-terminating nature of parental responsibilities: given the likelihood of parental exhaustion, senility, or death, children must in time be able to live without parents.

I do not expect this "Prospect Provision Principle" to win immediate adherents. It is offered merely as an example of a principle that stresses parental virtues, while respecting parental motivation and relative political autonomy. Institutions embodying some such principle will not make parents servants of the state, or servants of their children's desires. Over the long, unpredictable course of a parent-child relationship, the parental project might, if guided by this principle, prove rewarding to both parties.*(4)*

ACKNOWLEDGEMENT

I wish to thank my colleague Frances Myrna Kamm for her careful, helpful criticism.

REFERENCES

Feinberg, J. *Social philosophy.* Englewood Cliffs, N.J.: Prentice-Hall, 1973.
Ruddick, W. Parents and life prospects. In O. O'Neill and W. Ruddick (Eds.), *Having children: Philosophical and legal reflections on parenthood.* New York: Oxford University Press, 1979.
Scanlon, T. M. Rights, goals, and fairness. In S. Hampshire (Ed.), *Public and private morality.* Cambridge: Cambridge University Press, 1978.

FOOTNOTES

(1) The more familiar distinction is between negative and positive rights. I wish to avoid, however, the suggestion that non-interference is always inaction ("negative action") and assistance is always activity ("positive action"). 'Claim-right' may be confusing: some philosophers think that all rights are claims, liberty-rights being "claims against the world" not to interfere.

(2) This has perplexing effects on parents. See F. Scott Fitzgerald's story, "The Strange Case of Benjamin Button."

(3) On J. Schneewind's reconstruction of Western philosophical ethics, the goal has continuously been to find ways of resolving or avoiding disputes, regardless of cultural and legal differences or boundaries. If so, then rights are paradigmatic moral concepts in virtue of their role in adjudication.

(4) An earlier version of this proposed principle is applied to familiar cases of parents refusing standard treatments for their ailing children. See my "Parents and Life Prospects," in *Having Children: Philosophical and Legal Reflections on Parenthood.* An earlier, shorter version of this present address is printed in the *Proceedings of the General Education Seminar*, 1980, VI: *2* (New York: Columbia University Press).

COMMENT:

Response to "Children's Rights and Parents' Virtues"

Wade Robison

Department of Philosophy
Kalamazoo College
Kalamazoo, MI 49007

William Ruddick has five theses:

(1) "Liberty-rights (are) inappropriate for children", for children are unavoidably dependent upon "adult assistance."

(2) Even if children had such rights, "liberty-rights without supportive claim rights are of no use to children" and are "dangerous and exploitative."

(3) Children do have "the (claim-) right to become an adult" which, with a proper theory of child development, implies "the (claim-) right to have an adequate parent."

(4) The government should play the role of "mother's helper" though assistance requires minimum standards so that "parental aid could be withheld from socially eccentric parents whose goals and ways of family life were socially deviant."

(5) What is needed are not rights (not even claim-rights?), but virtues-- specifically, attentiveness, patience, self-love, forethought, and flexibiity.

(5) is independent of (1)-(4). I am not sure whether it is meant as a counter to any thesis about children's rights, including Ruddick's own, or as a supplement, and there is no argument regarding the accuracy or completeness of Ruddick's list of virtues. Why not reasonableness, for instance? But I am not in disagreement with the claim that parents ought to be virtuous, and I leave (5) to one side.

175

(4) is in part dependent upon (1)-(3). If children lack (what Ruddick calls) liberty-rights and have (what he calls) claim-rights, then government's role cannot be to enforce the former, but, at best, to aid in achieving the latter. There are problems with (4) independent of any problems with (1)-(3). For instance, who counts as socially deviant? The Amish, to mention one of Ruddick's examples? Christian Scientists? But these are matters requiring further development, and, rather than speculate, I leave (4) to one side.

I shall concentrate upon (1). For the rest of the paper, (4) included, hangs upon the claim that liberty-rights are inappropriate for children or, as Ruddick prefers to say, that children do not have liberty-rights (1, 5).

The only argument Ruddick suggests for this claim occurs in the example about his child wanting to leave home and live elsewhere. He says that "a mere offer of non-interference is an empty gesture to someone of her age and unavoidable dependence on adult assistance." As later remarks suggest, it is the *dependence* of children upon adults that is crucial, and if one were to try to sketch the argument out, it would begin like this:

P_1 - Children are unavoidably dependent upon adults.

P_2 - Liberty-rights are rights that others not interfere with one's actions.

I do not know how to complete this argument. For, first, I do not see the *relevance* of the claim that children are dependent upon adults to any claim that they have no liberty-rights or even, as in Ruddick's second thesis, that liberty-rights are of no use to children. And, second, I find Ruddick's views about liberty-rights and the difference between them and claim-rights enormously puzzling: he has left out the most important rights we all have, children included. Let me consider these points in turn.

It is easy to find counter-examples to the claim that because one being is dependent upon another the first therefore lacks liberty-rights. If a wife is unavoidably dependent upon her husband because financial conditions and a large family prevent her from being independent without his financial aid, it does not follow that she lacks a right, e.g., to work. It may be that she will not be able to work without his aid, but that is a different matter entirely. If we reverse the dependence relation for parents and children and take an elderly parent unavoidably dependent upon a child for financial support, say, do we say, or want to say, that the parent thereby has no right to, e.g., go out to a club to relax? The right of the elderly parent to relaxation is *of use* to the parent, for it provides a ground for a claim against the child--or against the state--to provide transportation. Indeed, any institutionalized person would provide a counter to Ruddick's theses. Someone who is ill in a hospital, or someone who is imprisoned, is utterly dependent upon others, but not without liberty-rights. And so on.

Ruddick has simply failed to distinguish between having a right and having the capacity to exercise a right independently of the help of others. We make this distinction in the law, and since we are talking about legal rights of children, there is no reason to accept the thesis that children, merely because of their reliance upon adults, lack liberty-rights.

To go on to argue that children have liberty-rights would be, though accurate, misleading. For it is not liberty-rights that are of fundamental importance to children. What are of fundamental importance are rights that Ruddick's classification of rights has squeezed out of existence. Let us look at that classificatory scheme.

Liberty-rights, Ruddick says, are rights we have to be "free from interference by other individuals." They require "only restraint, not assistance." The two examples he gives are actions people undertake-- leaving home and working. A liberty-right is distinct from a claim-right, Ruddick says, because a claim-right is an entitlement to the services of others, and the right to be free from the interference of others is not the same as the right to the services of others.

Those are all the rights Ruddick mentions, and they do seem exhaustive: what else can one demand of others except to be left alone or to be aided? But this apparent exhaustion is misleading in two ways.

First there are other legal relations besides the right/duty relation, and by squeezing all a child's legal relations into the right/duty mold, Ruddick has skewed his investigation.

A privilege is a legal capacity to do or forebear when others have no right to interfere. The distinction is simple and fundamental. A has a right regarding X if and only if there is at least a B who has a duty to A regarding X. So a right imposes a correlative duty. But a privilege does not impose a duty. It requires only that others have no right to interfere.

If we slide this expanded classificatory scheme, which is still incomplete, over Ruddick's theses, it is clear that Ruddick's example of a right to work is more appropriately viewed in our legal system as a complex of legal relations--in particular, a privilege to seek employment (others having no right to interfere) and at least a right not to be discriminated against in regard to employment opportunities. Ruddick's examples of leaving home and working direct our attention away from rights to privileges, and whatever we hold about the rights of children, presumably we are less inclined to think they have privileges. For we think that far from having no rights to interfere, parents are under special obligations to interfere. And that duty to interfere means the loss of privileges.

Ruddick's classification of legal relations into liberty-rights and claim-rights has apparently led him to argue as follows: there are claim-rights, which impose duties upon others to aid, and privileges, which require that others have no rights to interfere. But since children are unavoidably dependent upon adults, adults have a special duty to interfere--which must mean, or so he seems to argue, that children have no liberty-rights (privileges), but only claim-rights.

The conclusion is too broad--even if one agreed with the premises. For one needs to examine what specific duties parents have to children and thus which possible privileges children do not have--and, accordingly, which they do have.

But there is a second problem with the assumption that the classification of legal relations is exhaustive: it leaves out of consideration the most important legal relation of all. I have a right that others not harm me--by not kicking me, for instance, or by not spitting on me, even in passing. My right not to be harmed, though certainly dependent for its realization upon your actions, or omissions, is not a right I have *to do* anything at all. Children may not have the privilege of working and still have a right not to be harmed. Indeed, I would argue, they clearly have a right not to be harmed; they have it by virtue of being persons, and their rights not to be harmed deserve special attention--just as do the rights of the institutionalized, dependent spouses, the elderly, and so on--simply because they are dependent. Dependence is relevant not to the non-existence of a liberty-right, as Ruddick argues, but to a special concern that the most important kind of right be sustained.

It may be that Ruddick assumes that a child's claim-rights to become an adult and thus to have an adequate parent imply such fundamental rights as a right not to be harmed. Perhaps it does in this special case. Ruddick gives no argument, and there seems on the face of it no logical relation between a right that others shall forebear and a right that others perform. I think that in any case it is worth distinguishing the two. For children have long been abused--not conceptually, but actually, and one of the causes of that abuse has been the failure to extend to them the rights we adults have that others shall forebear. Children ought to be treated as miniature adults in that regard. That is not conceptual abuse, but a moral requirement--because they are persons, just like us.

REPLY TO ROBISON

William Ruddick

Department of Philosophy
New York University
New York, NY 10003

In reconstructing my paper, Wade Robison finds at least two confusions (having a right with its exercise; liberty-rights with legal privileges), two gaps (in my lists of rights and virtues), and a falsehood essential for my argument against children's liberty-rights (in his words, "...because one being is dependent upon another the first therefore lacks liberty-rights"). He does agree that there is a kind of right more important for children's welfare than any liberty-rights they share with adults, but it is a "right of forbearance" not to be harmed. As such, it is neither a right to non-interference nor a claim-right to the assistance of others. Since my proposed "child-rights" to become an adult with the aid of adequate parents are claim-rights on parents and the state, they do not fall under this "third kind of right." Moreover, children allegedly have this right not to be harmed in virtue of being persons, just as adults. My child-rights, by contrast, reflect differences from adults in capacities, forms of dependence, and life-prospects.

Here lies our basic disagreement in approach: Robison's proposals, criticisms and examples tend to assimilate children to adults, while I try to capture the differences. Understandably, he finds my account of parent-child morality obscure, while I find his familiar approach clear but simplistic. For example, consider the counter-examples he cites against the claim quoted above: Hospital patients, prisoners, financially dependent wives and elderly parents all have liberty-rights although "unavoidably dependent." I agree, but fail to see how these adult cases bear on the case of children whose "biographical dependence" on parents is very different from the financial and institutional dependence of adults constrained, voluntarily or otherwise, by marriage, age, illness, or prison. In some respects these adults are dependent on others in a childlike way for food, shelter, care and protection. But, on one plausible construction,

179

they differ from young children in a morally relevant way: they have all, with varying degrees of freedom, traded prior liberties for material security and care. They retain *some* liberty-rights, including the right to cancel the implicit contracts into which they have entered (prisoners excepted). Hence, their dependence is not truly "unavoidable." Moreover, their loss of other adult liberties generates special claim-rights: prisoners, under the Constitutional prohibition of cruel and unusual punishments, acquire protected rights to food and medical care, unlike the rest of us who are free to work for those necessities of life. And critics of conventional marriage would argue that a woman, in undertaking a disproportionate share of childcare, acquires a claim-right to her husband's assistance in working outside the home when their children need less home-care.

In short, these adults have reversed the usual transition from immature claim-rights to mature liberty-rights. In their childlike dependence, they do not enjoy the full range of liberty-rights that define maturity in our culture. For various reasons, they lack the capacities or opportunities to form and pursue projects of one's own without justified interference from others and without rightful assistance from others. Of course, most adults need the cooperation and emotional support of others, but for adults these are normally not a matter of right, as they are for children and incapacitated adults.

I do not intend, in opposition to Robison's approach, to assimilate these dependent adults to children. Unlike children, they have well-defined interests and self-conceptions in virtue of their undiminished adult capabilities and the individuated lives they have led. Their financial or institutional dependence is (usually) not part of a more complex "biographical" dependence on those who sustain them. It is that more complex dependence of one life within another that calls young children's liberty-rights into question, not a catch-all notion of dependence that occurs in the general "claim" that Robison attributes to me. The dependence generated by the incapacities of childhood is unique: until a child's life and interests are clearly individuated from those of its parents, Robison's notions of liberty-rights and legal privileges do not come into play. His distinction between having but not exercising a right presupposes a distinct individual with interests (and perhaps projects) that can be ignored or overridden by other agents. It is not clear that infants and young children are such individuals.

For some of the same reasons, I am not sure that they are persons in the full sense required by Robison's account of the right not to be harmed. Like fetuses, infants and (very) young children are perhaps best classified as *potential* persons, with capacities to acquire--with time and much aid--the capacities that define a person. But, as the philosophical abortion debate has shown, potential personhood provides uncertain protection in competition with (adult) persons with defined rights and interests. For young children, the right not to be harmed needs some stronger basis.

Moreover, that right entails more onerous duties than Robison's forbearance allows. Like an infant's right to life, an infant's right not to be harmed requires continuous adult efforts, since infants cannot sustain or protect themselves. If adults forbear, infants will quickly come to harm. For able-bodied adults in favorable circumstances, the right not to be harmed may be a "right of forbearance," but for children it must be a claim-right. Thus, like the right to life, the right not to be harmed takes one form for the young, another for the mature. Rather than a single right, it is better to think of the right not to be harmed as a class of differing age-relative rights, as is the right to life. It makes for moral and political confusion to define these "rights" in terms of the adult version alone, another instance of the assimilation of children to adults.

A final comment on political matters. Robison's fourth thesis is not mine, for it reverses the thought I expressed by saying:

> ...it would be necessary to define that standard of ade-
> quate parenting at which government assistance aims.
> Otherwise parental aid could be withheld from socially
> eccentric parents whose goals and ways of family life
> were socially deviant.

That is, a definition is needed to *avoid* undesirable governmental pressure on the socially deviant, *not* (as Robison's attribution has it) to facilitate conventional pressure. A clear statement of a government's conception of adequate parenting would, admittedly, discourage parents who disagreed from taking assistance meant to further that conception of childcare. (Christian Scientists would not send their children to a government daycare center that taught children standard views of health, disease, hygiene, and the like.) And I suppose there would be *some* conditions on the use of government aid (such as, no supplemental aid for bizarre therapies to which parents committed their children).

I do regret, on reflection, mixing politics and parental virtues. Government parental aid should probably be defined solely in terms of rights and other quasi-legal notions; parental virtues is a topic too novel and debatable to guide public family policy. Is reasonableness to be added to the list of parental virtues? Perhaps so, but again Robison seems proleptic: reasonableness is surely a virtue among adults and it is a trait that parents must exemplify as children grow older. But these examples, like limited exercises in the use of liberty, are part of the training for eventual adult life. They are not evidence for the view that children and adults are alike, morally speaking.

CHILDREN'S NEEDS AND PARENTAL LIBERTY:

A LIBERAL CONTRADICTION AND HOW TO ESCAPE FROM IT

Susan K. Perkins

Department of Philosophy
Swarthmore College
Swarthmore, PA 19081

Unless we are willing to consider human beings as simultaneous nurturers and recipients of nurture, we can never reach a coherent understanding of equal liberty for parents and children. The efforts of the great classical liberals to deal with the problems raised by the needs of children fail because they cannot make this leap. Instead, such thinkers are trapped between alienating the liberty of the parents and making liberty into a hollow form which guarantees no benefits of any substance to the children. Yet in *A Theory of Justice,* John Rawls has escaped from this dilemma. Understanding how he does so implies abandoning the understanding of human beings as merely those who pursue their own separate ends and find the aid of others a useful means to doing so; it suggests that in recognizing ourselves as dependent on the nurture of others, we must accept our role as the givers of that nurture. We must do so however much this role may conflict with our separate goals if we are to legitimize our own claims to the benefits liberty can offer us.

What distinguishes children from adults is their special needs. These are needs that they cannot meet themselves, which they depend on others to supply. The unborn child is the ultimate case of such needs: food, oxygen, warmth and shelter must come through the body of the mother. Yet the unborn child and the growing child also cannot provide for themselves. They need protection and care: to be cleaned and clothed, fed and watched over. They need psychological and mental nurturing as well: to be taught if they are to care for themselves, to be held and loved if they are to care for others, to be played with and excited if they are to develop the qualities and abilities we value in others.

Because children are thus dependent, it is not sufficient to define their rights in terms of freedom from interference by others. Left alone, the newborn child will die. Even given physical care and maintenance, the growing child will be a mental and emotional cripple, unable to care for itself or others. Most people do indeed feel in principle that these needs ought to be met. The difficulty comes in specifying who ought to do so, and deciding how much of the effort should be considered morally (or legally) required and how much treated as a voluntary, supererogatory good action.

This is the problem beneath a number of contemporary public issues. On the one hand, there is an effort being made to expand the definition of individual rights to include children's claims to have their needs met. The anti-child abuse and anti-child neglect movements reflect the urge to enforce such extended rights. Special juvenile courts and legal procedures are defended by assertions that the young have a right to be corrrected rather than punished by adults. Arguments about child support and about mothers working outside the home turn on who holds responsibility for meeting children's needs.

On the other hand, there are efforts afoot to protect the parents from the impositions of some of children's needs. Feminist defenses of women's liberty deny that mothers have duties correlative to certain claims made by or for children.   The abortion controversy polarizes around this issue; "pro-choice" denies an enforceable duty of the mother to bear the unborn child to term, and "pro-life" insists that one exists. Any solution to these problems must begin with a coherent view of the rights and duties of children and of those who are to take care of them.

A number of major liberal thinkers have dealt in passing with the question of who ought to take care of children and why. They argue variously that care fulfills parental desires, that it is required by a contractual obligation to the child, that it is a duty to God, and that it follows from maximizing general utility. I shall present each of these arguments briefly, and then follow its consequences for parent and child. I shall argue that each one fails to reserve real opportunity for self-determination to the parent or else is unable to assure that the child will receive enough care to use the liberty that is preserved. Moreover, if we truly are concerned with both goals, these solutions give us no idea of how to balance the costs to the two sides fairly.

* * *

The first argument used by liberals is that no argument is necessary. People want to have and care for children, according to this view. Complete freedom to pursue individual goals poses no problem, because parents will voluntarily take care of their offspring.

This 'argument from desire' occurs in several forms. In the *Discourse on the Origins of Inequality*, Rousseau (1952, p. 340) asserts that in the complete freedom of the 'state of nature', "the mother gave suck to her children at first for her own sake, and afterwards, when habit had made them dear, for theirs." He thus claims that an innate desire, independent of socialization, leads to care for the child. Somewhat differently, Hobbes (1952, p. 155) understands children as the means to parental ends. Care, he explains, is repaid later with respect and financial support. Since children are not often viewed as a source of income today, some modern economists (Becker, 1960; Blake, 1973) have tried to define benefits from children similar to those from other commodities; there has been a fascinating debate on whether children are consumer durables. Regardless of which of these cases is used, this argument can only work if the desire to care for one's children is strong enough and permanent enough to insure their welfare.

The evidence for a biologically innate instinct to nurture is weak. What special feeling exists for the child one has given birth to fades within a few days. The stronger and more enduring concern of an adult for any child is deeply linked to that adult's previous nurturing experiences. Among primates, if the adolescent is separated from adults, and not pushed into caring for the younger members of the family group, it will later be unable to care for its own offspring. The too familiar abused child/abusive parent cycle confirms the link in human life between earlier experiences and ability to care for children. Biological instinct alone provides neither the desire nor the capacity to care adequately for human children (Maccoby and Jacklin, 1974).

The will to care for children instead depends on a process of socialization. A society valuing good childcare can mold its young members to follow its existing pattern. Such a process depends on continuity in social values. If these values change or break down, the attitudes transmitted can be altered, and the desire to care for children may be weakened.

Indeed, certain changes in our society may well be having such an affect on this sort of socialization. Feminism has launched a frontal attack on the process which pressures women into nurturing behavior. New options for entertainment and life-styles have been shown to cut into the time put into parent-child interactions (Waite and Stolzenberg, 1976; Sawhill, 1977). Lowered literacy and rising juvenile delinquency rates are tied in ways not fully understood to changes in the ways children are raised. It is not altogether clear that such changes in our society, its values, and the behavior of its members are to the net benefit of its children.

The argument from desire is thus caught in a bind. The desires referred to will only be adequate to provide for children if a pattern of pro-nurturing socialization is maintained. Maintaining such a pattern when it is being weakened by other forces will require a conscious effort. Yet this effort itself must be justified by an argument about why people ought to care about children. This argument must come from some other premise. If such an argument is not made, then as desire to care for children weakens, the care of children will erode, and this argument will be inadequate to solve the problem of rendering people able to use their liberty. Taken alone, the argument from desire is inadequate. If desire is strong enough to provide for children, it is because the pressures of society have led to parents who feel that they have no alternatives. If it is not that strong, then the children are not protected by its assumptions.

*

Reference to a contractual bond is a standard liberal way to establish obligations, and is indeed applied to providing care for children. The usual premise is that the parents' decision to cause the child's conception implied an agreement to take responsibility for its welfare. Mill (1859) and Kant (1952) both argue that conception obligates the parents. A popular anti-abortion argument shows the same conviction: the mother's bodily rights are said to have been alienated by her sexual activity that led to the conception.

Trying to define precisely what obligations the contract entails reveals its problems. If it is said that whatever is best for the child is required, regardless of conflicting parental desires, then conception becomes the alienation of liberty altogether. This sort of bond is one that liberals generally are unprepared to accept; it certainly does not provide the freedom of choices for the parents we are looking for. Instead, if it were taken seriously, very few people would choose to have children. The costs would simply be too high.   Rather, some more limited obligation seems to be called for. Yet the line cannot be acceptably drawn. To show why, let me select a level of obligation, and then show how it could be challenged. Let us suppose that what is required is that the parent assure the child food, clothing, shelter, and literacy. This constitutes a base level of both maintenance and development, yet limits what the parent is asked to do.

This solution is unsatisfactory for the child. It includes none of the close attention or the expense necessary to acquire any sort of job skills or develop further talents. It offers none of the physical and psychological contact necessary for the child's happiness and well-being. It cannot provide the confidence and ambition necessary for real achievement. The child will survive under these circumstances, and perhaps be prepared for a low grade job. Yet any further advance for the child or the society it will join will be impossible without the strictly voluntary decision of others to make further provision for the child.

Yet if we look to any expansion of the parental obligations, we are abrogating the parents' life choices and chances to fulfill their own goals. What has been asked so far is already a major drain on the parents, especially in the first years of a child's life. These messy feedings and dirty diapers are not things we would take on lightly as our regular employment for any small wage. The costs involved in raising several children can easily swallow most of the parents' income and absorb the greater part of their time away from the job where that income is earned. If we talk about the extension of what is asked of the parents any further, the vision of the parental automaton living only to work and attend to household duties, objected to by feminist critics of "super-mom" and repudiated by counter-culture opponents of life dominated by the work-ethic, looms before us.

The basic problem is that, like King Solomon in his classic dilemma, we cannot split the difference between our two concerns here in a way that will satisfy both goals. No redefinition of the contract can be better for one side without further harming the other, and yet this solution itself is unsatisfactory.

*

There are two other options open to us from among the great liberal thinkers. These are simpler and more quickly stated, and their problems are readily apparent.

John Locke (1952, p. 36) and other religiously inclined people argue that the care of children is a duty to God. For those with such a belief, this is an easily accepted justification, that will quickly still any anxieties they may have about other desires they may be unable to fulfill because of responsibilities to their children. The trouble is that such beliefs are not shared by all members of society. If the actions they require are imposed on non-believing parents, these parents are again denied chances to fulfill their own goals altogether. If the believers do not make such an imposition, and rely instead on evangelization and voluntary conversion to bring others around, this sort of ethical grounding provides no security for the children of the unconverted. Faith and obedience to God's command, however valid, is not common enough in our society to solve the problem of parents' liberty and children's needs.

The utilitarian approach would proclaim that the net pain and pleasure resulting to members of society should determine what care children should receive. Yet it is a standard criticism of utilitarianism that it will permit the interests of any one person to be over-ridden if there is a sufficient benefit to others (Rawls, 1971a). If the calculations of utility favor the child's needs, the parents' happiness may be ignored. If the parents' choices yield greater utility, the child has no guarantee against the sort of neglect that will preclude the full exercise of the benefits liberty is supposed to provide.

* * * *

These problems exist regardless of whether we accept the premises of any of these arguments. The contract puts a great deal of weight on a single act which is often done for its own sake, and collapses in case of rape or sexual ignorance, since one can hardly be bound without one's consent or knowledge. Duty to God is a credible ethical basis only to those with a strong and specific faith. The utilitarian argument has been badly dented, if not crushed, by years of criticism on other scores. Yet what I have argued here is not that any of these cases for child care is wrong, but only that each pushes us to a choice between parental freedom and the care the child needs to enjoy the benefits of freedom.

Yet I think this conflict poses a basic dilemma for those drawn to liberalism by its claims to protect the individual. It suggests one of two things, depending on how the conflict within any of these cases for child care is resolved. Either the sphere of individual choices is in fact a small one, where the fulfillment of sexual desire or the decision to have children at all can close many of one's other options, or, though a broad sphere of choices are open to individuals, it is dubious that those individuals will have the capacity to make use of the options available. While some may receive the sort of care that will enable them to use their liberty fully, in the latter situation others will not, and this situation will lead to major arbitrary inequalities. Neither of the possible conclusions sustains the sorts of power and freedom for individuals that has given liberalism such great appeal.

The conflict between respect for the parent and concern for the child is a special version of the usual liberal problem about human nature. The traditional liberal concludes that what must be reconciled are individual freedom and social order. On the one hand, individuals have separate, subjective goals and do not want to be interfered with by others pursuing conflicting goals. The problem is that they need the cooperation and forbearance of others to achieve these goals. The great tension is to find the level of order that permits the fulfillment of individual goals by allowing such cooperation without imposing so many rules that such fulfillment is precluded altogether (Unger, 1975).

In the case at hand, however, the question is not of the balancing of interests of one individual in freedom and order. There is no equivalence or reciprocity in what is at stake. The parent is asked to make a great sacrifice of chances to fulfill other goals, and receives a reward that is valuable only relative to the worth of other options. The child is asking for life, health, happiness, and a chance at any options at all, and can give little beyond love in return. As pointed out in the discussion of the argument from desire, it is contingent on social factors beyond the control of either party whether what the child can give the parent is of value to the parent; the satisfaction from nurturing is in large part a result of socialization. A simple trade-off of interests cannot provide the order the child needs to benefit from freedom; neither can it convince the parent that the order established is worth the freedom lost.

* * * *

With this problem in mind, I want to review John Rawls' treatment of the child care issue. His *Theory of Justice* involves an impressive and complex derivation of his views, ending up as a defense of a liberal-looking political liberty with a graft of limits on permissible economic inequalities. To justify this position, Rawls argues that the evaluation of moral principles must be made independently of special self-interest. Interests resulting from one's race, sex, class, age, skill, or particular life goals or notion of "the good" are "morally arbitrary," according to Rawls, and entitled to no advantage in defining what is just. He therefore argues that, in order for a set of rules of justice to be valid and neutral, they must be those that would be accepted in an "original position" where such interests were unknown. He devotes considerable effort to defining what would be known and not known in such a position and to explaining what it would be rational to accept as rules in such a situation. A "veil of ignorance" is imposed on the parties so that they do not know what position (race, class, age, taste, notion of the good, etc.) they will have in society. All they know is that they must think through what will give them the best chance to get what they want regardless of their position; they are required to assume "mutual disinterest," that is, not to concern themselves with whether others can achieve their differing goals. Rawls (1971b) believes that his particular set of rules of justice will emerge from this "original position," and that therefore they should be accepted in general.

Let us now look at how Rawls deals with the issue of children's needs. He requires that the parties in the original position assume that they are heads of families concerned for their offspring. If this were not assumed, Rawls would get disturbing results; parties could decide that this generation should squander resources and pollute the environment, live recklessly and forget future planning. The decision to include such a consideration of children is therefore necessary in order for Rawls (1971b, pp. 128-129) to derive rules that are just between two generations.

Yet here he has contradicted the situation he set up before. He has said that position in society is morally arbitrary, yet he places all parties in the original position in the role of responsible parents, a role they might not have in reality at all. His parties are to be mutually disinterested, but here they are to be concerned with precisely the goals of others. He claims that individual notions of the good are not to be considered here, and then insists that on this score a conviction about concern for children, which he holds but some other people may not, must be accepted by all. If Rawls is not to be dismissed as simply contradicting himself here, an explanation must be found for why this issue warrants special treatment.

The explanation can be supplied by combining good sense with an understanding Rawls already uses in other areas. He argues that what the parties in the original position must concern themselves with is the distribution of "primary goods," among which he includes "rights and liberties, opportunities and powers, income and wealth," and "a sense of one's own worth" (Rawls, 1971b, p. 92). Regardless of social position or particular personal goals, these are the means that everyone will need in order to pursue his ends (Rawls, 1971b). I think that parental concern for children merits exactly this treatment. If one is to achieve one's goals, whatever they may be, one first needs to have support and nurture in one's early years. Rawls (1971b, p. 128) must work this realization into his original position (though perhaps not quite in the way he does it, as he, himself, allows).

Rawls might also argue from his concern with the consideration of morally arbitrary interests in the selection of moral rules. Adults defending parental liberty and ignoring children's needs are acting from such an interest. What is required in the original position is that those worst off be treated as well as can be; children's vulnerability can place them in such a situation. Indeed, the insistence on such concern has an added strength here, because each adult has in fact been in that "worst off" position (Rawls, 1971b).

Rawls may not have followed this insight through in his own theory and weighed what impact such requirements would have on the exercise of the liberties that concern him. The list of liberties that can be exercised equally by all may be smaller than he thinks as a result of the constraints on parental individuals imposed by the protection of children. Yet he has still moved the problem forward, by establishing a standard of equality and neutrality that operates across generational lines. The protection provided the parents must not make liberty meaningless for the child. At the same time, that given to the child must not altogether enslave the parent. One must instead balance what each may achieve with what that allows to others, seeking that balance which provides maximum benefit possible for both.

* * * *

We do not have to accept Rawls' approach to ethics or his result in order to recognize what has happened with his treatment of children's needs. When we looked at the isolated situation of particular parents and chldren, there was a non-reciprocal relationship; there was no way to balance what was to be given and received on the two sides. But if we look in a larger context at both lives, we then find an identical need and can argue for an identical response. If the attraction of liberalism has been the concern with the freedom and fulfillment of the individual, this suggests what the response should be. For equality's sake, it must be that which will sustain the highest chance to make use of freedcm for all.

This standard can be read back into the desire, the contract, or the utilitarian argument (the argument from God may prove more difficult, as beliefs are still imposed from without). It may also be used within a Rawlsian original position to select rules. Exactly what standard will emerge from it for practical use will require some further detailed thought.

Yet the acceptance of this standard involves a shift in the understanding of individual nature. It asks that we recognize ourselves and our own actions as the necessary means to the ends of others. We must see individuals as both in need of the help of others and capable of giving the help others need. If acknowledging this, we leave this help as merely optional, we must then concede that our own capacity to benefit from our liberty is a mere fortunate and accidental gift from others. I doubt that this can constitute a solid basis for any secure benefits of liberty to any of us; liberalism then would have no promise, no appeal, independent of the inexplicable charity of individual parents. Seriously considering such obligations may require major change from the levels of liberty some liberal thought has defended. Yet I think this is merely an indication of the weakness of such thought. We must remember that if such liberals did not intend their theories to be applied to a small subgroup of humanity, then why has the major practical application of liberal standards indeed been confined to an adult male elite class? By an elaborate sleight of hand, these liberties have only had to apply to those capable of living on such terms; such special legal "persons" do not know the dependency of childhood, the limitations imposed on women by the bearing and rearing of children, or the problems of those without the property, skills and privileges to consider themselves independent. Yet all along these "persons" have relied on such "non-persons" for their credibility. Once we decide to confer the same rights on all, and the same consequences of the behavior of others, it may be more difficult to credit the amount of self-satisfaction the initial elite group set as a standard. If we try to float the part of the iceberg once hidden beneath the elite first fraction on the surface, the entire operation may sink.

The point of this paper is to clear the ground so that the exploration of the sort of liberty that can be credibly undertaken by all individuals equally may begin. Any effort to operate directly out of the justifications for requiring child care presented by the classical liberals will run directly up against objections to its impositions on parents or its neglect of children. Only if it is acknowledged from the start that the grounds of the discussion have changed can the conflict be understood and resolved. The question must no longer be simply one of specifying reasons to behave in a way beneficial to others, as the liberal discussion of freedom and order, and its methods of approaching this problem have done. Rather, it must be a question of balancing the roles we recognize ourselves to have, as individual pursuers of goals and also as givers and as receivers of nurture. Only this sort of concern will lead to an understanding of rights and duties that speaks responsibly to both the liberty of parents and the needs of children.

REFERENCES

Becker, G. S. An economic analysis of fertility. In *National Bureau of Economic Research's Demographic and Economic Change.* Princeton, N.J.: Princeton University Press, 1960, pp. 209-240.

Blake, J. Are babies consumer durables? In *Population Studies,* March, 1973.

Hobbes, T. *The leviathan. Great Books* edition. Chicago: Encyclopedia Britannica, 1952.

Kant, I. *The science of right. Great Books* edition. Chicago: Encyclopedia Britannica, 1952, pp. 420-421.

Locke, J. *Concerning civil government, Second essay. Great Books* edition. Chicago: Encyclopedia Britannica, 1952.

Maccoby, E. E., and Jacklin, C. N. *The psychology of sex differences,* Stanford, CA: Stanford University Press, 1974, pp. 215-219, 317-373.

Mill, J. S. *On liberty.* London: 1859.

Rawls, J. Justice as reciprocity. In S. Gorovitz (Ed.), *Utilitarianism.* Indianapolis: Bobbs-Merrill Co., 1971, pp. 262-267. (a)

Rawls, J. *A theory of justice,* Cambridge, MA: The Belknap Press, 1971, pp. 90-161. (b)

Rousseau, J. J. *Discourse on the origins of inequality.* Translation by G. D. H. Cole. *The Great Books of the World* edition. Chicago: Encyclopedia Britannica, 1952, p. 340.

Sawhill, V. Economic perspectives on the family. *Daedelus,* Spring, 1977, pp. 117-118.

Unger, R. M. *Knowledge and politics.* New York: The Free Press, 1975, pp. 64-67.

Waite, and Stolzenberg. Intended child-bearing and labor force participation of young women. *American Sociological Review,* 1976, 46, 235-252.

COMMENT:

Response to "Children's Needs and Parental Liberty:

A Liberal Contradiction and How to Escape from It"

William Dibrell

Department of Philosophy
Central Michigan University
Mt. Pleasant, MI 48859

There are two principal projects undertaken in "Children's Needs and Parental Liberty". First a wide variety of accounts of the moral dimension of the parent-child relationship are criticized under the catch-all heading of a "liberal conception". Second, having found the liberal conceptions wanting, a way to talk about the just relationship between parent and child is suggested.

There are many important points made in the paper; few of these can be done justice in a short discussion. Here I would like to first focus on some of the critical points made and bring out weaknesses in certain of the key ones; and second, show that the final proposal of the papers, the sketch of what the just relationship between parent and child is, leaves us with at least two ways to understand how we might escape the "liberal's" problem.

The liberal views on taking care of children, each discussed separately, are that:

> ....care fulfills parental desires, that it is required by
> contractual obligation to the child, that it is a duty to
> God, and that it follows from maximizing general utility.

The discussion of the first, I will argue, is inadequate because it does not force us to the conclusion the author recommends. The discussion of the second will be given some attention; although the author and I agree that the contractualist view is not plausible, I am not sure about the reasons given in the paper. Points made on the third view reveal an important confusion. Because the last view is given only token mention it will not be treated here.

Against the view that no moral coercion is required in order that parents care for children, because parents naturally want to, it is argued that:

(1) There is no innate desire to nurture.
(2) What nurturing behavior there is, is due to sociali-
     zation.
(3) Where nurturing socialization is weak, either some
     other means of guaranteeing parental interest in
     child care is forthcoming or children will go without
     the necessities required for well-being (or in terms
     preferred in the paper --for what will render people
     capable of using their liberty).
(4) Nurturing socialization is in a weakened state today.

Therefore:

(5) Either some other means of guaranteeing parental
     interest in child care is found or children will go
     without the necessities required for well-being (Lib-
     erally paraphrased).

What we ultimately are supposed to conclude from the considerations supporting the above argument is that what is required for insuring nurturing behavior now and in the future is a moral argument or principle which can take the place of nurturing socialization. This is drawn from the third and fourth premises of the above in a rather interesting way.

The argument from desire is thus caught in a bind. The desires referred to will only be adequate to provide for children if a pattern of pro-nurturing socialization is maintained. Maintaining such a pattern when it is being weakened by other forces will require a conscious effort. Yet this effort itself must be justified by a statement about why people ought to care for children. This argument must come from some other premise.

Even without a direct conditioning of a desire to nurture (I'm not even sure what such conditioning would be, given that nurturing is a complex phenomenon) there are many possible sources, both conscious and un-conscious, that work and probably will continue to work in favor of nurturing behavior. The other premise (a moral argument of some sort) may not be needed in the way the author seems to be suggesting.

Granting that no direct desire to nurture exists and that some aspects of nurturing socialization are changing, what possible motives could move a person to nurture another? The options seem to be many: (1) a moral argument (this option preferred by the author); (2) a desire for intimacy (one of the few opportunities in life for intimacy is between adult and child in the nurturing situation); (3) a desire for a well finished product, that is, a child one is proud of; (4) a child one can live with (children can be difficult to live with if they are not getting the nurture they need). I can offer no evidence here for these motives; however, if they are plausible, these together with others perhaps could account for continued nurturing behavior even in a heterogenous society, heterogenous with regard to childrearing patterns. Finally, none of the above mentioned motives is particularly weakened by being conscious.

There may be no way to make sense of an innate desire to nurture but some or all of the above-mentioned motives could provide the needed premise(s) sought by the author. This, of course, does not rescue the desire argument but (2)--(4) are not moral reasons and so to think we must have a moral reason to nurture is not established. There is no reason given in the paper to think that (2)--(4) could not shore-up a weakening nurturing socialization.

I share with the author a certain scepticism concerning the contractual account of parental obligation to nurture children. Contracts between adults grounded in formal or informal promises do seem to give a clear account of many moral relationships but there is something odd with this as an account of nurturing responsibilities. Although I would not defend the contractual account, it has been popular and the criticisms in "Children's Needs and Parental Liberty" are well worth comment.

The problem the author sees with a contractual account is that we cannot show how to satisfy both the desire for parental liberty and the full needs of children on that account. There can be no fair contract between parent and child.

It has been argued by some that the duty to nurture is grounded in a tacit commitment made in getting pregnant. Taken at one extreme, it is argued that this account would constitute a complete alienation of parental freedom. But at the point where parental liberty is taken seriously children suffer.

I have no disagreement with the first point. The second point deserves more discussion. Physically isolated parents may have no means to secure the benefits of liberty, poor parents may have little chance at the enjoyment of liberty, but surely these are problems of isolation and poverty, not of parenthood. The author mentions the problems of feedings and diapers. These are real problems and these and other demands do seem to be in conflict with parental liberty. However anyone who wanted to maintain the feasibility of the contractual view would only need a creative solution to child care problems to make meeting childrens needs compatible with parental liberty. A kibbutz system is one example of a creative solution.

Clearly if we have in mind a one adult/one child (or perhaps more than one child) working relationship, as Mill and Kant probably did, then the criticism that there is no way to satisfy the goals of parental liberty and child care at the same time is reasonable. I do not think the author has found any logical flaw in the contractual view, however. If we were to grant that the tacit agreement exists (on whatever basis) then there is nothing offered here to force a contractualist to abandon that position. Again the contractualist need only argue that parents are obligated to arrange some guarantee of child care, not necessarily arrangements at the cost of parental freedom.

In the summary of the problems with the liberal conception of the parent/child relationship the author makes a point which is relevant to the contract conception but which is not developed during the criticism of that position.

> A simple trade-off of interests cannot provide the order
> the child needs to benefit from freedom; neither can it
> convince the parent that the order established is worth
> the freedom lost.

If a trade-off of interests were the basis of some sort of tacit agreement between parent and child (even in a one child/one parent situation) the liberal conception would indeed appear attractive. The notion of interest is relatively clear. If I were to agree to take care of you and you me, then a reasonable bargain might be struck. Does such a bargain make sense in the case at hand? Clearly the author believes not, I am not as sure.

It is argued that there is no basis for reciprocity between parent and child. After all, the child can give *little more* than love in return for nurturing. (The value of love may be a bit underestimated here. For many, love is worth almost any cost given that for many it makes an otherwise meaningless life worthwhile.) This case is overstated because it is underdescribed. Consider the often heard criticism that "X is an ungrateful child" where X is an adult offspring. The point of such criticism depends on the intuition that parent-child relationships where nurturing has taken place are relationships which eventually obligate children. Reciprocity can indeed exist between parent and child and this can be seen if we take a more comprehensive look at parent child relationships that involves more than the rather one-sided early years. Ultimately the author and I do not disagree on this because a more comprehensive view of some sort is a basic goal of the paper.

With regard to the critical sections of the paper, one final point. It is claimed that there is a certain dilemma involved in the view that one ought to care for children out of duty to God. The dilemma is that where belief is not prevalent, then either religious people impose their beliefs on others or children are not protected. Because of this we are to believe that the view that taking care of children is right because of God's law, even if it were true, is not worth pursuing. The confusion this reveals is between two sorts of issues: The correct account of the moral obligations that exist between parent and child and the basis of these obligations, and an account that can serve to motivate parents to care for children. Hopefully the correct account of the moral dimension can motivate but I see no reason why this has to be the case. Suppose, for example, the principle of justice indicated in the last section of the paper to be the correct way to understand the moral side of the parent/child situation. Should this account be criticized because few people attend to the progress of philosophy (certainly fewer than attest faith in divine commands)?

In summary, there may be some way to salvage the desire argument. Here I have tried to indicate some possible ways. The desire argument is not a moral argument and if successful might indicate that no moral argument is needed for the protection of children. The contract view as well could be redeemed but this may well lead us to a position not unlike the one ultimately argued for in the paper and to be considered presently. The duty to God argument, I think, is rejected in an unreasonable way; the real problems that exist with such a view are not mentioned.

My final comments concern the positive proposal made in the paper. The proposal offers a guideline that any solution to the conflict between parental liberty and children's needs would need to satisfy.

The solution to the 'contradiction' offered in the paper is actually independent of its introduction through a discussion of Rawls. Because of this I will go directly to the proposal.

Although I am not sure that each position discussed under the guise of liberalism has the flaws suggested, it is argued that each account forces us to a choice between parental liberty or child care. This is seen as an exclusive choice. What makes this uncomfortable for the liberal is the liberal's concern for individual freedom, which is defeated by either choice. On the one hand, parents can limit their freedom and give a child all that is needed for a good chance at enjoying liberty, or on the other hand, parents may enjoy freedom and children suffer a loss that makes their chance of enjoyment small.

The reason for this problem is finally identified when we learn that the levels of liberty which have been the goal of liberals are unrealistic in a society that takes equality seriously. This is perhaps the most crucial point made in the paper and dictates the escape from the liberal "contradiction". The escape is to abandon the search for a large share of personal freedom in favor of a smaller share more equally distributed. As the author put it:

The point of this paper is to clear the ground for the exploration of what sort of liberty can be credibly undertaken by all individuals equally.

Finally, we must not forget the basic problem; children's needs appear to be in conflict with any large share of freedom for individual parents. We are now asked to solve this problem by thinking about the levels of liberty that may be enjoyed by all equally. It appears to me that this solution suggests at least two alternatives. Following the guideline suggested we are led to a situation where parents are destined to be rather unfree and children, in their turn, when they are parents; or we are left still concerned for large shares of liberty and looking for social arrangements which do not require that any individual parent bear all the responsibility for nurture.

RIGHTS OF CHILDREN, RIGHTS OF PARENTS,

AND THE MORAL BASIS OF THE FAMILY

Ferdinand Schoeman

Department of Philosophy
University of South Carolina
Columbia, SC 29208

*Reprinted from *Ethics* 91 (October 1980) by permission of the
University of Chicago Press copyright 1980
The University of Chicago. 0014-1704/81/9101-0001$01.00

> He lets it (the state) dictate to him what is possible or
> permissible, instead of stipulating, as an unruffled part-
> ner, what is to be stipulated to the state of every time,
> namely, what space and what form it is bound to concede
> to creaturely existence.
>
> Martin Buber

Because moral and social philosophy have concentrated almost exclusively on abstract relationships between people, emphasizing either individual autonomy or general social well-being, certain key aspects of our moral experience--those aspects which deal with intimate relationships--have been virtually ignored. It is with this relatively untilled terrain of intimate relationships that the following analysis is concerned. Specifically, I try to show (1) why traditional categories employed by philosophers misrepresent moral features of intimate relationships; (2) that the significance of intimate relationships is such as to morally insulate persons in such relationships from state obtrusions; and (3) that it is the significance of intimacy, and not just a concern for the best interest of the child, that is essential to understanding the basis of the parents' moral claim to raise their biological offspring in a context of privacy, autonomy, and responsibility.

The discussion focuses first on the notion of children's rights and child welfare, then critically reviews certain proposals for regarding parents as having rights to rear their children, and finally suggests that the right to a private and autonomous relationship with one's biological children stems from the importance of intimate relationships in general.

Philosophers debate whether children, especially infants, are the kinds of beings who can have moral rights, whether rights talk in general has any point unless the being to whom rights are ascribed is in a position to exercise choice (which infants are not), and whether ascribing some rights to beings commits us to ascribing others (i.e., must one have a whole packet of general rights or none at all, or may one ascribe certain rights to one kind of being and other rights to other kinds of beings?).(1) Not only have many of these abstract philosophical issues about rights been argued inconclusively, but for the most part we can do without talk about children's rights and can express ourselves instead in terms of the needs and welfare of (small) children and the duties of their parents. I shall regard it as given that parents have a duty to protect their children from abuse and neglect, both physical and emotional, recognizing that what should count as abuse or neglect for legal purposes is difficult to determine and may even change from context to context (Wald, 1974-75; 1977). Also I shall assume that if a parent or guardian fails to promote the child's interest at some threshold level of adequacy, a form of intervention, ranging from counseling to imprisonment of the parent as well as loss of parental rights to the child, may be legitimate.

There is a different and more practical reason for hesitating to stress the rights of infants, vis-a-vis their parents. We typically pay attention to the rights of individuals in order in order to stress their moral independence, the fact that one individual constitutes a limit on what others, whether well intentioned or not, may legitimately do. In other words, the language of rights typically helps us to sharpen our appreciation of the moral boundaries which separate people, emphasizing the appropriateness of seeing other persons as independent and autonmous agents. While such emphasis constitutes an important point when it comes to structuring relationships between older children, and their parents, it may obscure the real point of moral criticism intended in the case of parent-infant relationships. When we are tempted to admonish parents for morally failing in their relationship to their young children, it is presumably and usually because we find them not furnishing the love, attention, and security we think it every parent's duty to provide. We find them short on caring and intimacy and insensitive to the state of dependency and vulnerability into which children are born and remain for several years.

Ideally the relationship between parent and infant involves an awareness of a kind of union between people which is perhaps more suitably described in poetic-spiritual language than in analytic moral terminology. We *share ourselves* with those with whom we are intimate and are aware that they do the same with us (Buber, 1947; Burt, 1977). Traditional moral boundaries, which give rigid shape to the self, are transparent to this kind of sharing. This makes for non-abstract moral relationships in which talk about rights of others, respect for others, and even welfare of other is to a certain extent irrelevant.*(2)* It is worth mentioning that the etymology of 'intimate' relates it to a verb meaning 'to bring within,' and that the primary meanings of 'intimate' focus on this character of being innermost for a person. It is also worth mentioning that establishing such relationships tends to be the primary reason adults in our culture give for wanting and having children (Hoffman, 1978).

The danger of talk about rights of children is that it may encourage people to think that the proper relationships between themselves and their children is the abstract one that the language of rights is forged to suit. So, rather than encouraging abusive parents to feel more intimate with their children, it may cause parents in intimate relationships with their infants to reassess the appropriateness of their blurring the boundaries of individual indentity and to question their consciousness of a profound sense of identification with and commitment toward their families. Emphasis on rights might foster thinking about the relationship between parent and child as quasi-contractual, limited, and utilitarian in objective. Moreover, such emphasis tacitly suggests that the relationship is a one-way relationship aimed solely at promoting the best interest of the child.

It is worth noting that the dependency of the child is, in most parents' consciousness, directed at them. As they see it, their child needs *their* warmth and concern. Such a consciousness on the part of parents must be generally conducive to the attitudes we want to promote. To the extent that the state takes over primary responsibilities for the satisfaction of children's needs, we might speculatively anticipate a weakening in the parents' sense of responsibility for their children. As parents are made less important in the lives of their children, they will feel less accountable and act less responsively--in sum, express a diminished sense of commitment toward their children.

There are many circumstances when the independence of children, primarily older ones, ought to be stressed; for these circumstances stress on children's rights makes sense. But when it is the dependence and vulnerability of the child that we want to emphasize, as we unfortunately must at times do, some different moral strategy would be more appropriate. And when we become conscious of the possibility that intimacy here, as in other relations, is a two-way sharing of benefits, primary emphasis on the rights perspective becomes even more distorting. To avoid misunderstanding I wish to reiterate however that in recommending a different moral startegy I am not to be taken as denying that infants have rights, either in relation to their parents or in relation to abstract others. Rather, I am questioning the moral advantages of extolling the rights of infants in our consciousness of their most important relationships.

Let me try to articulate briefly the principles at which we have arrived, and then proceed to describe and execute the objective of this paper. As persons, children ought to be thought of as possessing rights, but as infants in relationship to their parents, they are to be thought of primarily as having needs, the satisfaction of which involves intimate and intense relationships with others. As against society, we might yet think of infants and parents as having rights to conditions which permit or encourage, or at least do not discourage, the social and material conditions conducive to parent-child intimacy--a point we will return to below. What I want to discuss primarily is the moral basis for thinking that biological parents have a presumptive right to keep their children under their care in the setting of privacy, autonomy, and responsibility which is usually accorded the family.

For purposes of this paper, I shall mean by 'family' an intense continuing and intimate organization of at least one adult and child, wherein the child is extensively and profoundly dependent on the adult, in which the adult supplies the child with its emotional and material needs, and in which the parent is dependent on the child for a certain kind of intimacy. This relationship is to be understood as moral, not biological. Furthermore, the family is to be understood as entitled to certain rights of privacy and autonomy. The right of privacy entitles the adults of the family to exclude others from scrutinizing obtrusions into family occurrences. The right to autonomy entitles the adults of the family to make important decisions about the kinds of influences they want the children to experience and entitles them to wide latitude in remedying what they regard as faults in the children's behavior. Neither the right to privacy nor the right to autonomy associated with the family is absolute. These rights are to be conceived as rights against society at large. In relation to the children, they impose upon parents the duty to employ considered judgments in taking into account the child's needs, and eventually his rights. But in large part, such duties are unenforceable by the state because of the rights of privacy and autonomy already mentioned.

Just how much discretion should be left to the parents--how wide should their latitude be in structuring the environment of their children? For theoretical reasons to be advanced below, I follow Professor Michael Wald and others in setting strict threshold conditions (amounting to a clear and present danger criterion) which must be met before coercive state intervention is permitted. Wald (1974-75, pp. 992-993, p. 1005) argues that coercive intervention should be authorized only if (1) serious physical or emotional harm to the child is imminent and (2) the intervention is likely to be less detrimental than the status quo. He cites several practical factors in justifying his recommended policy of restraint: (1) typically, good alternatives to unfortunate family circumstances are not available; (2) it is difficult to predict which circumstances will have harmful long-range effects; (3) there is a lack of consensus about proper methods of childrearing and the ideal end product of childrearing; and (4) our social commitment to diversity of life-styles requires a great deal of tolerance in what should be permitted.

While such factors reflect important desiderata, it is notable that concern for the parent appears to be irrelevant in Wald's article, as in much of the legal literature of recent vintage.*(3)* Though I find this exclusion of the parents' perspective peculiar, very widespread and in need of remedy, it is to a certain extent understandable. For the infant, the family as here defined involves an intimate relationship with at least one adult. Since the psychological evidence (Bronfenbrenner, 1975; Goldstein, Freud and Solnit, 1973) suggests that children need this type of relationship for their cognitive and emotional well-being, we may conclude that children must be provided with such an arrangement (or, if you prefer, that they have a right to it). But from the child's perspective it doesn't matter whether the adult who will become its psychological parent is also its biological parent.

In what follows, I shall focus on the parents' perspective and attempt to address this question: Why should the biological parents be thought to have a right to raise their child in an intimate setting even before it is determined that their child will fare best under their care and guidance (*however* 'faring best' is defined)? Ultimately, what I shall want to emphasize is that the functional, efficiency-oriented approach to the family found in much of the literature defending family autonomy represents neither the only nor the best assessment of the moral basis of the family.

It should, however, be noted that not all social theorists see the family as an institution worth preserving. For not only does it provide a context for abuse and brutality in which the law has traditionally declined to take an interest, but it interferes with what might be called 'equality of opportunity' because it makes children depend on the spiritual and material resources of the family they happen to be born into (Rawls, 1971, p. 511; Fried, 1978, pp. 150-155; Clark, 1978). Though these points do constitute genuine moral worries which are theoretically inseparable from family institutions, pursuing such worries is not part of my present interest, though they will be touched on in the final portion of the paper.

* * *

Since surprisingly little philosophical attention has been devoted to the moral meaning of intimate relationships such as arise in family setings,*(4)* it should prove a useful exercise to see just what can be said in behalf of the biological parents' right to raise their offspring, obvious though it may appear. The right of biological parents (hereinafter referred to as just 'parents') with which I am concerned is not a right to certain services from their children, but a right against all the rest of society to be indulged, within wide limits, to share life with the child and thus inevitably to fashion the child's environment as they see fit, immune from the scrutiny of and direction from others.

It might be impatiently suggested that parents' rights to raise their children stem from an evolutionary phenomenon: parents' natural affections for their offspring and their infants' needs make for something like a pre-established harmony of interests. Since everyone, or almost everyone, benefits from this arrangement, and since provisions can be made for those few biological anomalies in which natural passions and natural needs do not correlate, what better basis could there be for our traditional arrangement? The suggestion might be given added weight by calling to mind the reported deleterious effects of impersonal, institutional efforts at raising children.

Three comments are in order in response. First, it has been observed that parental attachments may be more the result of enculturation than we naively suppose (Aries, 1962; Skolnick, 1973, pp. 60-62). Second, there is sufficient evidence to suggest that not all alternative modes of distributing children involve impersonal institutions in which children languish emotionally and intellectually (Bronfenbrenner, 1975, pp. 46-48). Third, and philosophically most significant, I wish to consider what we would think parents' rights would amount to if means equal or superior to those parents can typically supply could be found for benefiting the child outside the biological parents' domain? Would parents still have a claim on their children, as against society? And if so, what would its basis be? Is the parents' right to their children contingent upon the biological family's being the most efficient arrangement for benefiting children? Or is there some less incidental account of parental prerogative? (As indicated above, most recent proponents of family autonomy and state restraint have argued that promoting the child's interest is the primary or sole basis of their advocacy.(5) Though I am in agreement with these policy recommendations, I find that more needs to be said about their justification.)

One not very plausible account for the parent's right, despite the fact that the account can be traced back to Aristotle, involves looking at the child as the property of the parent, analogous to teeth and hair which have fallen out.(6) Since the child is the product of material and labor supplied prenatally by the mother, the child would seem to be the natural possession *par excellence* but for the fact that this product is a person. (I suppose that those who think that the newborn infant is not yet a person (Tooley, 1972) would have an easy time thinking of the parent as entitled to the infant in Aristotelian fashion.)

Another justification for our current arrangements might follow these lines: so long as children are adequately cared for under our present practices, then we can take into account parental preferences. True, these preferences as such do not constitute rights, but in our way of allocating benefits, once children's needs are satisfied, a precondition we have set into our scheme, then preferences should count in our determination of which claims will be recognized as entitlements.

This account of the basis of parental rights is not contingent solely on the fact of benefiting children, but makes essential reference to parents as persons with preferences which must be considered so long as the child's basic needs are met. But ultimately this justification of parental right is not satisfying, for all that would be necessary to override it would be a showing of some increased benefit to children in non-parental settings. True, the needs of the children and the preferences of the parents go some way toward showing that it is the parents, and not someone else, that should have rights to their children. But if marginally more good resulted for children from alternative set-ups, this fact could immediately outweigh parental preferences and militate against according parents' rights. I take it as a given that a parent's stake in her relationship to her children is based on something more profound than parental preferences, even when we add to such preferences a realistic scepticism about the state's competence to distribute children in a manner more advantageous to the children.

In discussing sources of authority, Elizabeth Anscombe (1978) recently has proposed that institutionalized practices which carry out important tasks thereby gain legitimization or authority. Miss Anscombe suggests that the parent's rights to obedience from her child and respect for her exercise of discretion from others outside the family evolve from the manifestly crucial functions parental authority performs. So long as families maintain their position of being necessary conditions for the performance of such functions, Miss Anscombe's argument captures common sense and preserves family entitlements. But the emergence of alternative, possibly superior (relative to the child), means of rearing children would deprive the family of its position as being necessary, and hence undermine its claim to rightful autonomy, except on a customary basis.

We must note that these last two theories, both fundamentally utilitarian, are by no means clearly false or even clearly wanting. Whether they are fully adequate must be judged in light of alternative dimensions we can manage to elaborate.

* * *

We have yet to supply the justification of three institutions which we, for the most part, take for granted. Why should the family be accorded rights to privacy and autonomy? Why should the family be given extensive responsibilities for the development of children? Why should the *biological* parent be thought entitled to be in charge of a family? I believe that the notion of intimacy supplies the basis for these presumptions, and would like now to elaborate an account more successful than those mentioned in the preceding section. But first I shall try to show why intimacy requires privacy and autonomy as its setting, and second why we should recognize a right to intimate relationships. I shall then argue that the parent's right to raise her children in a family stems naturally from the right to engage in intimate relationships, even when recognition of this right involves some comparative cost to the child.

At an earlier point in this paper, I described an intimate relationship as one in which one shares one's self with one or more others. It was suggested that via intimate relationships one transcends abstract and rather impersonal associations with others and enters personal and meaningful relationships or unions. Such relationships are meaningful because of the personal commitments to others which are constitutive of such relationships. For most people, such unions are not only central to defining who one is, but human existence would have little or no meaning if cut off from all possibility of maintaining or reestablishing such relationships. Though such relationships are undoubtedly culturally dependent in the form they take, they constitute one's roots in life or attachment to living even when the concerns of the relationship are independent of, or hostile to, the values of the culture and the welfare of others.(7)

Practically speaking, the strength or very possibility of intimate relationships varies inversely with the degree of social intrusion into such relationships generally tolerated.(8) The prospects of state intervention into a relationship depresses the sense of security of the relationship. It makes people hesitant to see their interests fused with those of another (Goldstein et al., 1973). The intimate sharing described as part of these close unions presupposes limited sovereignty on the part of those reaching out to and sharing with others to determine the conditions of the relationship. Without privacy and autonomy the relationship would be neither secure nor on the parties' own terms.

Privacy and autonomy provide the moral space within which concrete personal relationships can be formed independent of general social concerns. To give the state authority to regulate such relationships would inevitably result in a redirection or 'socialization' of these relationships. We see evidence of this shift in doctor-patient relationships wherein doctors are seen increasingly to have direct responsibilities for the health of the population, and not for the comfort of specific patients.(9) While it would be presumptuous of me to declare, without marshalling evidence, that such shifts in loyalties ought on balance to be forestalled, it should be recognized and made part of our reckoning that systems of meaning can be uprooted in the process of realigning commitments.

Professor Lon Fuller (1969 a, b) has devoted considerable attention to understanding principles of human association and the law's varying capacities to regulate diverse kinds of relationships. Fuller distinguishes two different principles of association, the relative mix of which in any particular relationship determining what the relationship is. One principle is shared commitment, the other is the legalistic. The legalistic aspect is that which makes explicit rules of duty and entitlement (Fuller, 1969a, pp. 6-8). While the former principle, shared commitment, is concerned with conditions of mind and degrees of inner resolution, the latter is concerned with overt, clearly definable acts (Fuller, 1969a, p. 14). As the legalistic principle comes to dominate the parties' image of their relationship with one another, the element of shared commitment tends to sink out of sight. State intervention into relationship, Fuller argues, tends to shift the emphasis of the relationship in the direction of formality and abstractness (Fuller, 1969a, p. 21). The very act of precisely sorting things out in conformity with the legalistic paradigm tends to wring out aspects of inner commitment (Fuller, 1969b, p. 34)

Fuller's analysis helps to indicate why intimate relationships must be accorded privacy and autonomy and why they deserve social and legal respect. Friendship, love and family represent institutions in which intimacy is central to the relationships. Because of the importance of these relationships to the self-image and meaningful existence of most people, the state, before intruding, should impose high standards like the clear and present danger test suggested above. The state should be very chary in trying to alter the terms of such relationships to serve social ends. As has been noted by others, while the state is quite limited in its ability to promote relationships, it can do much to destroy them (Goldstein, 1972, p. 637). The state threatens relationships by requiring the parties to think of themselves as primarily serving public ends and as having public duties. This intrusion beclouds the integrity of the trust and devotion that can arise between people. Though it may be that important ends are served by such intrusion, as, for example, when doctors are required to report suspected cases of child abuse, we should be willing at the very least to acknowledge the cost of such intrusions. Parenthetically, it is worthwhile noting that the state does find certain relationships privileged, like the lawyer-client relationship, even at some possible cost to public welfare.

Yet to show the importance of intimate relationships, even family relationships as characterized in this paper, is not yet to show that parents have any rights to their children. After all, adults can establish intimate relationships with other consenting adults. Assuring that children become part of an intimate and secure setting is not the same as assuring the biological parents of these children that they (the parents) will be part of this same setting.

The alternative to the natural and customary distribution of children to their parents is some kind of social decision determining who goes with whom. Such distribution schemes are not necessarily, from the perspective of the infant, inimical to intimacy, as the institution of early adoption establishes. But it does or may preclude such kinds of intimacy for those who are determined by popular social criteria to be not maximally fit or not maximally competent to really provide children with all that they need or can use. But such a preclusion would, I believe, represent an interference with a practice from which intimacy and with it life-meaning typically emerge.

Once this is acknowledged, I am not sure what else would have to be added before we could come to speak of such structures of meaning as investing individuals with a moral right to be free from intentional interferences. Presumably, part of what would be required would include a moral comparison of various elaborated social structures. Because I am not equipped to articulate such comparisons, I shall speak of moral claims, as distinct from moral rights, claims being justified on the basis of their importance to our present conditions. So rather than arguing that we have a moral right to family autonomy or that we should have a positive legal right to such autonomy, I will be content in encouraging a kind of appreciation for the meaning of the family over and above the recognition of its accomplishments as an institutions dedicated to the production of future citizens.

Though the infant is non-consenting, it does not represent a denial of its rights for it to be entrusted to its parents even if better surroundings are available, since we are assuming that minimal conditions for adequate upbringing will be met. (We are, after all, utilizing something like the clear and present danger test to protect children from abuse and neglect, though of course such standrads raise problems of their own.(10)) To set terms for emotional parenting more stringent than is required for the protection of children from abuse and neglect constitutes an interference in a person's claim to establish intimate relations except on the society's terms. We have already indicated reasons for thinking that such regulation transforms relationships into less intimate ones. Such allocation schemes could redefine the parenting role as one in which the objective is abstract social well-being, not intimacy and the kind of meaning found in commitment to particular others.

The practice of entrusting children to their parents ultimately limits the control of society to determine the life-style and beliefs of persons because it means there would be one important relationship a person could be in without the requirement of prior social approval. Since society cannot determine and should not try to determine who may have intimate relationships with whom, if a person chooses to have his relationships in a family setting, society should not interfere since that kind of choice is essential to intimate relationships in general.

Thus, as a way of transcending oneself and the boundaries of abstract others, and as a way of finding meaning in life and as a means of maintaining some kind of social and moral autonomy, the claim to freedom from scrutiny and control in one's relations with others should be thought of as a moral claim as important as any other that can be envisioned. It must not be up to society in general, without there being some special cause, to decide whom one can relate to and on what terms. Other things being equal, parents consequently are entitled to maintain their offspring and seek meaning with and through them.

Though there are many questions which plague the account of family privacy here advanced, there is one in particular I would like to raise and address because of the direction it suggests for further reflection. The problem is: Given the subjective basis of the importance of intimate relationships, how can it be used to defend privacy and autonomy within families in general since the members of many families manifestly fail to invest their relationships with the requisite kind of personal meaning? And looked at the other way, there are surely many relationships in which personal meaning is sought and found, but to which the law is and, as things stand, ought to remain oblivious. If we distinguish the substance from the structure of an intimate relationship, we can see the question as requiring that we justify our practice of according privacy and autonomy to people who comply only in form to meaningful relationships while denying them to other people who may be far more committed to one another but who fail to establish the formal, institutional accoutrements of close relationships.

In responding, we need to note that the state cannot employ the subjective or substantial criterion when judging whether privacy and autonomy are appropriate for a particular relationship. The state is unequipped to investigate souls, and even were it so equipped, it could set its standards and make its particular findings only at the expense of just the kind of intrusions which shatter the very relationships it would be seeking to protect. Consequently, it is essential that there be formal or ritualized means of 'privatizing' a relationship, on the basis of overt acts or habits, even though inevitably there will result two tragic consequences: Abuses of privileged privacy and intrusions into some morally deserving relationships.

Ultimately, what is being suggested here is that it is important for states to respect relationships the very point of which is to insulate the people so related form ordinary forms of social and legal control. The state needs to be cognizant of those means--culture specific and conventional though not necessarily popular--that people have for finding meaning; and it must do so by means of clearly structured and easily recognizable institutions of relating. It can do neither more nor less without changing the nature or possibility of such relationships. Any effort to gauge the meaning of a particular relationship that goes beyond superficially based presumptions will involve distorting intrusions. Consequently, what is important about the biological relationship between parents and children is the *conventional meaning* given to it within our culture. Since people do in fact vest the biological relationship with meanings of intimacy, the state must not interfere with that relationship unless the danger is serious, clear and imminent.

Most justifications of family autonomy that one finds in the literature have concentrated on the child's perspective and stressed the point that families, as we know them, represent the least detrimental means we have of child rearing. In contrast, my arguments on behalf of the family, though concerned with the well-being of children, have had as their chief focus an idea of human relationships. Consequently, even if someone could demonstrate that there were some more efficient and effective institution for promoting the interests of children than the traditional family, I would still think that the family would have a strong, though rebuttable, moral presumption in its favor. The implications of such a presumption extend beyond requiring high threshold conditions before the state intervenes coercively into family affairs. The presumption would seem to imply that the state should not, to the extent possible, make the family and parental responsibility otiose through the provision directly to children of services which parents are in a position to supply.

One final point. Some people have argued recently that while the family deserves the privacy and autonomy suggested above, in case the state is presented with a claim of rights violation by a child, the state is in a situation in which it must either find for the child or find for the parent, and that accordingly it should make its decision by regarding the interests and rights of the parents and child as being on a par. However plausible this picture of restricted options appears, it ignores one crucial alternative. Parents can be seen as representing the interests of the family as an integrated whole in addition to representing their own particular interests. Though entrusting individuals with the responsibility of making judgments for the common good when their own interests are involved does not accord well with modern constitutionalist conceptions, we should not discount on a *priori* grounds the prospects for such an arrangement being feasible in certain contexts. The context in which such kinds of representation can work are those in which people in fact conceive their roles and their very identity as requiring such an attitude. Informal custom rather than formal institutional means of resolving conflict of interest generally sufficed in ancient and medieval government, imbued with notions of virtues and right as they typically were.*(11)*

Given social expectations and governmental non-interference, important ends are served by relegating to parents the right to decide important issues for the family even when what is at issue is a conflict in interests between the parent as individual and the child as individual. I have been suggesting that if the state takes the attitude that conflict within families are the same as conflicts anywhere, the state will be adding considerable impetus to the evolution of the family as a non-intimate structure.

ACKNOWLEDGEMENT

I wish to express my appreciation to Amy Gutmann, Iris Young, Sanford Levinson, Glen Brooks, Tim Scanlon, Nora Bell, Herbert Fingarette, Rosamond Sprague, Mark Sheldon, Barry Loewer, Eugene Long, Patrick Hubbard, and Sara Schechter-Schoeman for helpful criticisms on earlier versions of this paper.

REFERENCES

Anscombe, E. On the source of authority of the state. *Ratio,* 1978, *20,* 1-28.

Aries, P. *Centuries of childhood: A social history of family life.* New York: Alfred Knopf, 1962, Pt. I, Ch. II, pp. 398-407.

Aristotle *Nichomachean Ethics,* 8:12.

Aristotle *Politics,* 1:1.1, 1:3.6, 1:7.16-17, 1:13.15, 3:6.7, 3:9.9-15.

Baier, K. The right to life. Paper delivered at Conference on Human Rights and Justice, University of North Carolina at Greensboro, Spring, 1978.

Blackstone, W. (Ed.) *Philosophy and environment crisis.* Athens: University of Georgia Press, 1974.

Bourne, R., and Newberger, E. 'Family autonomy' or 'coercive intervention'? Ambiguity and conflict in the proposed standards for child abuse and neglect. *Boston University Law Review,* 1977, *57,* 670-706.

Bronfenbrenner, U. *A report on longitudinal evaluation of preschool programs,* Vol. II. *Is early intervention effective?* D.H.E.W. Publication No (OHD), 75-25, 1975.

Bronaugh, R. (Ed.) *Philosophical law.* London: Greenwood, 1978, pp. 167-187.

Buber, M. Dialogue. In M. Buber (Ed.), *Between man and man.* London: Routledge and K. Paul, 1949.

Burt, R. Developing constitutional rights of, in, and for the children. In M. K. Rosenheim (Ed.), *Pursuing justice for the child.* Chicago: University of Chicago Press, 1976, pp. 225-245.

Burt, R. The limits of the law: Can it regulate health care decisions? *The Hastings Center Report,* 1977, *7(6),* 29-32.

Clark, L. Privacy, property, freedom and the family. In R. Bronaugh (Ed.), *Philosophical law.* London: Greenwood, 1978, pp. 167-187.

Feinberg, J. Duties, rights, and claims. *American Philosophical Quarterly,* 1966, *3,* 137-144.

Feinberg, J. The nature and value of rights. *Journal of Value Inquiry,* 1971, *4,* 263-277.

Feinberg, J. The rights of animals and unborn generations. In W. Blackstone (Ed.), *Philosophy and environmental crisis.* Athens: University of Georgia Press, 1974.

Flathman, R. E. *The practice of rights.* Cambridge: Harvard University, 1976.

Fried, C. *Medical experimentation: Personal integrity and social policy.* Amsterdam: North-Holland Publishing Company, 1974.

Fried, C. *Right and wrong.* Cambridge: Harvard University Press, 1978.

Fuller, L. Two principles of human association. In Pennock and Chapman (Eds.), *Nomos Volume XI: Voluntary Associations,* Yearbook of the American Society for Political and Legal Philosophy. New York: Atherton Press, 1969, pp. 3-23. (a)

Fuller, L. Human interaction and the law. *American Journal of Jurisprudence,* 1969, *14,* 1-36. (b)

Garvey, J. Child, parent, state and the due process clause: An essay on the Supreme Court's recent work, *Southern California Law Review*, 1978, *51*, 769-822.

Gierke, O. *Political theories of the middle ages.* Cambridge: Beacon Press, 1922.

Goldstein, J. Finding the least detrimental alternative. In *Psychoanalytic study of the child.* New Haven: Yale University Press, 1972, pp. 626-641.

Goldstein, J., Freud, A., and Solnit, A. *Beyond the best interest of the child.* New York: Free Press, 1973, *supra* note 6, 7, and 25.

Gutmann, A. *Children, paternalism, and education: A liberal argument.* Princeton, N.J.: Princeton University Press, photocopied.

Hafen, B. Children's liberation and the new egalitarianism: Some reservations about abandoning youth to their 'rights'. *Brigham Young University Law Review*, 1976, 605-658, esp. 644-670.

Hart, H. L. A. Are there any natural rights. *Philosophical Review*, 1955, *64*, 175-191.

Hart, H. L. A. Bentham on legal rights. In A. W. Simpson (Ed.), *Oxford essays in jurisprudence: Second series.* Oxford: Oxford University Press, 1973, 171-201.

Hegel *Philosophy of right*, sections 158-164 and 238-341.

Hoffman, L. The value of children to parents--a national sample survey. Paper read at the October, 1978 meetings of the American Public Health Association.

Kern, F. *Kingship and law in the Middle Ages.* Oxford: Blackwell, 1948.

Lyons, D. Rights, claimants, and beneficiaries. *American Philosophical Quarterly*, 1969, *6*, 173-185.

McCathren, R. Accountability in the child protection system: A defense of the proposed standards relating to abuse and neglect. *Boston University Law Review*, 1977, *57*, 707-731.

Melden, A. I. *Rights and persons.* Berkeley: University of California Press, 1977, pp. 166-224.

Murphy, J. Rights and borderline cases. *Arizona Law Review*, 1977, *19*, 228-241.

Nozick, R. *Anarchy state and utopia.* New York: Basic Books, 1974.

Rawls, J. *A theory of justice.* Cambridge: Harvard University Press, 1971.

Rosenheim, M. K. (Ed.) *Pursuing justice for the child.* Chicago: University of Chicago Press, 1976.

Schrag, F. Justice and the family. *Inquiry*, 1976, *19*, 193-208.

Skolnick, J. *The intimate environment.* Boston: Little, Brown Publishing Company, 1973.

Solnit, A. See Goldstein, J., Freud, A., and Solnit, A.

Tooley, M. Abortion and infanticide. *Philosophy and public affairs*, 1972, *2*, 37-65.

Wald, M. State intervention on behalf of 'neglected' children: A search for realistic standards. *Stanford Law Review*, 1974-1975, *27*, 985-1040. (Reprinted in *Pursuing justice for the child*, M. K. Rosenheim (Ed.). See M. Rosenheim.)

Wald, M. Symposium: Juvenile justice. *Boston University Law Review*, 1977, 57, 663-731.

FOOTNOTES

(1) It is perhaps worth mentioning two related conceptual proposals for thinking about rights of children in response to the worries just indicated. First of all, Professor Bruce Hafen (1976) has suggested that we distinguish between two kinds of legal rights: (1) legal rights which protect one from undue interference by the state and from the harmful acts of others; and (2) legal rights that permit persons to make choices which have significant long term consequences--choices which seem to require mature capacities. These latter rights, called 'choice rights', are not, Hafen argues, appropriately ascribed to children. Consequently children's rights include the right to be protected from their own immaturity. Arguing to a similar effect, Professor Jeffrey Murphy (1977) has distinguished between 'autonomy rights' and 'social contract rights'. While the role of autonomy rights is to mark out the special kind of treatment which is appropriate toward autonomous rational persons whose choices are to be respected, the role of social contract rights is to guarantee legally the satisfaction of certain moral claims--ones rational agents under a veil of ignorance would find morally reasonable to insure. The child's right to paternalistic treatment, argues Murphy, loses its sense of paradox when understood as a social contract right.

(2) See Hegel. But note that for Hegel, once civil society makes its appearance, the abstract relations which aim at social well-being come to predominate over rights of intimacy and privacy. Aristotle, though generally subordinating family relationships to the goals of the polis, does describe children as "another self" of the parents (*Nichomachean Ethics*, 8.12), and also says that justice is irrelevant between friends (*Nichomachean Ethics*, 8.1).

(3) Amy Gutmann has argued that the *only* legitimate account for the family in the liberal state is the best-interest-of-the-child account in an unpublished manuscript, "Children, Paternalism, and Education: A Liberal Argument."

(4) Notable exceptions include Francis Schrag (1976), Melden (1977) and Fried (1978).

(5) Hafen (1976, 651), Wald (1974-5), Goldstein, Freud, and Solnit (1973, 7 and 25).

(6) Aristotle adopts the view that the child is the parent's possession, actually comparing the child to a tooth and a piece of hair (*Nichomachean Ethics*). But since Aristotle also thinks that slaves are possessions toward which the master owes nothing, and since vis a vis their children Aristotle's view is that parents ought to make their benefit

primary (Politics 3:6.7), it is not the best of analogies that Aristotle picked to represent his own views of parent-child relationships. For a critical discussion of Locke's treatment of this view, see Robert Nozick (1974, pp. 287-291). It may be worth noting that we often use the possessive idiom to indicate a special relationship to something and not legal or moral proprietorship. An architect might say of a building, "That's mine!" or a child might say of a teacher, "That's my teacher," without suggesting ownership.

(7) Though Aristotle observed that the aims of friendship and political association differed, the former aiming at common social life and the latter at the good life, he regarded friendship as on a lower moral plain than political association and as a means to the good life. See *Politics* 3:9.9-15 and 1:1.1.

(8) Aires (1962) argues that our modern notion of the intimate family emerged as sociability (neighborly relations, friendships, and traditional contacts) diminished and presupposed a sense of the importance of privacy.

(9) Charles Fried (1974) represents a critical discussion of such proposals.

(10) In the Boston *University Law Review*, 1977, 57, see: Synopsis: Standards relating to abuse and neglect, pp. 663-668; Bourne and Newberger, pp. 670-706; and McCathren, pp. 707-731. Also, in M. K. Rosenheim (1976), see: Burt, R., pp. 225-245.

(11) See Fritz Kern and Otto Gierke. Also, John Garvey has argued that this policy toward the family is consistent with Supreme Court decisions, in "Child, parent, state and the due process clause: An essay on the Supreme Court's recent work" (1978).

COMMENT:

Response to "Rights of Children, Rights of Parents,

and the Moral Basis of the Family"

J. H. Pillote

Department of Philosophy
Central Michigan University
Mt. Pleasant, MI 48859

As I understand Professor Schoeman's paper, he seems to be making three main points: (1) the usual analysis of parent-child relationships in terms of rights and obligations does not do justice to the nature of the relationship; (2) an analysis which realizes the importance of intimacy (i.e., relationships which involve sharing ourselves with others) in the parent-child relationship more adequately captures the essential nature of the relationship; and (3) relationships of intimacy, because they require privacy and autonomy, are best maintained and fostered when coercive state intervention is prevented.

From these points, he reaches the conclusion that parents have a moral claim to raise their (biological) children without coercive intervention by the state, provided that certain basic conditions are met, e.g., that the child's basic needs are being met, the child is not physically or emotionally abused, etc.

Schoeman is careful to insist that none of this requires us to deny that children have rights. As he says, *qua persons* children have rights, but *qua children* it is more important to focus on their needs. He also states that to the extent that we relate to others in quasi-contractual terms, our sense of commitment is lessened. In relationships of intimacy, e.g., parent-child, wife-husband, lovers, friends, etc., the relationship is changed--even, at times, destroyed--when rights and obligations significantly enter the relationship. I believe that recently publicized cases of "palimony" suits and pre-nuptial contracts illustrate this point.

There is a great deal in Schoeman's paper that I agree with. In this age of instant and disposable relationships it is refreshing to see someone realize that relationships of intimacy are important to cultivate even though they require considerable effort to develop and grow.

However, since time is short, I think it will be more productive to restrict my comments to certain questions that I believe need answers, rather than focus on the many areas of agreement I have with Schoeman.

The first question I have is: is it true that the family does in fact provide the intimate relationship for its members that is being claimed? I believe that, in many instances, the answer is clearly affirmative. Most parents love their children and derive great pleasure from them. I believe the same can be said of children's love for their parents. Even in cases where we may believe, from our perspective as "outsiders", that there is no warmth in the relationship between parent and child, there still may be considerable love between them and a genuine "sharing of oneself" with each other.

However, we have to admit, not the possibility, but the actuality, of child abuse where, for whatever reason, the parent is not exhibiting or feeling love and concern for the child. Now in cases where the abuse is considerable enough so as to deprive the child of its basic needs, Schoeman admits the legitimacy of state intervention. But what about the lesser cases? What about the cases where the child's basic needs are being fulfilled, but the child is deprived of love, at least to the extent that the child *feels* unloved? (We could also ask here about the cases where the parent is deprived of the child's love.) That these cases occur, and occur frequently, is testified to by the number of children who run away from home each year and the number of parents who spend only a nominal amount of time with their children.

However, perhaps the situation is not so bleak as it appears in these cases. There is no reason to assume that the family is the sole source of intimacy for individuals. Children, as well as adults, find friendships and love relationships of various kinds outside the family. Even in families where parents and children have great affection for each other there is no reason to ignore the fact that they may each have other relationships in which considerable affection and sharing of oneself occurs.

There still remain cases, though, where the child's well-being is not being provided for in the family. To talk here of the parents' moral right to raise their children makes sense if we consider state intervention on behalf of the child the only viable alternative. Surely, given our present society and the options it provides, i.e., state institutions, foster homes, etc., the child is probably best provided for by his/her own parents. But if viable alternatives were available, I believe more defense would be required to support the claim that parents have a moral right to raise their children. Perhaps if we really thought that children were important we, as a society, would place more value on good child-care from infancy through adolescence, and we would not be caught in the dilemma of leaving a child in a family where his/her well-being was not being provided for adequately or removing the child from the family and placing it in an environment where there is not likely to be much more provided than basic custodial care. Perhaps we need to look for ways to *supplement* the family in the child's life, rather than *replace* it.

My next question has to do with the unequal opportunities afforded children of different families. Schoeman recognizes that "making children depend on the spiritual and material resources of the family they happen to be born into" constitutes a "genuine moral worry." However, I do not find any further discussion of this problem in his paper. If preserving and strengthening the family has as one of its consequences the further entrenchment of basic inequalities in society, perhaps we ought to examine more seriously alternatives to the family.

Approaching the problem from the parents' view, rather than the child's, I have other questions. Is the picture of the family as presented in Schoeman's paper a realistic one? The form of today's family is changing. No longer is the predominant pattern the traditional nuclear family, with mother at home taking care of the children and the household, and father working outside the home. Today, this model is becoming a rarity. It is more likely that if it is a two-parent family, both parents are working outside the home. And it is becoming more and more common to have single-parent households. While it is certainly possible to have intimacy between parent and child in these circumstances, I believe we would all agree that it is more difficult and considerable effort needs to be devoted to maintaining the relationship.

Also, as more and more women are demanding a chance to pursue goals in addition to motherhood, to require even more of them would further limit their chances to fulfill the other goals. I am speaking of women here for two reasons. I believe it is still usually the woman upon whom the responsibilities regarding children fall in a two-parent family, and I believe in most one-parent families it is the mother who is the parent. Let me stress: I am not advocating that women continue to play this role, nor am I denying that many men are spending more time with their children. I am simply claiming that, at present, the responsibilities of child-rearing still fall mainly on women and that to increase the responsibilities increases the burdens on women. It seems to me that stressing the importance of intimacy in families might be parallel to stressing the importance of "romantic love" in marriage, i.e., both are ways, intended or not, of keeping women "in their place."

While we do not have enough time to go into a detailed examination of the history of the family, I believe it is clear that its forms and functions have varied throughout history and vary even at the present time in different societies. The family as we primarily know it, i.e., the nuclear family, serves the function of our particular social and economic system.   The family is no longer a productive unit in the sense of producing goods for consumption or trade, but is more of a reproductive unit in at least three ways: (1) it reproduces the species; (2) it reproduces the next generation of workers and citizens; and (3) it reproduces-- "replenishes"--today's workers.

This last function of the family is one that ties in with the claim that family relationships are primarily relations of intimacy. For, on the model suggested, it is the institution of the family, and the various relationships within it, that serves to provide the basic needs for intimacy that individuals have, both as children and as adults.

However, if sharing oneself with others is as important as Schoeman suggests it is--and I am in basic agreement with him on that point-- perhaps we are looking in the wrong place for that need to be fulfilled. Perhaps the family, in its present forms, is not capable of fulfilling the basic intimacy needs of its various members.   To demand of the family that it be a primary source for intimacy and that the state not intervene except in exceptional circumstances is to allow the very real possibility that we are abandoning children to the vagaries of the particular family they happen to be born into.   Since the state can offer no genuine alternative to the family, the question of state intervention is funda- mentally irrelevant.   Perhaps our collective energy would be better directed toward developing other ways of providing for these needs of intimacy than is presently available.

THE IDENTITY OF THE CHILD AND THE RIGHT TO INTEGRATION

Joseph Evans

Immaculata College
Immaculata, PA 19345

In this paper I propose to develop a principle (a philosophical principle) which bears directly on the rights of children and which should prove useful to many people working in many different fields. The principle states that when a free society imposes its values upon people and particularly upon children, then a division arises in individual consciousness and with it arises the right of the individual to achieve integration. This right is prior to all others with the exception of the right to life itself.

The rights of children must be determined before schooling, family life, cultural life, and even economic and political life can be organized in a more satisfactory way. In turn, these rights cannot be determined until the question of the identity of the child has been answered more satisfactorily. Philosophy provides a perspective in which the question can be answered more fully than it has been up to the present time.

I shall claim that there is a prevailing notion of the identity of the child, and that this notion can be identified and analyzed. I shall further claim that a more realistic and comprehensive notion can be developed using the prevailing one as a point of departure, and using the knowledge that has become available in recent years in a number of disciplines. The right to achieve integration is based on the more adequate notion of identity.

The prevailing notion of childhood is ordinarily traced back to Rousseau, to his theory of education, and to his followers in the field of education (Silberman, 1970, p. 214; Johnson, Collins, Dupuis, and Johansen, 1973, p. 246; Meyer, 1975, p. 214). More recent history reveals a convergence on this notion. Studies of adolescence, education, childhood, the family, and popular culture show that there is the same romantic idea

219

of the child which is prominent in each area and that this prominence has only been intensified during the last half of the twentieth century (Shorter, 1977; Kett, 1977; Greenleaf, 1978; Rakoff, 1978).

When this notion is analyzed a number of features stand out very clearly. The child, as well as the adolescent, is seen in terms of a store of positive personal and social experiences. The features of this identity are: it is cumulative, it is experiential, it is strictly positive, and it is sufficiently broadly social that it includes the personal.

These features are best seen in operation. According to this conception of childhood a particular person is to be formed, in his earliest years, by providing him a series of positive experiences. At home, with his parents, brothers and sisters, peers, at school, and in his cultural life, the child is to be accorded a consistent kind of positive experience. In every setting the child is to be shown useful and viable forms of behavior, allowed to develop along these socially preferred lines, and encouraged to express himself and his own point of view even when it is not identical with social convention. Throughout this entire process negative experience is to be kept to a minimum or eliminated entirely. The child is to be protected from the destructive or damaging effects of criticism, failure, personal attacks, rejection, etc.

When a course of development follows this prescribed path, the young person will have amassed as much positive experience as possible, and will, as a result, be as complete a human being as possible. He will be fully competent to function in society in a variety of settings and be comfortable and confident in each one. He will be able to deal with a variety of people, and he will have begun to exercise all of the talents and abilities which he possesses. He will find the whole world open to him and suffer from no fears or inhibitions. All of this will be as true of his private or personal life as it is of his public life.

This notion prevails as the preferred or ideal identity of the child. It shapes social arrangements, social conventions, and, ultimately, the life of every individual. It is obviously superior to the notion which preceded it, where the child was seen, and then treated, as someone to be disciplined, ordered about, and made into a physical laborer at a fairly early age (Eisler, 1977; Wallace, 1978). The newer identity has allowed the child to become more vital, more curious, more imaginative, more knowledgeable, more interested in his own life, more critical, more experienced, and more resistant to the imposition of rigid authority. In many ways the child has become the embodiment of the libertarian aspirations of the earlier centuries of the modern period.

But there is also something wrong with all of this. The child is just as much the embodiment of the ills and evils of the modern world. Children have become too undisciplined, too resistant to authority, too interested in their own personal preferences, too disinterested in the world around them, too selective in their personal interests, and, in the last analysis, too indifferent to their own overall human welfare. The reason for this is that their own basic right to integrate themselves is consistently and systematically ignored.

The new positive course of childhood and adolescent develoment is simply too positive. It is artificially positive. The true course of contemporary childhood development is diverse and divided. When this division is deliberately obscured and ignored in favor of the emphasis on positive consistency, an artificial condition is created which, in turn, produces the new and somewhat destructive state of mind which we find today. I shall not attempt to document the existence of this state of mind; rather, I shall assume that its existence is well-known. (It appears in discussions of the family, the schools, the law, etc.) I shall proceed to analyze the division that causes it and establish the right that promises to diminish or eliminate it. This will be done on a conservative rather than a reactionary basis. That is, there will be no suggestion that we should go back to treating children in the old-fashioned manner. The emphasis will be on preserving the best features of the prevailing notion of the child while attempting to overcome its inherent tendency to generate destructive behavior.

The prevailing notion of the child comes out of a romantic tradition in philosophy, literature, psychology, educational theory, etc. It has been employed for several generations as a powerful cultural instrument to gain for the child a new, free, and prominent place in society. But the limitations of this notion are now quite obvious, and it is time for it to be modified. The modification I shall propose is based upon the recent advances in both philosophy and social history.

Social history shows that the romantic conception of the child has come into greater and greater prominence during the nineteenth and twentieth centuries. The same social history also reveals the most fundamental misconception which has been perpetuated by the romantic tradition. The romantic idea of an idyllic, positive environment for child development is misconceived, because the last two centuries have provided the child with an increasingly diverse environment. (Compare the (brutal) simplicity described in Wallace (1978) pp. 44 f., 180 f., 326 f., and in Shorter, (1977) pp. 169 f., with the diversity described in Kett, (1977) pp. 258 f., in Shorter, pp. 205 f., and in Greenleaf, (1978) pp. 124 f.) As a result, the prevailing notion consistently falsifies the reality which the child must deal with, and distorts the perspective of the child and his ability to understand reality.

Social history shows the stark simplicity of childhood only about one-hundred-fifty years ago. Since that time social realities have changed and introduced a radical diversity in place of the simplicity of childhood. Marriage has changed greatly, giving to the child a parental environment where disagreement and conflict are more likely. Education has become much more important, giving to the child a new set of relationships and responsibilities outside the home.   Social life has changed, giving the child a set of peer associations which are strikingly independent of the family. (See Kett (1977) and Shorter (1977), pp. 120 f.) Cultural life has changed dramatically, giving to the child a set of ideals and aspirations which are unprecedented in human history. At the same time, family life has been prolonged, giving to the child a more extended period during which these diverse forces may exert their influence.

The simplicity of childhood has been replaced by diversity and complexity. We may find privileged individuals in earlier centuries whose childhood was characterized by some of these social innovations, but even these few did not experience many of the innovations. Today all children experience all of them.   A radically new pattern of childhood and adolescence has arisen over the past two centuries, and the reality of this pattern is the reality for today's child.

Diversity is not division. If social history shows how diversity takes the place of simplicity, it has yet to be shown that diversity produces division and the need for integration. For this it is necessary to turn to philosophy and to some of the basic themes that have occupied philosophers in recent times.

The Hegelian tradition has established the priority of human cultures.(1) People do not live in a natural setting as much as they live in a cultural setting, where basic ideas and beliefs are shared and where life is organized around beliefs. This is an important principle for today's young person because his life is influenced by several cultural centers (the family, the school, the popular culture, the peer group). For perhaps the first time in history the individual, and the child in particular, is subjected to a diversity of cultural ideals and recommended beliefs.

The response to established cultural diversity produces division within the individual. This response will be analyzed according to three principles which have been developed in the philosophy of mind and action. The first two principles are internalization and self-constitution. When a person is exposed to a set of cultural figures, images, ideals, etc., he internalizes them (Grice, 1974-75). Either directly or indirectly, either sooner or later, he takes them into his own memory and imagination. They become established in the mind of the individual as the correct answers to certain important questions or as the basis for individual priorities, commitments, and actions.

For example, an individual internalizes the principle of equality at a very young age by attending school. He becomes accustomed to educational practices which embody this principle, and very shortly learns to recognize deviations from it. He may never have used the word, but he has internalized a basic cultural principle through his affiliation with a cultural center (the school) and the activity of his own mind.

Internalization initiates self-constitution. The human agent is neither an empty vessel, a physiological machine, nor a socially conditioned automaton. The individual constitutes himself as the first step in performing actions.(2) He condenses his experiences, interprets himself and the situation he is in, decides who he is and what he intends to accomplish, and then proceeds to perform particular actions. Unless the individual determines who he is, he is unable to know what is expected of him, what his possibilities are, what his prospects of success and failure are, etc.

Basic cultural ideals play a prominent part in the process of self-constitution. For example, the child who internalizes the principle of equality employs that principle in self-constitution. He literally sees himself as someone who is equal and ought to be treated equally. This kind of self-determination then provides a foundation for actions. When the individual is treated in a way which he perceives as a violation of his own constitution, he may sulk, complain, protest or whatever, but the action rests directly on the original determination he has made about who he is. Self-constitution enables a human being, starting at an early age, to assert that he is equal and how he proposes to achieve equality in his everyday life.

Self-constitution takes basic cultural ideas and ideals, which have already been internalized, puts them into a more personal form, and projects them as the basis of human possibility, expectation, and action. As a result, specific human intentions arise. This is the third principle to be employed here. When the individual formulates practical intentions he is oriented toward action, and the world takes on a double aspect. Things stand as they actually are, but they also stand as they might possibly be. The individual intends a result or an outcome which action will make real, but which, as yet, is not a reality (Anscombe, 1969).

All of this provides a description of how an individual, living in a particular culture, employs its ideals to form his own character or personality, and how he develops a set of human intentions to direct his actions. In the twentieth century, the individual, and especially the young person, lives in a diversified world, where different cultural centers provide him with several cultures and several sets of cultural principles and ideals.(3) The culture of the school varies considerably from that of the family, from that of the popular culture, and so on. The individual is required to internalize, in effect, several different cultures and to constitute himself in a variety of ways.

When a single individual, living in a free and diverse society, internalizes competing or diverging cultural ideals, he necessarily constitutes himself accordingly. That is, he sees himself and then literally makes himself to be the kind of individual which is repeatedly suggested by the influential centers of organized life. And when this happens, division arises. The person divides himself into several persons within his own mind and imagination. By constituting himself in an appropriate way for each of several cultural centers, the young person becomes several different persons instead of a single, unified person, and he beomes divided against himself.

A pluralistic social order is not divided against itself. It simply reflects freedom and cultural diversity. But when this diversity becomes personalized, and is translated into the living reality of a single human being, it generates division. Very simply, when a child is required to be a number of different persons, it produces a unique brand of confusion. The child, within himself, becomes a number of different persons, and is consistently faced with the task of being some of these, all of these, or just one of these, according to his own internal dynamics.(4)

Psychology has acquired an impressive body of data which helps to illustrate this phenomenon. When an individual is diversified within his own self-constitution, a continuous competition arises among the various coherent selves. The individual cannot simply assign one self-constitution to one social setting. An internal dynamic allows two or more of these self-images to come into play in a given situation. The individual cannot simply assign one self-constitution to one social play in a given situation. The individual is then divided within himself. The various images do not coordinate, because they have been formed according to opposing cultural principles. They oppose each other and leave the individual divided.(5)

A common example of this is the junior high school student. The school requires that he constitute himself according to the principle of equality (along with other principles, such as independence, rationality, etc.). The same child has an extensive experience at home, with his peers, and watching television. In each of these other settings he is encouraged to constitute himself according to vastly different principles (the inequality of uniqueness, self-expression, personal attention, etc.). When he sits in the classroom he is constituted in different ways, and the difference produces division. He cannot be sure who he is. He cannot be comfortable being any one person, and his actions reflect a commensurate restlessness and lack of interest and commitment.

Most of the dubious behavior on the part of children which we observe today can be traced back to their response to established cultural diversity. Internalization and self-constitution in a pluralistic society produce a divided consciousness and divided intentions. In this divided state of mind the child is receptive only to those things which appeal to his preferred constitution or image of himself. He becomes resistant to other, perhaps more constructive activities because they do not conform to his preferred images. And, on some occasions, he simply does not know who he is or even who he prefers to be.

The child of today is divided within himself and proceeds to act in dubious and destructive ways. He has a fundamental right to overcome this division and to integrate himself. The present emphasis on positive experience not only fails to acknowledge this right, it actually promotes division. The prevailing notion of childhood identity forbids parents and teachers and everyone else from dwelling on matters which are not pleasant, and this kind of division is not inherently pleasant.*(6)* It is ironic that freedom and diversity are very strongly desired, but the division they generate is unsettling, confusing and destructive.

The right to be integrated is established by the most fundamental considerations of justice and fairness. If a child is born into a pluralistic society where cultural diversity is established, then that child deserves the opportunity to benefit from that diversity and not to be divided and destroyed by it. The very purpose of the diversity should be carried out in individual life, and, whereas division inhibits this achievement, integration promotes it. If integration is the activity which enables the child to begin to carry out the diverse aims of the social order, then he has the right to be integrated. Society cannot deprive him of his right to achieve integration.

These considerations elevate integration to the level of a general (i.e., having both legal and moral dimensions) right, but this status also has important practical ramifications which can be seen by reviewing the cultural dynamics of modern Western civilization. The pre-modern order was replaced by modern institutions and practices through the effective employment of the notion of individual rights. Conceived as a right, a particular aspect of human endeavor can be translated from theory and aspiration into large scale, practical reality. The disintegrated, unnecessarily anti-social state of mind which is so common today ought not to exist, and the process of integration promises to eliminate and to transform this state. But, at present, integration is largely a 'nice idea' reserved for academic discussion and very limited psychoanalytic application. In order that it be given the important place it deserves (institutionally, educationally, legally, morally, etc.) it must first be conceived as a right. In this form it constitutes the crucial step in the transformation of a (philosophical-psychological) theoretical idea into a useful activity in the mainstream of contemporary life.

As long as society remains committed to the prevailing notion of childhood identity, this right will be violated consistently and systematically. The last point to be raised, therefore, is how integration might be given its appropriate place and how the prevailing notion must be modified. Although it is unpleasant and even upsetting for a child to be reminded or have to admit that these divisions exist within himself, the alternative is even more destructive. That is, when unpleasantness is denied or put aside for the sake of positive experience, the division of consciousness not only occurs, but it continues to produce its divisive consequences without constructive resistance or opposition.*(7)*

Integration, on the other hand, confronts the unpleasant fact of division (or potential division) in order to unite opposing self-images. An experience which is not immediately pleasing is promoted in order to eliminate or moderate the negative experiences which generally follow once division becomes established. The child should be encouraged to admit or recognize his opposing self-images in order to deal with them effectively and constructively. Integration is no more than the practice of dealing with the most basic elements of psychological reality in order to allow them to reinforce and support each other instead of competing with and opposing each other.

The incompatibility between the two points of view can now be seen quite clearly. The prevailing conception of positive child development believes in the simple obliteration of unpleasant memories and experiences. This is thoroughly incompatible with the necessity, in integrating processes, to return consciously and deliberately to such experiences in order to incorporate them, in the most constructive way, in a unified personal consciousness. Theories of simple, positive socialization seem not to understand that upsetting images and memories must be dealt with directly and continuously or they will persist and undermine the social and personal development of the individual. The two approaches are actually in conflict insofar as integration acknowledges the ambivalence of the human condition and the prominence of drama, inconsistency, pain, and uncertainty in human affairs, while the prevailing positive view projects a picture from which these elements have been eliminated.

Trying to say what would facilitate integration is like trying to say, in the year 1700, what would facilitate public education or democratic government. The outlines of the future cannot be seen clearly. At the institutional level it is easy to make some general statements. The legal dimensions of the right to integration ought to be implemented in education. The schools ought to teach the skills of integration and provide opportunities to the child for the exercise of these skills. The moral dimensions of the right ought to be implemented in the home. Parents ought to be integrated persons and promote integration in their children. The popular culture ought to promote integration rather than disintegration, but it is not clear whether this is a legal or a moral matter. In all cases this calls for fundamental institutional reforms.

Two further questions must obviously be asked. First, how can these reforms be accomplished? It will not be as easy as it might seem. In order to introduce institutional practices which focus on personal conflict our cultural commitment to the opposite view must be reconsidered, and it is never easy to change such basic commitments. Second, what are the skills of integration? They are conversational skills and they include the ability to articulate the fundamental conflicts which form the center of personal consciousness. At present, psychoanalysis leads the way in providing knowledge about the nature and the variety of these conflicts. But psychoanalysis actually views personal conflict in narrow and peculiar ways. Perhaps the greatest need in the facilitation of integration as a right is the need for a more comprehensive and more useful framework for understanding and articulating personal conflict.

In play, through stories, in conversation, in classroom themes and exercises a child can be encouraged to identify his own multiple self-images, how they compete or threaten to compete with each other, and how they might actually support each other in everyday life. If a child has a right to integrate himself, then society should be organized to facilitate integration. Parents, grandparents, older brothers and sisters, teachers, authors, television producers, manufacturers of educational materials, educators, and others ought to be able to promote personal integration in children. They ought to possess the skills and employ the materials which would open up the child's inner world for his own edification and eventual integration. Schooling, family life, and cultural life ought to adopt a new and better version of childhood identity and give to personal integration the highest priority possible.

In terms of an example, the integrated junior high school student would be familiar with himself in the various configurations he takes on in his own imagination. He would have articulated his peer or social self which prefers a free and unfettered expression and an undisciplined life. He would have articulated his classroom self which is less expressive and more disciplined. Most important of all he would have explored the unpleasant division between these two selves, and how this division threatens his own growth and development, the success of his schooling, and many of his own intentions as well as those of his parents and teachers and his own peers. On the basis of years of this kind of conversation and insight the child would possess a certain power which he would not otherwise have. He would have the power to control his own self-constitution and intentions. He would be able to exercise his various self-images as long as they were in support of each other, and when they were not he would be able to sense the threat that this poses and avoid certain courses of destructive behavior.

Integration can only occur within the child. It requires a more developed consciousness than is ordinarily possible in society today, and it produces a power that the child would not ordinarily possess. The child has a right to this power over himself and to participate more uniformly in the social order. The only apparent disadvantage associated with integration is its tendency to produce seriousness. Children certainly have the time and the capacity to achieve integration, but it would also tend to make them more serious than they are today. They would have to pay some continuous attention to certain unpleasant matters which presently they are encouraged to ignore. This would add a serious side to the life of the child, and it is something which must be evaluated. Too much seriousness inhibits an individual. It makes things seem more formidable than they really are. In any actual program or practice for the purpose of fostering integration this would have to be guarded against. But there is a seriousness which is appropriate to life today and which is needed. An appropriate seriousness would not be out of place and would be welcome.

If this analysis is correct, it is up to many people working in many areas where the life of the child can be affected to invent and establish ways by which integration can be accomplished, because it is the child's right and it should not be denied.

REFERENCES

Anscombe, G. E. M. *Intention,* 2nd ed. Ithaca, NY: Cornell University Press, 1969, 51 f.

Eisler, B. (Ed.) *The Lowell offering.* Philadelphia: Lippincott, 1977.

Greenleaf, B. K. *Children through the ages.* New York: McGraw-Hill, 1978.

Grice, P. Method in philosophical psychology. In *Proceedings and addresses of the American Philosophical Association,* 1974-1975, *XLVIII,* 23-53.

Johnson, J. A., Collins, H. W., Dupuis, V. L., and Johansen, J. H. *Foundations of American education,* 2nd ed. Boston: Allyn and Bacon, 1973.

Kett, J. F. *Rites of passage.* New York: Basic Books, 1977.

Meyer, A. E. *Grandmasters of educational thought.* New York: McGraw-Hill, 1975.

Rakoff, V. The illusion of detachment. In S. C. Feinstein and P. L. Giovacchini (Eds.), *Adolescent Psychiatry,* Vol. VI., 1978, pp. 119-133.

Shorter, E. *The making of the modern family.* New York: Basic Books, 1977.

Silberman, C. E. *Crisis in the classroom.* New York: Random House, 1970.

Wallace, A. F. C. *Rockdale: The growth of an American village in the early industrial revolution.* New York: Knopf, 1978.

FOOTNOTES

(1) This tradition obviously includes Marx and the avowed Hegelians, but also many of the neo-Kantians and turn-of-the-century thinkers who emerge out of neo-Kantian thought, such as Dilthey, Weber (the Weber of a more "spiritualistic causal interpretation of culture and history." See the Talcott Parsons translation of the final paragraph of *The Protestant Ethic and the Spirit of Capitalism.*) Heidegger, and Lukacs (and the whole Frankfort school up to and including Habermas).

(2) A summary of the various forms this principle takes is given in Bernstein, R., *The Restructuring of Political and Social Theory,* New York: 1976, parts II, III, and IV.

(3) Pluralism is generally acknowledged, but the "end of ideology" thesis has obscured the fact of cultural pluralism. This thesis has been

attacked often, but with little effect. See, for example, MacIntyre, A., *Against the Self-Images of the Age*, Notre Dame: 1978, 3 f.

(4) This phenomenon has been noted in literature and psychology (from Sigmund Freud to Samuel Beckett), but it has not been clearly correlated with cultural plurality and diversity.

(5) The case studies of the psychoanalytic tradition constitute such evidence. See, for example, Feinstein and Giovacchini, 1978, n. 2.

(6) The works of Bruno Bettelheim illustrate this and also that children are able to carry out integration even under the most adverse circumstances. See, for example, *Truants from Life*, New York: 1955.

(7) John Dewey's insistence on "continuity" in all human experience provides an example of this extreme emphasis on the positive to the exclusion of the divisive.

COMMENT:

Response to "The Identity of the Child and the Right to Integration"

Lawrence B. Schiamberg

Department of Family and Child Ecology
Michigan State University
East Lansing, MI 48824

I will begin this commentary by agreeing with Evans' basic conclusion: "If this analysis is correct, it is up to many people working in
many areas where the life of the child can be affected to invent and
establish ways by which integration can be accomplished, because it is the
child's right and it should not be denied." I will, however, qualify this
broad agreement with two caveats. There are several points in Evans'
paper where we differ in our interpretation of child development and the
child's world. These differences will constitute the majority of my comments. Given my agreement with Evans' general conclusion (and I think
other social scientists would likely be similarly disposed), I think the
essential problem is one of trying to do something feasible about the issue
of personal disintegration. I am talking about practical issues of ends,
means, and the "politics" of child development. Put another way, if we
have a problem, what--if anything--can be done about it? (The concept
of "progress" and its correct philosophical and historical status may well
be involved here. However, that topic is the subject of a recent book and,
perhaps, beyond the scope of Evans' paper).

As to my differences with Evans' interpretation, I will list each one
and describe each rather briefly.

(1) In the first place, the time frame of childhood is never
adequately delineated in this paper. Childhood can range from the infant-
toddler age on through the phase of adolescence. What is meant by
childhood? Who are we talking about? In some parts of the paper, the
term "young person" is used while in other parts (perhaps more frequently)
the term "child" is used. Are we talking about toddlers and preschool

children (1½ to 3 years of age), young school children (6 to 10 or 11 years), early adolescents (11 or 12 to 17 or 18 years), later adolescents (17 years and beyond), or, indeed, all of the above.

This is not a trivial consideration since Evans' notions of children and their "right" to integrate themselves hinge, in part, on their level of functioning. Without straining common sense, the toddler would presumably integrate himself/herself with far less reliance on verbal or complex cognitive skills than some adolescents. The latter's "information-processing" skills would presumably allow them to do far more incisive analyses of their life situation. By using the word "child" or "childhood", Evans may be obscuring these complexities or to use his terms--creating an unrealistically "positive" view of child functioning. Furthermore the question of self-integration has long been recognized as a vital component of adolescence (Erickson, 1963, 1968). There is no need to argue for its validity in that phase of life.

(2) My second difference with Evans has to do with his description of this unrealistically positive view of childhood which he sketches for us in rather broad strokes. The evidence for this "zeitgeist" or world view of childhood is not well documented. Rather, it is assumed to be the case. Presumably, if enough of us "feel", at the gut level, that Evans is right, then he must be correct.

Let us, for the moment, grant Evans his view of childhood as far too positive and, thereby, ultimately destructive of children. The question which I think needs to be raised is not *where* this view comes from but *why* this view has emerged as so prominent in middle-class America. Having granted Evans the uncontested validity of his "zeitgeist", I shall now take the liberty of broadly answering my own question. Specifically why do we adults *need* to propagate an unreasonably positive, serendipitous and uncontrollably happy view of childhood for ourselves and our children? We probably do this because we adults may also live in a world which does not place a high value on "integrated" human beings. Does the foreman at the automobile factory really care if his workers have it "all together" from a personal perspective? Does the corporation executive really care if the plant workers perceive their work and work-related experiences as "meaningful"? Hopefully, the foreman and corporation executive do "care" about our "right" to self integration. Many of us adults have, however, learned not to be so optimistic. The sometimes harsh realities of life teach us that there are a few "good days" and a few "bad days" and lots of gray Monday morning coffee-stained days. But alas, do we want this kind of life for our children? "Of course not," comes the thunderous clamor through every respectable shopping center and pet store in the country.

We adults like to think of ourselves as "child-oriented" and concerned about the welfare of children. This may be true to some extent. However, we also seem to have a marvelous ability for transferring "our" problems to our children. We do this so subtly that both we and our children actually come to believe that these problems are "owned by " or "belong to" our children. We are simply looking out for the welfare of our children. Right? A classic example of this "selfless-selfishness" is the whole issue of children's television. Many adults are outraged--and rightly so--by the violence and explicit sexual behavior which can be viewed on T.V. by young children. The "ownership" of this problem is cleverly passed on to children. Note the "slight of hand." One wonders why the television programming is so potentially offensive to children but *not* to adults. Why don't adults voice their complaints about television programs that are so blatantly mediocre that only violence, explicit sexual conduct and low-brow language can hold one's attention? Why don't adults speak for themselves? The answer is both simple and unfortunate--they do not believe that they "own" the problem.

In summary, I would suggest that the very first step in overcoming the narrowly and destructively positive view of childhood described by Evans (assuming that it exists) is for adults to become aware of their "selfless-selfishness." This is not to suggest that adults retreat into a world of self-concern and narrow self-interest. Rather, it seems to me that a first step in the direction of encouraging "self-integration" for children is for adults to do it themselves.

(3) A third concern which I have with Evans' paper is his assumption that cultural diversity leads almost inevitably to a divided self in children. I think Evans underestimates the skills and resilience of young children. Evans states his position as follows: "A pluralistic social order is not divided against itself. It simply reflects freedom and cultural diversity. But when this diversity becomes personalized, and is translated into the living reality of a single human being, it generates division. Very simply, when a child is required to be a number of different persons, it produces a unique brand of confusion.... They oppose each other and leave the individual divided."

In footnote #4 Evans acknowledges that "this phenomenon has been noted in literature and psychology (from Sigmund Freud to Samuel Beckett) but it has not been clearly correlated with cultural plurality and diversity." Once again Evans appears to be on weak footing in presenting evidence for a critical notion in his paper. Freud and the psychoanalytical tradition have long been criticized for offering just such "subjective evidence" based on case studies limited in both number and representativeness.

The error is compounded when Evans--again with only limited evidence--makes the following statement. "Most of the dubious behavior on the part of children which we observe today can be traced back to their response to established cultural diversity?"

It is, in my estimation, just as likely that children's dubious behavior is the result of imitating and modeling the dubious behavior of adults whose "selfless-selfishness" allows them to help children without first helping themselves.

I would like to turn now to the second major caveat or reservation which I have about this paper. I consider it important enough to treat it as a separate issue rather than simply identifying it as a fourth area of disagreement following the prior ones. Specifically, if we grant the assumption that the "right" to personal integration is necessary and important for children, then the real problem is the practical one of how to get from "here" to "there".

The issue of self-integration is not a new one and has long been recognized as a critical issue in child development (Bronfenbrenner, 1979; Coleman, 1974). Although the words "self-integration" may not have been used, the general idea is the same. Bronfenbrenner (1979) has used the term "alienation" to refer to the isolation of youth and children from significant others (e.g., adults other than teachers or parents). Such alienation or isolation results in inadequate self-development and self-integration. Likewise, James Coleman (1974) recognizes the problems of the isolation of age grades from one another as a critical problem in self organization and the maximization of human potential. Unlike Evans, however, Bronfenbrenner's and Coleman's ideas have incorporated the *social prerequisites* for self-integration. In other words, self-integration does not occur in a vacuum of cognition or thinking apart from first-hand experience. Evans' view of self-integration is, it seems, much more limited. "Integration...confronts the unpleasant fact of division...in order to unite opposing self-images.... The child should be encouraged to admit or recognize his opposing self-images in order to deal with them effectively and constructively. *Integration* is *no more than* (italicizing mine) the practice of dealing with the most basic elements of psychological reality in order to allow them to reinforce and support each other."

Perhaps the limitations of Evans' view are illustrated again in the following statement: "Integration can *only* occur within the child." It is the view of Bronfenbrenner (1979), Coleman (1974) and this writer (Schiamberg, 1973, 1981, forthcoming) that revisions or modifications in the "social arrangements" (e.g., work experience, community activity) of childhood and adolescence are both a prerequisite and an accompanying reinforcer of self-integration. Once again the ownership of problems becomes important.

In conclusion, a good case could be made for the assertion that our society does *not* provide enough diversity in the social arrangements of children and youth to promote self-integration. Note that this is the opposite of the position taken by Mr. Evans and others who assume that we have too much diversity.

REFERENCES

Bronfenbrenner, U.   *The ecology of human development.*   Cambridge: Harvard University Press, 1979.

Coleman, J. S. *Use: Transition to adulthood.* Chicago: The University of Chicago Press, 1974.

Erickson, E. *Childhood and society,* 2nd Ed. New York: Norton, 1963.

Erickson, E. *Identity: Use and crisis.* New York: Norton, 1968.

Evans, J.   Identity of the child and the right to integration.   In A. Cafagna, R. Peterson and C. Staudenbaur (Eds.), *Philosophy, children and the family.* New York: Plenum, 1981.

Schiamberg, L. A cybernetic-systems approach to human development. *Cybernetica,* 1977, *20,* 43-55.

Schiamberg, L., and Smith, K. U.   *Human development and human ecology: A systems perspective.*   New York: Macmillan, 1981 (Forthcoming).

THE RHETORIC OF TOYS

David W. Black

Department of Philosophy
Pennsylvania State University
University Park, PA 16802

Are there bounds and borders to the world of play? If so, how are these borders defined? And what, if anything, might be learned through play? These questions suggest that play exhibits an autonomy that is in some measure describable or distinct. But what is at issue in a description of play? Is it enough to simply point to this and that experience, claiming that the one is play and the other is not? Or, must one ask: How does play come into being? How is it possible that we recognize an act of play?

In this paper I want to argue that any definition of play must take into account the objects used in play. The toy, far from being incidental to play, is part and parcel of the experience itself. The toy allows the child access to an environment, a perceptual locus, a place in the world. The child plays *together* with his toys. Thus, the character of a toy, in part, determines what games can be played with it. In this sense, not only does the child manipulate the object but the object also manipulates the child. The child finds himself in a world which is, to some extent, fashioned from the features of toys, features which must be considered in terms of their normative influence. Play is linked to the expressivity of the toy, the flexibility of the object, its texture and design, its color and size. Toys provide means for the child to explore his powers of imagination by serving as a link to the external world. In this role, toys become a part of the very essence of play. Hence when examining play, a consideration of the nature of toys becomes inevitable.

* * *

Before considering toys, one must return to a decription of play. The nature of play bears on the nature of toys; and it is therefore impossible to speak about the essence of toys without giving some prior consideration to the nature of childhood experience. In effect, one must begin with the following question: What does it mean to play?

As Maurice Merleau-Ponty (1964, p. 95) observes, external relation for the child is not a simple reflection or a "process of sorting out data. Rather it is a more profound operation whereby the child organizes his experience of external events--an operation which is thus neither properly a logical nor a predictive activity." When a child plays, he is taking delight in the sights and sounds of his world. He appears to enjoy perceptual forms apart from classifying or categorizing them. Merleau-Ponty stresses that this organization of experience is primarily proto-cognitive. He says: "There is perhaps no place for the question of the child's conception of the world, the child would actually have to totalize his experience under general concepts" (Merleau-Ponty, 1964, p. 95). It is this apparent lack of totalization that makes the nature of play so interesting. The child, while seemingly unconcerned with conceptual anslysis, remains fascinated by the intensity of objects. In spite of his conceptual naïveté, he distinguishes among aspects of his world. The child is intrigued by the sensible relatedness of things. He is concerned with perceptual integration, what Piaget (1954, pp. 46-47) calls the "totality of pictures emerging from nothingness."(1)

The objects of the child's world are distinguishable but they are not sorted in terms of concepts. They are recognizable by what I will call their *internal rhetoric*, their self-perpetuating schema. This rhetoric in no way suggests logical distinctiveness. Such objects are understood in terms of their self-distinctiveness. The rhetoric of an object is what allows it to stand out, to occupy a place in the world. This is a much more concrete individuality than that afforded the object through conceptualization. The child sees objects as vital entities, capable of interaction and change. One might say that the child views the object as affective rather than neutral.

R. G. Collingwood (1924, pp. 105-106) observes that the "enjoyment of play is sensuous, precisely as far as, and in the same sense in which, that of art is sensuous: where sensuous means intuitive, immediate, innocent of explicit reason." This innocence of play distinguishes it from the utilitarian or cognitive act. When Collingwood claims that play is "innocent of explicit reason," he means that the activity is free from the intervention of the category. One need not call concepts into action to justify the activity of play. Play is discovery for its own sake. It is an open and innocent participation in what Piaget (1960, p. 221) calls the "animism" of the world.

If the concept is operative in the child's manipulation of objects, it is highly subordinate to the percept. It is the perceptual nature of toys which causes the child to become enamored of them. It is not the concept of a circus which causes a child to play with his circus wagon--it is the image of a circus that fascinates the child. When a child pretends he is at the circus he is not so much conceptualizing as visualizing the experience. The child pretends he is at the circus, not out of some conceptual need, but out of his fondness for the phenomenon itself. The circus wagon helps in recalling the spectacle of the circus. Such wagons with their bright localized colors and intriguing serpentine designs epitomize the circus by bringing the perceptual atmosphere directly to the child. In a single, graspable circus wagon the child has manageable access to the glamor of a specific environment. He is given means to find again the experience he delighted in before.

To pretend is not to think, it is to enter into a situation. It is to put oneself in a precise place. When I *think*, I *abstract* from my place and, in effect, obviate my situation. Where I am is no longer of prime concern. I have taken a step back from my place in order to "explain" or understand it. From this standpoint of *second-order* experience, the physical condition of the child's circus wagon makes little difference to my conceptual attempt to see the wagon as an instance of a universal. Whatever else it is, it is still a circus wagon even though it is an imperfect example which is in need of repair. The broken-down circus wagon can represent all circus wagons. It is no wagon in particular and every wagon in general. Here the concept becomes restrictive. The wagon is simply an instantiation and as such it is measured against an external paradigm, a paradigm that is captured only in abstract thought, only in the ideal world of the universal. But when the same wagon is experienced in the rhetorical mode, the color and condition of the object make *all* the difference. If the colors are faded, if a spoke is missing from the wheel, the situation suggested by the wagon is limited because the perceptual possibilities, the vitality, and the potential forms of the object are radically reduced. If the vital perceptual nature of the wagon depends on its rhetorical or first-order form, then the qualities displayed by the object function together intrinsically to sustain that form. An adaptation in any of the qualities constitutes not only a change in that particular element but also in the form it helps sustain. Thus, when pursuing a rhetorical understanding, one need not venture beyond the mode of presentation. The value of play does not lie in some categorical or representational scheme. As Collingwood (1924, p. 106) points out, "of play, as of art, the justification is its own splendour."

This intrinsic splendor of play seems to defy abstraction. One cannot improve play by introducing rules and regulations. The rationalization of play does not make it better; it turns it into something else. This is why Johan Huizinga (1955, p. 3) maintains that "the *form* of playing resists all analysis, all logical interpretation. As a concept, it cannot be reduced to any other category." For this reason, play often occasions the absurd, the silly, the useless perception, a perception which carries meaning in itself. As Huizinga (1955, p. 3) explains, "you can deny, if you like, nearly all abstractions: justice, beauty, truth, goodness, mind, God. You can deny seriousness, but not play." Play is impossible unless the "order" of the world is suspended. The world of play is variable, mutable, flexible and imprecise. A world which is ordered under *a priori* regulations imposes restrictions on triviality. The world of seriousness is a world of stability. The world of play accommodates change.

Childhood seems to be enlivened by a contrast between the intense and the extended. At bottom, such a contrast makes possible the distinction between the playful and the useful, the silly and the serious. Silliness denies extension. It directs one's attention toward something local. Laughter, for example, is an intense experience. It is localized and individual. The silly act seems to direct one's attention toward one's place. To ride on top of a teeter-totter, to board a contraption bound for nowhere, is to take delight in the ridiculousness of one's place. Bouncing up and down on the teeter-totter, one is carried along for the ride. The act, in the eyes of logic, is absurd. One isn't getting anywhere; no progress is being made. Yet such silliness is part of even the most basic forms of play.

As Susanne Langer points out, play is bound to gesture. She argues that if the purpose of a play were, as is normally supposed, "to *learn by imitation,* an oft repeated act should come closer and closer to reality, and a familiar act be better represented than a novel one; instead we are apt to find no attempt at *carrying out* the suggested actions of the shared day dreams that constitute young children's play" (Langer, 1942, p. 136). The child is fascinated by the intrinsic form of his gestures. Gesture and intention become interdependent. When children play, they take delight in the silliness of certain gestures. What does not fall within the scope of gesture, what extends beyond the child's grasp, is unattainable and inapprehensible. Through gesture, the child seems to understand what in his perceptual world is graspable and manageable--for example, the teeter-totter ride--and what is awesome or extensive--for example, the noise and hoopla of a carnival midway. When the young child rides the teeter-totter he can *manage* the ridiculous gesture. But when confronted with the carnival midway, the child cries, his perceptual world has grown sublime; it has become too large for him to grasp. His world is no longer intensive and gestural. To understand and appreciate the complexities of the midway, one must extend one's interpretation beyond the gesture to categorical understanding. The concept of the midway allows us to synthesize the noise and hoopla under an intellectual category of interpretation.

Play appears to begin, then, with the simplest of gestures; it appears to begin with the grasp. The young child loses his fascination with objects if he cannot clutch them or stick them in his mouth. Children tend to cling unrelentingly to their favorite doll or stuffed tiger. These objects stand within the child's grasp. They are manageable phenomena, central to the child's experience and easy for him to manipulate and hold. The child carries his teddy bear *with* him as if to say, "this is *mine.* It is part of *my* place, *my* situation." The child is unconcerned with the synthetic or abstract unity of his experience. He is interested in that which is peculiarly his. He is concerned with the recognition of his own place. The arbitrary or silly gesture, the gesture produced for its own sake, lies at the bottom of such recognition. It offers the child access to the sensible relatedness of his place. The intense or integrative gesture is self-justifying. Children giggle when they run around in circles. They laugh when they rock back and forth on a swing. There is no logical justification for these acts. They are actually absurd. Yet it is the absurdity that the child finds delightful.

The final question to be posed, then, is: how are toys to be linked with the act of play? If play is an activity which provides meaning in itself and if this meaning appears at the perceptual level in the form of the absurd or silly gesture, what might one conclude about the normative nature of toys? I should like to suggest four perceptual or rhetorical schemata which I think might be helpful in understanding the toy's relation to play. I offer these schmata as a means for making sense out of the notion of a toy. These intuitive forms, however, overlap and determine one another. They may be too few in number. There may be more rhetorical schemata that one might add to the list. I therefore offer the list not as a pronouncement on the ultimate nature of toys, but rather as a point of departure. I think that such inquiry is particularly important today, since we live in an age which is witnessing a remarkable change in the design and construction of toys.(2) I present these schemata, then, not only as descriptive notions, but also as a means for understanding how the rhetoric of toys might contribute a normative dimension to play.

The schemata I propose, then, might be summarized as follows: (1) the toy ought, I think, to contribute an intuitive *mutability*, that is, one ought to be able to bend, slacken, maneuver or expand the object in new and different ways. One should actually be able to break down one's experience of the object into component parts and deal with these parts severally and autonomously. (2) I would suggest that the toy display *uselessness*, that it not be judged as a means to an end or as reflecting some external standard. The use of the toy, if there is one, is defined each time it is played with. (3) I think that the toy ought to display *rhythm*, that there should be a perceived movement in the design of the object. The toy ought to be able to maintain its *own* continuity or integrity in terms of a continuous intrinsic pattern. And, (4) the toy ought to include, I think, a sense of *hyperbole*. The pattern of the toy ought to reflect extreme distinction. The toy should exhibit intensity. It ought to be made attractive through exaggeration. Let me now return to each of these schemata individually.

When I refer to *mutability*, I am, of course, referring to change. But I have in mind a most general sense of change. Quite simply, I feel that it is important that toys remain free of any "final form." Toys that are designed to perform a highly specialized function approximate final form.

That is, one finds it impossible to tamper with the detail of such toys without distorting their value. For example, if a spaceship that emits a stream of smoke is more highly prized than a similar rocket of less complicated design, then one must learn to play with the rocket in such a way as to accommodate its detail. If I crush the fantail or forget to pour the "super steam" into the toy, I no longer own the toy I originally purchased but rather the less complicated toy I chose to avoid. In this case, the introduction of detail finalizes the form of the toy. The "uses" of the toy are more strictly predetermined in the case of the more detailed rocket. Thus, if I am playing a complicated game, my behavior is governed by an equally complex set of rules.

I think that the final form of the toy must arise during the act of play itself. It becomes extremely difficult to regard play as an end in itself when the form of the toy is predetermined. When toys are assigned specific functions, a conceptual or categorical order supersedes the perceptual order of play. There becomes a right and a wrong way to play with toys. I think of the well-meaning mother who instructs, "trucks don't travel upside-down across the bottom of the table, they travel on the top of the table," and with these words the mother then demonstrates the *proper* way to play with the toy, as if in the child's world trucks must obey the law of gravity. The child is unconcerned with gravity, not because he is naive or ignorant, but because he is concerned with something else. As the child explores the sights and sounds of his world, the final form of the toy remains undetermined. If the toy is immutable or inflexible there is little to be perceived or discovered. The toy's form and function become finalized. Conception replaces perception as the standard of value.

When I argue that *uselessness* is a schema of the rhetoric of toys, a possible misconception must be avoided. The notion of use must be distinguished from the notion of value. When I claim that a toy is useless, I do not mean that it lacks value. In fact, I mean quite the reverse. When I think of the word use, I think of what the word means. When I "use" an object, I value it as a means to an end. The object I use has no intrinsic significance. It is important only as a tool. The toy, on the other hand, finds its value intrinsically. It is a useless phenomenon in the sense that it is "appreciated" rather than "employed." The use of the toy, if there is one, changes from day to day. If, for instance, one examines the kaleidoscope, one finds a simple cylinder which, when rotated, produces colorful designs. One enjoys the designs; one values them. Yet, it would be improper to claim that the kaleidoscope is useful. In fact, playing with a kaleidoscope might be called a waste of time since there is no purpose to such an act. Yet, to program play, to use one's time wisely, is to defeat play. The toy must hold its own in the imaginative world of the child. When the toy becomes strictly purposive, it surrenders its integrity. Play is a denial of time; it is indeed a "waste of time," and therein lies its value.

A word might be said here about the educational toy. An educational toy is of value only insofar as it is a means to an end. It helps the child bridge the gap between perception and conception and thereby plays an important role in the older child's experience. Yet, it is not properly a toy. An educational device is didactic; a toy is fun-loving. Because the educational toy is both didactic and fun-loving, it is only partially effective in either of its roles. An educational toy reflects an external standard. It puts the activity of play to work. The silly or fun-loving act is now seen as serious. An unrestrained imagination complicates the button-down business of play. The educational toy must be skillfully designed. The developmental psychologist is called in. Exacting blueprints are made. The toy is no longer self-justifying; it is now something to be "used"--something which has a job to do. The toy differs from the educational toy in just this sense.

How is it that toys exhibit *rhythm*? This, too, is a peculiar trait. Rhythm, I would suggest, injects vitality into the toy. If the world of play is affective rather than neutral, then the aspects of this world must display a sense of liveliness. The criss-crossing lines of tinker-toys, the spinning colors of a top, the rocking of the swing set, all exhibit rhythm. each of these toys displays integrity because each conveys vitality. The vitality or liveliness of these toys is sustained by their rhythm or continuous movement. Toys which emulate adult life are crude effigies; they are lifeless replications rather than productive, self-sustaining wholes. The Barbie doll is an abstract idea. There is nothing vital or integral about the doll itself. Barbie is not *my* doll; she is *everyone's* doll. She is the paragon of dollhood. Barbie is not a toy; she is a concept. She and her various friends lack any sense of rhythm. They have no pulse, no integrity.

A child can learn to recognize a toy by its rhythm. The colors and lines of a circus wagon make the object instantly discernible. Toys which convey rhythm take on an existence of their own. The child need not introduce external rules when he plays with such toys. These toys suggest their "own" rules, rules which the child uncovers, not prior to, but during the act of play. The rhythmic object invites play. It begs our participation. A conceptual object succumbs to the child. A rhythmic object responds to the child. When I spin a kaleidoscope, I receive a sense of feedback from the toy. It responds, in this way, to my imagination. The same is true of a kite which, when caught by the wind, bobs and weaves with a will of its own. Kites and kaleidoscopes exhibit vitality and integrity because they display a recognizable, internal pattern of movement. Rhythm sustains the autonomy and continuity of the object.

Closely related to rhythm is *hyperbole*. It is important, I think, that toys not only convey a sense of rhythm, but that their rhythm be exaggerated, ridiculous, or highly stylized. The toy is no ordinary object. It is strikingly significant. It displays a lack of decorum and generates integrity through its decadence. A toy is not a chaotic collage of disconnected sense; it does display rhythm and form. But its rhythm is not subtle. It is rather loud and obtrusive, outlandish and overdone, readily recognizable by even the most naive of perceivers. If play is to remain an intense experience, toys must be, in some way, overdone. The world of play is a world of hoots and whistles. When the rhythm of a toy is streamlined, it is no longer readily perceived. The concept must be called into action since a cognitive process is required. When the design of a toy is extremely subtle, its perceptual significance is blindly sacrificed.

The circus clown, for example, appeals to the child because clowns exhibit hyperbole. The costume of a clown is bold and perceptually intrusive; and the clown wears makeup to exaggerate the features of his face. No one's nose is as big and as bright as a circus clown's. Exaggeration is employed to draw attention to the rhythm and design of a "happy" face. A happy face has its own integrity, internal rhythm and form. The circus clown brings this rhythm to the child's attention. The child, therefore, takes delight in his perception of this crazy, outlandish character who seems to defy any descriptive classification. The bright colors and obtrusive designs of a clown's happy face are what first attract the child to the performer. The child's experience is perceptual. The clown walks by and the child simply "points" in the clown's direction, as if to say, "look, see, enjoy this perception with me." The clown is seen as something unusual, out of the ordinary, radically different from the child's day-to-day experience. Through hyperbole, the child comes to recognize the sensible integrity of an object by apprehending its radical difference and singularity. Whatever else it may be, a child's toy is clearly a "this." However, the thisness of the toy is not determined by its function or conceptual essence. It is rather found in the internal and hyperbolic rhythm that is readily perceived in the object.

* * *

In this paper I have argued that the normative value of toys is found in their sensible nature. In his experience of toys, I have argued that the child is concerned with the *perceptual integrity* of the objects, and that the autonomy of any act of play depends directly on the rhetorical or presentational form of the toy. Given the toy's perceptual nature, I have tried to isolate certain rhetorical features which, I think, contribute to the spirit of play. By listing these features, I have tried to suggest a point of departure for further inquiry into the nature of toys.

If there are indeed bounds and borders to the world of play, the perceptual side of childhood seems to be active in the delineation of such boundaries. I think it is therefore important to consider how the rhetorical form of an object functions in any geography of juvenile experience. It is the child's place, the child's environment that directly informs the act of play. The child's imagination is conditioned by the sights and sounds which confront him. It is because the objects of childhood are vital and not abstract, affective rather than neutral, that a consideration of the rhetoric of toys is, I think, philosophically essential.

REFERENCES

Collingwood, R. G. *Speculum mentis.* Oxford: Clarendon Press, 1924.

Huizinga, J. *Homo ludens: A study of the play elements in culture.* Boston: Beacon Press, 1955.

Langer, S. *Philosophy in a new key.* Cambridge: Harvard University Press, 1942.

Merleau-Ponty, M.   The child's relation with others.   (William Cobb, Trans.)   In J. Edie (Ed.), *The primacy of perception.* Evanston: Northwestern University Press, 1964.

Piaget, J. *The construction of reality in the child.* New York: Ballantine Books, 1954.

Piaget, J. *The child's conception of the world.* Totawa, NJ: Littlefield Adams, 1960.

FOOTNOTES

(1) Piaget continues: "Proof that this interpretation is the right one, however painful it may be to our realism, is that the child makes no attempt to search for an object when it is neither within an extension of the gesture made, nor in its initial position; here obs. 28-33 are decisive."

(2) The toy has become increasingly complicated in design. Rules and regulations accompany each item.   Today the child is not only provided with a toy, but is also given instructions for its use. Certain computerized toys actually "reward" the child by playing a delightful tune when the proper manipulations have been completed. The computer robot is programmed play, technical play, dead serious play. Far from centering around the ridiculous gesture, technical play actually condemns the absurd or nonconforming act.

COMMENT:

Response to "The Rhetoric of Toys"

Alice Whiren

Department of Family and Child Ecology
Michigan State University
East Lansing, MI 48824

Play has been defined by motive, by content, and as voluntary activity (Ellis, 1973). In the English language the word 'play' is used to encompass the broad range of behaviors of animals that are not obviously essential to survival. A host of other words have been used to describe the various activities humans use as play (Huizinga, 1949).

The concept of *play* is somewhat similar to the concept of *plant*. Both are general words that define a class of instances. Each has many particular forms with unique characteristics. Exploration, sensorimotor investigation, dramatic play, testing play, games and practice play and sports are classifications commonly used to describe childhood play. It appeared that "The Rhetoric of Toys" was written in response to the characteristics of artifacts which uniquely stimulate the first three of these forms of play, though Black failed to clarify this point. It should be noted that exploration, sensorimotor investigation, and dramatic play are the predominant forms of ludic behavior in children under six years of age; an age period frequently referred to as the "age of toys." However toys, in some form, are used throughout the human lifetime and are not restricted to childhood. Electronic games, pleasure boats, playing cards, puzzles, and sports equipment are examples of materials used by adults in their play. Many of these objects have similar attributes of the "toy" as described by Black though all discussion of adult use is omitted from his paper. Play, then, is a category of behavior exhibited by some animals, including man, having no obvious survival value, that may or may not be related to the specific use of specialized artifacts.

The circumstances in which play may or may not occur need to be stated. It should be noted that unsatisfied primary and acquired drives can preempt playful behavior. In order to be free to play, the basic needs

247

of the player, such as security, food, and warmth, must be met. However, even when these conditions exist, the child may or may not play. Novel objects, or toys, as discussed by Black *do* stimulate play in the child.

How then can play be distinguished from non-play behavior? Neuman (1971) analyzed with great care the traditional definitions of play as well as current research that describes playful behaviors. She proposed three criteria that distinguish playful behaviors. Briefly stated they are: (1) *The locus of control of the activity is invested in the individual.* The player has control of the activity, the player being the decision-maker. (2) Secondly, the *motive of the behavior is intrinsic.* The players engage simply for the processing of the act itself. Therefore, there would not be any immediate or deferred external rewards. (3) The last criterion is that the *player is freed from the constraints of reality.* Though total freedom from constraint is not possible, suspension of time, pretending situations, and imagining that one object represents another are familiar examples.

Should the toy, as an artifact, be introduced into the definition or conceptualization of play? Black modifies Neuman's criteria by describing the toy as having sensory properties that to some extent shift the locus of control from the child to the artifact. Clearly the interaction between the object and the child is complex in and of itself. It is perhaps more mutable than Black suggests, in that the skilled child's *use* of the toy during play is likely to *exceed* the expectations of adults for variation, refinement and permutation.

Though the concept of *toy* was used by Black, he did not differentiate between a plaything and a toy. A plaything can be any natural object such as a stick (used as a spoon, a gun, or conductor's baton), an article of clothing (hats, high heeled shoes or purses), or a saucepan (used as a helmet, a pail, a drum). Though each of the objects has meaning in itself, perhaps usefulness in addition to importance to the owner, the child's incorporation of the object into a dramatic play theme drastically alters the meaning of that object during the play episode.

A toy, on the other hand, is an artifact constructed for the sole purpose of stimulating play. The number, variety and availability of toys tends to increase with the complexity of technologically advanced cultures. Such advancement tends to produce the related need of adults to simplify complex, unsafe or physically distant experiences to more manageable chunks for children. The toy in itself may be useless in the sense suggested by Black but may serve a broader function for the child and the culture as it *stimulates* play behavior. For example, in her research on socio-dramatic play, Smilansky (1968) fully illustrates the relationships between cognitive development, play experience, and culture. Schwartzman (1978) has integrated research and theory on play as it appears in many cultures.

What then is the meaning of the toy? Black's schematic of the toy as posing intuitive *mutability, uselessness* when judged as a means to an end, *rhythm* of design and a sense of hyperbole are conceptually descriptive of the heuristic value of toys. However, the child's play stimulated by the toy is not static. Though child behavior is dominated by perceptual cues during early development which is reflected in the content and style of play, the use of the toy changes over time as the child changes. This change is toward increasing complexity and abstraction. In other words, the younger child's play may be truly dominated by the sensory qualities of the toy but the older, more mature and skillful player tends to *assign meaning* to his toys which may or may not be related to the sensory qualities of the object. Pantomime is probably the most extreme form of abstraction of objects. The objects are omitted altogether, leaving only the gesture.

The meaning of the toy is further complicated by consideration of *various* adult perspectives. The artist who designed the toy, the manufacturer who built it, the store owner who displayed and sold it, the great aunt who bought it, and the psychologist who assessed its effect on the child, all use *different* conceptualizations as to the quality and value of a particular toy. All of these meanings and perspectives are valid as each of the adults' decisions affect the availability of the toy for the child. Clearly, though, the heuristic significance of the object is likely to be considered directly or indirectly from other perspectives and perhaps should be the primary qualification of excellence in such artifacts.

In summary, the concept of play as a broad category of experience remains elusive. The toy does contribute to the particular forms of play in early childhood but its primary meaning is assigned by the child rather than being wholly inherent to the artifact. Playthings, toys, and sports equipment are all used in various forms of play over a lifespan. These objects remain, however, tools and though related to play are not central to this form of experience.

REFERENCES

Ellis, M. J. *Why people play.* Englewood Cliffs: Prentice Hall, 1973.

Huizinga, J. *Homo ludens: A study of the play element in culture.* New York: Routledge and Kegan, 1949.

Neuman, E. A. "The elements of play." Unpublished doctoral dissertation. Champaign, IL: University of Illinois, 1971.

Schwartzman, H. B. *Transformations: The anthropology of children's play.* New York: Plenum, 1978.

Smilansky, S. *The effects of sociodramatic play on disadvantaged preschool children.* New York: Wiley, 1968.

PART IV

MORAL EDUCATION

MORAL EDUCATION: INTRODUCTION

Craig A. Staudenbaur

Department of Philosophy
Michigan State University
East Lansing, MI 48824

Theories of moral education seek to answer the question whether virtue can be taught, and if so, how? Eminent philosophers have been concerned with these questions, from Socrates to John Dewey, and psychologists, educators, and sociologists have added to what is now a mountain of literature on the subject. I can not adequately survey this literature; I shall try only to fit the essays in this section into a philosophical context.

The assumption behind most of the literature on moral education is that virtue can be taught. In the Western tradition, the first educators to defend this view were the sophists. Protagoras, in Plato's dialogue of that name, argues forcefully that virtue can be taught; that it is taught to children first by their parents, then by their teachers, and then by the laws of the city and the force of public opinion. Socrates argues against Protagoras, and concludes the dialogue by pointing out that we cannot know whether virtue can be taught unless we know what virtue is. Many philosophers would agree that the task of saying what virtue is is the most difficult philosophical task for a theory of moral education. Disagreements about this question characterize the history of efforts towards a theory of moral education, and figure prominently in the essays in this section as well.

What is virtue? Socrates complains that Protagoras hasn't said, but if we look carefully at Protagoras' initial speech, it is not hard to delineate the concept of virtue presupposed in his theory of moral education. Moral virtues are those shared opinions the possession of which allows one to get along in society without interpersonal and social friction. And, like other opinions, they are taught by indoctrination. Because of their importance we add praise and blame, reward and

253

punishment, to moral instruction, to make sure that the individuals learn their moral lessons thoroughly (*Pr.* 325b-326e; cf. Vlastos, 1958).

Much of the educational literature of the 1940's and 50's echoes the Protagorean view. It sees the goal of education as the instillation of those beliefs and values which will enable the student to achieve a harmonious social adjustment (Beck, Crittenden, and Sullivan, 1971). One problem with this view is that, if the society to which you are harmoniously adjusted is an unjust society, then the education which promotes that adjustment may be promoting injustice. This point is made by Eric Hoffman in the paper in this section entitled "Educating for justice in an unjust society." It would seem that an obvious reply to Hoffman is that while the Athenian slave-holding society might promote injustice through "social-adjustment" moral education, our own democratic society will not. But Eric Hoffman's argument is that our democratic society is not fully democratic. It is a capitalist society, and the means of production are not organized along democratic principles. "Our economic institutions, the institutions through which adults receive their primary social definition, are authoritarian, hierarchical and undemocratic. Effective socialization must therefore reproduce the consciousness (and moral character) that accepts these relations as either inevitable or just." Hoffman recommends that moral education should promote virtues like justice even though these do not fit the individual harmoniously into society; he proposes that moral education should be "revolutionary" in its effects in an unjust society.

Ronald Suter, in his "Comment on educating for justice in an unjust society" agrees with Hoffman that moral education is not to be confused with socialization, but for different reasons. The "socialized adult" who acts on opinions because others share them is not acting morally. Suter argues, "The Gospel of getting on the bandwagon is not a moral position. Anyone who accepts the ready-made opinions of others about what is good and right, has not yet learned how to think morally, for moral reasons do not guide this person's judgment and conduct." The same point is made by Socrates in many of the early Platonic dialogues. Socrates rejects Protagoras' view that virtue is shared opinion, and taught by indoctrination. Teaching virtue by indoctrination would only be appropriate if the teacher had knowledge of what virtue is. In most of Plato's early dialogues, Socrates insists that he does not have this sort of knowledge and that consequently he is not a teacher of virtue. In the *Protagoras* and the *Meno*, he argues that virtue cannot be taught, apparently because, as he argues in the *Apology*, no human has knowledge of virtue. Only the gods have wisdom or knowledge of these important matters; Socrates is wise because he recognizes his human limitations. But Socrates does not conclude that because we don't have knowledge, we should be content to teach other people our opinions on moral matters. Rather, each person must examine moral opinions for himself, and "life without this sort of examination is not worth living" (*Ap.* 38a, 1961, p. 23).

Plato was less skeptical than Socrates about the possibility of humans attaining to moral knowledge, at least when he wrote the *Republic*. The *Republic* is a long essay on moral education; it provides an answer to the question of whether virtue can be taught. It suggests that both Protagoras and Socrates were partly correct. Some virtue is based on shared opinions, as Protagoras believed. And in the ideal state, children would be indoctrinated in those beliefs which were determined to be good both for the citizens and the state. (And in the bad state, this indoctrination will produce vice rather than virtue, as Hoffman argues in his essay.) But the virtue produced by indoctrination would not be perfect virtue, although it would be adequate for the producing and guardian class. The highest class in the state, the philosopher-rulers, would have virtue based on knowledge. After years of philosophical examination of moral opinions, they would arrive at a stage of moral knowledge. Plato posited stages of virtue corresponding to cognitive stages. Only the philosopher-ruler would pass sequentially through all of the cognitive stages (eikasia, pistis, dianoia, theoria) and arrive at complete moral development.

Most of the papers in this section are concerned with the theory of Lawrence Kohlberg, which like Plato's, is based on the assumption that virtue is knowledge, that moral development is primarily cognitive, and that it is stage-sequential. Kohlberg argues that moral development proceeds through the following three levels, which correspond roughly to the three levels of moral development postulated by Dewey and Piaget (Kohlberg, 1976). There are two stages at each level; six stages in all (Kohlberg, 1971a, 1971b).

I.   Preconventional level. At this level the child interprets "good" and "bad" in terms of physical consequences of action, in terms of reward and punishment. It may be divided into the following two stages:

      Stage 1.   *punishment and obedience orientation.* Actions are seen by the child as good or bad depending on whether the consequences are rewarding or punishing.

      Stage 2.   *instrumental relativist orientation.* "Right action consists of that which instrumentally satisfies one's own needs and occasionally the needs of others."

II.   Conventional level. Maintaining conformity and loyalty to the expectations of the individual's family, group, or nation defines right and wrong at this level. The two stages are:

Stage 3.   *interpersonal concordance or "good boy-nice girl" orientation.* Good behavior is what pleases or is approved by others. Behavior is frequently judged by intention; "he means well".

Stage 4.   *"law and order" orientation.* Right conduct consists of doing one's duty, respecting authority, and maintaining a given social order.

III.   Post-conventional, autonomous, or principled level. At this level an effort is made to define moral principles which are valid independently of authorities or groups. This level has two stages:

Stage 5.   *social-contract legalistic orientation.* "Right action tends to be defined in terms of general individual rights and in terms of standards that have been critically examined and agreed upon by the whole society." While the emphasis is upon socially determined rules, there is the recognition that these rules may be changed through rational scrutiny.

Stage 6.   *universal ethical-principle orientation.* "Right is defined by the decision of conscience in accord with self-chosen *ethical principles,* appealing to logical comprehensiveness, universality, and consistency."

Moral development proceeds through these stages sequentially, and in an invariant order (1971 b). Although the content of morality may be taught, at the earlier stages (Protagoras' theory of virtue and how it is taught might be more or less correct for level II for example), moral development is not taught, and the form which morality takes at each stage is not taught (Peters, 1971). Moral development proceeds through role-playing on the part of the child, is primarily cognitive, and is the natural result of the child's intellectual confrontation with his social environment (Kohlberg, 1971a; Peters, 1971). The principles which operate at stage six are, in their general form, universal principles of justice which can be found at the highest stage of moral development in all societies (1971a, 1971b). In other words, the stages represent degrees of moral adequacy, with the highest stage of development the only completely morally adequate stage (1971a).

Kohlberg believes that all of these conclusions are based on empirical studies and that the theory of moral development has ramifications for ethical theory as well as for educational theory. Protagoras' theory of moral education, like other indoctrination theories of moral education, is based on an inadequate theory of what virtue is. It is relevant to the earlier stages of moral development, but not to the higher ones.

Of the papers in this section which deal primarily with Kohlberg, Friquegnon's is very critical of Kohlberg's theory. Friquegnon rejects the heart of Kohlberg's theory; that moral development is basically a stage-sequential development which ultimately produces moral knowledge, if the highest stage (stage six) is reached. Kohlberg attributes his view to Socrates, but Friquegnon argues, correctly I think (although the problem of what Socrates believed is a difficult one), that Socrates did not believe that humans could attain to moral knowledge. Friquegnon thinks that what Socrates really believed, and what she herself believes, is that moral concepts, because of their "essentially contested" nature, require continual reexamination; we can never rest content in the belief that we have arrived at moral truths which, because we know them to be true, can be straightforwardly taught to others. Friquegnon argues that the belief that moral knowledge can be attained leads to moral authoritarianism in moral education. On the other hand, Socratic cognitive humility encourages a democratic system of moral education.

Fitzgerald agrees with the basic thrust of Friquegnon's criticism of Kohlberg. After a useful survey of the literature critical of Kohlberg, Fitzgerald singles out and endorses a point made by Gibbs. "Kohlberg's great error, and one that Piaget avoided, was to transpose a descriptive theory of the development of children's moral reasoning, to moral reasoning during the adult years (Gibbs, 1979)."   This transposition changes a psychological-educational theory into a philosophical theory about the nature of moral knowledge. And it is to the resulting philosophical claims of Kohlberg that Friquegnon objects.

Levande's essay, "Content and structure in moral development; a crucial distinction," expresses "a debt of gratitude" to Kohlberg for his willingness to "take on" the areas of philosophy as well as psychology and education. Even though Kohlberg's theory may be defective, Levande argues, it is something that scholars from different backgrounds and disciplines are reacting to, and the resulting cross-fertilization of disciplines should lead to progress in the study of moral development. Levande focuses her criticism of Kohlberg's theory on a single issue. Kolhberg claims to be able to distinguish the form from the content of moral reasoning. He claims that while the content of the different stages varies across cultures, the form of moral reasoning does not, and for this reason his theory of moral development holds across cultures. Levande criticizes both of these claims. She argues that the distinction between form and content in moral reasoning is not as clear-cut as Kohlberg believes, and that the cross-cultural studies which have been done do not support Kohlberg's view that moral development progresses through the same sequence of stages in every culture.

If Kohlberg's theory resembles Plato's in its cognitive stage-sequential emphasis, Bertrand Russell's resembles Aristotle's in the central role of the concept of habits of character. According to Ferree and Vaughn, in their essay "Bertrand Russell's approach to moral education in early childhood," Russell believes that the central business of education in the early years of childhood is "education of character," which consists primarily in the development of sound moral and intellectual habits. Russell singles out four characteristics which are crucial to good character; "vitality, courage, sensitiveness, and intelligence." He also discusses, often in considerable detail, a host of other habits and ways to foster them, but he does not provide any general theory of virtue or typology of virtuous habits to connect his various discussions together (unlike Aristotle). "His major concern," according to Ferree and Vaughn, "is not to offer a typology of habits but to show how desirable habits are to be promoted." Ferree and Vaughn do not fault Russell for his failure to address more theoretical philosophical issues; they attempt to expound his theory and contrast it with a variety of other views on moral education, including Kohlberg's. They suggest, in a brief defense of Russell's position, that his view that moral education consists essentially in providing the optimum environment for the development of sound habits of character is basically correct.

Suter, in his comment on Ferree and Vaughn's paper, agrees with them and with Russell that "genuine moral education involves the intentional fostering of desirable habits;...". However, Suter is not persuaded that much is to be learned from Russell's specific recommendations, and offers some criticisms of Russell to illustrate his skepticism.

It is hard to summarize the points of agreement of the papers in this section, since they set themselves diverse tasks. They do all refer to a greater or lesser extent to Kohlberg, so we might infer that they agree that Kohlberg is an important figure in moral education theory. Most of the papers are critical of Kohlberg. I suspect most of the authors would be sympathetic to Frequegnon's argument against Kohlberg's view that when one attains the sixth stage of moral development one has attained to the "knowledge of the good." But they would also side with Socrates against Protagoras that moral virtue is not merely shared opinion taught by indoctrination (which does not carry us beyond the second or conventional level, in Kohlberg's scheme). And I suspect that all of our authors would be sympathetic to Russell's view that educators ought to attempt to foster good moral and intellectual habits like courage, sensitiveness, justice, generosity, kindness, truthfulness, and the dispositions to seek clarity, consistency, self-knowledge, and judgmental autonomy.

But if there is this degree of agreement, can't we conclude that there is such a thing as moral knowledge, which is shared at least by the authors of the essays in this section (who have all attained the sixth level, perhaps, in Kohlberg's scheme)? This is a difficult philosophical question which is not to be settled as definitely as Friquegnon's essay might lead the unwary reader to believe. If we think of moral knowledge in the way that Plato did in the *Republic,* as resembling mathematical knowledge in precision and certainty, then Friquegnon is correct in arguing that moral knowledge is unattainable. No sensible person spends his intellectual energies continually reexamining mathematical truths; we know that two plus two equals four, and having once understood this, we don't have to be always ready to reexamine it. But most moral philosophers believe that moral principles are not like mathematical truths in this respect. It is reasonable to subject moral principles to continual examination, since they are not known with precision and certainty; if they were, it would be unobjectionable if they were taught in an authoritarian way. If Kohlberg means that we know the good at the sixth stage in the way that we know the truths of arithmetic, then he is surely wrong, and Friquegnon's arguments against his theory are definitive. But there are other ways to characterize moral knowledge. Aristotle, who thought that it was possible to attain to moral knowledge, also warned that this sort of knowledge was not like mathematical knowledge. In a famous passage in the *Nicomachean Ethics* he says that a mark of education is to expect only as much precision in each kind of study as the nature of the subject admits of, and that in ethics, "we must be content to indicate the truth with a rough and general sketch" (*N.E.,* 1094 b, 1962, p. 5). Some Aristotelians would admit that the sort of knowledge demanded by Kohlberg's theory is not impossible of attainment. But before that question can be answered clearly, we must get clear about the nature of moral knowledge, and exactly what sort of knowledge Kohlberg's theory is committed to. The contrast between the two different views of moral knowledge represented in this section (the "moral principle" approach of Kohlberg, and the "moral habit" approach of Russell) is a good introduction to that enterprise.

Finally, I should mention the obvious; that many of the diverse points of view on moral education are not represented in these essays. A major contemporary development is the values clarification movement; this is discussed briefly in Ferree and Vaughn's essay. I would also like to direct the reader's attention to the materials and methods developed by Matthew Lipman and his colleagues at the Institute for the Advancement of Philosophy for Children at Montclair State College. Lipman has written a novel for children in grades 7 through 9 called *Lisa,* which raises various ethical issues for discussion. A teaching manual is available to accompany the novel, entitled *Ethical Inquiry.* Other viewpoints are represented in the references at the end of the papers, especially the papers by Fitzgerald and Hoffman.

REFERENCES

Aristotle. *Nichomachean ethics.* Tr. M. Ostwald. New York: Bobbs-Merrill, 1962.
Beck, C. M., Crittenden, B. S., and Sullivan, E. V. (Eds.). *Moral education: Interdisciplinary approaches.* New York: Newman Press, 1971.

Gibbs, J. C. Kohlberg's moral stage theory. A Piagetian revision. *Human Development*, 1979, 22, 89-112.

Kohlberg, L. Stages of moral development as a basis for moral education. In C. M. Beck, B. A. Crittenden, and E. V. Sullivan (Eds.), *Moral education: Interdisciplinary approaches*. New York: Newman Press, 1971. (a)

Kohlberg, L. From is to ought: How to commit the naturalistic fallacy and get away with it in the study of moral development. In T. Mischel (Ed.), *Cognitive development and epistemology*. New York: Academic Press, 1971. (b)

Kohlberg, L. The cognitive-developmental approach to moral education. In D. Purpel and K. Ryan (Eds.), *Moral education...it comes with the territory*. Berkeley: McCutchan, 1976.

Peters, R. S. Moral developments: A plea for pluralism. In T. Mischel (Ed.), *Cognitive development and epistemology*. New York: Academic Press, 1971.

Plato. *Apology*. Tr. H. Tredennick. In E. Hamilton and H. Cairns (Eds.), *The collected dialogues of Plato*. New York: Random House, 1961.

Plato. *Protagoras*. Tr. B. Jowett and M. Ostwald. New York: Bobbs-Merrill, 1958.

Vlastos, G. Introduction. In Plato, *Protagoras*. New York: Bobbs-Merrill, 1958.

Vlastos, G. Introduction: The paradox of Socrates. In G. Vlastos (Ed.), *The philosophy of Socrates*. Garden City, NY: Doubleday, 1971.

KOLHBERG AT THE "IS-OUGHT" GAP

Marie-Louise Friquegnon

Department of Philosophy
William Patterson College of New Jersey
Wayne, NJ 07470

In an impressive monograph on moral developmental psychology, entitled "From is to ought," Professor Lawrence Kohlberg makes some rather extraordinary claims about both psychology and philosophy, claims that are so appealingly audacious that the reader feels as Adam should have felt when offered a bite of the apple from the tree of knowledge, that is, inclined to search, if not for a serpent, at least for a worm. Kohlberg, thoroughly familiar with philosophical literature from Socrates to Rawls, appreciates the arguments of the Wittgensteinians as to why psychology cannot be value-neutral. He maintains that psychology should engage in dialogue with moral philosophy and claims that his own empirical studies, conducted in accordance with the highest standards of experimental research, have enabled him to arrive at solutions to the most vexing problems of substantive and procedural ethics. In his view the logical relations among ethical principles, as well as the stages of development of moral consciousness both in the child and in the human race, reveal a pre-established harmony, somewhat like Leibnizian clocks that simultaneously peal the arrival of enlightenment.

In the peroration of his monograph, Kohlberg claims that he has rediscovered the Socratic truth about ethics, as follows:

> First, virtue is ultimately one, not many, and it is always the same ideal form regardless of climate or culture. Second, the name of this ideal form is justice. Third, not only is the good one, but virtue is knowledge of the good. He who knows the good chooses the good. Fourth, the kind of knowledge of the good which is virtue is philosophical knowledge or intuition of the ideal form of the good, not correct opinion or acceptance of conventional

261

beliefs.   Most psychologists have never believed any of
these ideas of Socrates. It is hard to understand if you
are not at stage 6 (1971, p. 232).

This magnificent apple requires close inspection. Socrates was not
an ethical relativist, but he nevertheless recognized, and indeed insisted,
that the Form of the Good could at best only be glimpsed through a glass,
darkly. That is why he kept saying that if the Delphic oracle was right in
calling him the wisest man in Greece it was only because he, Socrates,
was wise enough to realize that he knew nothing. Yet Kohlberg has
interpreted Socrates to have claimed that he knew a great deal, as
summarized in the above quotation, and Kohlberg seems to believe that he
shares with Socrates (but with few others) the most important and
profound kind of knowledge, namely, knowledge of what is both right and
good, and that if we follow his advice, we can educate our children to join
him and Socrates on the lofty pinnacle of "Stage Six."

After long study of Kohlberg's work I have become convinced that
there is a worm in his apple of moral wisdom. Because of what W. B.
Gallie (1964) has aptly called the "essentially contested" nature of moral
concepts, there simply cannot be any one universally true set of moral
principles that is apodictically known to Kohlberg or to any one else, and
in view of the "is-ought" gap engendered by this essential contestability,
no one, not even Kohlberg, can validly derive from any alleged psychological "facts" of child development such a set of true moral principles.
Consequently, the moral education of children must not presume to mould
them, however gently and with an appearance of tolerance, toward a
preordained morality.   Moral education is more like exploration of
unknown territory than it is like hothouse horticulture. It employs some
maps but, like those of Columbus, they are tentative and inaccurate, and
the parent or teacher must learn moralty together with the child.   In
brief, I shall defend democratic moral education against Kohlberg's moral
authoritarianism.

Kohlberg claims to have accomplished some remarkable feats. He
claims to have united empirical science with philosophy and to have
solved the fundamental problems of ethics and metaethics, problems that
baffled Plato, Aristotle, Kant, Hume and everyone else. (In all fairness I
should point out that, with an air of disarming modesty, Kohlberg (p. 224)
admits that he might be mistaken in a few details.) Further, he claims to
have discovered the basic structure of universal moral development and to
have provided both the scientific and the philosophical basis for a theory
of education and child rearing. If he has indeed accomplished half of this,
his work will be immortal. When I began to read his papers and those of
his followers I was attracted by the audacity of his aims and by the
sophistication of his knowledge of psychology and philosophy. I was also
impressed by his ecumenical interest in drawing philosophy and science
closer together and by his recognition of the importance of moral
leadership in child rearing. But in examining carefully his evidence and

his conclusions, I found them slipping like sand between my fingers. His system of ideas appears to me now to be a brilliantly constructed house of cards that delicately support each other in a complex structure, but one that collapses into a jumble at the slightest touch. I shall document its structural weaknesses later on. At this point I shall confine myself to explaining what seems to me to be a systematic fault within the overall vision. Kohlberg's work suffers from what Wittgenstein described as fixation on a picture. Kohlberg's picture of the ideal relation between parents and children is that of a gardener with his garden. The gardening model, I should add, is at least an improvement on the machine model of most of Kohlberg's American predecessors, whom Kohlberg rightly criticizes. The machine model, in which child development is envisioned as a product of conditioning processes that work like pulleys and gears, has been favored by behavioristic psychologists from Pavlov to Skinner, who deny that there is an irreducible difference between purposive behavior and inanimate movement. Nevertheless, Kohlberg's gardening picture is still too rigid to suit mankind. It drags us back to the outmoded Aristotelian natural teleology, to the belief that there is a built-in ideal goal state of the species which each individual must reach if he or she or it is properly nurtured. We can say with a fair degree of certainty what kind of soil a tree needs to grow to maximum height, how much sunlight it needs and how much rain. But our criteria of the ideal state of a plant are relative to our human interests. A Bonzai gardener prefers stunted trees, while an English country gardener wants them to grow as large and wild looking as possible. Once we are agreed on the desired goal of plant development, we can have a horticultural science of the means to achieve it. However, when it comes to children, we can neither agree on the end-state to be aimed at, nor be sure of the means of getting there. As Plato pointed out in the *Protagoras*, if we did have such knowledge, good parents would invariably produce good children. But they don't.

Kohlberg assumes that he knows what is the ideal end of moral development and that he has also discovered just how to achieve it. He wants all human beings to achieve moral consciousness of a kind that he calls "stage six," which he considers to be the very highest possible stage of moral development, comparable to the perfection of a prize winning artichoke at a state fair. I shall criticize his theory of stages later on. Here I wish only to point out that Kohlberg is misusing the gardening model in applying it to raising children. If we cannot even agree on the ideal end-state of a plant, how can we do so for a person?

Kohlberg's gardening model might be appropriate if two gigantic assumptions of his were true, namely, that we can have absolute knowledge of moral truth, and that science and ethics can support each other, science providing the means and ethics the ends. I intend to show that both these assumptions are unsound, and that consequently the gardening model is inconsistent with the democratic ideal of education to which Kohlberg gives lip-service. If we had absolute knowledge of moral truth we would be justified in using force to make everyone conform to it. But we don't, so we aren't.

In what does the vaunted superiority of Kohlberg's "stage six" consist? Each successive stage of moral development, according to Kohlberg, is superior to those below it because it resolves more moral conflicts. I quote from Kohlberg (p. 208):

> "Stage five and its extensions cannot yield a universal morality on which all men could agree. It yields a set of procedural principles...but it does not yield substantive moral obligations or choices on which men will agree..."

Kohlberg implies that his own view does yield such "substantive moral choices" and so resolves all moral conflicts. Indeed, his stage six *must* resolve all moral conflicts, or else there would have to be a seventh stage. But this criterion of the truth of a system of morality, that it resolves more moral conflicts than other systems, cannot be sufficient to ensure moral superiority. Kohlberg admits that there can be different moral conclusions about the same situation, even at stage six. In admitting this, he is inconsistent with his main argument for substantive moral absolutism. In any case, the resolution of moral conflict cannot do the work Kohlberg wants it to do, of proving the superiority of stage six. Moral conflicts can be resolved, and often are, by the most barbaric methods, for example, by Nazi propaganda and terror. No doubt Kohlberg would protest that Nazi terror did not really resolve moral conflicts but only seduced or frightened the Germans into a self-deceptive belief that moral conflicts had been resolved. But in that case, the criterion of moral adequacy is no longer *any* resolution of moral conflicts, but some specific kind of resolution that, on some *other* ground, Kohlberg finds satisfactory. Thus he needs a new criterion for judging when this criterion is properly satisfied. The new criterion would be, to say the least, not easy to find.

What other criterion does Kohlberg offer for demonstrating the superiority of stage six? He seems to claim that stage six is the logical terminus of the previous five stages:

> Moral judgment is a role-taking process which has a new logical structure at each stage,...paralleling Piaget's logical stages; this structure is best formulated as a justice structure which is progressively more comprehensive, differentiated, equilibrated than the prior structure (p. 195).

Kohlberg seems to be claiming here that a child is progressively better able to understand other people's points of view as he moves to higher stages of moral development. But such progress does not, as he seems to believe, automatically make the child a more just person. Every confidence man is adept at understanding the points of view of his victims, for only so could he take full advantage of them. Adeptness at role-taking may guarantee good acting and effective salesmanship, but it does not ensure moral integrity.

So justice and "role-taking" are not integrally connected. It seems more reasonable to hold with Hume that certain moral *sentiments,* such as benevolence and sympathy, are at least as essential to moral development as are the stages of conceptual understanding emphasized by Kohlberg. It is hard to accept Kohlberg's claim that considerations of justice resolve more moral conflicts than does a benevolent attitude toward one's fellowmen. In any case, we have already noted the question-begging circularity of the conflict-resolving criterion of moral superiority.

Having said what I think is wrong with Kohlberg's fundamental vision, I shall now summarize Kohlberg's main findings and then proceed to a detailed documentation of where I think he goes wrong.

Over a fifteen year period, Kohlberg made careful studies of children's responses to hypothetical moral problems described to them. He found that their responses became increasingly more "moral" as they developed intellectually, and that their responses progressed through three "levels", each divisible into two stages. Only those children who reached the third level were considered by Kohlberg to be capable of distinctively moral judgment.

On the first level, which Kohlberg calls "preconventional," the child's decisions are said to be governed by fear of punishment (stage one) or by hedonistic considerations (stage two). At this stage there is already some sense of reciprocity, of the "you scratch my back and I'll scratch yours" type. The next level is the conventional level. People follow the rules of their social group for the sake of winning approval (stage three) or because of excessive respect for law and order (stage four). At the third level which is the "postconventional" level, people make moral judgments and reason morally either in terms of rights and obligations which are established and modified by agreed upon procedures (this is the contractarian stage five) or in terms of two universal moral principles, namely, justice and respect for persons, constituting the exalted and elusive stage six.

Similar studies carried out in non-western and in primitive societies convinced Kohlberg that his theory of six stages of moral development applies cross-culturally. He holds that this explains both similarities and differences among cultures that have been described by anthropologists. Individuals in each culture pass through the same successive stages but at varying rates, both for individuals and for cultures. In some cultures, no one reaches level three, that is, stages five and six (p. 174).

In order to draw any reliable conclusions from Kohlberg's statistical findings, we must first become clear as to just what these six stages are stages *of,* that is, as to what he means by a stage of moral development. Does he mean good conduct, or sound moral judgment, or sophisticated ethical reasoning, or conceptual and verbal competence at giving reasons for actions? In different passages in which he tries to explain what he means he seems to shift from one of these meanings to another as if he thinks them equivalent.

One of the most striking paradoxes that I find in Kohlberg's empirical studies is that they say little about the actual moral conduct of the children studied. They deal almost entirely with answers given by children to questions about what they would do and why they would do it in various hypothetical problematic situations. Thus all his scientific evidence is evidence only of verbal competence--the ability to formulate plausible reasons for action. Kohlberg's implicit assumption that conclusions can be drawn about moral judgment and moral conduct from such evidence is dubious, to say the least. What of all those who do good and honest deeds without being able to explain why it is right to do them, such as Huckleberry Finn in protecting Jim, or, for that matter, many of us who suspect ourselves and others of casuistic glibness when we or they give ready solutions to tragic moral dilemmas?

Thus even if Kohlberg has really discovered levels of ability to use moral language in an increasingly sophisticated way, this hardly entitles him to draw conclusions about moral improvement. On the other hand, when he stresses benevolent feelings and role-playing, these surely can develop quite independently of a person's ability to express or even to understand his reasons for action.

To this criticism Kohlberg might reply that each of his stages is a stage of *both* conceptual *and* emotional development. Indeed, he confronts this issue squarely and makes the additional claim, based on some empirical studies, that there is a fairly high correlation between "the maturity of an individual's moral judgment and the maturity of his moral action" (p. 228). But any correlation lower than 1 is much too modest, since as we have seen, Kohlberg agrees with Plato that to know the good is to choose it. Something has gone wrong if there are *any* cases of negative correlation. In fact, several things have gone wrong: first, moral judgment is not the same as competence at giving reasons; secondly, there is no reason whatsoever to trust the judgment of empirical psychologists or even of school teachers when they rate children for moral character and conduct--are they next to tell us whom to vote for in political elections? And thirdly, since Kohlberg claims that moral knowledge *entails* goodness of conduct, it is as silly to look for empirical correlations of this relation as to try to confirm that two plus two equals four by placing two pairs of shoes side by side and triumphantly counting four shoes.

There is also a serious problem in Kohlberg's treatment of the concept of moral development. He calls stages one and two "pre-moral" and he holds that stage six is the only fully moral stage, although he is charitable enough to concede, at times, that perhaps people on stage five reason morally, if not adequately (p. 226). Yet he grants that children can appreciate basic values such as the value of human life at every stage, and can sympathize with others and employ a rudimentary sense of justice. In this regard he mentions that his own son performed his first moral action at the age of four when he had not yet toddled beyond stage one (p. 191).

But if the earlier stages are also stages of genuinely moral judgment and conduct, then what gives stage six its "characteristic superiority?" It may be more sophisticated to refrain from killing one's neighbor after deliberating on Hare's principles of reversibility or on Kohlberg's principles of justice and respect for persons, but why is it more moral than to abstain from murder simply because one feels it is wrong? And this feeling, by the way, can be just as *autonomous* as stage six reasoning. Huck Finn refused to turn in Jim, the runaway slave, not because he could refute a racist argument for slavery, but because of his deep feeling of loyalty to Jim. In so doing, he opposed the pressures of his society and his church. "Well, I guess I'll just have to go to hell," said Huck.

Perhaps the most serious defect in Kohlberg's division of moral development into allegedly empirically discoverable stages is the circularity of his procedure. He concedes to a critic that his theory has built into it assumptions about the relative value of the various stages (Alston, p. 274; Kohlberg, pp. 214-218). But if this is true, then his vaunted scientific findings could not fail to confirm his moral theory, for the theory makes the alleged evidence true by definition.

This problem haunts Kohlberg when he assesses the situations or moral conflict to which the children studied are asked to respond. The investigator must judge whether a certain hypothetical situation is one that calls for a moral response, and which response is morally the best.

The trouble is that one cannot arrive at moral truth from empirical facts alone, no matter how carefully the observations are carried out. One needs a moral theory to identify moral "data", so that the very notion of moral "data," in the sense relevant to empirical science, is philosophically anomalous.

For example, suppose Kohlberg's research assistants were to ask children for their responses to the following situation: A small boy is told by his father to come straight home from school to work in the family store. But at school a friend who is in trouble needs the boy's shoulder to cry on and asks him to go with him for a coke. Should the boy go straight home or accompany his troubled friend?

Suppose a child were to respond that he ought to go home because otherwise his father will punish him. Kohlberg would put this response down to stage one judgment. Yet this might well be unfair. How can we be sure that this hypothetical situation is one of genuine moral conflict? If the father of the boy is an overbearing tyrant, then obeying him to avoid brutal punishment would be the perfectly appropriate thing to do--can we expect small children to be heroic revolutionaries? In any case, the important point is that, in order to grade the response in the Kohlbergian fashion, the observer must make a moral judgment of the situation as *requiring* a certain moral response, and this sort of moralizing is simply not the job of empirical science. Kohlberg's experimental "data" are not data at all, but disguised moral judgments of extremely doubtful validity.

The trouble is precisely what Hume, in his famous "is-ought" passage and Hare, in *The Language of Morals*, said it is, that one cannot derive moral truths from empirical observations alone, no matter how carefully the observations are carried out and no matter how they are statistically analyzed. For one needs a moral theory and a capacity for sound moral judgment to know *what* to observe, that is, to identify and classify correctly the moral facts of the matter.

Thus in order to evaluate Kohlberg's psychological theory of stages of moral development we must first decide whether he has really discovered the true principles of morality and also whether he has taught his researchers how to apply those principles to concrete situations. This is a large order, to say the least.

Let us take a careful look at Kohlberg's system of philosophical ethics. He tries to combine Kantian formalism with the prescriptivist meta-ethics of R. M. Hare and then remedy the shortcomings of this "procedural" meta-ethics by adding two alledgedly substantive principles (also derived from, yet mysteriously not fully appreciated by Kant), namely, the principles of justice and respect for persons. The combination of these ingredients is supposed to resolve all problems of moral conflict.

For Kant, morality meant acting in accordance with universal rules, but he gave us no way of handling conflicts between such rules. Hare dealt with this problem by substituting reversibility of roles for universalizability, thereby, I think, adding a pinch of intuitionism to his Kantian-prescriptivist souffle. Given a situation where one must choose between two rules, one should perform an imaginative reversal of roles and so act toward a second person as one would want that person to act toward oneself were the roles reversed. (How this procedure would work for sadists and masochists is anyone's guess. Perhaps we should then redefine a sadist as someone who refuses to beat a masochist.) In Kohlberg's best known example, where children are asked if a man should steal a drug for his sick wife when the pharmacist demands more than the man can pay, the pharmacist, the husband, and the wife must view the situation from each other's point of view and then, presumably, they will agree on what is the right thing to do.

Hare was less optimistic than Kohlberg about the effectiveness of this procedure in resolving moral conflicts. Kohlberg recognizes this and criticizes Hare's relativism, whereby different agents may come to different moral conclusions on the basis of different principled commitments. As Hare put it, a Nazi might sincerely believe that all Jews should be killed and be willing to apply this principle to himself should he turn out to be Jewish after all.

Kohlberg tries to improve on Hare's view in the direction of moral absolutism. Clearly, he must do so, if his theory of fixed stages of moral development is to bear its heavy philosophical burden without breaking its back. For he must justify the assumption that he, Kohlberg, and his fellow psychologists and educators know what is the morally right thing to do, if they are to assign their subjects' responses to the appropriate stage of development.

Only if there were one right answer to a moral dilemma would we be justified in guiding children toward "the truth" in the way we guide them to the right solution to a problem of arithmetic. This is the sort of ethical discussion that used to take place in religious seminaries, where students were "helped" to see the truth of the religious dogma, and in Chinese Red Guard discussion groups, where workers were "helped" to appreciate the wisdom of Mao Tze Tung.

Far from stimulating genuine moral reflection and development, this kind of moral horticulture of our little seedlings is destined to produce at best only clever casuists. The bright student quickly figures out which responses are expected of him and serves up whatever will get him a high grade. A teacher directed to guide students toward Kohlberg's stage six responses might very well succeed even if both teacher and students commit every moral crime imaginable, just as long as they give the right verbal answers.

Worse yet, the Kohlbergian claim to possession of absolute wisdom supports moral fanaticism and authoritarianism. If one knows without question that action A is morally wrong while action B is right, then one is justified in forcing another person to do B rather than A, the degree of justifiable force depending only on the gravity of the consequences of A and B.

It might be objected that if we cannot be sure of our moral convictions there is no point to moral education of our children, nor to discussion of moral problems. But this would follow only from the denial of the possibility of objective *justification* of moral judgments, that is, from a more extreme ontological scepticism, rather than the modest epistemological scepticism I am here proposing. The recognition that moral concepts have essentially contestable criteria requires modesty toward one's claim to moral wisdom, rather than scepticism about any distinction between right and wrong. This, I believe, was Socrates' real position, rather than the one imputed to him by Kohlberg. For Socrates, the art of dialectic can help to discredit false and inconsistent moral judgments and thus bring us closer to the elusive truth, but we cannot ever be sure that we have arrived at our final destination.

Philosophy can also help to identify situations in which univocal moral solutions cannot be found because of conflicts of principles and obligations. A doctor may have to choose between saving his patient and saving his own child. It seems doubtful that there is one correct resolution of such a dilemma. But recognizing this very fact of irresolvable conflicts represents some progress in understanding the need for ethical tolerance, which is just the sort of tolerance that Kohlberg's moral absolutism rules out.

REFERENCES

Alston, W. P. Comments on Kohlberg's "From is to ought." In T. Mischel (Ed.), *Cognitive development and epistemology.* New York: Academic Press, 1971.

Gallie, W. B. Essentially contested concepts. In *Philosophy and the historical understanding.* New York: Schocken Books, 1964.

Hare, R. M. *The language of morals.* Oxford: Oxford University Press, 1952.

Kohlberg, L. From is to ought. How to commit the naturalistic fallacy and get away with it in the study of moral development. In T. Mischel (Ed.), *Cognitive development and epistemology.* New York: Academic Press, 1971.

COMMENT:

Response to "Kohlberg at the 'Is-Ought' Gap"

Hiram E. Fitzgerald

Department of Psychology
Michigan State University
East Lansing, MI 48824

In 1932 Jean Piaget's, *The Moral Judgment of the Child*, was published. This work stimulated much of the current research concerning the development of moral reasoning. Piaget argued that the child first is a moral realist who views rules as absolute, fixed, and unchangeable. Moral judgments are based on consequences external to the child. Around 9 to 13 years of age the transition to moral relativist occurs--intentionality now providing the basis for moral judgments. In the broadest sense, Piaget proposed a two-stage sequence of moral development: initially, the child uses objective moral reasoning and later uses subjective moral reasoning when confronted with problems requiring moral judgments. Contrary to popular impressions, Piaget did recognize the role that parents might play in facilitating the transition to moral relativist. For example, in *The Moral Judgment of the Child*, he asserts that "those parents who try to give their children a moral education based on intention, achieve very early results...." (1932, p. 130).

Without question, Lawrence Kohlberg has attempted the most systematic elaboration of Piaget's theory (Kohlberg, 1963a, 1963b, 1969, 1971, 1973a, 1973b; Kohlberg and Gilligan, 1971; Kohlberg and Kramer, 1969). Kohlberg's original research, his 1958 doctoral dissertation, involved the cross-sectional study of children and adolescents and was designed to identify age trends in moral reasoning. That is, he wished to identify age trends in moral reasoning that would be independent of such factors as social class, sex, race, culture, or history. From these cross-sectional data he constructed a 3-level, 6-stage descriptive account of the development of moral reasoning, thereby arriving at an invariant stage-sequential model. Kohlberg then sought longitudinal confirmation of his original heuristic model. Unfortunately, the longitudinal follow-up revealed discrepancies with the invariant stage-sequence notion. Some

271

children seemed to skip stages, whereas others regressed to previous stages (Gibbs, 1979). For example, stage 5 and 6 sixteen-year-olds regressed to stage 2 moral reasoning during their college years. To solve this problem, Kohlberg argued that although the college age responses to moral dilemmas were similar in *content* to those of stage 2 moral relativists, the responses were different in *form*. Whereas the thinking of stage 2 moral relativists was aimed at justifying moral judgments to an individual actor, the thinking of the college age moral relativists was aimed at "defining a moral theory and justifying basic terms or principles from the standpoint outside that of a member of a constituted society" (Kohlberg, 1973). Thus, argued Kohlberg, college age moral relativism is more properly viewed as a transitional phase, a stage 4½, marking the shift from conventional to post-conventional levels of moral reasoning. In other words, stage 2 moral relativists are just that, whereas stage 4½ moral relativists deal with meta-ethical subjective relativism (Turiel, 1974). Kohlberg's attempts to account for "skippings" and "regressions" moved him completely away from a heuristic descriptive theory of moral reasoning, to a theory infiltrated by subjective idealism, formal logic, apriorisms, and absolutisms (Sullivan, 1977). Now, rather than merely describing various age-related types of moral reasoning, Kohlberg is moved to the assertion that he has isolated the structure or form of morality from its content. In a Bergsonian sense, Kohlberg seems to have shifted from an interest in discursive "knowledge about" moral reasoning to an intuitive "knowledge of" moral reasoning. Not only does the gardener now know how to till the soil and when to plant the seeds, but knows *a priori* that the crop will win the blue ribbon at the county fair.

During the past decade, Kohlberg's developmental theory of moral reasoning has been criticized as enthnocentric (Simpson, 1974), ideological (Sullivan, 1977), elitist (Fraenkel, 1978), abstract (Aron, 1977), 'perniciously individualistic' (Hogan, 1975), subjectively idealistic (Braun and Baribeau, 1978), lacking an underlying general ethical theory (Peters, 1971), proposing nothing more than a classification of habitual styles of moral reasoning (Alston, 1971), overextending the concept of stages (Gibbs, 1977, 1979), and relying on empirical studies that are hopelessly methodologically flawed (Kurtines and Grief, 1974). For example, responding to Kohlberg's contention that individuals in preliterate societies progress more slowly through the lower hierarchical stages of moral reasoning than do individuals in Western societies, and become fixed at lower levels, Simpson (1974) cites the following response to one of the more famous of the Kohlbergian dilemmas, "should the husband steal the drug to save his wife's life?" The respondant's answer was:

"Yes....The inherent worth of the individual human being is the central value in a set of values where the principles of justice and love are normative for all human relationships."

Simpson asks, "Is this a measure of success at Philosophy 800, or a measure of the development of moral reasoning?   Oh pity the poor savages in state colleges, our ghettos, in villages and tribes abroad who cannot express themselves so neatly, so profoundly, and so elegantly" (Simpson, p. 95). As respects methodological issues, Kurtines and Grief (1974) have offered a devastating critique, noting problems related to the construction, administration, and scoring of the Moral Judgment Scale (the major instrument used to assess Kohlberg's stages), reliability and validity of the scale, and the paucity of empirical support for the theory other than that offered by Kohlberg himself.

Professor Friquegnon's name now may be added to this list of Kohlbergian dissenters. She quite properly chides Kohlberg for asserting that he has captured the elusive Ideal Form that moral philosophers have been chasing since the dawn of human existence.   While deontologists might be correct in asserting that the meaning of ethical terms goes beyond observable facts on which ethical judgments are made, we first must have some ethical facts. Unfortunately, it seems that Kohlberg has not yet provided them.

Friquegnon (1980) reminds us that Kohlberg's theory is based on "evidence of verbal competence or the ability to formulate plausible reasons for action;" that there are observer biases built into the analysis of responses to moral dilemmas; that there is little, if any, correspondence between moral reasoning and moral action; and that Kohlberg is unclear as to which meaning of 'stage' he intends. Does a stage of moral development refer to 'good conduct,' 'sound moral judgment,' 'sophisticated ethical reasoning,' or 'conceptual competence at articulating reasons for actions?'

Now at some point I suppose that it is at least fair to ask what all of this fuss is about. Is it because Kohlberg has proposed a stage-sequential theory of moral development that places primary emphasis on cognitive structures underlying the development of moral reasoning? I think not. Is it because he asserts that there is a universal principle of justice? Not entirely. Is it because he implies that since there is a Stage 6, a universal principle of justice, he has provided, in Professor Friquegnon's words, "both the scientific and the philosophical basis for a theory of education and child rearing?" I think so. Collectively, the criticisms offered by Professor Friquegnon are made in defense of "democratic moral education against Kohlberg's moral authoritarianism." While I am not completely certain that I understand what "democratic moral education" is, it is clear that it is not related paradigmatically to "machine" or "garden models" of child rearing. If Friquegnon is opting for pluralism, then I would like to suggest that democratic moral education might best be viewed as a multivariate process conceptualized within either a systemic, organismic paradigm or a dialectical one. Kohlberg's great error, and one that Piaget avoided, was to transpose a descriptive theory of the development of children's moral reasoning, to moral reasoning during the adult years

(Gibbs, 1979). I am in complete agreement with Gibbs' (1979) assertion that "....the emergence of philosophical reflection in human development is a valuable object of study in socio-historical, existential, and humanistic terms, but *not* in Piagetian stage-sequential terms" (p. 107). Gibbs' proposed revision of Kohlberg's theory posits two phases of moral development, the standard (child) phase and the existential (adult) phase, and suggests that stage-sequencing applies only to the development of moral reasoning during the child phase.

Among the many tasks involved with growing up are those related to learning the ground rules for social living. One set of rules the child must learn involves the generally accepted moral standards by which actions are judged to be "good" or "bad." While it is a fundamental thesis of socialization theory that children *learn* values, attitudes, and beliefs, I am not aware of any contemporary theory of socialization that regards the child as a passive participant in the process. Children do think, they do evaluate, they do reason, and they take into consideration differences between what models say and what models do. Values, attitudes, and beliefs and moral decisions based upon them emerge from transactions among children and parents, siblings, peers, neighbors, relatives, teachers, priests, and the multitudes to whom children are exposed via the media. Ample empirical evidence attests to the fact that children's moral behavior, including their values and moral judgments, are influenced by such factors as parental discipline techniques (Hoffman, 1970), parental value orientations (McKinney, 1971; Oljenik and McKinney, 1977), family rearing climates (Baumrind, 1971), and cultural values (Bronfenbrenner, 1962), but none of these factors have been shown to pre-determine the child's moral end state. Even if we were to organize child rearing and education to guide children to the "truth" or to "a categorical imperative of justice," we can be assured that not all children would play the game according to our rules. Professor Friquegnon can be assured that "democratic moral education" is in no serious danger from "Kohlbergian authoritarianism."

REFERENCES

Alston, W. P. Comments on Kohlberg's "From is to ought." In T. Mischel (Ed.), *Cognitive development and epistemology.* New York: Academic Press, 1971.

Aron, I. E. Moral philosophy and moral education. A critique of Kohlberg's theory. *School Review,* 1977, *85,* 197-217.

Baumrind, D. Current patterns of parental authority. *Developmental Psychology Monographs,* 1971, *4,* 1-103.

Braun, C. M. J. and Baribeau, J. M. C. Subjective idealism in Kohlberg's theory of moral development. A critical analysis. *Human Development,* 1978, *21,* 289-301.

Bronfenbrenner, U. Soviet methods of character education: Some implications for research. *American Psychologist,* 1962, *17,* 550-564.

Fraenkel, J. R. The Kohlbergian paradigm. Some reservations. In Scharf (Ed.), *Readings in moral education.* Minneapolis: Winston Press, 1978.

Friquegnon, M. L. Kohlberg at the is-ought gap. Paper presented at the conference on Philosophy, Children and the Family. East Lansing, MI. March 29, 1980.

Gibbs, J. C. Kohlberg's stages of moral judgment: Adminstrative Critique. *Harvard Educational Review,* 1977, *47,* 43-61.

Gibbs, J. C. Kohlberg's moral stage theory. A Piagetian revision. *Human Development,* 1979, *22,* 89-112.

Hogan, R. Theoretical egocentrism and the problem of compliance. *American Psychologist,* 1975, *30,* 533-540.

Hoffman, M. L. Moral Development. In P. H. Mussen (Ed.), *Carmichael's Manual of Child Psychology,* (Vol. 2), 1970.

Kohlberg, L. *The development of modes of moral thinking and choice in the years ten to sixteen.* Unpublished doctoral dissertation, University of Chicago, 1958.

Kohlberg, L. The development of children's orientations toward a moral order: I. Sequence in the development of moral thought. *Vita Humana,* 1963, *6,* 11-33. (a)

Kohlberg, L. Moral development and identification. In H. W. Stevenson (Ed.), *Yearbook of the National Society for the Study of Education.* Chicago, IL: University of Chicago Press, 1963. (b)

Kohlberg, L. From is to ought. How to commit the naturalistic fallacy and get away with it in the study of moral development. In T. Mischel (Ed.), *Cognitive development and epistemology.* New York: Academic Press, 1971.

Kohlberg, L. The claim to moral adequacy of a highest stage of moral judgment. *Journal of Philosophy,* 1973, *70,* 630-646. (a)

Kohlberg, L. Continuities in childhood and adult moral development revisited. In P. Baltes and K. W. Schaie (Eds.), *Life-span developmental psychology.* New York: Academic Press, 1973. (b)

Kohlberg, L., and Gilligan, C. The adolescent as a philosopher. The discovery of the self in a postconventional world. *Daedalus,* 1971, 1051-1086.

Kohlberg, L., and Kramer, R. Continuities and discontinuities in childhood and adult moral development. *Human Development,* 1969, *12,* 93-120.

Kohlberg, L. Stage and sequence: The cognitive developmental approach to socialization. In D. A. Goslin (Ed.), *Handbook of socialization theory and research.* Chicago: Rand McNally, 1969.

Kurtines, W., and Grief, E. B. The development of moral thought: Review and evaluation of Kohlberg's approach. *Psychological Bulletin,* 1974, *81,* 453-470.

McKinney, J. P. The development of values--prescriptive or proscriptive. *Human Development,* 1971, *14,* 71-80.

Olejnik, A. B., and McKinney, J. P. Parental value orientation and generosity in children. In H. E. Fitzgerald and J. P. McKinney (Eds.), *Developmental Psychology: Studies in Human Development* (Rev. ed.). Homewood, IL: The Dorsey Press, 1977.

Peters, R. S. Moral development: A plea for pluralism. In T. Mischel (Ed.), *Cognitive development and epistemology.* New York: Academic Press, 1971.

Piaget, J. *The moral judgement of the child.* New York: The Free Press, 1965/1932.

Simpson, E. L. Moral development research. A case study of scientific cultural bias. *Human Development,* 1974, *17,* 81-106.

Sullivan, E. A study of Kohlberg's structural theory of moral development. A critique of liberal social science ideology. *Human Development,* 1977, *20,* 325-376.

Turiel, E. Conflict and transition in adult moral development. *Child Development,* 1974, *45,* 14-29.

CONTENT AND STRUCTURE IN MORAL DEVELOPMENT:

A CRUCIAL DISTINCTION

Diane I. Levande

School of Social Work
Michigan State University
East Lansing, MI 48824

Studies of moral development in the Piaget and Kohlberg tradition have been the subject of growing and challenging debate as evidenced by the presentations today. Philosophers attack Kohlberg's particular brand of philosophical reasoning. For example, R. S. Peters (1976) criticizes Kohlberg for his reluctance to consider other philosophical systems by suggesting that Kohlberg simply does not do his homework. At the same time it is not unheard of for some philosophers to allow that Kohlberg's abilities as a social scientist, especially as a researcher, may really be quite good.

Social scientists, on the other hand, have been complaining about the theoretical formulations and research methodology in studies of moral development for some time, while occasionally admitting that Kohlberg may have something in his philosophical and educational approaches. To complete this scenario, I recently heard an educator give Kohlberg high marks for his empirical work, medium marks for his philosophical foundations, but a failing grade in the design and implementation of moral education programs.

I do not come here to either praise or bury Kohlberg, but it seems to me that we owe a debt of gratitude to him for his willingness to take on at least the areas of moral philosophy, moral development, and moral education. To produce a body of work which scholars from diverse backgrounds can analyze, react to, and build upon might be noted as quite an accomplishment. Even if we have serious differences with the work in progress, as is obviously the case, this renewed vigor in the study of moral development may provide the necessary corrections, additions, or innovations leading to firmer foundations in this complex and important area. And, the cross fertilization between disciplines and professions may well be worth it.

Setting gratitude aside for a moment, there are at least a few questions which might be raised concerning the study of ethnic ethics, or more generally, questions about the comparison of cultures and subcultures according to the tenets of cognitive-developmental theory as applied in the area of morals. A major issue which we have heard raised today relates to the question of what is universal in moral development and what is relative to culture or person. As has been indicated, one of the most frequent findings in the numerous studies attempting to test the moral development stage concept is the age-relatedness correlation: The older the child, the more likely he or she will be found at a higher level of moral reasoning in both the Piaget and Kohlberg schemes. Studies, with some exceptions, have replicated this finding across cultures, subcultures, sexes, and socio-economic levels. Kohlberg has no problem explaining this finding. According to his theory this result is expected since all people employ the same basic moral concepts, at least as related to justice, equality, and reciprocity. All individuals go through the same stages of reasoning about such concepts, and furthermore, all pass through such stages in the same invariant, logical order, though it is recognized that rate of progress and how far one progresses in terms of stages or levels can and does vary.

In order to maintain the age-related, invariant stage position a crucial distinction is made between structure and content in moral reasoning. Content refers to the meaning or substance of a person's beliefs influenced by such variables as culture, subculture, socialization experiences, and personality characteristics. Structure indicates how a person thinks about the meaning of his or her beliefs, and this reasoning process is held to be universal in the cognitive-developmental framework. There are some critical issues related to this separation of structure and content which we might briefly explore. Those issues include the influence of content on moral functioning when divorced from structure, how content and structure may act on each other, and the methodological problem of determining what is content and what is structure.

In our common everyday experience it is often contended that passion or emotion, rather than reason, guides our moral beliefs and actions, and that in order to really understand functioning in the moral domain, we must pay attention to meaning (or content) and the accompanying feelings. As R. S. Peters (1971) indicates, "This links with another central aspect of morality, to which Kohlberg pays too little attention, namely, the intimate connection between knowing the difference between right and wrong, and caring."

Speaking of the relative importance of content and structure, Derek Wright (1971) states, "It is not unreasonable to suppose that why a person thinks an action is wrong is much less important than that he thinks it wrong." Selman (1976) indicates that few professionals who work with children in the clinical sense view the structure of moral development as applicable to the psychological handling of children's social and emotional behavior. While maintaining that his research and experience has demonstrated the aplicability of the structural component to both educational and clinical intervention, Selman aptly characterizes the clinical situation as one in which the amount of data generated by the child client is overwhelming. While more attention might be focused on the structural aspects of such data, the content of this information remains equally important. Alston (1971) summarizes this point appropriately, "After all, morality is content as well as form, and to understand a particular person's moral character we need to know both."

Thus, there is at least some justification for considering that the content of moral beliefs is a potent influence, perhaps, as some suggest, the most salient influence in relation to moral action or behavior.

If structure and content in moral development exist as separate components (and some argue that this is a false dichotomy) there also is the related issue of how these two aspects influence each other. One view is that structure determines content. Kohlberg (1976) for example, indicates the relative importance of structure in determining content when he states, "Content influences will vary with the developmental stage. We are most susceptible to the influence of others, such as our peers, at the Conventional Stage of moral development."

However, a significant body of research on Piaget's dimensions of moral judgment indicates that content can impact upon structure in a highly significant way, and this research is directly related to the data reported today. The most researched dimension in Piaget's theory of moral judgment is Immanent Justice: The belief that the physical universe helps maintain the moral order. Piaget's classic story on the dimension involves the boy who steals and runs away, crossing a rickety old bridge in his escape. Will the bridge collapse as the boy crosses it as punishment for his stealing? According to this theoretical framework those who respond yes, or indicate in open-ended responses that this will happen, are expressing a more immature judgment than those who indicate that whether or not the bridge collapses is unrelated to the boy's stealing.

In summarizing the research data on this dimension of moral judgment, Hoffman (1970) found substantial support for the progression away from a belief in Immanent Justice with increasing age. However, a few noteable exceptions were found. For example, Medinnus (1959) found a situation or content specific factor on Immanent Justice with a decreasing belief in this concept with increasing age on one story, but an increasing belief in Immanent Justice with age on another story. Havighurst and Neugarten's classic study (1955) of ten American Indian groups shows a predominant trend toward an increasing belief in Immanent Justice in adolescence and adulthood among this population. Hart (1962) found that men hospitalized for mental illness manifested a greater belief in Immanent Justice than non-hospitalized "normal" males. One interpretation of these findings might be that culture, sub-culture, group values and beliefs, and individual personality variables can overwhelm structure.

The dimension of Moral Realism (judging all acts in terms of consequences rather than intent) also has been the subject of investigation. This dimension holds that the person who does more damage, tells the biggest lie, or whatever, is judged as worse, regardless of motive or intent. This view represents the immature moral judgment. Once again, a developmental trend is found toward intentionality with increasing age but some exceptions in these studies suggest that structure and content interact. Likona (1976) has shown that increases in the consideration of intentions may be specific to the story being presented. In his first story a boy told his father he had a headache in order to get out of shoveling snow and this boy was considered naughtier than a boy who got so excited that he said a kneehigh snowfall was way over his head. In the United States, first graders from both middle and lower income groups almost always say the intentional deception (the headache excuse) is worse. Piaget's Swiss children of the same age said almost the opposite. In a second story, however, only 50% of the U.S. children consider intentions when a boy who tries to deliberately trick his sister by telling her the wrong time is not judged as bad as a boy who unwittingly tells his brother the wrong time, causing him to miss a bus.

We could continue with such illustration on the dimensions related to punishment as well but the point is that some studies do exist which have not verified the age-related progression in moral development. Most often the interpretations of these findings suggest that culture, sub-culture, or socialization influences overwhelm the structural system.

Perhaps the most crucial question involves what is structure and what is content, or the separation of these two aspects. A critical challenge to cognitive-developmental theory in this area comes from those who argue that so called structural changes in moral reasoning may simply represent different levels of verbal ability developed through appropriate reinforcement. Simpson (1974) argues that those at Kohlberg's Stage 6 are not functioning independently of their socialization but instead have been thoroughly socialized into the company of intellectual elites who value and practice analytic, abstract, and logical reasoning.

In an effort to clarify the separation of structure and content in evaluating responses, Kohlberg (1976) has revised his assessment methodology moving from what was known as "aspect scoring" to "issue scoring." Either method of scoring is a complex undertaking which requires specific training. Some researchers are critical of the revised system, maintaining that you can't change the rules in the middle of the game. Kohlberg, however, maintains that this change is a perfectly legitimate methodological refinement. It is difficult to assess which group is at the higher level of moral development on this issue!

Aside from the difficult task of categorizing or scoring children's responses to moral dilemmas, the method used to present such moral conflict situations is also worth considering. Some studies have demonstrated that varying the format of presentation by using pictures instead of verbal stories, or by employing forced-choice responses rather than open-ended response categories can change the level of moral judgment. Variations in story content from simple to complex situations or from minor to severe consequences can also cause judgments to fluctuate. Magown and Lee (1970) demonstrated that stories assessing Immanent Justice tended to elicit high-level answers when the story was based on conditions familiar to the subject, and low-level responses when the story was based on situations taken from foreign cultures. Havighurst and Neugarten (1955) found just the reverse with Navajo children on the changeability of rules: Immature judgments were more likely to be shown on situations close to home while more mature judgments (in Piagetian terms) were given for culturally more remote situations.

In summary, it seems most appropriate for research in moral development which is explicitly directed toward the comparison of groups from diverse cultural, ethnic, and/or socio-economic backgrounds to take into consideration the critical issues involved in the content and structure distinction.

REFERENCES

Alston, W. P. Comments on Kohlberg's "From is to ought." In T. Mischel (Ed.), *Cognitive development and epistemology.* New York: Academic Press, 1971.

Hart, H. C. Piaget's test of immanent justice responses compared for several patient-nonpatient populations. *Journal of Genetic Psychology,* 1962, *101*, 333-341.

Havighurst, R., and Neugarten, B. *American Indian and white children: A sociological investigation.* Chicago: University of Chicago Press, 1955.

Hoffman, M. D. Moral development. In P. H. Mussen (Ed.), Carmichael's *Manual of child psychology,* 3rd ed., Vol. 2. New York: Wiley, 1970.

Kohlberg, L. Moral stages and moralization. In T. Likona (Ed.), *Moral development and behavior.* New York: Holt, Rinehart and Winston, 1976.

Magowan, S., and Lee, T. Some sources of error in the use of the projective method for the assessment of moral judgment. *British Journal of Psychology,* 1970, *61*, 535-543.

Medinnus, G. Immanent justice in children. *Journal of Genetic Psychology,* 1959, *94*, 253-262.

Peters, R. S. Moral development: A plea for pluralism. In T. Mischel (Ed.), *Cognitive development and epistemology.* New York: Academic Press, 1971.

Peters, R. S. Why doesn't Lawrence Kohlberg do his homework? In D. Purpel and K. Ryan (Eds.), *Moral education...it comes with the territory.* Berkeley: McCutchan Publishing Corporation, 1976.

Selman, R. Social-cognitive understanding: A guide to educational and clinical practice. In T. Likona (Ed.), *Moral development and behavior.* New York: Holt, Rinehart and Winston, 1976.

Simpson, E. Moral development research: A case for scientific cultural bias. *Human Development,* 1974, *17,* 81-106.

Wright, D. *The psychology of moral behavior.* New York: Penguin Books, 1971.

BERTRAND RUSSELL'S APPROACH TO

MORAL EDUCATION IN EARLY CHILDHOOD

George Ferree and Scott R. Vaughn

College of Education
Michigan State University
East Lansing, MI 48824

In his *Autobiography*, Bertrand Russell reports: "When my first child was born, in November 1921, I felt an immense release of my pent-up emotion, and during *the next ten years* my main purposes were parental" (1969b, p. 211, emphasis ours). The decade to which Russell refers-- Russell, incidentally was fifty at its outset--was indeed for him a period of great involvement in and reflection upon child-rearing and education in a broader sense. During this time Russell published two major books as well as numerous articles on education, and he and his second wife, Dora, founded and conducted their celebrated if sometimes controversial Beacon Hill School.

Russell's first full-length treatise on education, *Education and the Good Life*, published in 1926, addresses itself explicitly to the matter of the moral education of young children. In this paper we should like to elucidate and criticize certain of these views of Russell on moral education and to make some brief comparisons with contrasting positions.

A GENERAL SKETCH OF RUSSELL'S POSITION

It is well to note initially that Russell in his writings on moral education does not occupy himself elaborately with metaethical considerations. Although he does engage in brief metaethical deliberation elsewhere (1962, pp. 90-96; 1969a, pp. 228-252), one looks in vain in *Education and the Good Life* for attempts to demarcate moral from nonmoral discourse or for efforts to elucidate the meaning of ethical terms. Nor does Russell engage in extensive second-order reflection upon his manner of justifying what he in Aristotelian fashion calls the virtues he would promote in the young. Rather Russell seems to assume, correctly or incorrectly, that the moral terms he employs are sufficiently clear for his purposes and that his efforts at justification, when he makes them, stand up fairly well for the popular readership he is addressing.

The business of deliberate education in the early years, according to Russell, is *the education of character,* which he distinguishes from "education in knowledge, which may be called instruction in the strict sense" (1926, p. 10). The basic features of one's character are inevitably formed during the early years--by the age of six, on Russell's view-- hence the special importance of moral education in early childhood. The principal task of the educator at this stage is to provide the sort of "physical, emotional, and intellectual care of the young" (1926, pp. 60-61) which will result in a desirable character.

For Russell there are "four characteristics which...jointly form the basis of an ideal character": vitality, courage, sensitiveness, and intel- ligence" (1926, p. 60). These virtues do not somehow emerge in the young inevitably, maturationally, but are the product of education--just as are also their corresponding vices: laziness, cowardice, hardheartedness, and stupidity (1926, p. 83).

Vitality, for Russell, is a physiological feature, a kind of robust, vigorous health which brings with it satisfaction in being alive and an active curiosity about the world. "Courage," on Russell's use, ranges over an array of features, including, noteworthily, the absence of irrational fear. Sensitiveness, for Russell, in its highest form is the capacity for abstract sympathy, an active regard for others, including those remote in space and/or time and those who are not objects of special affection. "Intelligence," according to Russell, ranges over "both actual knowledge and receptivity to knowledge" (1926, p. 73).

Russell acknowledges that his list of four features may not be complete, but he thinks "it carries us a good way" (1926, p. 60). He justifies his choice of these features by citing the consequences to which a widespread fostering of these features in human beings would lead.

> A community of men and women possessing vitality, courage, sensitiveness, and intelligence, in the highest degree that education can produce, would be very dif- ferent from anything that has hitherto existed. Very few people would be unhappy. The main causes of unhappiness at present are ill-health, poverty, and an unsatisfactory sex-life. All of these would become very rare (1926, p. 82).

With regard to poverty Russell explicitly suggests: "*Sensitiveness* would make people wish to abolish it, *intelligence* would show them the way, and *courage* would lead them to adopt it" (1926, p.82, emphasis ours). Russell repeatedly affirms his conviction that people having the sort of character he commends would be able to cope well with their problems, would find personal well-being, and would contribute to a better world for all. He does not offer extensive arguments in support of the probability of these contentions, his chief intention being, rather, to offer specific, how-to-do-it advice to moral educators--who, in the main, are parents.

THE CONCEPT OF HABIT IN RUSSELL'S POSITION

In his discussion of the concrete details in which his ideals are embodied, it is clear that for Russell moral education is a matter of deliberately fostering certain *habits* in the young. "The secret of modern moral education," he suggests, "is to produce results by means of good habit" (1926, p. 114). "The new-born infant has reflexes and instincts but no habits" (1926, p. 88). Nonetheless the young child has an enormous capacity for and inclination toward the acquisition of habits, and those habits acquired in the early years have a profound impact upon later life. Thus Russell says:

> The rapidity with which infants acquire habits is amazing. Every bad habit acquired is a barrier to better habits later; that is why the first formation of habits in early infancy is so important. If the first habits are good, endless trouble is saved later. Moreover, habits acquired very early feel, in later life, just like instincts; they have the same profound grip. New contrary habits acquired afterwards cannot have the same force; for this reason, also, the first habits should be a matter of grave concern (1926, p. 89).

The habits which Russell wishes to foster in the young are of course those required for a person to be vital, courageous, sensitive, and intelligent; but Russell does not make any systematic attempt to show how the vast array of particular habits which he discusses in *Education and the Good Life* are subsumable under or are otherwise capable of being mapped by reference to these four terms. He considers how youngsters come to be respectful of life, kind, generous, just, truthful, constructive, well-mannered, and so on; but he does not, save incidentally, speak of these habits with explicit reference to his basic four ideals. His major concern is not to offer a typology of habits but to how desirable habits are to be promoted.

Desirable habits are not in any basic way promoted, on Russell's view, by hortatory injunction. Courage, for example, is not something a youngster *wills* upon himself as he responds to the admonition "Be brave!" Rather the courageous youngster is one who has had a variety of experiences which over time have *disposed* him to act in courageous ways. He may be disposed, for example, to endure hurts without making a fuss because in his experience of small mishaps he has not been given too much sympathy. Or he may be inclined readily to go to bed in a dark room because his experience has never exposed him "to the suggestion that the dark is terrifying" (1926, p. 104). For Russell there is no single, specific disposition called "courage" but rather a whole array acquired in a variety of settings. Thus it is entirely possible for one to be courageous in a great many contexts and yet to lack courage in others. The notion that a person either possesses courage in some absolute way or not at all is obviously wrongheaded for Russell.

Russell offers no explicit analysis of his concept of habit, but from his use of the word "habit" and his employment of terms denoting particular habits it is clear that he regards habits as learned *ways* of thinking, feeling, and doing. Thus all of the following are equally manifestations of habit: *regarding* the truth as establishable in a certain manner, *prizing* the truth, and *telling* the truth. Habits, then, are *dispositions*--Russell explicitly employs this term on occasion-- dispositions to respond in certain characteristic ways in certain sorts of situations.

The crucial question for the moral educator is how to foster desirable dispositions--and to deter the bad. While Russell does recognize a doctrine of positive and negative reinforcement, he offers few gener- alized rules in answer to this question, proceeding, rather, case by case. The disposition terms he employs in his discussion of some cases are highly specific--e.g., "punctuality"--whereas in some other cases Rus- sell's disposition terms are of a much more generic sort--e.g., "intelli- gence," "courage," etc. Punctuality may be characterized fairly directly and completely as the disposition to arrive on time. Intelligence, however--like courage, which we mentioned earlier--is a matter not of just one but a variety of dispositions: the disposition to observe carefully, to seek out relevant evidence, to be consistent, to project probable consequences, and so on. Generic disposition terms, then, range over a whole host of specific disposition.

These specific dispositions are best fostered in the young, Russell suggests, in the context of particular cases. The ideal learning situation is one in which everything is "concrete and demanded by the existing situation" (1926, p. 182). Russell explicitly says: "It is much easier to grasp a concrete instance, and apply analogous considerations to an analogous instance, than to apprehend a general rule and proceed deduc- tively" (1926, pp. 174-175). Thus Russell enjoins the parent who is teaching his son:

> Do not say, in a general way, "Be brave, be kind," but urge him to some particular piece of daring, and then say, "Bravo, you were a brave boy"; get him to let his sister play with his mechanical engine, and when he sees her beaming with delight, say, "That's right, you were a kind boy" (1926, p. 175).

Russell clearly does not limit the occasions for deliberate moral education to those useful, "teachable" situations which just happen to come along in the course of everyday living--although, to be sure, he recognizes the enormous importance of making the most of them. He is also quite willing--indeed, regards it as obligatory--for the moral educator deliberately to bring about circumstances that encourage good habits. If ordinary circumstances do not suffice, the moral educator should *contrive* them. Beacon Hill School--the school which Russell and his wife founded to educate their own children--was just such a contrivance on a large scale.

It is not the intent of the present paper to detail or to evaluate the vast array of specific methods Russell offers for bringing about various dispositions. Russell himself in his *Autobiography,* written some forty years after *Education and the Good Life,* is self-critical, recognizing that some of his suggestions in that 1926 volume were harsh and that his psychology was perhaps overly optimistic. "Nevertheless," he says, "as regards values I find nothing in it to recant" (1969b, p. 312). Nor does Russell disclaim in any way his general posture on what moral education is. He seems to have continued to regard moral education as the *intentional fostering of desirable habits.*

RUSSELL'S POSITION CONTRASTED WITH SOME OTHER VIEWS

An Existentialist View

The views of some current writers and researchers on moral education diverge patently in certain respects from those advanced by Bertrand Russell. Some avowedly existentialist thinkers, for example, have frontally attacked the view that education--moral education or any other education--is the intentional formation of fundamental dispositions in the young by parents and teachers. The stance of these existentialists--decidedly Sartrean in character--is that "one is the author of his own dispositions" (Morris, 1966, p. 110). Cultural alternatives along with the possibilities offered by the child's own received psycho-physical equipment provide options to the child--including the option to be rational and the option to make any one of an array of emotional responses. But it is the child who selects or rejects these and other options available to him for self-creation. It is wrong-headed and futile, on this existentialist view, for the moral educator to enjoin or exhort the young to become this or that. The business of education is strictly to provide options, and to help the young to explore those options if they so decide.

As we have already noted, Russell also holds that hortatory injunctions and appeals to the will are indefensible, largely ineffectual means for bringing about good character. On the matter of formation of fundamental dispositions, however, Russell and the existentialists decidedly part company. Russell's view is that during the early years, long before the child has developed the capacity rationally to consider alternatives or to select from among them, the educative influences of this environment are gradually, inexorably shaping his character to a considerable extent. Even the style of his thinking is determined very early in life. Russell is not saying that after the first few years--say the first six--a good character cannot go bad. "There is no age," says Russell, "at which untoward circumstances or environment will do no harm" (1926, p. 239). And, happily, there is no age at which character cannot be altered for the better.

Such alterations for the better, even in Russell's scheme of things, for a given person may be the result of a rational scrutiny of his own dispositions and of a deliberate effort to change them. But this capacity for the inclination toward rational self-scrutiny and self-improvement-- for those who have it--is itself, on Russell's view, considerably the product of their early education. Moreover, the great array of dispositions come by in early childhood profoundly grip the person, are resistent to change, and seldom, if ever, are replaced by habits of the same force (1926, p. 89). Vast numbers of adults spend their lives battling, as it were, ways of thinking, feeling, and doing acquired in the aptly labelled *formative* years. Utterly irrational feelings of guilt about sexual activity, for example, plague most of in the Western World. Unfortunately, such feelings do not magically go away immediately, once and for all, once a person has made an existential decision not to have them. Russell would have a person's early education spare him the anguish of such irrational guilt.

The Values-Clarifiers' View

The so-called values clarification movement in the United States is another approach to moral education with which Russell's views are considerably at variance. Proponents of the values clarification orientation seem to be saying that the task of the moral educator is to *encourage*--this is their word--the young to become completely clear on what their values are, not to foster any particular values.

Perhaps Russell would point out that clarity is itself a value and that to seek to dispose youngsters to clarify their values necessarily commits value clarifiers to the active promotion of a whole range of dispositions in the young--for example, the disposition to examine presuppositions, to consider the consistency of a value with other values, to project consequences for action, to consider alternatives, and so on. These are dispositions which value clarifiers themselves stress (Roth, Harmon, Simon, 1966, pp. 38-48, 259-261).

Russell, of course, has no quarrel with the fostering of such habits. Clarity for him is exceedingly important--perhaps one of the key components of what he calls intelligence--but the possession of the habits essential to clarifying one's values does not by itself constitute a sufficient condition for a desirable character. Nor does Russell suppose that the dispositions needed to clarify values, as helpful as they are, are likely to generate the full range of features appropriate to a desirable character. Russell would have the young become vital, courageous, sensitive, and intelligent--that is, to come by the wide array of dispositions that these four ideals necessitate. Values clarifiers, by way of contrast, eschew the active promotion of any dispositions, albeit as we have observed, they do not--cannot--avoid it.

Lawrence Kohlberg's View

The research of Lawrence Kohlberg on the stages of moral development seriously challenges some of the key views of Bertrand Russell on moral education. Kohlberg (1973) has found that across cultures moral development proceeds in an "invariant developmental sequence" the first discernible stages of which are characterized as follows:

> Stage 1:   Orientation toward punishment and unquestioning deference to superior power. The physical consequences of action regardless of their human meaning determine its goodness or badness.

> Stage 2:   Right action consists of that which instrumentally satisfies one's own needs and occasionally the needs of others. Human relations are viewed in terms like those of the marketplace. Elements of fairness, of reciprocity and equal sharing are present, but they are always interpreted in a physical, pragmatic way. Reciprocity is a matter of "you scratch my back and I'll scratch yours" not of loyalty, gratitude or justice (p. 133).

These two stages, usually occupied by children aged four to ten, Kohlberg calls the *preconventional* level. There are two more levels, the *conventional* and the *postconventional*, each of which has two stages. The most developed stage of moral development, stage 6, Kohlberg describes thus:

> Stage 6:   Orientation toward decisions of conscience and toward self-chosen *ethical principles* appealing to logical comprehensiveness, universality and consistency. These principles are abstract and ethical (the Golden Rule, the categorical imperative); they are not concrete moral rules like the Ten Commandments. Instead, they are universal principles of *justice*, of the *reciprocity* and *equality* of human rights, and of respect for the dignity of human beings as *individual persons* (p. 134).

Russell, of course, does not in any way express recognition of such stages. He repeatedly maintains that after the age of six, if moral education has been carried out aright--a crucial proviso--"it ought not be necessary to give much time or thought to moral questions, since further virtues as are required ought to result naturally from purely intellectual training" (1926, p. 239). Russell does not deny that further moral development will occur or is needful; he denies only that *intentional* moral training after age six is necessary.

Kohlberg maintains that progression through the stages of moral development can be accelerated deliberately by educators but only to a quite modest degree. Certainly Kohlberg would never claim that even the most precocious and thoroughly educated of children could achieve stage 6 by age six. Russell, however, may be construed to maintain that a proper early education can go a long way toward fostering by age six the very sort of moral orientation that stage 6 describes.

On the other hand, there is another way of interpreting Russell on this matter. It may be that he does *not* believe that the most *principled* sort of ethical orientation--the kind embodied in Kohlberg's stage 6--can be achieved by age six but that it can come only later in life when the habits of intelligence are fully developed. Stage 6, for Russell, could be one of those later moral developments that would occur quite naturally, provided one's moral education prior to age six was proper. If this is Russell's stance, his posture is much more compatible with that of Kohlberg. But even on this interpretation Russell seems to expect and wants to promote a far greater moral development by age six than Kohlberg sees possible. As we have already observed, Russell thinks that the six year old, with a proper education, can have a fairly sophisticated, abstract sympathy for other human beings.

As we noted earlier, Russell in his *Autobiography* explicitly recognizes that *Education and the Good Life* was "unduly optimistic in its psychology" (p. 312). Were Russell writing today, the research of Kohlberg could well incline him, assuming he regarded it as scientifically tenable, to expect less by age six and to see the necessity of deliberate moral education over a considerably longer span of the growing youngster's life. It might also incline Russell to believe that the principal dispositions he wishes to bring about are not the product of Watsonian conditioning but rather the result of the interaction of the child's psychophysical tendencies and capacities with certain sorts of environments. That is to say, Russell in his discussion of how habits are brought about might well lay greater stress upon what theorists like Piaget and Kohlberg call developmental stages. But Kohlberg's work does not require Russell to abandon his vision of the ends of education, nor does it undermine his belief that such ends can and should be promoted actively.

A BRIEF DEFENSE OF RUSSELL'S POSITION

In conclusion, we should like to make some brief remarks supportive of the Russellian view that the moral educator should *deliberately* seek to foster certain dispositions in the young. This view is of course not unique to Russell. Many thinkers--including John Dewey--have espoused the same or a similar position, and we suspect many ordinary people in an uncritical manner tend to think of moral education in this way.

Children as long as they "live and move and have their being" are going to come by some dispositions as they grow up, whether or not anyone pays any heed to the matter. The crucial consideration is, as John Dewey (1916) once pointed out, whether we should let chance environments do the work, with whatever dispositions fortuitously happen to be fostered by them (p. 22). We certainly concur with Dewey and with what we take to be the similar position of Bertrand Russell on this matter that habit formation in the early years is far too important to be left to chance. The objection characteristically raised against this posture is that deliberately fostering habits in the young somehow violates the autonomy of the child. The child is said to be indoctrinated, brainwashed, less free!

But whether such strictures are warranted, it seems to us, hinges upon what sorts of habits are actually fostered. It is true that there are habits which make people uncritical, fawning, uncreative, insensitive, vapid automatons. But there are also habits that enable people to be critical, self-directed, inventive, self-assured, and deeply aware of their own aesthetic potential. There are habits that positively aid a person in the planning of his own life and in the carrying out of his plans in the world. Habits of this latter sort, far from robbing the child of his autonomy, we submit, render autonomy genuinely possible.

If we lived in some ideal world in which the sundry influences upon the child quite easily, unconsciously generated desirable habits, obviously we could let uncontrived, chance environments do the work. But we may question whether it is reasonable to suppose that our kind of world conduces to the following sorts of habits: a high degree of self-esteem; the capacity to distinguish sound from unsound arguments; a commitment to truth; the courage to stand by one's honestly held convictions; a sense of justice that recognizes oneself as a person among persons, all of whom have some reasonable claim upon the resources of the planet; and so on.

It is precisely with such habits that Bertrand Russell is concerned in *Education and the Good Life.* Some of his specific techniques for promoting them are admittedly suspect, but the sort of person they are intended to bring about could never obsequiously kowtow before the herd, to use one of Russell's favorite expressions. Russell himself, may we note, lived what he preached.

REFERENCES

Dewey, J. *Democracy and education.* New York: The MacMillan Co., 1916.

Kohlberg, L. The child as a moral philosopher. In B. Chazan and J. Soltis (Eds.), *Moral education.* New York: Teachers College Press, 1973.

Morris, V. *Existentialism in education.* New York: Harper and Row, 1966.

Roths, L. E., Harmin, M., and Simon, S. B. (Eds.) *Values and teaching.* Columbus, OH: Merrill Books, 1966.

Russell, B. *Education and the good life.* New York: Liveright, 1926. (Published under the title *On education: Especially in early childhood* in England.)

Russell, B. *Human society in ethics and politics.* New York: Mentor Books, 1962.

Russell, B. *Power.* New York: W. W. Norton, 1969. (a)

Russell, B. *The autobiography of Bertrand Russell 1914-1944.* Boston: Bantam Books, 1969. (b)

COMMENT:

Response to "Bertrand Russell's Approach to

Moral Education in Early Childhood"

Ronald Suter

Department of Philosophy
Michigan State University
East Lansing, MI 48824

Professors Ferree and Vaughn have given us a very clear and accurate account of Russell's approach to moral education in early childhood. I agree with them, and with Russell, that genuine moral education involves the intentional fostering of desirable habits; that parents and teachers should attempt to educate character and promote the virtues in the young; and that such education is not, and should not strive to be, morally neutral.

But their paper raises two questions for me. First, is it correct to suggest, as they do, that values-clarifiers would disagree about the aims of moral education? It is true that they believe that helping the young to become clearer on what their values are is an essential task of moral education. But this does not imply that they oppose the fostering of particular values. Quite the contrary. For if they are themselves clear-headed--and professed clarifiers better be!--they will be aware that their very enterprise commits them, as Ferree and Vaughn recognize, to fostering certain values, in particular, the values of clarity, consistency, the importance of overcoming confusion, of gaining self-knowledge, of thinking things through, and of considering alternatives to, as well as the consequences of, proposed actions.

Maybe Ferree and Vaughn would reply that values-clarifiers have, as a matter of fact, been rather confused on some of these issues. I do not know enough of the literature to judge whether this is so. But recently I came across one well-known values-clarifier who seems to appreciate all these points. In an article in the *National Forum* (Winter, 1979), entitled "A Re-View of Values Clarification," Merrill Harmin, one of the original

293

authors of *Values and Teaching*, grants that values-clarifiers want to encourage the above mentioned values, in order to assist students to
"become more intelligently self-directing" (p. 24). He adds that values
clarification neither implies that anything anyone believes is equally good
nor that the moral educator must refrain from making value judgments
(ibid). He suggests, finally, that already in the first edition of *Values and
Teaching*, the authors quite consciously "made many value judgments"
(ibid). So it may be that values-clarifiers do not in general disagree as
much as Ferree and Vaughn believe on the aims of moral education.

I turn now to my second question, which concerns Russell's means of
achieving these aims. I am not at all convinced by what I have heard or
read that there is much to be learned from his specific recommendations.
For example, we seem to be told by Russell that we should not give the
child too much sympathy for small mishaps, then the child will endure
better later hurts without making a fuss. Either this is a tautology--of
course we should not give *too much* sympathy; by definition, we should
give just the right amount--or it is being suggested that we treat children
in a rather harsh and unsympathetic manner which seems unlikely to
achieve the desired effect. And listen to Russell's nonsense about
happiness. He says that in "a community of men and women possessing
vitality, courage, sensitiveness, and intelligence, in the highest degree
that education can produce...very few people would be unhappy. The main
causes of unhappiness at present are: ill-health, poverty, and an unsatisfactory sex-life. All of these would become very rare" (quoted by Ferree
and Vaughn). Would that it were so simple! Russell once observed that
the philosopher needs "a robust sense of reality." I submit that his sense
of reality was none too robust when he made this glib, simplistic, and
overly optimistic remark about happiness. (It's almost as bad as *Love
Story*'s definition of love.) Anyway, I wish Ferree and Vaughn would
someday give us a detailed critical evaluation of the specific methods
Russell offers for bringing about the desirable dispositions and that they
would enlighten us on how these moral aims are to be achieved. For this
is the important issue: how virtue is to be taught, not whether moral
educators should strive to teach it.

EDUCATING FOR JUSTICE IN AN UNJUST SOCIETY

Eric Hoffman

Department of Philosophy
SUNY at Fredonia
Fredonia, NY 14063

INTRODUCTION

My aim in this paper is to clarify the significance of the social and political assumptions underlying the program for educational reform that is emerging from the work of Lawrence Kohlberg and his followers. I will presume some familiarity with Kohlberg's research on moral development and moral education, but my main point can be made outside the framework he develops. Kohlberg is interested in devising and implementing programs that will promote the moral development of those who participate. They involve not only discussion of moral dilemmas, but the actual development of democratic structures for collective decision-making about institutional policies.(1)

The social and political background in which these programs are undertaken will, however, condition the prospects for any kind of widespread success. Following the general argument set out by Bowles and Gintis (1976), I want to argue for two interconnected conclusions: (1) that the moral development of Americans is blocked by the maintenance of capitalist institutions, and (2) that no program in moral education that has liberal rather than socialist presuppositions can succeed widely in promoting moral growth.

I will explain, first, how social institutions are connected with the moral development of members of a given society. Next, I will argue that on a socialist analysis of contemporary American institutions, the promotion of moral development requires that people be exposed explicitly to socialist analyses and proposals. Finally, I will consider how liberals avoid this conclusion and I will suggest some of the dangers of adopting liberal presuppositions in attempting to promote moral growth in capitalist America.

I

According to Hersh, Palitto and Reimer (1979, pp. 7-8) "any discussion of the role of the school in values and moral education must begin with the assumption that the education is to take place within a social and political milieu called 'democracy'." If we do not make this assumption, they suggest, then we assume that certain values *must* be taught, and "moral education" becomes simply a matter of teaching them. In a pluralistic democracy, however, moral education is the promotion of moral growth, which ensures simply that *whatever* values people accept are accepted for sound reasons.

John Rawls makes the point behind this assumption more clearly in his discussion of moral development in *A Theory of Justice.*(2) According to Rawls, two factors are independently necessary and collectively sufficient for ensuring the development of most individuals in a particular society to moral maturity. The first factor is cognitive or intellectual development. Children cannot effectively take the wishes of their parents into account until they are able to understand what the wishes of the parents are and how they express them. I will assume, with Rawls, that all human beings, except for a scattered few who are victims of disease or accident, have the natural intellectual capacity to achieve any level of moral development. My concern is with the second factor. On Rawls' account, moral development requires that all social institutions--from the family to the schools to the government--must be just. Moreover, this justice must not be an abstract and distant idea, but a manifest reality that the child understands to be in his or her interest at every point along the way. The infant, for example, comes to love and respect his or her parents as moral authorities because they manifestly love the infant, meeting his or her needs and affirming his or her worth as a person.

Thus, the reason for assuming that moral education must take place in a democracy is that only the background justice of social institutions can ensure moral development. If social institutions are unjust, moral development will be stunted. The dynamic processes of growth will reach an equilibrium prior to full development. A child uncertain of a parent's love may seek an authority figure throughout his or her life and thereby sacrifice the possibility of achieving moral autonomy. Freud, among others, has made these processes familiar with respect to the "politics" of the family. "Injustices" at this level may foster neurotic character defenses which stabilize immaturity. What is less familiar and more controversial is the complex of mechanisms whereby injustices in larger institutions encourage or permit the stabilization of moral immaturity. Marxian accounts of ideology provide one way of conceptualizing these processes, but the basic insight is not specific to Marxism.

Nonetheless, the reasoning behind the assumption of democracy that the new advocates of moral education are inclined to make is puzzling. I

understand well what Rawls' reasoning is. He is concerned primarily with
a theoretical question, viz. whether his principles of justice are really
superior to their alternatives. His discussion of moral development is part
of a broad argument aimed at showing that people socialized in a society
governed by his principles would come to accept these principles. The
stability of such a society recommends it over a society governed by
principles that people would be less likely to accept as they grew to
maturity. Thus, Rawls' assumption of background justice serves an
important theoretical function.

The case of the moral educators is somewhat different. Their
interest is a practical one; they want to promote moral growth. It would
therefore seem as though their social and political assumptions need to be
based on an *empirical* description of the society in which moral education
is to take place. It will not do to assume a "democratic milieu" simply
because, for theoretical reasons, one needs to assume it if the program is
to succeed. If we do not actually live in a democratic society, then a
program predicated on the assumption that we do is bound to fail.

II

In implementing a program in moral education, one is intervening in
an ongoing process of socialization. To understand the possible impact of
one's program, one must, therefore, understand that ongoing process. My
assumption is that the advocates of moral education generally understand
this ongoing process as the preparation of children, in the United States at
least, for life in a democracy. The skills, capacities and virtues they must
develop are, therefore, those required for full participation in democratic
institutions. Children must come to understand the rules for free,
rational and cooperative discussion and the justification for these rules.
Furthermore, they must become capable of participating in responsible
collective decision-making about important matters. I do not want to
contest here that these are indeed features of "moral maturity". My
question concerns the justification for moral education programs. The
reasoning here goes from an assumption about the nature of the society
for which children need to be prepared to the kind of preparation they
need. If this assumption is false, however, what happens to the conclusion?

Everyone admits, in theory anyway, that there may be a conflict
between our interest in socializing children and our interest in promoting
their moral growth. If socialization is conceived as the process by which
a child is prepared to function in the adult life of a given society, then
socialization in an unjust society is a process in which people are prepared
to perpetuate injustice. People must be encouraged to develop a "false
consciousness" such as that which we now recognize as important in the
stabilization of feudal institutions. The victims of injustice may view
their situation as inevitable, or they may be convinced that they somehow
deserve their fate. People easily understand this point as it applies to

historical or otherwise distant societies, but they sometimes fail to see its relevance to their own. Moore (1978) analyzes at some length several cases that contradict our natural assumption that oppression and suffering will always be a catalyst for revolt. His discussions of ascetics, of Untouchables and of prisoners in Nazi Concentration Camps illustrate the fact that the "moral authority" of the oppressor can be powerful enough to enable people to take pride in their suffering. Successful socialization in an unjust society is a process by which people become, at the very least, insensitive to injustice.

Such a process, of course, straightforwardly contradicts the aims of moral education. Moral education in an unjust society is, as Kohlberg himself says, "revolutionary" (1970, p. 65f). Like philosophy, moral education requires that actions, motives and institutions be subjected to rational examination and changed if they are found wanting. Moral education is a process in which people are led to develop the ability to conduct such a rational examination and the character to commit themselves to act on it results. In an unjust society, there is a conflict between socialization and moral education; but it should be added that, if the society is relatively stable, the conflict is generally and continuously resolved in favor of socialization. Much of what characterizes "moral maturity" in an unjust society is acquiescence to and support for the dominant social relations. Thus, one is "morally mature" when one is fully socialized.

Before applying this analysis to the United States, let me forestall some misunderstandings with a few remarks about socialization and moral maturity. First of all, it should be emphasized that my argument focuses on institutions, not individuals. Nothing I have said should be taken to imply that morally mature individuals do not exist in an unjust society. Social institutions shape and constrain individual development; they do not rigidly determine it. In the first place, institutions always leave some room for individual choices and idiosyncratic circumstances, and, in the second place, unjust institutions will tend to be characterized, to some extent, by struggle for change. Thus, some people will escape the strongest forces opposing moral development and some people will over- come them.

The dynamics of socialization in an unjust society and the impli- cations for moral development might be clarified if we consider a simple model, involving only two groups, the beneficiaries and the victims of injustice, and employ a distinction between the processes by which the social structure is reproduced and the struggles against its reproduction. At first, let me abstract from the struggle for social change and consider an unjust society reproducing its structure. The victims must be socialized to their status as victims, developing the traits of servility, self-sacrifice and resignation, traits from which they derive self-esteem. They are considered "morally immature" by the beneficiaries of injustice because they do not pursue responsible positions or handle responsibility well when it befalls them. They are not capable of full participation in rational discussion and collective decision-making.

Of course, we want to respond that this "moral immaturity" is not their fault, that it is due to their socialization and to the lack of an opportunity to develop the requisite skills and attitudes. Furthermore, we might add, the beneficiaries of injustice do not manifest much moral sensitivity in permitting their own individual and class interests to override moral considerations. Responses such as these, however, depend upon our having recognized the injustice *as* an injustice, precisely what the reproduction of injustice forbids. We have, in other words, adopted the perspective of those struggling *against* injustice. While there is some truth in the attribution of "moral immaturity" to the victims--they do lack the capacity for full participation in democratic institutions--the same attribution might be made, from a different angle, to the beneficiaries. They, too, are incapable of participating in democratic institutions as a consequence of their socialization to decision-making for others and the associated character traits. In this model of an unjust society, there are no democratic institutions to participate in. Therefore, if moral maturity is genuinely characterized by the capacity for participation in democratic institutions, then moral maturity in an unjust society is linked with a commitment to the struggle to create them. And moral education must be an attempt to foster such commitment by exposure to injustice and to the struggle against it.

Kohlberg attempts to sidestep the charges of bias in his measure of moral maturity by distinguishing moral reasoning from moral *character* and moral *action.* His stages capture only the increasing sophistication of reasoning, not the substantive values or virtues characterizing different social groups. Yet, the attempt to achieve objectivity through formalism fails, since Kohlberg's measure favors those whose social roles demand more "reasoning": the educated over the uneducated, men over women, etc. This must surely be part of what explains the correlations of "moral maturity scores" with social status, gender and culture.(3) But, while it is important to recognize the bias of the instrument, it is equally important to reject a relativism that denies the relevance of "moral reasoning", in Kohlberg's sense, to participation in democratic institutions. Or, to put it another way, we must affirm that injustice really does harm people by impairing their rationality and crippling their capacity to participate. Part of what explains these correlations must *also* be that socialization has overridden moral education, stunting moral development to stabilize injustice.

But we have turned now to the empirical questions about American culture and its moral dynamics. I cannot argue here that the model just explicated fits capitalist America; even those in what passes for full possession of the data disagree about this.(4) And, in any case, the American situation is immensely more complex. Nonetheless, I want to suggest that the model is far more accurate than is usually supposed and to trace the implications its greater acceptance would have for moral education in capitalist America.

Socialists believe that corporate capitalist America is profoundly unjust and profoundly undemocratic. The explanation for the moral immaturity of most Americans is at least partially grounded in this fact. We are often told that we live in a democratic society, but perhaps the best that can accurately be said is that our *political* institutions are somewhat democratic. Our economic institutions, the institutions through which adults receive their primary social definition, are authoritarian, hierarchical and undemocratic. Effective socialization must therefore reproduce the consciousness (and moral character) that accepts these relations as either inevitable or just. One of the important mechanisms by which this is accomplished is through the constant emphasis on political democracy and deemphasis of economic autocracy. As Bowles and Gintis write (1976, p. 54):

> For the political system, the central problems of de-
> mocracy are: insuring the maximal participation of the
> majority in decision-making; protecting the minorities
> against the prejudices of the majority; and protecting the
> majority against undue influence on the part of an un-
> representative minority. These problems of "making
> democracy work" are discussed at length in any high
> school textbook on government. For the economic sys-
> tem, these central problems are nearly exactly reversed.
> Making U.S. capitalism work involves: insuring the mini-
> mal participation in decision-making by the majority (the
> workers); protecting a single minority (capitalists and
> managers) against the wills of a majority; and subjecting
> the majority to the maximal influence of this single
> unrepresentative minority. A more dramatic contrast one
> would be hard pressed to discover. High school textbooks
> do not dwell on the discrepancy.

Since it is the autocratic economic system which, according to socialists, provides the main constraints on other social institutions, e.g., political and educational institutions, autocracy and not democracy is the fundamental reality of American life.

The two main agents of the socialization process, the family and the educational system, mediate the assignment of children to social functions in such a way that existing social relations are reproduced. Families and schools do not operate in a vacuum, but in a determinate context that conditions the possible outcomes of their efforts. Moreover, since in capitalist America, socialization, i.e. the reproduction of capitalist social relations, is inconsistent with the full moral development of Americans, the latter, despite all the good will of parents and teachers, must be sacrificed.

If correct, this means that any wide-spread program aimed at moral development must include critical discussions of socialist analyses of social relations and proposals for social change. Even more, they must include the affective dimensions of education that encourage commitment to the struggle against capitalism, a struggle whose history is often suppressed and whose participants are hidden or stigmatized.(5) I do not mean to suggest either that this is all there is to moral education or that moral education is all there is to the socialist programs for social change. The educational reform movement must conceive itself as part of a broader movement. These particular constraints on moral education derive from the socialist analysis of and program for overcoming the injustices of American capitalism. No moral education program that ignores these injustices is serious about promoting moral growth.

Someone might object that I am encouraging indoctrination, not moral education. Such an objection, however, misunderstands either the nature of democratic socialism or the concept of moral education. Democratic socialism, most simply, is the realization of democracy in economic life, and it differs from our present "democracy" in that it is democracy in primary social institutions affecting the everyday life of Americans, rather than "democracy" as an ideological tool to foster a false sense of personal responsibility for social status. To socialize children to this illusion is the injustice, the "indoctrination": to morally educate them is to help give them the strength to resist attractive illusions and to oppose injustice however it is disguised.(6)

III

Liberals attempt to avoid these conclusions by offering a different set of assumptions about contemporary American society. First, they argue that while socialists, feminists and others make some valid points about American society, the injustices to which they point are neither so profound nor so intractable as they would lead one to believe. "We have already made great and important strides," they say "toward eliminating the injustices of which they make so much and the future holds further progress. Through democratic procedures and educational reform, the injustices in American society are being overcome right at this very minute. We have a long way to go, but we shouldn't forsake reason and intelligence for passion and impatience."

This background assumption that social change is proceeding at roughly the proper pace enables liberals to take a more piecemeal approach to particular problems and to rely on reason, rather than struggle, to overcome injustice. In contrast with the socialist claim that our institutions of socialization are constrained to reproduce capitalist social relations, liberals grant families and schools more autonomy as agents of social change. Indeed, liberals typically focus on the conflict *between* the family and the school, arguing against the view that moral education belongs only in the home. The liberal advocates of moral education point out that the question is not *whether* the child will be morally educated at school but *how*. Families are necessarily authoritarian structures. Whatever the intentions of the parents (particularly if anything like a Freudian analysis is correct), the child is not likely to be able to develop the modes of reasoning typical of Kohlberg's "conventional" level unless he or she is meaningfully involved with peers. Schools can facilitate this development by adopting more participatory and democratic structures and they can block this development by adopting authoritarian structures.

Thus, even without the deeper socialist analysis, liberals face serious obstacles in their efforts at promoting moral growth through the schools. There are the parents, who sometimes view with suspicion the idea that the school should "teach values" to their children. There are the teachers, who are sometimes nervous both about relinquishing their institutional authority as teachers and about asserting their moral authority as facilitators of controversial discussions. And there are administrators, who have financial, managerial and educational responsibilities that make "moral education programs", particularly ones that don't promise to solve their immediate problems, like vandalism and cheating, seem frivolous and utopian. The liberal advocate of moral education faces enough obstacles, particularly in these days of "back to basics", without incorporating socialist concepts into the bargain. Yet, if the socialist analysis is correct, they ignore this constraint at the risk of failing in their basic mission.

The liberal line of thought presupposes what I would call a "misunderstanding" theory of injustice. Liberals typically assume that injustice, at least in a society "like ours", can be overcome primarily through rational discussion and moral persuasion. Parents, teachers and administrators "misunderstand" the true nature of education, and because of this misunderstanding, they create and support structures that are not in the genuine interests of children. Social practice lags behind our theoretical understanding because outworn traditions in parenting and education remain fixed in people's minds. (I should add that this theory is deeper than the "corrupt individual" theory, which is also popular and which sometimes supplements the misunderstanding theory.)

The problems with the misunderstanding theory is that it neglects the fact that misunderstanding is often *motivated* by values other than the disinterested pursuit of truth. Just as individuals are sometimes unable to hear the good advice of a friend, so whole social groups may be unable to understand how institutions block their development, however clearly it is explained. To turn our attention from the level of understanding to the level of the *determinants* of this understanding, however, is to recognize that the struggle for justice may require more than appeals to the understanding of those with various kinds of power. The socialist understanding of injustice is more structural in holding that injustice is to be analyzed in terms of social structures that constrain the consciousness of the participants in these structures. Social production and reproduction under capitalism is governed by the interest of capitalists in making profits; it is not governed, as it will be in a socialist society, by our interest in satisfying human needs. Injustice has beneficiaries, as well as victims, who quite "rationally" pursue their interest in the maintenance of unjust institutions. It is not a "big misunderstanding", and educational and family structures should not be analyzed as though it is.

The liberal focus on the school/family interaction is symptomatic of the misunderstanding theory. It suggests that the socialization process can be controlled in isolation from the "adult" institutions into which the child is being socialized. More accurately, it points to the liberal dream of promoting greater social equality through the equalization of educational opportunity. The strategy, however, has not worked. This, at any rate, is the conclusion to which several of the major studies of the matter have been led (Bowles and Gintis, 1976; Mosteller and Moynihan, 1972; Jenckes, 1972; Delone, 1979). Now it is possible of course, that people just didn't do it right, that the particular strategies adopted were not as good as some we can develop with our increased experience and knowledge. But I find more plausible the explanation of socialists like Bowles and Gintis.

Their argument is that periods of educational reform are best explained by reference to new needs of the economic system. In each of the three periods they describe, capitalist production required a fundamentally new kind of worker. Although the educational reformers of the time were inclined toward grandiose claims, both the extent and the limits of actual educational reform are best explained by viewing the educational system as an institution for producing the kind of worker that was needed at the time.

Moreover, despite the liberal educational reformer's competition with the family for the mind of the child, liberals are ambivalent about the family. The consensus has been to view the family as a "pre-social" institution into which social and political authorities have no right to intrude (Zaretsky, 1976; Ketchum, 1977). The internal dynamics of families are not matters of public concern. Although contemporary liberals are less inclined to exempt the family from consideration in this respect, even Rawls (1971, pp. 301, 510 f.) with hesitation but without argument, assumes that families will exist in a perfectly just society. In any case, what liberals neglect in their focus on the relations between family and school is that the division of labor between the two is largely determined in capitalist America by the requirements of the economic system in which both are embedded.

The moral education programs of the Kohlbergian educational reformers, even those advocating "revolutionary" changes in classrooms and schools, limit their "revolution" to the educational system. This is not only reflected in the repeated assertion that we live in a democratic society, but in the concomitant absence of emphasis on struggle and solidarity with the victims of injustice. *(7)* "Moral development" is viewed as a dimension of proper socialization rather than a radical challenge to that socialization. If we really lived in a democracy, this would be true, but then we wouldn't need special compensatory programs for the promotion of moral growth.

IV

I suspect that the advocates of moral education programs will meet the same fate as earlier liberal educational reformers. The monuments of their efforts will bear little relation to their ideals. Aside from the straightforward opposition which they face, they face the more subtle danger of being co-opted. They will "succeed" and find that in succeeding they have lost the "revolutionary" essence of moral education. What will remain are "citizenship" programs, Sunday School discussions and figurehead student-faculty councils. Perhaps they will succeed to a greater extent in middle-class communities which need to produce white-collar workers rather than blue collar ones.

It may appear as though I am opposed to moral education programs. Quite the contrary. I believe that Kohlberg's basic theory is a valuable contribution, despite its often ignored limitations, and that the programs he and others are developing and evaluating work, to some extent, in promoting the moral growth of those who participate. My point is rather that a serious concern for promoting moral growth on a larger scale requires a clearer understanding of the actual socialization process in which moral education programs intervene. Educating for justice in an unjust society requires an understanding of the mechanisms by which injustice is stabilized, a firm critical consciousness of the concrete contradictions between these mechanisms and real moral education, and a commitment to the struggle against injustice.

Societies, like individuals, undergo a process of moral development; and, like individuals, they grow only through conflict and its resolution. The struggle for socialism as the next stage in the moral development of American society requires, among other things, the kind of educational reform that Kohlberg and his followers advocate; but the success of such reform depends on viewing it as part of a wider "moral education program" that challenges the basic institutions of American capitalism.

ACKNOWLEDGEMENTS

This paper is a slightly revised version of the one presented at the Conference of Philosophy, Children and the Family. I am indebted to my commentator Ronald Suter and to members of the Philosophy Department at the University of Massachusetts, Boston, for helpful criticisms of the earlier version.

REFERENCES

Bowles, S., and Gintis, H. *Schooling in Capitalist America: Educational reform and the contradictions of economic life.* New York: Basic Books, 1976.

Braverman, H. *Labor and monopoly capital: The degradation of work in the Twentieth Century.* New York: Monthly Review Press, 1974.

DeLone, R. H. *Small futures.* New York: Harcourt, Brace and Jovanovich, 1979.

Edwards, R. C., Reich, M., and Weiskopf, T. E. *The Capitalist System.* Englewood Cliffs: Prentice-Hall, 1978.

Erickson, V. L. The development of women. In P. Scharf (Ed.), *Readings in moral education.* Minneapolis: Winston, 1978.

Fisk, M. History and reason in Rawls' moral theory. In N. Daniels (Ed.), *Reading Rawls.* New York: Basic Books, 1974.

Gilligan, C. In a different voice: Women's conceptions of self and morality. *Harvard Educational Review,* 1977, 47, 481-517.

Hersh, R. H., Paolitto, D. P., and Reimer, J. *Promoting moral growth: From Piaget to Kohlberg.* New York: Longman, 1979.

Jenckes, C. *Inequality: A reassessment of family and schooling in America.* New York: Basic Books, 1972.

Ketchum, S. A. Liberalism and marriage law. In M. Vetterling-Braggin, F. A. Elliston, and J. English (Eds.), *Feminism and philosophy.* Totowa: Littlefield, Adams, 1977.

Kohlberg, L. Education for justice: A modern statement of the platonic view. In N. F. Sizer and T. R. Sizer (Eds.), *Moral Education.* Cambridge: Harvard University Press, 1970.

Kohlberg, L. Cognitive-developmental theory and the practice of collective moral education. In M. Wolins and M. Gottesman (Eds.), *Group care: The education path of youth Aliyah.* New York: Gordon and Breach, 1971.

Kohlberg, L. Indoctrination vs. relativity in value education. *ZYGON,* 1971, *6,* 285-310.

Kohlberg, L., and Turiel, E. Moral development and moral education. In G. Lesser (Ed.), *Psychology and educational practice.* Glenview: Scott, Foresman, 1971.

Moore, B. *Injustice: The social bases of obedience and revolt.* White Plains: Sharpe, 1978.

Mosteller, F., and Moynihan, D. P. (Eds.) *On equality of educational opportunity.* New York: Vintage, 1972.

Nicholson, L. What *Schooling in Capitalist America* teaches us about philosophy. *Canadian Journal of Philosophy,* 1978, VIII, 653-663.

Norton, T. M., and Ollman, B. (Eds.) *Studies in socialist pedagogy.* New York: Monthly Review Press, 1978.

Rawls, J. *A theory of justice.* Cambridge: Harvard University Press, 1971.

Shor, I. *Critical teaching and everyday life.* Boston: South End Press, 1980.

Sullivan, E. V. Structuralism *per se* when applied to moral ideology. In P.
    Scharf (Ed.), *Readings in moral education.* Minneapolis: Winston,
    1978.
Wolf-Wasserman, M., and Hutchinson, L. *Teaching human dignity: Social
    change lessons for every teacher.* Minneapolis: Education Explo-
    ration Center, 1978.
Wood, A. W. The Marxian critique of justice. *Philosophy and public
    affairs,* 1972, 1, 244-282.
Zaretsky, E. *Capitalism, the family and personal life.* New York: Harper
    and Row, 1976.

FOOTNOTES

(1) For an overview of Kohlberg's theory, see Hersh, Paolitto and
Reimer (1979); see especially Kohlberg's Foreword in which he explains
the new interest in moral education in terms of the "rediscovery of the
moral principles behind the liberal faith". Kohlberg's work is available
from the Center for Moral Education at Harvard University. It should be
clear in what follows that the basic criticisms apply to other sorts of
educational reform. Kohlberg's is of particular interest both because of
its psychological research basis and because of its "radical" implications
for the democratization of schools.

(2) What follows is an interpretation of Rawls, who nowhere explicitly claims that the two factors I mention are collectively sufficient
for moral development.

(3) See Kohlberg (1970, 1971) for the correlations with social status.
Erickson (1978) and Gilligan (1977) give some evidence for parallel
criticisms of Kohlberg from the perspective of gender. Gilligan's treatment is especially important, but it remains at an empirical level,
suggesting in places that women's moral development as it occurs in a
sexist society should be taken as a model for women's moral development
per se. For a critique of Kohlberg's *theory* that focuses on the dimensions
that suit it to be a liberal ideology, see Sullivan (1978).

(4) Bowles and Gintis (1976), Braverman (1974), Edwards, Reich and
Weiskopf (1978) and the literature they cite provide some of the empirical
and methodological bases for the socialist view. See Nicholson (1978) for
some methodological analysis focused specifically on Bowles and Gintis.

(5) Some thinking about socialist pedagogy is presented in Norton
and Ollman (1978). Shor (1980) gives a more extended theoretical and
practical treatment with particular regard to higher education. Wolf-
Wasserman and Hutchinson (1978) collect a great deal of experience and
pedagogical philosophy oriented toward struggle, commitment and change.

(6) This response mirrors Kohlberg's perennial affirmation of the
legitimacy of moral education (Kohlberg, 1972). The basic idea is that to

avoid both indoctrination and moral relativism, we must affirm some values, and the appropriate ones are those associated with participation in democratic institutions. I have followed Kohlberg and others (e.g., Dewey) in accepting this line of thought.

(7) Fisk (1974) emphasizes the opposition between struggle and moral theory as understood by Rawls (and by implication, Kohlberg). I have ignored throughout the widely discussed view of Wood (1972) which holds, on many of the same grounds, that Marxists cannot criticize capitalism as *unjust*, although they may criticize it on other grounds.

COMMENT:

Response to "Educating for Justice in an Unjust Society"

Ronald Suter

Department of Philosophy
Michigan State University
East Lansing, MI 48824

Eric Hoffman rightly points out that there may be a conflict in socializing children and promoting their moral growth, conceiving here of socialization as "the process by which a child is prepared to function in the adult life of a given society." Both Hoffman and Kohlberg draw the corollary that moral education in an unjust society is "revolutionary." Thus moral people like Mother Theresa, Solzhenitsyn, and Martin Luther King can be seen as functioning as revolutionaries in largely unjust societies.

Drawing on the work of Kohlberg and his followers, one of Hoffman's major contentions is "that the moral development of Americans is blocked by the maintenance of capitalist institutions." But sometimes he overstates himself. For instance, he says that "in capitalist America, socialization, i.e., the reproduction of capitalist social relations, is inconsistent with the full moral development of Americans." If socialization in capitalist America ruled out, logically, the full moral development of individuals, as he here implies, the existence of fully developed moral people like Martin Luther King and Joan Baez would be a logical impossibility; but obviously it is not since they exist. (If you have reservations about my examples, simply replace them with some of your own favorite moral heroes or heroines.) Consequently, the stronger version of Hoffman's thesis, that socialization in capitalist America is inconsistent with full moral development, should be dropped.

But is the weaker thesis, which says that the maintenance of capitalist institutions merely conflicts with moral development, itself defensible? It is not clear to me how Hoffman makes his case for this. Certainly Kohlberg might say that capitalists, qua capitalists, are only moved by considerations of profit; thus when they are on the job, they think at the stage two level, which he says is an extremely low level of moral thinking. I, myself, believe this is too complimentary: it is a misnomer to call such egoistic calculating moral thinking at any level, for "It is to my advantage" or "I shall make a profit from it" are never moral reasons, much less the only moral reasons, as egoists suppose. Kohlberg thinks that most adults usually merely conform to the prevailing customs and practices, whatever they are; that is, they operate at the conventional level, which he says is to operate at the third or fourth level of moral thinking. Again, I think we should take issue with Kohlberg's characterization of such thinking as moral. The Gospel of Getting on the Bandwagon is not a moral position. Anyone who accepts only the ready-made opinions of others about what is good and right, has not yet learned how to think morally, for moral reasons do not guide this person's judgment and conduct. "Everybody or most everybody does it or approves of it" is not a moral reason for doing something. Nevertheless, we can agree with Kohlberg that neither of these groups, neither the profit maximizer nor the conventionalist, exhibits a very high level of moral thinking.

It seems that we are to contrast this poor showing in moral development in capitalist America with the way things will be under democratic socialism, which Hoffman says "is the realization of democracy in economic life." Hoffman continues: "Social production...in a socialist society [will be governed] by our interest in satisfying human needs," not by the interest of capitalists in making profit. Consequently, those running the means of production under democratic socialism will be operating at the very highest moral levels, if we accept Kohlberg's account of moral thinking. This is apparently true by definition of both 'democratic socialism' and of 'thinking at the very highest moral levels.'

What conclusions should we now draw from this contrast between capitalist America and ideal democratic socialism, which unfortunately is not to be found anywhere? The big message seems to be that socialization in the latter ideal society will neatly accord with promoting moral growth, unlike socialization in capitalist America. But that thesis has now become an analytic truth or one based on the definition of the terms used. Hoffman has not shown that there is in fact any existent or possible society more conducive to moral development than our own. In short, there seems to be something disappointingly truistic about Hoffman's thesis. He appears merely to offer us a choice between an idealized alternative and a real one, and of course the idealized one comes out looking much better, from a moral point of view. But what of it? Such are not the choices we face in life.

Now it might be said that this criticism is unfair, that one choice we do face is to accept the real society or to choose to work toward the ideal one. That is a real choice, and Marxists will choose the latter. But what does the choice to work toward the ideal society consist in? Surely it is neither necessary nor sufficient to say you are working for it. But what must you do or refrain from doing to work for it? Were Thoreau, Tolstoy,

Anita Bryant, or Stalin working for it? How are we to tell? What behavioral criteria can we appeal to, if any? Until these questions are answered--and Hoffman does not answer them here--it is not at all clear what the alleged choice of working towards an ideal Marxist society amounts to.

In conclusion, let me merely point out a minor misrepresentation of Rawls by Hoffman. Accordingly to Hoffman, Rawls contends that "moral development requires that all social institutions--from the family to the school to the government--must be just." Rawls does not contend this. Nor would he, since he is well aware of the existence of people like Gandhi, Martin Luther King, Mother Theresa, and Solzhenitsyn, who all functioned quite effectively--even powerfully--as adults in societies none of which were, or are today, perfectly just.

MEDICAL DECISIONS THAT AFFECT CHILDREN: INTRODUCTION

Craig A. Staudenbaur

Department of Philosophy
Michigan State University
East Lansing, MI 48824

Medical decisions which affect children involve a number of areas of medical ethics: euthanasia of defective infants, experimentation on human subjects, allocation of scarce medical resources, child abuse, proxy consent, paternalism, to name just a few. At least two basic approaches to these issues may be distinguished. A subject-centered approach would concern itself primarily with the interests or rights of the child affected by the medical decision. A social-policy approach would concern itself primarily with the effects on or costs to society of different approaches to medical decisions involving children. The essays in this section, like most of the current essays on topics in medical ethics, are primarily subject-centered, concerned with how one establishes what are the interests and rights of children and how these bear on medical decisions.

All of the papers in this section are concerned with the application of the notions of "informed consent" and "proxy consent" to medical treatment of children. The law requires that a physician who undertakes treatment of a patient get that patient's consent; if the patient is a child or legal minor, the consent of a proxy (the parent(s), guardian, or court) is required. "Informed consent" is a doctrine which has emerged recently from case law, codes of ethics, and government regulations. "The basic elements of informed consent are: (1) that the physician or researcher disclose to the patient or subject the procedures proposed to be done; (2) disclose the material risks and benefits of the procedure; (3) disclose the alternatives to the proposed procedure and their material risks and benefits; (4) that the physician or researcher obtain the voluntary permission of the patient or subject to do the proposed procedure" (Miller, 1979). Informed consent must be based on knowledge, and recent court cases suggest that the knowledge required in order that the consent be informed, meet the "reasonable person test"; namely, "what would a

315

reasonable person in the patient's position want to know" (Miller, 1979). It is not always clear at what point a child becomes a "reasonable person" capable of giving informed consent. In many states the law allows mature minors to give consent to therapeutic procedures, in some cases (for example, in the treatment of venereal disease) without their parents even being informed. But it is clear that a young child cannot give informed consent; and an infant or a neonate cannot give any sort of consent. In these cases, a proxy (usually a parent) gives consent on behalf of the patient. Our papers in this section inquire into the nature and justification of proxy consent to medical intervention in the lives of children, especially infants or neonates, since this is the class of subjects which presents the most difficulty for the concept of proxy consent.

In "Proxy consent in the medical context: the infant as person," William Bartholome concludes, that "The proxy consent of parent(s), guardian or courts must be obtained in order to morally justify a medical intervention on behalf of an infant." This conclusion, along with several others concerning medical treatment of infants, he derives from the principle that the infant has a right to be treated as a person. Before we look at his argument for this principle and his application of it to the conclusion concerning proxy consent, it would be well to summarize Anne Donchin's treatment of the issue in her paper, "On the grounds of parental consent in determining the treatment of defective newborns."

Donchin believes that no adequate justification has yet been given for parental proxy consent to treatment of infants. She takes the case of defective neonates and considers five arguments which have been given for parental consent to treatment. It has been argued that parents are in the best position to determine the *good* of the child, to determine the *wishes* of the child, to know what the child *ought* to want, they have principle responsibility for the *consequences* of treatment, and can best determine the effect of treatment on the *family* of the newborn child. Donchin examines each of these arguments and finds them unconvincing. She argues that the fundamental mistake comes from trying to apply the concept of informed consent by extension of the concept in proxy consent. Proxy consent to treatment for neonates cannot be informed consent, even by extension of the concept, since what is essential to informed consent is that it be voluntary. The patient, once he or she understands the treatment, must have the freedom to consent or refuse consent, even if that freedom is exercised to produce what is clearly a wrong choice. Even if we could determine the choice an infant *ought* to make, if it were a reasonable adult, we cannot determine what desires, wishes, and preferences would operate in that child as an adult, and so we cannot determine what decision it *would* make. So we cannot make a decision for the child which really represents the decision the child would make if it were an autonomous adult. Donchin argues that we should not operate with the model of adult informed consent in approaching the issue. We should base decisions on the ground of what is the good of the child, and recognize that we cannot treat the child as an autonomous moral agent in making these decisions for it. She believes that the parents are generally in a better position to represent the child's good than anyone else, so that the current practice of requiring parental consent to medical treatment should be continued, even though this consent cannot be justified under the rubric "informed consent".

William Weil, in his comment on Donchin's paper, approaches the issue from a practical point of view: what should be done when the decision-makers disagree? If the parents disagree with each other or with the health care providers? Generally such disagreements are resolved by the courts or their representatives. Weil discusses the tendencies of each set of decision-makers and suggests a "pragmatic solution" to disagreements over treatment.

William Bartholome also expresses reservations about the application of accepted notions of proxy consent to situations where decisions are required for medical intervention into the lives of children. He makes some of the same points that Donchin makes; that children are "morally opaque" to parents as well as to others, and that there is no way to know what a child's wishes will be when it becomes an autonomous adult. Bartholome seems to be arguing that because of this opacity, because we have no way of knowing the infant's future wishes, we should ignore this dimension of the decision (a crucial one for the concept of informed consent) and base the decision concerning medical intervention simply on what is *prima facie* right, wrong, good or bad. For Bartholome this means that the decision turns on the question, what are the infant's rights?

Bartholome argues that the fundamental right of the infant is the right to be treated as a person. Bartholome presents several arguments for his view that infants have this right. If the infant is to develop as a person, it must be treated as a person. If intervention by society into the lives of abused children is to be justified, it must be justified in terms of the concept of children as persons. Children and infants have interests, and only beings who are persons or developing persons have interests. Where there is equality of intrinsic value, there is equality of right to attain that value. The intrinsic value of things like relief from pain seems equal to infants and adult persons. For all of these reasons, children have the right to be treated as persons.

Some of these arguments Bartholome presents in considerable detail; in other cases he refers to their fuller treatment by others. He then applies the conclusion that infants have a right to be treated as persons to the issue at hand, and tests his principle against several case histories. Finally he presents a series of "claims" which he believes "can form the basis of policy guidelines for the provision of medical services to infants."

Bartholome's paper covers a great many issues and discusses several difficult concepts; informed consent, proxy consent, values, interests, moral rights, the concept of a person. It is not surprising that some of these concepts are not fully discussed.   One issue not fully clarified surrounds the question, what is a person, and do infants have the right to be treated as a person because infants *are* persons or because they are *developing* persons?   The question of what is a person, and when an organism is a person, is a central question in medical ethics. Is an infant a person? A fetus? Is it rather a potential person? Is an ovum or a sperm a potential person? Various theories of how to handle the concept of person have been developed and applied to the medical context. Most theorists distinguish between "human" as a biological category and "person" as something with moral status, something which is a "subject of rights" (Reich and Ost, 1978).   Tooley (1973) argues that a defective human newborn is not a person and does not have some of the rights, for example, the right to life, that a person has. Englehardt (1974, 1975), while agreeing that fetuses and infants are not persons in a strict sense, argues that they should be treated as if they were persons, since they are potential persons. Bartholome also takes this position; since infants have interests, they are potential or developing persons, and as such have the right to be treated as if they were persons. Bartholome presents a series of conclusions which are based, he believes, on his fundamental claim. Some of these are: proxy consent of parent(s), guardian or courts must be obtained for medical intervention into the life of an infant; the infant's interests are to be considered rather than the family, parents, etc.; any medical intervention which would render impossible the future enjoyment by the patient of a fundamental human right is *prima facie* wrong.

Bruce Miller, in his comment on Bartholome's paper, agrees that insofar as an infant is a *developing* person, it has certain rights which impose obligations on others with respect to medical interventions. However, he does not believe that infants have the right to be treated *as* persons. Miller discusses the relation between interests and rights and concludes that Bartholome's argument, that because infants have interests they are persons, is unsound. Miller argues that infants are not persons. "If a person is someone who is, inter alia, capable of reasoned choice, then an infant cannot be a person." But Miller agrees that an infant may be regarded as a developing person, and as such has certain rights. "Infants and children have rights with regard to their future right to be treated as a person, but it is not itself the right to be treated as a person."

The difference between treating an infant as a person and treating it as a developing person is illustrated by Miller in several ways. A person is an autonomous moral agent and has the right to make choices which restrict his or her own future.   An infant cannot make such choices because it is not an autonomous agent. But the infant, as a developing person, has what Miller calls the right to an open future. Choices should not be made for the infant which would restrict his or her *future* capacity to act as an autonomous agent. For example, if some treatment proposed for an infant would restrict future options and it could be postponed without harm, it should be postponed until the child is old enough to make a decision on that treatment which is voluntary and based on the desires which the child develops in the course of becoming an adult. And a child should be allowed and encouraged to make choices which help him or her develop as a person. When the child is old enough to start to make decisions, it might then be treated *as if* it were a person (even before it *is* a person, i.e., an autonomous moral agent) if this treatment helps it to develop into a person.

The infant's right to an open future is an example of what Miller calls a non-exercise right, a right which the infant or child has, which imposes obligations on others, but which the child does not exercise itself. It is a negative right in the sense that it requires that others refrain from doing certain things. To take an extreme example, it obliges a parent to refrain from deciding on behalf of a male infant that the child should become a castrato; such a decision would obviously be an infringement on the child's right to an open future. Miller discusses the rights of infants in terms of the distinction between exercise and non-exercise rights, and concludes that infants have some non-exercise rights which adults have, and some non-exercise rights which adults don't have. The reader may wish to compare Miller's essay with some of the essays in Part III on children's rights, where the authors disagree over the question of whether adults and children have the same rights. Finally, Miller applies his theory of infant's rights to several medical case histories which Bartholome had introduced and discussed in his paper.

There are many interesting issues discussed in these essays, and some interesting disagreements develop in the papers and comments on them. One issue which is not explicitly explored is whether *all* infants have the rights which Bartholome and Miller attribute to infants. That they do would seem to follow from Bartholome's arguments, at least from some of them. If infants are persons or developing persons because they have interests, since all infants apparently have interests (the interest in avoiding pain, for example), it would seem to follow that all infants have the basic right to be treated as persons. But Miller rejects this argument. And his conclusion also differs: infants have the right to be treated as *developing* persons. But if a person is someone who is capable of reasoned choice, it is clear that some infants will never develop into persons. Miller comments on one case: "If the retardation were profound, the infant would not become a person, but remain an infant." Does such an infant have a right, then, to be treated as a developing person? If not, what rights does it have? Does it have the right to life? This is an especially important question in the case of defective newborns, as Donchin's paper illustrates. It is clear that these issues are very controversial and a great deal of work needs to be done by philosophers, health-care professionals, and others who work with infants and children before anything resembling a reasoned consensus begins to emerge in these areas.

REFERENCES

Engelhardt, H. T., Jr. Ethical issues in aiding the death of young children. In M. Kohl (Ed.), *Beneficient euthanasia.* Buffalo, NY: Promotheus Books, 1975.

Engelhardt, H. T., Jr. The ontology of abortion. *Ethics,* 1974, *84,* 214-234.

Miller, B. L. Informed consent in medicine: Legal and philosophic issues. *Committee on Philosophy and Law Newsletter: American Philosophical Association,* 1979, *8,* 2-10.

Reich, W. T., and Ost, D. E. Infants: Ethical perspectives on the care of infants. In W. T. Reich (Ed.), *Encyclopedia of bioethics,* Vol. 2. New York: Macmillan and Free Press, 1978, pp. 724-742.

ON THE GROUNDS FOR PARENTAL CONSENT IN DETERMINING

THE TREATMENT OF DEFECTIVE NEWBORNS

Anne Donchin

Department of Philosophy
Medgar Evers College
City University of New York
Brooklyn, NY 11225

Recent advances in medical technology have made it possible to substantially extend the life expectancy of defective newborn infants.(1) By the 1960's application of this technology had become so widespread that it was the common practice of most major United States' hospitals to offer maximal treatment to all such infants despite the severity of their impairment. By the end of the decade some physicians involved in the care of these children had begun to question the advisability of this practice. Where an infants' life prospects were, at best, bleak they suggested that nontreatment might be preferable to active intervention. Reservations were voiced most frequently about treatment of the congenital malformation of the spinal cord known as spina bifida myelomeningocele. The infant is born with a lesion in the spinal column and paralysis below the level of the lesion. The higher the lesion the more severe the disability. Controversy soon began to surface in the medical journals between a group of physicians who advocated a policy of *selective* treatment of infants with such congenital malformations and those who now found themselves challenged to justify the prevailing practice. The controversy grew more complex as it was found that infants selected for nontreatment frequently survived nonetheless and their prognosis was often bleaker than would have been the case if they had been treated initially. Their death could not be accurately predicted.

As the controversy deepened it became apparent that the issues at stake extended far beyond the special province of the physician. Medical judgments were inextricably interwoven with legal, ethical, moral and social issues of vital concern to all of the affected parties. If treatment is to be denied an infant on the presumption that, were he to live, his handicap would be so severe that his early death would have been preferable who should participate in such a decision? What role should the physician play? The child's parents? Legislative and judicial bodies?

As these issues surfaced in the controversy, traditional relationships between physician and parent came to have a changing significance. Consent of parents is customarily requested for treatment decisions if for no other reason than to authorize the cost of treatment. But what role ought parents to play where *non*treatment is at issue? References to the 'informed consent' of parents were frequently invoked. Duff and Campbell (1976), for instance, stressed the importance of recognizing parents' right to information about their children as the basis of their 'informed consent' to whatever decision the physician recommended. Other participants in the controversy expressed reservations about ever obtaining genuinely informed consent from parents under such stressful conditions and where so many technically complex issues were involved. Lurking beneath the surface of the discussion were serious reservations about the applicability of the informed consent model to these cases, reservations that in the heat of the controversy eluded explicit formulation. Though all of the physicians who spoke out acknowledged the need to obtain parental consent, whether for treatment or nontreatment, they differed considerably over the significance of this practice and the appropriate role of parents in reaching such decisions.

In this paper I will examine the basis for this practice. By 'basis' I do not mean the historic origins of the practice but the *principles* presupposed by it. I will sort out the justifications that have most often been offered for vesting in parents the power to decide treatment for their children and then evaluate each of these justifications.(2) I wish to show that some of the arguments commonly used to justify this practice rest on confusions, most conspicuously the confusion of presuming that the word 'consent' is used univocally in both 'parental consent' and the 'informed consent' that is required to treat a competent adult. Once we have resolved this confusion, it will become apparent that parental consent on behalf of children rests upon considerations very unlike those that the competent adult needs to take into account in granting, or withholding, consent for his own treatment. Though my evaluation of this issue provides no decision procedure for specific cases, I believe it will clarify relevant factors involved in deliberations about particular cases and be of use to physicians and other parties who participate in treatment decisions involving those who are in no position to consent on their own behalf.

Five distinguishable bases for justifying parental discretion in deciding the treatment of defective newborns have been offered. I shall briefly state each of these and then discuss them individually in detail. I doubt that any of these justifications are wholly incompatible with any other so it is conceivable that in a particular instance some combination of the five might be offered.

1. Parents are in the best position to determine the *good* of the child, that is, whether a specific course of treatment is likely to promote the child's well being or diminish his human potentialities.

2. Parents are in the most advantageous position to assess their child's future *wishes*, that is, what the child, himself, would want were his cognitive faculties and his tastes sufficiently developed to express his own preferences.

3. Parents are the best spokespersons for what the child *ought* to want, that is, what the child *should* see as his moral duty either toward himself or toward others.

4. Parents hold the principal responsibility for the *consequences* of whatever decision is made. If the child is treated, then both the burden of financial responsibility and custodial care fall primarily on them.

5. Parents can best determine what would promote the good of the entire *family*, whether the presence of the handicapped child in the family would enhance family relationships or destroy family cohesiveness.

1

Parental responsibility to safeguard the *good* of their offspring is universally acknowledged. In those cases where courts have limited parental discretion, they have appealed to this test to justify their action. Though the physician shares this responsibility his role in deciding matters pertinent to the newborn's welfare is usually viewed as secondary, particularly in the United States, though actual practice might not conform to such priorities. However, it is far from clear *why* we presume that the child's parents are the most suitable individuals to decide matters pertinent to his welfare. Some argue that parents have a "natural" concern for the well-being of their child though we are all familiar with cases where the child's well-being is sacrificed to the parent's passions or greed or self-interest. However, there is some reason to suspect that, where a positive treatment decision might commit a parent to considerable expense and substantial modification in lifestyle, the parent's own interest might preclude a judgment on the basis of the child's future welfare.*(3)* Taking this possibility into account it has sometimes been argued that since we need some general *rule* to guide decision making on behalf of children, it is more appropriate that we *presume* the legitimacy of parental authority than allow the presumption to rest with any other party, say, the physician or the State, since parent are *least* likely to abuse this authority. Moreover, where abuses do exist there are procedures for divesting the parents of this presumptive authority. Goldstein, Freud and Solnit (1979) have ably defended this position.

Moreover, parental authority is already limited with regard to certain kinds of choices. Formal education and vaccination are obvious examples.   The prohibition against infanticide is another.   However, recently a number of suits have been initiated in the United States on the grounds that life itself is under certain circumstances an injury to the living person, and some physicians have argued that we have a duty not to inflict life on another person in circumstances where that life would be painful and futile (Engelhardt, 1979).   Were such a duty established, and, if it were not overridden by other conflicting duties, it would suffice to justify active euthanasia.   John Freeman, a pediatrician at Johns Hopkins Hospital who has played an active role in the controversy over the treatment of severely defective newborns, defends a similar position (1972).   What is most noteworthy about this position is the claim that the child's good would be better served by his death than his continued existence, a claim which implies that life itself is not a good but at most a condition for other goods which may or may not be realizable for a specific individual.   Were such a claim recognized, however, there is no reason to presume that such a power ought to be vested in the child's parents unless it were also presumed that withholding treatment and terminating life were morally equivalent.   If this were to be shown then, since we already grant parents the authority to withhold treatment, we ought also to extend to them the authority to terminate life under comparable conditions.   Freeman, himself, takes this position, a position which, I believe, rests on a confusion between the situation of the neonate and the adult.

2

The claim that parents are in the most advantageous position to assess their child's future wishes would seem to have little application in the case of defective newborns since they have not yet had opportunity to formulate any wishes to guide us in representing their desires and preferences.   However, this argument is commonly used among Jehovah's Witnesses in denying permission for blood transfusions for their children. They claim that, were the child able to express his own wishes, they would rest upon the beliefs of the community of Jehovah's Witnesses within which he is being reared.   Where such arguments have been presented in courts they have ruled that this allegation is without foundation.

Yet the considerable range of disagreement among physicians and parents over the kinds of impairments that would preclude a "meaningful existence" suggests that the practice of projecting our own personal preferences and lifestyles onto the newborn might be fairly widespread. Ambulation is indispensable to the life of the athlete but plays a comparatively peripheral role in the life of the scholar.   Lack of bowel and bladder control is enormously important in gregarious surroundings, far less so in a more solitary situation.   The adult who uses his head for a living attaches overriding importance to normal intellect--which is appropriate for *him* given his developed preferences and goals.   But for the infant who has not yet exercised *any* of his potentialities or talents what grounds do we have for attaching to him any particular wishes at all?

The presumption that *anyone* is qualified to represent the wishes of the infant rests, I believe, on a misunderstanding. Since we grant to adults the freedom to decide their own fate without interference, a freedom that rests on the presumption that one's own desires about one's future have priority over anyone else's we search about for someone who can best represent the *child's* freedom since he is unable to express his own wishes. However, the neonate does not yet possess the *conditions* that would underlie such a freedom. This 'right' granted to adults, the right to pursue one's own ends in one's own way, has no application to the newborn at all.

3

The position that parental authority rests on knowledge of what the child *ought* to want has been argued most forcefully by Richard McCormick (1974). He maintains that the child would not only consent to therapeutic procedures if he had the relevant capacities, but the child *ought* also consent to certain non-therapeutic procedures because: "To pursue the good that is human life means not only to choose and support this value in one's own case, but also in the case of others when the opportunity arises...for we are social beings and the goods that define our growth...are goods that reside also in others...Therefore when it factually is good, we may say that one *ought* to do so (as opposed to not doing so). If this is true of all of us up to a point and within limits it is no less true of the infant" (p. 12).

Though McCormick's argument is directed principally toward the issue of using children as subjects of experimental research, his argument presupposes a doctrine of proxy consent that merits independent evaluation. For, as Paul Ramsey (1976) has pointed out in response to McCormick, this interpretation of the doctrine of proxy consent regards the child as if it were the subject of *moral obligations*, that is, as if it were capable of assuming adult responsibilities, e.g., respecting the rights of others, rendering aid to those in need and a host of other obligations of justice, charity, etc., which bind us together into moral communities.

Moreover, McCormick's position ignores a distinction fundamental to the doctrine of informed consent *proper*, that consent cannot be *exacted* from the adult as we exact obligations from him (the payment of debts, for instance). As a moral agent he is empowered to *withhold* his consent, and we are bound to respect his choice whether that choice promotes his own good or the good of others. Whatever obligations he might have to contribute to the good of others these are not the 'perfect' obligations of justice (which can be exacted of an individual) but the 'imperfect' obligations which charity imposes on members of a moral community.(4) I have no choice but to pay my debts and keep my promises, but though I am in a sense obligated to promote human welfare, this obligation does not bind me to promote the welfare of any *particular* individual. Here there is moral space to exercise my own judgment and rely on my own preferences. This "right" possessed by me to exercise choice in determining whose good I will work to promote obligates others to refrain from interfering with my exercise of that right.

However, if we were, as McCormick proposes, to decide *for* the infant that he is obligated to participate in non-therapeutic research out of concern for the general good, then we would, on the one hand, be presupposing that he is already initiated into our moral forms of life while, on the other hand, denying him the freedoms to which the initiated are entitled. Informed consent--whether for one's own benefit or for that of another--presupposes moral agency, that is, the *right* that one's own choice be honored and the obligation to avoid interfering with another's choice. The presumption that parental consent might be founded upon knowledge of what the infant *ought* to want violates principles that lie at the foundation of our moral life.

4

It is often argued that since parents must assume the principal responsibility for the care of the child, they should have the principal voice in determining his treatment. Raymond S. Duff and A. G. M. Campbell (1976) maintain that treatment decisions concerning severely defective children "can be made only by those who care most for the patient and who must bear the consequences." They argue for the authority of family and physician to choose even the death of the patient--by either active or passive means-- unless: "three conditions occur: first, if harm is being done to someone; second, if a better alternative is available; third, if it (society) can demonstrate the capacity and the will to support those on whom it imposes an unwelcome choice" (p. 492). Presumably *all* of these conditions would need to be met before social intervention would be deemed appropriate.

This position bears a close resemblance to an argument often used in justifying a woman's right to elect abortion. However, there are important differences between the two situations. The survival of the nonviable fetus is wholly dependent upon the mother, and it can be argued that she has, at most, an imperfect duty to sacrifice her own well-being and her own interests for the sake of the fetus. But the survival of the newborn does not depend on the care and nurture of any particular individual. It is necessary only that *some* capable adult assume responsibility until it is able to care for itself.

Also, the presumption, underlying Duff and Campbell's position, that altruism in families is strong and that "the foundations of altruism may be inborn" cannot be readily reconciled with reports of the incidence of child abuse. Though we might have good reason to presume that the primary authority over newborns ought to rest with the parents, this authority might be grounded on considerations that do not commit us to such a doctrine of human nature. For instance, the presumptive authority of parents might be based on the principle that the extension of social authority to such cases might be *more* likely to lead to abuses than a social arrangement that left treatment decisions in the hands of parents; that the burden of proof should be on society rather than the individual to prove that a given decision is *not* compatible with the child's welfare. (Of course, as matters stand presently we have no uniform social policy of either sort.)

5

Some have argued that the well-being of the infant ought not to be the sole consideration in treatment decisions, for such decisions ought also to take into account the well-being of other members of the family. Advocates of this position usually presume that only the family, itself, is in a position to make this determination, but some favor including the physician in the decision process. Duff and Campbell's (1976) treatment of the issue seems to derive in part from this presumption for they claim that: "Choices will vary because an experience of caring for a very defective person may be rewarding for one family but destructive for another. Thus, in apparently similar medical situations physicians may advise differently" (p. 491).

Duff and Campbell, themselves, are preoccupied in offering practical moral advice. They offer little by way of reasons why we ought to accept their advice apart from a few scattered references to the sufferings of the parties involved in the care of the child. But on what grounds can we justify a decision procedure which condones treatment for an infant born into a family with one set of values and preferences, but nontreatment for an infant with *identical* abnormalities who happens to have fallen into a family with a different cluster of values? Were these incompetent adults, rather than infants, it would be difficult to defend such a practice against the charge of unfairness, the charge that we were treating equals unequally.

A defender of this position might fend off this charge, however, by pointing to the very considerable differences between the newborn and the adult incompetent, arguing that we do not owe to the newborn the obligation of fair treatment. Engelhardt (1975), adopting this view, argues that the child is not due the recognition that we grant to 'persons' for he does not 'belong' to himself as the adult does but the child belongs to the parents in a sense that it does not belong to anyone else, even to itself.

Here we return again to a view that the child, somehow, is an extension of the parent and that parental preferences are definitive in determining the treatment of defective newborns. Though Engelhardt does not appeal explicitly to the doctrine of proxy consent to support his position, nonetheless his view rests on the presumption (shared by those who hold that doctrine) that parental desires and preferences are to be accorded the space that would be given to the child's own desires were he able to formulate any. His position differs from proxy consent in that he does not presume that the adult's desires *represent* those the child would have, but only that the *scope* we allow to free choice in granting consent be vested in the parents.

CONCLUSION

There are serious questions, I believe, in accepting the model of adult consent in formulating issues pertinent to deciding treatment for newborns. Unreflective acceptance of this model leads us to search after substitutes for the child's 'wants' and 'oughts' that have no possibility of satisfaction. The only uncontested ground upon which we might base such a decision is the good of the child, whether a course of treatment would promote his well-being or inhibit it. However, as Smith (1974) has pointed out, in decisions to withhold treatment the temptation is to compare this particular infant with his prospects to 'normal' children and theirs, a comparison we avoid in decisions affecting adults at the fringes of life. There we can more readily see that, whether or not life itself has positive value or is only a condition for realizing other goods, comparison between this particular individual and others is inappropriate in deciding care. Such considerations enter only at another level where economic circumstances intervene.

Of course parents are particularly prone to such comparisons for they naturally desire a 'normal' child. Hence they are unlikely to be ideal decision-makers. Yet, as Goldstein *et al.* (1979) argue forcefully, they are generally most able to provide continuity of care for the child, whatever the outcome might be, and society imposes on them a special duty toward the child which takes precedence over their individual preferences. Hence, given the assumed capacity of parents to make health choices for their children and to provide continuous care, there is reason to believe that they might be in the most apt position to represent the child's good. Moreover, since the duty to care is imposed upon them, there is further reason to delegate such authority to them. This has been the tacit policy in the past and, despite the technical complexities of this issue, a persuasive case has yet to be made for altering it.

ACKNOWLEDGEMENTS

This paper was originally prepared for incorporation in a teaching module prepared by the Project on Ethics and Values in Health Care at Columbia University College of Physicians and Surgeons. I wish to express my gratitude to fellow members of the Project for stimulating me to sort out the issues, to the Project directors for permission to put the material to another use and to the National Endowment for the Humanities who supported us all.

REFERENCES.

Duff, R. S., and Campbell, A. G. M. On deciding the care of severely handicapped or dying persons: With particular reference to infants. *Pediatrics*, 1976, *57*, 487-493.

Engelhardt, H. T., Jr. Ethical issues in aiding the death of young children. In Marvin Kohl. (Ed.), *Beneficent euthanasia.* Buffalo: Prometheus Books, 1975.

Fost, N. Proxy consent for seriously ill newborns. In D. H. Smith (Ed.), *No rush to judgment.* Indiana: Poynter Center, 1977.

Freeman, J. Is there a right to die quickly? *Journal of Pediatrics*, 1972, *80*, 904-905.

Goldstein, J., Freud, A., and Solnit, A. J. *Before the best interests of the child.* New York: The Free Press, 1979.

Kant, I. *Critique of practical reasoning and other writings in moral philosophy.* (Translated by L. W. Beck.) Chicago: University of Chicago Press, 1949.

McCormick, R. Proxy consent in the experimental situation. *Perspectives in Biology and Medicine*, 1974, *18*, 2-20.

Ramsey, P. The enforcement of morals: Nontherapeutic research on children. *Hastings Center Report*, 1976, *6*, 21-30.

Robertson, J. A. Legal issues in the nontreatment of defective newborns. In C. A. Swinyard (Ed.), *Decision-making and the defective newborn.* Springfield, IL: Charles C. Thomas, 1978.

Smith, D. M. On letting some babies die. *Hastings Center Studies*, 1974, *2*, 37-46.

FOOTNOTES

(1) I have serious misgivings about the use of the word "defective" since it might be taken to imply a negative valuation of the infant's status. I employ it nonetheless since it has achieved standard currency in the literature as a designation for infants born with congenital malformations which seriously threaten their capacity to achieve 'normal' development. However, I hope my use of the word does not in any way prejudge the issue in question.

(2) There are some notable exceptions to this practice, cases where parents have denied consent for treatment and state courts have appointed a guardian for the express purpose of consenting to a medical procedure. However, no *criminal* charges have been brought against parents, even in these instances. For a comprehensive discussion of this issue see Robertson (1978).

(3) Norman Fost (1977) takes this position. He argues that because of a parent's own self-interests, they are not the proper advocates for an infant born with severe defects. He suggests that such decisions be made by an impartial committee who can collectively approach the decision that would be made by an ideal ethical observer.

(4) Here I employ a distinction borrowed from Kant: see his distinction between perfect and imperfect duties in (1949).

COMMENT:

Response to "On the Grounds of Parental Consent in

Determining the Treatment of Defective Newborns"

William B. Weil, Jr.

Department of Pediatrics/Human Development
Michigan State University
East Lansing, MI 48824

Professor Donchin has presented an excellent discussion of some of the issues involved in the area of parental consent for defective newborn infants. Yet she has provided us no final decision on what one is to do at 3:00 in the morning in the newborn intensive care unit when a decision is required in the next 60 minutes. I, too, have no solid answers to this problem but I would like to present two sets of comments. First I would make some remarks regarding the five issues presented by Professor Donchin regarding parents as decision-makers; then I would like to point out some of the advantages and problems relative to each group of potential decision-makers; and finally, I'll present a pragmatic solution.

The first argument for parental consent which Professor Donchin discusses states that parents are in the best position to make decisions because first, they are in the best position to determine the *good* of the child. This is reinforced by the concept of the natural concern of parents for their children, but it is also a problem because of the potential for parental self interest. I would point out that although there is parental concern for normal newborn infants in other animal species, it is remarkable that in almost all species but man, the parents either destroy or expel a newborn that is defective. As far as parental self interest is concerned, this produces a problem when the parent decides that a child should not be treated because then it is difficult to know whether they see this for the good of the child or for their own good. It is not particularly a problem if they decide to go ahead with treatment.

The second issue that Professor Donchin raises is that the parents are in the best position to determine the child's future wishes. She points

331

out this claim is probably difficult to apply to newborn infants but I would indicate that it is probably true if the child is to be reared by its own family. Under those circumstances, the value system that the child would develop would be the one that that family has and then the child's future wishes would probably coincide with those that the parents would expect.

The third point is that the parents are in the best position to determine what the child *ought* to want. Professor Donchin points out that this violates the principles of adult consent, that is, that to give a consent freely it is not necessary to be concerned with this particular type of moral obligation. She assumes that the *ought* is a moral obligation. Therefore, one could argue that this would require the child to make decisions that would increase survival, but such a presumption hardly applies to what a defective child ought to want. Such a child ought at times to want to die; in that way the child would be less of a burden to others. Thus the *ought* does not preclude a decision either for or against intervention.

The fourth point is that the parents are in the best position to assume responsibility for the child but the parents would not necessarily be the ones that might be responsible for the child as he/she matures. As a matter of fact, in one way or another, society has a share of the responsibility for all such children through sharing in the medical insurance premiums and the taxing required to support legislatively mandated education for the handicapped.

Finally, Professor Donchin addresses the view that the parents are in the best position to take into account the good of the family. She raises the question that there is some concern simply because the child's future would depend on the value system of one family. I would indicate that yes, that's true, but it is that particular family who will be involved and perhaps it's appropriate that the family's and the child's value systems would coincide.

Other issues that Professor Donchin did not raise are important. One is how one resolves the question of parental disagreement, i.e., the situation where one parent wishes to do one thing and one the other. This probably occurs more often than we know about since it is probably often resolved by one parent dominating the other. Yet there are some ethical questions of how this should be resolved.

Finally, it is quite clear that the basic question is what rights does an infant have? Professor Ruddick (chapter 8 above) indicated that the infant has the right to become an adult and the right to have appropriate parenting. Whether these rights apply to the defective newborn or not is hard to ascertain.

I would now like to turn to the problems that are associated with each of the sets of decision-makers. The parents are one set, the medical care providers the second set, and the third set are the Courts or the State. The parents have a tendency to put their family's needs first and generally this would tend to lead to a decision not to treat more often than it might lead to a decision to treat. However, parents lack an understanding of the future health care problems that a defective child might face and because there is no way for them to comprehend fully all of those future problems, they might decide to go ahead and treat such a child. Alternatively one could argue that they might have such fantasies about the future, these fantasies being much worse than reality, that they might decide against treatment.

The health care providers have a basic problem because there seems to be an underlying desire on their part to do something rather than to do nothing. One might speak of the health care providers as human interventionists and when one intervenes one is doing something. It is hardly considered intervening when one chooses not to act. Therefore, the health care provider has a basic orientation to treat. On the other hand, the health care provider might be overly concerned on the basis of his/her knowledge about the possible complications of a particular condition and that concern, which is based on seeing the worst possible end results of treatment, might lead to no treatment.

The Courts themselves have some problems. They have a tendency in general to take the safe way out and the safe position is generally a recommendation for treatment. The Courts also have difficulty because they are the least understanding about the needs of the family and they also are the least understanding about the medical problems that are involved. Therefore, on the basis of knowledge, the Courts are least well informed and whatever decision they make can be said to be an uninformed one.

These potentially are all disadvantages that occur to each of the decision makers. They are disadvantages because they suggest that the decision to treat or not to treat is based on something other than the immediate value system of the situation and the child's needs.

There are, on the other hand some advantages for each of these decision-makers. For the parents, clearly the advantages are that they know the child's future environment better than anyone else--the one in which the child would be reared. For the health care provider, they know the medical and future problems that are likely to ensue. The advantages of the Courts are that they are impartial and they in a sense can see the view of society at large.

This then leads to my pragmatic solution which would be that if the parent and the health care providers agree on a course of action, then that is the course of action that should take place. If the parents disagree among themselves and can't resolve this or if the parents agree but disagree with the health care providers, then such a disagreement would be resolved by the Courts or their representatives.

I realize that this is not the ideal way of attacking this problem from a philosophical point of view, but it is one that will tend to work at 3 o'clock in the morning in the premature intensive care unit.

PROXY CONSENT IN THE MEDICAL CONTEXT:

THE INFANT AS PERSON

William G. Bartholome

Department of Pediatrics
The University of Texas Medical School at Houston
Houston, TX 77025

INTRODUCTION

This paper is the attempt of a parent, and pediatrician, and one concerned with the problems of medical ethics to examine critically the notion of proxy consent. I am motivated to write this paper by the finding that discussions of proxy consent in the literature (Shaw, 1973; Freedman, 1975; Jonsen, et. al., 1975), with few exceptions, are "too clean," "too simple," "too tidy" to account for a large number of problem situations which I have encountered in my life as a father and as a pediatrician. I cannot promise a systematic formulation or anything resembling a complete theory of proxy consent. My aim is primarily to muddy the waters, to point out ways in which accepted notions and concepts do not fit or fail to take into account the complexity of situations in which such consent is called for. I will argue that the accepted notions are inadequate primarily because they allow parents and others involved in the lives of infants and children a degree of comfort and assurance that is inappropriate to what is at stake in being a parent or in attempting to provide a service to children. The accepted notions would have us believe that infants and children are "transparent," or "knowable" in ways that even our closest friends and associates are not. What I am asking of parents, pediatricians, child care professionals and others is to "see" and "feel" the difference between the statement: "I know my infant child would have me do "x" on his/her behalf" and the statement "I assume my infant child would have me do "x" on his/her behalf."

Although proxy consent is a requirement for the provision of medical services to any "incompetent" person, I will limit my discussion to proxy consent for children. I do this both because my discussion will

335

speak to these other cases by implication and because what is morally at stake may not be the same in the case of the infant and that of a "mentally incompetent" octogenarian.

In order to avoid the difficult problem of determining when a young person is able to give his/her "informed consent" to medical care, I have chosen as my "patient" the infant. Clearly this is an issue which any theory of proxy consent must address, but I feel that the issue of proxy consent becomes less problematic, at least from a moral point of view, as the patient develops the capacity to make choices and to communicate these choices and their reasons to others. Many parents feel that decision-making on behalf of their children is least complicated when they are infants and most complicated when they are teenagers. This widely accepted feeling is not only wrong, but symptomatic of the inadequacy of popular conceptions of justifiable interventions into the lives of children. In selecting the infant I have selected the most difficult case.

Finally, I will not discuss in any detail what may seem at first sight to be an irrelevant question, namely: How do we justify interventions into the lives of animals? This question is important because the accepted notion of proxy consent fails to adequately account for our intuitive feeling that the justification of an intervention into the life of a human infant should somehow differ from our justification of an intervention into the life of a pet. Do we owe infants more than humane treatment? Do they have a right to more? One of the central questions to be raised and answered is: Is the human infant a member of the human community, a person?

CASES

I elected to include a section on cases for the purpose of forcing you to think about the notion of proxy consent "at the front line," in situations in which acceptance of the traditional concepts does not seem to fit. If the cases make the reader uncomfortable, they achieve the intended end.

Case 1

Tay-Sachs Disease is a recessive genetic disease, i.e., both parents must be carriers of the gene and there is a one in four risk of having children with the disease. The disease is a fatal disease marked by rapid deterioration of the brain beginning in the first year of life with death occurring usually by age three. Methods have been developed for both detecting the carrier state and for making the diagnosis in the fetus. Since the disease is primarily confined to Jewish people of Eastern European heritage, it is possible by screening this population to identify all carriers, "at-risk" couples, and to monitor all the pregnancies of the "at risk" couples. Mrs. R. and her husband are both carriers of the disease. Their first child was affected and died at twenty-six months of age. Their second child is a four-year-old girl who is not affected but has a one-in-two chance of being carrier. Her parents bring her to the screening center requesting that she be screened for the carrier state. They argue that if she is identified as a carrier they will encourage her as she grows up to date non-Jewish men, and to marry a non-Jew or at least ask any young Jewish man with whom she is becoming "emotionally involved" to be screened for the carrier state.

Case 2

Mr. and Mrs. S. have a six-week-old girl with a large capillary cavernous hemangioma of the face ("strawberry birthmark"). They bring the infant to a plastic surgeon and request that the lesion be removed surgically or treated with radiation. The surgeon explains that radiation treatment would lead to extensive facial scarring and that it would be impossible to remove the lesion surgically without permanently disfiguring her face. He explains that a high percentage of such lesions regress spontaneously without significant scarring and that some respond to treatment with drugs. He recommends that they wait and offers to follow the infant for the problem. However, the parents claim that they cannot stand the way people look at their daughter and that they have trouble looking at her. They state they can't wait any longer even if it means risking permanent scars. They argue that she can have plastic surgery later in life to remove scars or remedy any disfigurement. The surgeon, sensing their determination and worried that any surgeon who would operate on the infant would likely be less competent, agrees to do the surgery.

Case 3

After an extensive analysis and a ten-year study of neonatal circumcision, the American Academy of Pediatrics in 1971 issued a position paper which points out that there is no medical justification for routine circumcision of the newborn infant. The Academy strongly urges all members to point out this finding to parents. Three pediatricians who make up the pediatric staff at a small community hospital decide that they will no longer provide this service to newborn infants unless there is a demonstrable medical need. The obstetrical staff at the hospital agrees and the policy is made public. Mrs. J. gives birth to a male infant. Although she had been given a copy of the policy statement on admission, she claims to have the right to determine if her son is to be circumcised or not. She also claims that since the hospital is the only one in the area which provides obstetrical and nursery care they must do the procedure. Her lawyer discusses the situation with the legal representative of the hospital and the pediatrician is ordered by the hospital director to do the procedure.

Case 4

At four weeks of age, infant B.J. was diagnosed as having Turner's Syndrome. This abnormality of the chromosomes is characterized by short stature, failure of normal ovarian development with subsequent failure to mature sexually and sterility, and mild learning disabilities. This patient also has coarctation of the aorta which is associated with the syndrome. At three months of age the infant develops intractible heart failure. The parents are told that she will require surgery to correct the narrowing in the aorta. The risk of mortality with surgery is estimated to be fifteen to twenty percent and essentially one hundred percent without it. The parents decide that in view of the other problems which their daughter has the surgery should not be done and "nature" should be allowed to take its course. The surgeon after pleading with the parents for several weeks is unable to change their decision and the surgery is not performed. The infant dies three months later. The surgeon's husband tells her: "You did all you could. They were confident that they had the infant's best interests at heart. They know they were doing what she would have wanted. After all, they are in a better position to know." The surgeon reminded her husband that the infant had been in her care longer than it had been home and said: "Neither they nor I were in a position to know that much about her."

It is my hope that I have sensitized you. I would ask that you attempt to use your power of imagination and stay in this tangle of claims and counter claims for the rest of the paper. In the concluding section of the paper, I will analyze these cases from the point of view of the infant as person.

THE INFANT AS PERSON

I have borrowed my paper title from Paul Ramsey's *The Patient as Person* (1970), primarily because I am very much indebted to him and his book which pointed me on the way to this argument. The most particular debt I owe to Ramsey is for what is both said and provocatively left unsaid in a footnote:

> To base "Good Samaritan" medical care upon the implied consent of automobile accident victims is quite a different matter. A well child, or a child suffering from an unrelated disease not being investigated, is not to be compared to an unconscious patient needing specific treatment. To imply the latter's "constructive" consent is not a violent presumption, it is a life-saving presumption, *though it is in some degree "false"* (accent mine).

Why would Ramsey claim that proxy consent to a life-saving medical intervention was "in some degree false?" What Ramsey is trying to tell us is that there is always something uncomfortable, unsettling, or "false" about giving consent for an intervention into the life of another human being; someone else's life and well-being are at stake, yet we are asked to provide consent. Ramsey's feeling that something is false about this situation is something that is felt on almost a daily basis by pediatricians and by other professionals who have infants and children as patients or clients. It is also a feeling that all parents have had about major interventions of their own into the lives of their children. That particular, unsure, uncomfortable, uneasy feeling is a combination of doubt and what Albert Schweitzer must have meant by reverence. We parents and professionals who deal with children get that feeling because we are aware of both who we are (with all our limitations) and who they are: dependent, vulnerable, and yet, real persons.

The higher-order claim or principle for which I will argue in this paper is essentially Kant's claim. If one accepts this fundamental Kantian principle, in order to apply it to the case of the infant in a society that accepts a pluralistic concept of "the good", a list of seemingly radical second-order principles or policy guides is required. More later on this.

This fundamental principle can be stated in a variety of ways. Kant's second formulation of the "categorical imperative" is: "Act in such a way that you always treat humanity, whether in your own person or in the person of any other, never simply as a means, but always at the same time as an end" (1964, p. 96). What Kant is saying is that a human being must always be treated as a human being. It may be possible to defend the position that the infant has the same *prima facie* human rights as the adult, but I am not attempting to defend that position. I am attempting to defend the position that the infant has a more basic, absolute right on which a list of *prima facie* rights is or at least, may be based. This right is simply the right to be treated as a member of the human community; the right to be treated as "more than" an animal or an inanimate object. Both Rawls (1972) and Morris (1968) have called this "the right to be treated as a person."

The argument I will use to defend the claim that infants have this basic right is not a systematic position. I will present five arguments any of which provide the outline of what is needed to defend this principle in a systematic way. I will present a brief version of each argument and point the reader to secondary material in which the arguments are carefully worked out in a detailed manner. I present five defenses in outline form rather than one systematic position both for the sake of brevity and for the purpose of demonstrating that it is possible to defend the principle in a variety of ways.

THE RIGHT TO BE TREATED AS A PERSON

Before presenting arguments in support of this right, it should be pointed out that much recent talk about rights is so loose and conflicting that it is often difficult to know what is being talked about. Most recent writers have found it necessary to educate their readers in terms of what a right is. I will follow the terminology used by Feinberg (1966), Morris (1968), Hart (1955) and McCloskey (1965) and argue that a right is not a claim or a particular kind or form of claiming. It can form the basis of a claim or be claimed, but a right is most fundamentally an entitlement. And as all of these authors point out, a right does not depend for its existence on its recognition by others. Often, as in this case, what is being claimed is that a person's right(s) ought to be recognized. That is to say, it should not be accepted as evidence against infant's right(s) that they are not given explicit recognition in this society. I am not saying that rights or talk about rights does not require a community or even a community with certain constitutive characteristics (see Golding, 1968).

Secondly, an entitlement does not depend on its bearer or possessor having any relevant power or capacity; rights are distinct from powers. In fact, one need not necessarily have the power or capacity to claim the right. Rights can be claimed in support of a third party. Thirdly, rights do not depend for their existence on the holder's knowledge, awareness, or capacity to enjoy the right in question. If you fall asleep you may not be aware of your rights, you may not be able to enjoy them, but you clearly don't lose them. As a result of an accident or intoxication you may lose knowledge, awareness, enjoyment, and even the capacity to claim rights, but you don't lose your rights. You may not enjoy your right to life if you are extremely depressed, but you don't lose it. To have rights or entitlements it is only necessary that a being be a member of a community of rights-holding persons. If you are a member of a community of rights-holding beings, you have those rights regardless of your knowledge, awareness, capacities, or powers in regard to them.

ARGUMENTS ON BEHALF OF THE RIGHT
TO BE TREATED AS A PERSON

1. Infants have special rights. Special rights depend on the existence of at least one general right: the right to be treated as a person.

The first argument follows closely that made by H. L. A. Hart in "Are there any natural rights?" (1955). I would argue that infants must be recognized as having special rights that are the correlative of certain kinds of obligations. Hart points out that "special rights" have many sources such as promises, various forms of special authorization, and both special and natural relationships. Although I would be willing to argue that a formal promise made to an infant was morally binding and that the infant could be said to have a right to what was promised, I will limit the discussion to rights which are generated by natural and special relationships.

I would argue that as a result of the natural relationship between parents and children, that parents have moral obligations *vis a vis* infants, e.g., to provide adequate food, shelter, etc., or to find others who will fulfill these parental obligations. I would argue, following Hart, that such obligations give rise to a right or entitlement of the infant against his/her parents to adequate food, shelter, etc.

Secondly, I would argue that when an infant is born into the care of a physician or brought to a physician for care that the physician (or someone to whom the responsibility has been delegated) is obligated to provide medical care to the infant. (Such an obligation to the infant is clearly recognized in the law of torts.) This moral obligation of the physician arising from this special relationship gives rise to a special right of the infant against the physician to medical care.

I would argue, again following Hart, that these rights depend on the existence of what he calls general right(s). An infant cannot be held to have these legal/moral entitlements unless he/she has at least one more basic right. At a minimum, the infant must be recognized to have the right to be treated as a member of the human community, as a person. If a society recognizes that infants have these "special" rights, it must also grant that infants have at least this one general right.

2.   In order to develop as persons, infants and children must be treated as persons.

This argument is alluded to by Morris (1968):

Brought to our attention, if we ascribe them [children] the right [to be treated as a person] is the legitimacy of their complaint if they are not provided with opportunities and conditions assuring their full enjoyment of the right when they acquire all the characteristics of persons. More than this, all persons are charged with the sensitive task of not denying them the right to be a person and to be treated as a person by failing to provide the conditions for their becoming individuals....There is an obligation imposed upon us all, unlike that we have with respect to animals, to respond to children in such a way as to maximize the chances of their becoming [more developed] persons.

However, one gets the feeling that Morris is pleading with the reader rather than trying to prove his case. This impression is made all the more vivid by his reference to infants and children as both persons and beings who will or are to become persons.

A much powerful argument which parallels the above is made by Ladenson (1975) on behalf of the right to freedom of expression. His argument, based on material derived from Dewey and the Deweyan tradition in philosophy of education, is that the development of personal autonomy is impossible without freedom of expression. My argument is that if the role of parents, if the end of parenting, is the formation of highly developed persons i.e., persons who are free, autonomous beings, capable of reasoned choices, it is essential that infants and children be treated as persons. If an infant is not treated as a person, this process of development is in a fundamental way rendered impossible.

3.   If members of society or persons they delegate desire to have the right to intervene on behalf of abused or neglected infants they must recognize their right to be treated as persons.

The third argument is more pragmatic, but for anyone interested in or involved with the problem of child abuse and/or neglect it is a very real one. I would argue that in order to justify intervention on behalf of an abused or neglected infant it is necessary that infants be recognized to have rights against both their parents and against society. This is especially the case if society wishes to designate certain persons or categories of persons as obligated to intervene. It is necessary to grant that infants are not "part of" their parents nor are they owned by or the property of their parents. We feel that we are not justified in intervening on behalf of an animal if its owner feels that the animal should be put to sleep. We believe that given some limitations on what is "humane" treatment, pets are the property of their owners. If, however, a set of parents elected to put their child to sleep because he was "lame" or too much trouble, we would argue not only that these parents were not fulfilling their obligations to treat their child "humanely," but that we had an obligation to intervene on behalf of the child, and that the infant had a right, was entitled, to our intervention. If the owner of a dog, deeply concerned with the problem of overpopulation in his area, elected to have his puppy sterilized, we would argue that this was his right since it did not involve inhumane treatment. Some would even praise the owner for his "social responsibility." However, if this same man, deeply concerned with the population problem, elected to have his infant daughter sterilized, we would argue that he had no such right. In fact, we would argue that we or someone with delegated responsibility had an obligation to prevent him from so acting. I would argue that the basic factor justifying our intervention must be that the infant is a member of the human community and has a right to be treated as such. If infants were not members of the human community and had no right to be treated as such, such interventions would be much more difficult to defend.

4.   Infants have "interests" in how they are treated. Only beings who are persons or developing persons have interests. Infants are developing persons and must be seen as such.

My fourth argument is based on what at first sounds like a very legal term, namely interests. Morris (1968) argues that infants possess the right to be treated as persons "as an individual might be said in the law of property to possess a future interest." Smith (1973) argues that the only factors which are to be taken into account in decision making about defective newborns are the "interests" of the infant and the health care delivery system. Although Goldstein's provocative book, *Beyond the Best Interests of the Child* (1973) clearly demonstrates how this argument can be turned against children, I think that Goldstein and others who have discussed this issue miss an important aspect of what can be called the interests of the infant. H. J. McCloskey's definition of an interest is crucial. He argues that an interest is "that which is or ought to be of concern to the person/being. Moral rights can be possessed by beings who can claim them, or by those who can have them claimed on their behalf by others and whose interests are violated or disregarded if the rights are not respected" (McCloskey, 1965).

I would argue that the infant has interests, e.g., it would make a difference to the infant when he became aware of himself if during his infancy his parents had elected to amputate his thumbs to prevent his thumbsucking. The infant/child now aware of his body could rightly claim: "You certainly didn't have my interests in mind when you amputated my thumbs!" Such a claim could also clearly have been made on his behalf when he was an infant. Such claims are made almost daily by family counsellors, by parents, and even by mothers-in-law on behalf of their new grandsons or granddaughters. If it is granted that the infant has interests, i.e., has something at stake even though he/she is an infant, then we must grant that we are talking about a being who is a person or at least is a developing person. I would argue with McCloskey (1965) that "until it is clear [beyond doubt] that they [infants] can never really be said to have interests, we [must] treat them as if they do." I have rarely seen an infant about whom such a claim could be made with any degree of certainty. Some would argue that this claim can be made, for example, about anencephalic infants. I would only observe that such a claim is clearly implicit in the terminology widely used in both the medical and lay communities to describe such infants. They are called "monsters" in order to clearly rule them out of the human community and to distinguish them from infants with a variety of severe defects and diseases whom we wish to include. This tension and its significance is clearly seen in the extremely heated debate over "mere words" in the abortion issue. We have to be able to include or not include beings in the human community on this basic level. There is no in-between; you are either in or out, and it's damn important which you are!

5.   Life, well-being, and freedom have both extrinsic value, i.e., value to or for others or society, and intrinsic value, i.e., value to the individual. The intrinsic value of things like relief from physical suffering seems to be equal for all. Therefore, all ought to have an equal right to relief from physical pain. This argument can be generalized to include equality of intrinsic value and rights to life, well-being, and freedom.

Alternately, we have no rational basis on which to compare intrinsic values quantitatively; therefore, equality of right.

We come to know about an individual's valuation of things like life, well-being, or freedom primarily by communicating with that individual over a long period of time. If we were to claim to know that the intrinsic value of life, well-being, or freedom for a particular individual was less or greater than that for others, we would have to know that individual intimately. Our ability to communicate with infants is severely limited. Therefore, our ability to know the extent to which a particular infant values or will value his/her life, well-being, or freedom is essentially non-existent. We are forced to assume equality of right to life, well-being, and freedom: the right to be treated as a person.

The final argument is the most complicated of the five, but may well be the most important in terms of its implications for treatment policy. The material on which it is based was presented by Gregory Vlastos (1962) and Richard Wasserstrom (1964). Their arguments have been challenged by a potent critic: Kai Nielsen (1968). None of these authors apply their argument to the infant, but Vlastos implies that it is possible to do so.

Vlastos begins by arguing that we seem to "acknowledge personal rights which are not proportioned to merit and could not be justified by merit. Their only justification could be the value which persons have simply because they are persons...". He argues that "individual human worth" can be understood, at least primarily, to refer to the individual's well-being, and freedom. Both well-being and freedom have extrinsic value, i.e., value to others and society, and intrinsic value, i.e., value to and for the individual. The value to others of the life and well-being of a drug addict may be significantly less than that of, for example, a president. But the value of well-being to and for each individual must be seen as equal. For Vlastos (1962), "one man's freedom and well-being are as intrinsically valuable as any others." Equal intrinsic value then translates into equal *prima facie* right to well-being and freedom.

Nielsen argues that Vlastos does not prove, but rather, assumes that intrinsic worth or value of life, well-being, and freedom are equal. He argues that we can and do compare individuals according to their worth or value. We do this, according to Nielsen, by a "total value equation." We sum the value of the individual's well-being and freedom for others and society and their value to the individual, i.e., we sum extrinsic and intrinsic value. But even Nielsen seems to admit that there may be some cases in which it can be demonstrated that intrinsic value is essentially equal. Vlastos (1962) uses the example of relief from acute physical pain. Essentially, all of us seem to have an almost equal aversion to this form of suffering, i.e., our intrinsic valuation of such an experience seems to be universally negative to essentially the same degree. If it can be established that all people have an essentially equal aversion to acute physical pain, then it is difficult to defend relieving the acute pain of one person rather than that of another, except for some stringent moral reason. That is, they both have an equal *prima facie* right to the relief of the pain or to the avoidance of the painful situation. Vlastos would use a similar argument to establish equal rights to, at least, well-being and freedom.

Wasserstrom (1964) develops the argument in a different manner. He argues that we may not be able to demonstrate that the intrinsic value of things like life, well-being and freedom are the same for all people. That is, we may not be able to demonstrate that each individual values his/her life, well-being, and freedom equally. Wasserstrom argues that "we have no meaningful or reliable criteria for comparing or weighing capabilities for enjoyment or for measuring their quantity or quality." What we can demonstrate is our inability or lack of these measurement criteria. If one is dealing with something that all seem to possess and value, and which we cannot measure, the only reasonable assumption is an assumption of equity. An example might be helpful. John seems to value his freedom. It has significant value for him. Mary's freedom means a great deal to her. Since we have no reliable criteria for measuring their individual valuations of their freedom, we must assume that John and Mary value freedom essentially to the same degree. The intrinsic value of their freedom is equal. Therefore, each has equal right to freedom.

If you would argue that this argument fails, you have two options. The most popular one is to ignore that anything like intrinsic value exists or is significant for decision-making. What your life means to you is not a significant issue in according moral rights.

Or you can argue that the intrinsic value of things like well-being and freedom can be compared; that we can claim and defend a position that A's life or freedom is more or less valuable to A than B's life or freedom is to B. I think most people, at least intuitively, would argue that comparing what my life means to me with what your life means to you is to compare us in ways that seriously undermine our individuality. I would argue that the only way I could come to know anything about what your life means to you is through communicating with you over a long period of time (years). If you told me that you didn't value your life or didn't value it as much as you did, for example, vanilla ice cream, my reaction would be to say that I didn't know you well enough to know what you really meant by that claim. To claim that I can know how much you value your life, your well-being, or your freedom, I would have to claim that I knew you almost as well as you know yourself. If one adds any doctrine or theory of the unconscious, it must be admitted that we are somewhat opaque, or less than completely knowable, even to ourselves. To claim that kind of knowledge about another human being (with the possible exception of life-long friends or perhaps a spouse of some fifty years) is to this author the ultimate in human hubris.

If it is granted that another "adult" member of the human community is opaque to us to this degree in terms of the intrinsic value of life, well-being, or freedom, is not a member with whom we cannot even communicate, in any morally significant way, even more opaque? Who is to claim to know how valuable an infant's life or well-being is to him/her? The infant is not even aware of his/her existence as a valuing self! To claim to know that an individual infant will not value his/her life or not value it highly is to pretend to have access to a crystal ball. Anyone who would make such a claim is claiming access to knowledge or feelings that do not yet exist!

It might be objected: "But you are claiming to know that the infant will value his/her life, well-being, and freedom when it becomes possible to do so!" I reply that I know no such thing. I live in a world where the most down-trodden of my fellow creatures place a value on their lives that staggers those of us who are more fortunate. We often find it impossible to understand why these people do not put an end to their "miserable" existences. Yet those who do take this bold step seem to come predominantly from the ranks of those of us who "have it made." *I make an assumption,* nothing more, nothing less. However, my assumption is open to challenge by the central actor in the drama. I allow my assumption to be subject to the review of my most astute critic, the infant on behalf of whose life, well-being, or freedom I have intervened.

APPLICATION OF THE RIGHT TO BE TREATED AS A PERSON TO THE INFANT

In an extremely provocative article on proxy consent, Richard McCormick (1974) confronts Paul Ramsey on the issue of the validity of proxy consent to the involvement of children in non-therapeutic research. The central issue is that of what it means to be treated as a person. McCormick asks Ramsey: "Why is their [parents] consent considered null here [in non-therapeutic research] while it is accepted when procedures are therapeutic?" McCormick claims that Ramsey has not adequately "unpacked" the notion of proxy consent. McCormick argues that "parental consent is morally legitimate where therapy on the child is involved precisely because we know that life and health are good for the child, that he would choose them because he ought [is morally obligated] to choose the good of life, his own self-preservation as long as this life [i.e., that of the infant] remains, all things considered, a human good." McCormick (1974) proceeds to argue that children, including infants, ought to want to participate in non-therapeutic clinical research that offers hope of genuine benefit and involves no "discernible risk or undue discomfort for the child."

I think McCormick's argument that children, especially infants, have moral obligations to the human community is highly problematic. For example, how can an infant have a moral obligation to do or be anything when he/she is not even aware of his/her existence as a self? However, McCormick is arguing that infants are moral persons, i.e., that any intervention into the life of an infant or child requires a moral justification. McCormick has provided us with part of the content of the right to be treated as a person. The right to be treated as a person requires that any intervention, e.g., medical intervention, must be justified morally.

However, McCormick's argument makes this author extremely uncomfortable. The unspoken claim behind McCormick's argument is that infants and children are what I would term morally transparent to, at least, their parents. In the case of infants and children, we, or at least their parents, can identify their actual (as opposed to their *prima facie*) obligations and duties: what is actually morally right/wrong, good/bad, for that particular infant or child to do or be. Ramsey (1970) finds this not only strange, but dangerous, and I agree. He would claim that even in the case of proxy consent for therapeutic interventions the consent is in some sense "false". Why? Ramsey believes that one of the fundamental reasons why consent is essential to the practice of medicine is that none of us is or has access to a perfect moral judge. Ramsey would argue that when we intervene in the life of another human being we are armed only with our assumptions about what that person would want or would feel was morally justifiable. For Ramsey to treat an infant as a person requires that we be aware of the fact that we are interfering in the life of another human being based on an imperfect knowledge of what is actually right/wrong, good/bad for that person. We have access to no better knowledge.

John Rawls (1972) has argued that to treat a human being as a person demands that he be treated in ways that the individual himself can see as justifiable. He allows us to act on behalf of others, but asks that such interventions be guided by the "individual's own settled preferences and interests in so far as they are not irrational, or failing a knowledge of these, by the theory of primary goods. As we know less and less about a person, we act for him as we would act for ourselves *from the standpoint of the original position* (i.e., with the veil of ignorance!). We try to get for him the things he presumably wants whatever else he wants. We *must* be able to argue that *with the development* or the recovery of his rational powers the individual in question *will* accept our decision on his behalf and *agree* with us that we did the best thing for him" (Rawls, 1972, p. 249. Accents mine.)

I am much more comfortable with Rawl's argument, but I am concerned that his "theory of primary goods" (which he calls a "thin" theory) can be used to render other human beings morally transparent in which case it is as "thick" as McCormick's claim that parents have virtually perfect knowledge of their infants and children as moral persons.

What is missing? I would argue that what is missing is what could be termed an adequate doctrine of inviolability. I have argued that infants are more morally opaque than adults. William May (1974), in an article that he wrote in response to Richard McCormick (1974), argues that the most appropriate principle in ethics for the situation of medical intervention into the lives of infants and children is that developed by Simon, Powers, and Gunnemann (1972), namely the "Kew Gardens Principle." This principle was developed in the attempt to find a method of dealing with the case of Kitty Genovese in the Kew Garden Section of Queens who was killed as scores of people looked on. The principle has four elements: need, proximity, capability, and last resort. If one approaches the issue of proxy consent from the framework of this principle, the key element is that of need. Parents or their delegates clearly fulfill the criteria of proximity, capability (along with the physician), and are often the last resort. Intervention, in order to be justifiable, must be in response to the fact that "some human good (life itself, health, justice) is being destroyed or imperiled in another human being." May (1974) points out that a medical intervention into the life of the infant where no "need" existed for such intervention is thus *prima facie* wrong. One of the key ingredients, then, in justifying proxy consent in the medical context is necessity. "The ultimate reason why this is justifiable lies in the obligation incumbent on parents and others to care for children and other human beings *who stand in need of help*" (May, 1974. Accent mine.).

I have argued that the right to be treated as a person includes at least three major considerations or questions: (1) Can it be argued that this particular intervention is morally justifiable? (2) Am I as certain as I can possibly be that this particular infant will be able to see my action on his/her behalf as morally justifiable? And, (3) is my intervention in response to a demonstrable, significant need of the infant's, i.e., cannot be delayed without significant risk to the life, well-being, or freedom of the infant? At least these three questions must be considered when a medical intervention (or non-intervention) into the life of an infant is under consideration. Look again at the cases which are presented in the first section of the paper. Let us apply the claim that infants have a right to be treated as persons to each case. I do not claim that my way of applying the principle is right, but rather, that using this principle does "push" one in the direction outlined in seeking resolution of these cases.

Case 1

Mr. and Mrs. R. have demonstrated no significant need to know if their daughter is a carrier of the disease. Their daughter is clearly in no need of this information at age 4. She may elect to have the test done at any time. Clearly, since what is involved is her decision about marriage and reproduction, the decision should be hers.

Case 2

Mr. and Mrs. S. are willing to expose their daughter to significant risk of permanent facial deformity to avoid the feeling they get when people look at their daughter in a certain way. The infant is not even aware of the way people look at her. This intervention seems clearly not justifiable from a moral point of view and the surgeon's "lesser of two evils" approach is suspect.

Case 3

The circumcision is clearly not in response to a demonstrable medical need. It also can clearly be delayed with no significant risk to the infant. (That the risks of the surgery would be higher for the older child is a factor he can take into account when he make his decision about his foreskin.) Mrs. J.'s claim to a right to have her child's foreskin removed appears groundless.

Case 4

This case seems to be one in which the parents could be said to have had the "best interest of the child at heart." It is also an excellent example of how dangerous that concept can be to infants and children. The parents decided that their daughter would have a strong negative interest in her life because of her handicaps. Yet, they provide no evidence for this claim. What would count as evidence? The crucial piece of evidence is unobtainable. One must assume that the child would value her life despite the handicaps and be open to being found wrong by the child at a later date.

GENERAL PRINCIPLES FOR POLICY DECISION-MAKING IN THE PROVISION OF MEDICAL SERVICES TO INFANTS

I will now present a series of "claims." This series of claims can form the basis of policy guidelines for the provision of medical services to infants. The claims are based largely on what is a more basic claim which was discussed in the body of this paper, namely, that infants are members of the human community and that this fact must be reflected in the treatment accorded them by parents, physicians, and society at large.

(1) The proxy consent of parent(s), guardian or court must be obtained in order to morally justify a medical intervention on behalf of an infant. This strict moral requirement can be waived only in the event of an immediate and grave threat to the life or health of the infant in a situation in which the time necessary to obtain such consent would or would be likely to lead to severe, and/or irreversible harm to the infant.

(2) Although a necessary condition of the morality of any medical intervention except in emergency situations as described, such consent is never a sufficient condition of the morality of the intervention, i.e., is never all that is required to justify the intervention.

(3) When a medical intervention is considered and/or undertaken on behalf of an infant, the infant is the party whose "interests" are at stake, i.e., the infant is the patient. Clearly the fact that the infant exists as part of a family must be taken into account as it should be

when a medical intervention is considered or undertaken on behalf of an adult who is a member of a family.

(4) Because the infant's ability to communicate his/her "interests" to parents, physicians, and society is essentially non-existent, the infant is one of, if not the most, "morally opaque" member of the community. For the infant, moral justification of interventions must depend on assumptions based only on what is *prima facie* right, wrong, good, or bad.

(5) Any medical intervention into the life of an infant for which there is no demonstrable need is *prima facie* wrong.

(6) To undertake any medical intervention that can be delayed without significant consequences on the life or well-being of the infant until the infant has developed the capacity to share in the decision-making process is *prima facie* wrong.

(7) Any medical intervention which would have as one of its consequences rendering impossible the future enjoyment of any fundamental human right is *prima facie* wrong.

(8) The traditional distinction made between "ordinary" and "extraordinary" medical interventions is not applicable to the infant unless it can be established that the infant is: (a) dying, and (b) the intervention is likely only to prolong that process. Any medical intervention on behalf of an infant who is not dying and is (a) undertaken in response to a demonstrable need; (b) cannot be delayed without significant morbidity to the child; (c) does not preclude the future enjoyment of a fundamental human right; (d) offers reasonable hope of success; and (e) can be provided to infants with similar needs in an equitable manner by the delivery system is *prima facie* obligatory.

They principles outlined above may overlap and it may well be possible to formulate and to state them in more precise terms. My purpose is to demonstrate that some list of claims like these can be established from what I think is a prior claim, namely that an infant has the right to be treated as a person. Acceptance of this "higher-order" principle pushes one toward accepting this list or a very similar list as "second-order" principles which are to be utilized to establish policy or to guide one in attempting to justify a medical intervention (or non-intervention) into the life of an infant.

I have argued that the accepted doctrine of proxy consent must be refined. I have presented a series of problematic cases in order to make the reader sensitive to these deficiencies. Five arguments were provided as fertile ground to be examined in support of this right and three necessary conditions for its application to the case of the infant are proposed. Guidelines for establishing a policy for newborn medical care were proposed. A list of principles such as these can be defended if it is granted that infant have a basic, absolute human right, namely the right to be treated as a person.

REFERENCES

Freedman, V. A moral theory of informed consent. *Hastings Center Report*, 1975, *5*, 32-39.

Feinberg, J. Duties, rights, and claims. *American Philosophical Quarterly*, 1966, *3*, 137-144.

Golding, M. P. Towards a theory of human rights. *The Monist*, 1968, *52*, 521-549.

Goldstein, J., Freud, A., and Solnit, A. J. *Beyond the best interests of the child*. New York: Free Press, 1973.

Hart, H. L. A. Are there any natural rights? *Philosophical Review*, 1955, *64*, 175-191.

Jonsen, A. R., Phibbs, R. H., Tooley, W. H., and Garland, M. J. Critical issues in newborn intensive care. *Pediatrics*, 1975, *55*, 756-764.

Kant, I. *Groundwork of the metaphysic of morals*. New York: Harper and Row, 1964.

Ladenson, R. F. A theory of personal autonomy. *Ethics*, 1975, *86*, 30-48.

May, W. E. Experimenting on human subjects. *Linacre Quarterly*, 1974, *41*, 238-242.

McCloskey, H. J. Rights. *Philosophical Quarterly*, 1965, *15*, 115-127.

McCormick, R. A. Proxy consent in the experimentation situation. *Perspectives in Biology and Medicine*, 1974, *18*, 2-20.

Morris, H. Persons and punishment. *The Monist*, 1968, *52*, 475-501.

Nielsen, K. Skepticism and human rights. *The Monist*, 1968, *52*, 573-594.

Ramsey, P. *The patient as person*. New Haven: Yale University Press, 1970.

Rawls, J. *A theory of justice*. Cambridge: Harvard University Press, 1972.

Shaw, A. Dilemmas of 'Informed Consent' in children. *New England Journal of Medicine*, 1973, *289*, 885-890.

Simon, J., Powers, C., and Gunneman, J. *The ethical investigator*. New Haven: Yale University Press, 1972.

Smith, D. M. On letting some babies die. *Hastings Center Studies*, 1973, *2*, 1974, 37-46.

Vlastos, G. Justice and equality. In R. B. Brandt (Ed.), *Social justice*. New Jersey: Prentice-Hall, 1962.

Wasserstrom, R. Rights, human rights and racial discrimination. *Journal of Philosophy*, 1964, *61*, 628-640.

COMMENT: What Rights do Infants Have?

Response to "Proxy Consent in the Medical Context:

The Infant as Person"

Bruce L. Miller

Department of Philosophy and
Medical Humanities Program
Michigan State University
East Lansing, MI 48824

PART I

There is an ambiguity in Dr. Bartholome's position on the rights of infants. It is an ambiguity that is not uncommon and it goes to some of the most fundamental issues about rights. In order to show the distinction which is missed four different sorts of entities will be considered: a rock, a cat, an infant, and an adult. I will examine each one of them in a hypothetical situation concerning the question of their location at a given time.

Suppose that the rock is on a bookshelf holding up books. The owner of the rock is pleased to have it there; it looks attractive, reminds him of a trip to the mountains where he obtained it, and it does a fine job of holding up books. If it pleases the owner, he may throw it away or use it to hold papers on his desk, but it is of no consequence to the rock where it is. It makes no nonmetaphorical sense to say that the rock would be better off on the desk. The owner of the rock has an interest in the rock and an interest in where it is, but the rock has no interests of its own. In deciding where to put the rock, the owner can consider his interests and the interests of other persons, but he cannot consider where the rock should be in order to advance the interests of the rock.

Now the cat. Imagine that the cat is sleeping on the floor in the study of its owner. The owner is reading a book and it pleases her to have the cat there; it looks attractive and shows the cat's dependency. It might come about that the owner is not pleased to have the cat in the study; it might become an irritant rather than a pleasure. The owner may wish to have the cat out of the house. Unlike the rock, it is of consequence to the cat where it is; if the cat is put out in the snow it may suffer miserably. The owner of the cat has an interest in the cat and an interest in where it is; the cat also has an interest in where it is. In deciding where the cat is going to be, the owner can consider her own interests and the interests of the cat.

Our infant is in a crib, in the study where its father is reading a book. The child had been content to lay there and gaze about, but now it is crying because it is hungry, and its mother is not home yet to breast feed it. After a bit it becomes an irritant to the father to have the infant crying; it interferes with his reading. He could take the baby and put it in the nursery where its crying won't disturb him; that may please the father, but it may make the child less happy; it may cry all the harder and become so upset that its feeding will not go well. In deciding where the baby should be the father can consider his own interests, the interests of the infant and the interests of the mother. However, it would not make sense to ask the baby to decide where it would rather be. The baby may be happier in the study than in the nursery, and that would be evidenced by how much the baby cries, but the infant cannot decide the question of where it should be, the father must.

Suppose two adults are seated in a room; both are reading books and it is late at night. One of them has a dreadful cold and is coughing uncontrollably. The well adult is irritated by this and wishes that the other would go to bed. He could say, "Look, both of us will be better off if you were in bed, so I'm going to put you there." In doing so the interests of both of them could have been considered by the well adult. The sick person might protest, "I suppose you are right, but I really want to finish this book. I know its irritating to have me coughing, but I like to read here." Like the cat and the infant, the sick person has interests, but the sick person, unlike the cat and the infant, can make decisions in respect of these interests. The sick person can decide to sacrifice her immediate interests in finishing the book to the longer term interest of getting well and to the interest of the well person in not being irritated by the continual coughing, or she could decide just the opposite. Unless there is some understanding or agreement to the well person's authority over the sick person, it is up to the sick person to decide where she will be. The well person can only recommend or request.

PART II

In section 3 of his paper, "The infant as person," Bartholome (1981) says that the fundamental principle he wants to argue for can be stated in a variety of ways. He quotes Kant's categorical imperative in one of its well known versions, "Act in such a way that you always treat humanity, whether in your own person or that of another, never simply as a means, but always at the same time as an end." Bartholome says that this means that a human being must always be treated as a human being, that there is a right to be treated as a member of the human community, as more than an animal or inanimate object, and that this has been called "the right to be treated as a person."

The ambiguity shows here and continues throughout the paper. On the one hand, the right Bartholome has in mind could be the right to have one's interests taken into account and fairly considered, i.e., the right not to be treated simply as a means. Our rock has no interests and hence can have no such right. The cat does have interests; they can be thwarted or advanced by the treatment of others. Does the cat then have the right to be treated as a person? That sounds odd for the cat is not a person. We might say that the cat has the right to have its interests fairly considered. Even that is controversial; few would deny that cats have interests; many would deny that cats have rights. Because it has interests, a cat has a necessary, if not sufficient, condition for having the right to have its interests considered. On the other hand, the right Bartholome has in mind could be the right to make one's own choices and have them respected. Our rock can have no such right for it cannot make choices; the cat can have no such right for it cannot make choices. Its preferences can be manifest in its behavior, and in that limited sense we can say that the cat makes choices. But there is no evidence that cats can consider alternatives, assess their consequences, evaluate the alternatives and then choose a course of action based on that evaluation.

Our sick adult has interests and can therefore have the right to have those interests taken into account. The sick adult can also make choices about which of her interests to advance, and therefore can have the right to make choices and have those choices respected. If the well adult disregarded the choice of the sick adult and forced her to go to bed, this right would be violated. The right to have one's interests fairly considered may not have been violated. If the well adult did weigh the interests of the sick person in reading the book and in doing what is best to get rid of the cold, as well as the interest of the well person in not being irritated by the coughing, the right was not violated. Using Kant's language, the person would not have been treated as a means only.

Which of these rights does the infant have? I think the infant is more like the cat than the adult. They both have interests which it is their right to have fairly considered. Since neither have the capacity for choice, neither can have the right to have their choices respected. I hasten to add that I am not claiming that infants and cats are alike in all respects, nor that the interests of cats and infants are equal, nor that cats and infants have the same rights.

The distinction that comes out of my examples is an instance of a more general distinction made by others. Joel Feinberg (1973) has distinguished between active and passive rights; the former are rights to act, to do something; the latter are rights not to be done to, to be let alone. A similar distinction is made by Phillip Montague (1980). Exercise rights are rights to engage in some intentional action, e.g., the right to free speech, the right to protect oneself against an aggressor, the right to go where one choses; non-exercise rights are rights that others treat or not treat one in a certain way, e.g., the right not to be killed, the right to a fair wage, the right to privacy and the right to have one's interests considered. These distinctions are not quite the same, but their difference is slight given our purpose. Using these distinctions, the ambiguity in Bartholome's paper is whether the right of an infant to be treated as a person is an active (exercise) right or a passive (non-exercise) right, or both. Does Bartholome's employment of the right in consideration of his cases clarify the matter?

PART III

In three of the four cases, Bartholome's position rests only on giving adequate or fair consideration to the interests of the infant. In the case involving circumcision, he simply restates the view of the American Academy of Pediatrics; there is no demonstrable medical need for circumcision; it is not in the interest of the infant. More fully, the pain and possible infection caused to the infant by the procedure is not off-set by any benefits, e.g., fewer infections throughout life. The implication is that the parents are either mistaken about the benefits of the procedure or are considering their own interests rather than those of the child. The argument is similar in the case of the birthmark and in the case of the infant with Turner's Syndrome. The question Bartholome addresses in both is what is in the interests of the infant. In the birthmark case Bartholome claims without hint of reservation, that surgery would not be in the interests of the child, but only in the interests of the parents. In the Turner's Syndrome case Bartholome is less confident; he uses the case to show the difficulty of determining what is in the interests of an infant. It seems to be his position that the child should be saved because there can be no evidence on the crucial question of whether the child has an interest in existing with Turner's Syndrome; he does not take the firmer position that it is in the interests of the infant to be saved.

The case of the parents with the child at risk for being a carrier of Tay Sachs disease comes closer to involving the right to be treated as a person in the sense of having an active (exercise) right. The parents wish to know whether their four-year-old daughter is a carrier so they can take action to avoid the possibility that their daughter will have a Tay Sachs child. Bartholome (1981) says:

> [the parents] have demonstrated no significant need to know if their daughter is a carrier of the disease....She may elect to have the test done at any time. Clearly, since what is involved is her decision about marriage and reproduction, the decision should be hers.

Bartholome's argument goes beyond the passive (non-exercise) right to have one's interests taken into account and seems to reach the active (exercise) right to make one's own decision. At age four, the child does not have the exercise right to elect to have the test, but she will have the right in several years. What sort of right can an infant have with respect to the future capacity to have active (exercise) rights? A child could be said to have the right not to have his or her future capacity to make choices overly restricted. A parent or other person who acted on a child in such a way that the child's future was severly limited would be acting against the future autonomy of the child by determining that some options in life are closed. Joel Feinberg (1980) calls this right the child's right to an open future.

> This right holds autonomy rights in trust for children. When sophisticated autonomy rights are attributed to children who are clearly not yet capable of exercising them, their names refer to rights that are to be *saved* for the child until he is an adult, but which can be violated "in advance" so to speak, before the child is even in a position to exercise them. The violating conduct guarantees now that when the child is an autonomous adult, certain key options will already be closed to him. His right while he is still a child is to have these future options kept open until he is a fully formed self-determining adult capable of deciding among them (p. 125).

I will assume with Feinberg that children have the right to an open future. It is interesting to note that this right is not an exercise right; the child's right is a non-exercise right that others not treat the child in such a way that the future exercise right to autonomy is improperly restricted. The right to future options is not the right to have a future right, for the child will have that right when he or she becomes a competent adult. The right to future options is rather the right to have one's future exercise rights to autonomy be effective. For example, when a person becomes a competent adult, he or she will have the right to choose an occupation. If while a child the person did not receive a basic education in reading and writing, the exercise of the right to choose an occupation is severely restricted. The right of the child is the right to acquire capacities and skills that increase the options that will be open when the child gains the exercise right to autonomy.

Can the right to an open future serve as the basis for the right Bartholome appeals to in the case of the four-year-old who is a Tay Sachs carrier? Among the autonomy rights of an adult woman are the rights to determine whether to marry and whether to have children. An adult woman who is a Tay Sachs carrier has the right to decide whether she will run the one-in-four risk of having a child with Tay Sachs disease by marrying a carrier and having a child with him. How would this option be closed? Obviously, if the parents have their daughter sterilized, the option to have children would be closed. The option to marry would not, but it would be limited. The parents do not propose sterilization; they wish to encourage their daughter to date non-Jewish men, or, if she does date Jewish men, to ask them to be screened for carrier status. If this is a violation of the right to an open future, then it would seem that any parent who attempted to determine what sort of person their children marry is violating the right. This comes dangerously close to denying parents the right to transfer values to their children. The problem in the case is not one of whether the rights of the daughter to an open future will be violated, rather the problem is whether the test should be done in the interests of the daughter and her parents. If it is not done, the parents will worry that the daughter may be a carrier and this can have negative impact on her. If it is done, and the daughter is a carrier, the parents' attempt to influence her away from Jewish men could have a negative impact on the daughter. If she is discovered not to be a carrier, there is nothing for the parents to worry about and no pressure is placed on the daughter. So it might be argued that they would all be better off if they knew. However, this does not take account of when the parents would tell the daughter, how they would tell her, how they would try to influence her relationships with men, whether the daughter would feel shame that she is defective, etc. Also involved are the questions of ethnic identity. Encouraging the daughter to date non-Jewish men could run counter to strong pressures to marry "one's own kind." Whether it does or not will depend on aspects of the social environment. What is best is so connected with the personalities of the persons involved and conditions specific to time and place, that no blanket approach should be taken.

I cannot say, on the facts Bartholome presents, whether the parents should or should not know whether their daughter is a carrier. I do believe that her right to an open future is not violated if the parents have her screened. The question in the case is what is in the best interest of the child, taking into account parental influence on the child. The right to have her interests taken into account and fairly considered is paramount in this case, and could be violated if the parents project too much of their anxiety into the situation.

PART IV

I want now to consider Bartholome's "Arguments on behalf of the right to be treated as a person." This will again show the importance of the distinction between exercise and non-exercise rights; it will also show the complexity of the relationship between interests and rights and that infants' rights must receive special consideration in arguments for rights. Two of Bartholome's arguments are basically the same: 1 and 3. The argument is essentially this: "Parents, physicians and others have obligations to infants, e.g., to protect their life and secure their maturation, to intervene in their behalf in case of abuse or neglect; correlative to these obligations are special rights of infants; these special rights of infants presuppose the general right to be treated as a person." The special rights that infants have are non-exercise rights, e.g., the right to be fed, sheltered, given needed medical care and protected from abuse and neglect. If the general right to be treated as a person is, or includes, the exercise rights of autonomy, e.g., the right to make choices and have them respected, then having non-exercise rights does not imply the general right to be treated as a person. The reason is simply that exercise rights require the capacity to make choices while non-exercise rights do not. An infant, a severely retarded human being and a cat are on similar ground here; all three have interests, and thus can have the right to have those interests fairly considered, but none of them have the capacity for choice, and hence, not the right to make choices.

Can it be argued that having interests is a sufficient condition for the right to be treated as a person? In one of his arguments that is just what Bartholome (1981) does. He says this:

4. Infants have "interests" in how they are treated. Only beings who are persons or developing persons have interests. Infants are developing persons and must be seen as such.

The first point to notice about this argument is that the second sentence is plainly false. Cats and many other animals who are not persons, and never will become persons, have interests. Having interests is not sufficient to distinguish human animals from non-human animals. So it cannot serve as the ground for the right to be treated as a person. Can we never argue from interests to rights? There is a tendency to do so, but it can be explained by the fact that most of the things we agree persons have a right to are also things practically everyone has an interest in, in the sense of being consciously aware of how much they desire it and being ready to complain if they are, or will be, denied it. Consider the right not to be killed; we recognize that right and recognize that all persons have a strong interest in not being killed. Other examples abound: the right to freely move about, the right to be relieved of suffering, the right to seek happiness. For all of them, there is a corresponding interest that nearly everyone in nearly every circumstance ardently pursues. Yet there are other rights which do not interest nearly all persons: the right to vote, to run for public office, to refuse medical treatment, to donate all your money to charity. There are interests to which no rights correspond, e.g., an interest in owning a yacht, an interest in playing the piano as well as Rubenstein, an interest in writing poetry. There are rights related to these interests, e.g., the right to pursue these things without interference, but the interest in having a yacht does not by itself grant the right to a yacht. Interests and rights are intimately related; rights recognize and protect interests and having interests is a necessary condition for having rights, but having interests, or having an interest in a particular thing, is not sufficient for having rights, nor for having a right to a particular thing. Just what is sufficient will not be addressed here.

A piece of the last argument which was not considered is the idea that infants are developing persons; this of course distinguishes them from cats and other non-human animals, and is a possible basis for some rights of infants that the former do not have. One of Bartholome's arguments for the right to be treated as a person hangs on this claim about infants. He puts it very simply. "In order to develop as persons, infants and children must be treated as persons." This has certain shortcomings which are avoided in a passage from Morris used by Bartholome (1981).

> ...All persons are charged with the sensitive task of not denying them [children] the right to be a person and to be treated as a person by failing to provide the conditions for their becoming individuals....There is an obligation imposed upon us all, unlike that we have with respect to animals, to respond to children in such a way as to maximize the chances of their becoming [more developed] persons.

Bartholome adds the phrase "more developed" in the last sentence. It shows the difference between his view and Morris'. Bartholome claims that infants and children are persons and have the right to be treated as persons. Morris makes a different claim; it is that infants and children have the right to be treated in such a way that they will become persons and then be able to exercise the right to be treated as persons. Bartholome (1981) complains about an ambivalence he sees in Morris between regarding children as persons and as beings who will become persons. He wants the argument this way:

> ...if the role of parents, the end of parenting, is the formation of highly developed persons, i.e., persons who are free, autonomous beings, capable of reasoned choice, it is essential that infants and children be treated as persons. If an infant is not treated as a person this process of development is in a fundamental way rendered impossible.

If a person is someone who is, inter alia, capable of reasoned choice, then an infant cannot be a person. Morris is right when he implies that infants are not persons but potential persons and must be treated in a way that ensures they will become persons. How parents treat a child in order to foster its development as a person depends in large measure on the age of the child. If we restrict our consideration to infants, as Bartholome wishes to, then the most important things that can be done are to give the infant a protective environment, affection and attention in order to develop a sense of security and self esteem of a crude sort. If we consider older children, then we can treat them as if they were persons in order that they become persons. We give them some decisions to make but stand ready to interfere if the consequences are harmful, immoral, illegal or otherwise not tolerable. In some cases we are willing to let them make decisions whatever the consequences; that is a good way to learn decision-making; further, too much protection can stunt their development as persons. Infants and children have rights with regard to their future right to be treated as a person, but it is not itself the right to be treated as a person.

PART V

I want to draw this comment to a close with direct answers to the question in the title; "What rights do infants have?" First, infants have many non-exercise rights that adults have, e.g., the right not to be killed, the right not to be caused needless suffering, and other rights of personal security. An infant has these rights in the same way that adults do; they impose obligations on others not to do certain things to infants; they are negative as opposed to positive rights in the sense that they require others not to do certain things. Infants have other non-exercise rights that adults have, e.g., the right to food, shelter, protection from harm of others, and other rights of well-being or happiness. In adults these rights can be exercise rights, e.g., the right of an adult to pursue well-being; further, in adults these rights are again negative, they impose the obligation on others not to interfere. For infants the situation is different. The right to well-being cannot be exercised by an infant, and hence for them it is not a negative right but a positive right; others, usually parents, have the obligation to provide the infant with shelter, protection from harm and well-being.

Second, infants have a special class of rights that adult persons don't have; again, these are non-exercise rights, but they are rights held in respect of the future exercise rights of the persons who the infants will become. There are two sorts of rights here, and they are found in Morris (1970) and Feinberg (1980). On the one hand there is the right to be treated in such a way that an infant will come to have the capacity to be a person, and to exercise the rights of a person. This is the right emphasized by Morris, but also found in Feinberg somewhat. On the other hand there is the right to future options, the right not to have options closed over which one can exercise the rights of a person. This right is the focus of Feinberg. These two rights will shade into each other, but there is a distinction to be made. Take the following extreme case. Suppose the parents of a child believe they know the one true path for their child and do all they can to direct the child in that path; they do not allow the child to make any choices, to even become familiar with alternative ways of doing things; further they shame the child's efforts at decision-making, belittling his or her capacity to know what's right. Such a child will likely arrive at adulthood without the capacity to make decisions. The adult will lack self esteem, be insecure without a parental figure, and unable to decide what to do except follow the path the parents laid down. For such an adult, the right to be treated as a person means practically nothing; he or she makes no choices of any magnitude, so there are not choices for others to respect. In order to be a person, certain capacities must be developed, the capacities for utilization of freedom and autonomous choice. Those adults who most clearly lack these capacities are the mentally ill. Morris (1970) links the treatment owed to children and the treatment owed the mentally ill.

> When an individual is ill he is entitled to that assistance which will make it possible for him to resume his functioning as a person....Those human beings who fill our mental institutions are entitled to more than they do in fact receive; they should be viewed as possessing the right to be treated as a person so that our responses to them may increase the likelihood that they will enjoy fully the right to be so treated. Like the child, the mentally ill person has a future interest we cannot rightly deny him (p. 134)

This right to develop the capacity to have the exercise rights of autonomy is distinct from the right not to have one's options closed. Consider another extreme case: parents who have their male child castrated to preserve a beautiful soprano voice. For a less grotesque and more likely example, consider a parent who decides that his child will become a farmer who uses primitive methods of farming and hence the parent sees no need for anything but a rudimentary education in reading, writing and arithmetic. Such a child might not be otherwise stunted in personality development. As an adult this person will have the capacity to make choices, but his choices will be restricted. If the socio-economic conditions change so that primitive farming is no longer a feasible way to survive, the adult will find it very difficult to find another way to make a living. Suppose the adult decides that he doesn't like the life his father wanted him to live, and would rather be working at some trade. This option may be closed for all practical purposes, depending on many factors. These two rights shade into each other when we consider those capacities which are essential to being a person, and which if possessed in some degree above the minimum for personhood, open more options. Self esteem, in the sense of confidence in one's ability to succeed at tasks one takes on, must be present in some degree if one is to have the capacities of choice at all. With no self esteeem, an adult is not a person; he or she will lack the capacity for autonomous choice. If one has a great deal of self esteem, one is not more of a person, but is able to consider more options, able to enter into more risky or unfamiliar courses of conduct. Developing a certain amount of self esteem in children is required of parents to fulfill their children's right to become a person; developing a strong sense of self esteem is important to the child's right to future options.

These two rights comprise a special class of rights; they are possessed by infants and children, and by some of those who are mentally ill; they are not possessed by adult persons. By becoming adult persons, their right to do so has been recognized. As adult persons they have the right to future options, but not in the same way a child has that right. Adult persons have the right to keep their own options open and to develop their ability to take advantage of future options; children cannot do this.   Another difference is that the right to future options is an exercise right for an adult, others are simply under an obligation not to interfere. For children, the right to future options is a non-exercise right and others are under the obligation to provide future options for children.

PART VI

A final issue. Are the two special rights of children likely to be of significance in decisions regarding medical care of infants and children? In the version of his paper submitted to the National Commission, Bartholome (1977) presents two cases which involve the special rights of infants and children.

> Mrs. B. had her right breast removed for cancer in 1973 at the age of 32. Because of her age and a suggestive family history, an extensive analysis was undertaken of the incidence of breast cancer in her family. It was discovered that her grandmother, her mother, two of her mother's three sisters, and her own sister (age 37) had had cancer of the breast. It was felt that she and her family had a genetic predisposition to the development of this tumor. She elected to have her opposite breast removed in 1974.   This breast showed evidence of microscopic tumor development. Her younger sister, age 23, had her breasts removed that same year. Study of her breast tissue revealed no evidence of tumor. However, in late 1974, Mrs. B.'s 15-year-old daughter was found to have cancer of the breast and had both breasts removed. In February 1975, Mrs. B. gave birth to a girl. As a result of the influence of maternal hormones, the breasts are completely delineated at birth and it is possible to remove all breast tissue. It seemed possible to do what would be a major surgical procedure under local anesthesia, save the infant the risk of developing breast cancer, and allow her to avoid the serious psychological trauma of the possibility of having to have her breasts removed after puberty. Mrs. B. gave her consent to the operation. (3.26)

> Mr. and Mrs. R. have just had an infant son. The child is healthy and the examination is unremarkable except for the presence of severe talipes-equino-varus deformity of both feet ("clubfoot"). An orthopedic specialist is consulted and strongly recommends immediate casting to begin treatment and to prevent the necessity of multiple extensive surgical procedures at a later date. She points

out to the family that late surgical treatment often fails
and that intervention in infancy is essential if the child is
to walk normally.   Mr.   R. tells the physician that he
cannot stand the thought of his son having to wear casts
on his legs for the first six months of his life. He claims
that to torture the baby in this manner is inhumane and he
will not permit it. His wife agrees. The hospital lawyer
is consulted and tells the physician that since the intervention is not life saving and since correction can at least
be attempted (in spite of poor chance of success) at a
later date that the parents' refusal to give consent should
be respected. (3.27)

Bartholome (1977) comments on these as follows:

> Mrs. B.'s daughter was clearly at risk of developing cancer
> of the breast after puberty. Her mother's wanting to save
> her the trauma of having her breasts removed is clearly
> understandable, but the procedure could have been de-
> layed at least 15 years without significant risk to the
> child and she could have shared in this admittedly dif-
> ficult decision. (3.50)

> Mrs. R.'s infant has a clear need. His parent's refusal to
> give consent to the intervention may well result in his
> being crippled for life. The physician is clearly obligated
> to take whatever legal steps are necessary to see that this
> need is met. If the issue is not one of legal negligence
> (most courts would argue that it was), it is at least serious
> moral negligence of the infant as person. (3.51)

Both cases pose a possible violation of the right to an open future.
The infant at risk for breast cancer will lose the option for normal
maturation of her body and the option to nurse her own baby. There is no
reason to close that option at infancy; the infant is under no immediate
risk of illness. In the case of the child with clubfoot, the right to future
options is recognized by doing the recommended treatment rather than
delaying it. Delaying the procedure increases the risk of permanent
incapacitation which would clearly close future options. Neither of these
cases involves violation of the right to become an autonomous person. In
both cases, doing or not doing the procedure will not in any direct way
prevent the child from having the capacity to exercise autonomy rights.

The right to become a person could be violated if the following set
of circumstances obtained; 1) an infant has a disease; 2) the disease poses
a risk of significant cognitive disfunction if not treated, but not a risk of
death; 3) there is a treatment which will substantially reduce or eliminate
the risk of cognitive disfunction. The proviso that there is no risk of
death is used to avoid cases where an infant's right to life mandates

treatment, and no need exists to appeal to the right to become a person. There are diseases where there are risks of death or significant neurological damage, e.g., bacterial meningitis. It would be an upside-down approach in such a case to appeal first to the right to become a person, and only secondly to the right to life. There are not many cases where decisions about medical treatment are decisions to preserve or eliminate the potential to become a person. PKU may be one example. If the infant with PKU is not put on the low phenyl alanine diet, there will be significant retardation. If the retardation were profound, the infant would not become a person, but remain an infant. If the retardation were moderate or slight, the infant would become a person, but one with limited options. It is possible then that the right to become a person is at stake for an infant with PKU; at minimum, the right to future options would be violated if the proscribed diet is not followed.

Bartholome succeeded in his primary purpose; "to muddy the waters, to point out ways in which accepted notions and concepts do not fit or fail to take into account the complexity of situations in which such consent (for medical treatment for infants) is called for." I hope he will think I have withdrawn some precipitate.

REFERENCES

Bartholome, W. Proxy consent in the medical context: The infant as person. *Research involving children: Appendix to report and recommendations.* The National Commission for the Protection of Human Subjects of Biomedical and Behavioral Research, DHEW Publication No. (OS) 77-0005, 1977, 3.23-3.54.

Bartholome, W. Proxy consent in the medical context: The infant as person. *Philosophy, children, and the family.* New York: Plenum Press, 1981.

Feinberg, J. *Social philosophy.* Englewood Cliffs: Prentice-Hall, 1973.

Feinberg, J. The child's right to an open future. In W. Aiken and H. LaFollette (Eds.), *Whose child: Children's rights, parental authority and state power.* Ottowa: Littlefield Adams, 1980.

Montague, P. Two concepts of rights. *Philosophy and public affairs,* 1980, *9,* 371-386.

Morris, H. Persons and punishment. In A. I. Melden (Ed.), *Human rights.* Belmont: Wadsworth, 1970.

AUTHOR INDEX

Alston, W. P., 267, 272, 279
Ames, B., 10
Anderson, N., 51
Annas, G., 49
Anscombe, G. E., 205, 223
Aries, P., 27, 40, 58, 59, 60,
    61, 62, 63, 204
Aristotle, 6, 7, 25, 26, 35, 258,
    259
Aron, I. E., 272
Bales, R. F., 48
Barash, D. P., 83
Baribeau, J. M. C., 272
Barker, E., 19
Bartholome, W. G., 316, 317,
    318, 319, 353, 354, 356,
    357, 358, 359, 360, 363,
    364, 365
Bartky, S. L., 115
Bateson, G., 29, 34, 35, 41
Baumrind, D., 274
Beaver, W. R., 34
Beck, C. M., 254
Becker, G. S., 185
Benn, S. I., 135
Bennis, W. G., 31
Black, D. W., 145, 146, 247,
    248, 249
Blake, J., 185
Bloch, M., 39
Bowles, S., 64, 295, 300, 303
Brandel, F., 40
Braun, C. M. J., 272
Bronfenbrenner, U., 163, 203,
    204, 234, 274
Brophy, J., 47
Buber, M., 199, 200
Burt, R., 200
Campbell, A. G. M., 322, 326,
    327
Castan, Y., 40
Charlemagne, 58
Chodorow, N., 102
Clark, L., 203
Clifton, L., 104

Cohen, H., 137, 138, 139, 140,
    158
Coleman, J. S., 234
Collingwood, R. G., 238, 239
Collins, H. W., 219
Cortes, J. B., 48
Crittenden, B. S., 254
Curie-Cohen, M., 47, 49
Decker, A., 47
Delone, R. H., 303
Demos, J., 41
Dewey, J., 291, 341
Dibrell, W., 141
Dinnerstein, D., 94, 95, 118
Donchin, A., 316, 317, 319,
    331, 332
Donzelot, J., 13
Duff, R. S., 322, 326, 327
Dupuis, V. L., 219
Dworkin, R., 155
Eisler, B., 220
Ellis, M. J., 247
Engels, F., 27
Englehardt, H. T., Jr., 318,
    324, 327
Epictetus, 50
Erikson, E., 33, 232
Espenshade, T., 53
Evans, J., 143, 144, 145, 231,
    232, 233, 234
Farson, R., 150
Febvre, L., 39
Feinberg, J., 134, 135, 138,
    150, 167, 339, 355, 357,
    361
Ferree, G. F., 258, 293, 294
Fitzgerald, H. E., 257
Flandrin, J., 5
Flay, J., 12, 13
Fraenkel, J. R., 272
Freeman, J., 324
Freeman, V., 335
Freud, A., 203, 206, 207, 323,
    328, 342
Freud, S., 296
Fried, C., 203

367